ORDINANCES

OF THE

MAYOR, ALDERMEN AND COMMONALTY

OF THE

CITY OF NEW YORK.

REVISED A. D. 1859,

BY D. T. VALENTINE.

ADOPTED BY THE COMMON COUNCIL, AND PUBLISHED BY THEIR AUTHORITY.

NEW YORK:
CHAS. W. BAKER, PRINTER, 29 BEEKMAN STREET.
1859.

PREFACE.

This edition of the City Ordinances has been revised under circumstances which rendered necessary their adoption by the city government. Since the last revision (by David Graham, Esq., in the year 1845,) the Constitution of the State has been remodeled, and provisions have been introduced which annulled the operation of many of the ordinances of the city previously existing; several State laws have also been passed which affected the powers of the municipal government and established regulations to which it was necessary to make the ordinances conform. In addition to these circumstances, three amended charters were passed (those of 1849, 1853 and 1857,) to meet the requirements of which the ordinances were, in some degree, altered at those successive periods; but by their conflicting provisions, additional complications ensued in the body of the ordinances.

Appreciating the necessity of a careful performance of the duties intrusted to him, the undersigned did not rely entirely upon himself in the preparation of this revision, and to his attorney, John Paulding, Esq., he deems it due to acknowledge services entirely satisfactory. An analysis of the charters and all the recent State laws was made with a view to a more certain detection of conflicting provisions, and several of the departments were re-organized by the Common Council. When the ordinances were prepared, they were from time to time submitted to the Common

Council, by whom they were ordered to be printed in a documentary form, and were thus brought to the notice of the members of the city government and the officers of the departments. With some additional amendments to make them conform to the practical workings of the departments, they were finally submitted in a body to the Common Council, and having passed the Board of Aldermen on the 6th day of June, 1859, and the Board of Councilmen on the 13th day of June, 1859, they were approved by the Mayor on the 20th day of June, 1859. Such ordinances as passed between the last-mentioned date and the time of placing the work in the printer's hands, have been likewise incorporated in the work. The ordinances thus adopted are embraced between pages 37 and 478 (inclusive) of this volume.

DAVID T. VALENTINE,

Clerk of the Common Council.

CONTENTS

OF THE VARIOUS CHAPTERS OF CITY ORDINANCES.

CHAPTER I.

Of the Mayor, and the officers appertaining to the Mayor's office.

CHAPTER II.

Of the Legislative Department.

CHAPTER III.

Of the Department of Finance.

CHAPTER IV.

Of the Street Department.

CHAPTER V.

Of the Law Department.

CHAPTER VI.

Of the Croton Aqueduct Board.

CHAPTER VII.

Of the City Inspector's Department.

CHAPTER VIII.

Of Miscellaneous Provisions respecting the Executive Departments and their officers.

CHAPTER IX.

Of the Sinking Fund.

CHAPTER X.

Of the Fire Department.

CHAPTER XXI.

CHAPTER XXII.

CHAPTER XXIII.

Of Cleaning the Streets and herein of the Removal of Snow and Ice and the Sale and Cartage of Manure.

CHAPTER XXIV.

CHAPTER XXV.

CHAPTER XXVI.

Of Vessels, Wharves, Piers and Slips.

CHAPTER XXVII.

Of Sales in the Public Streets.

CHAPTER XXVIII.

CHAPTER XXIX.

CHAPTER XXX.

CHAPTER XXXI.

CHAPTER XXXII.

CHAPTER XXXIII.

CHAPTER XXXIV.

Of Weights and Measures.

CHAPTER XXXV.

Of the Public Markets.

CHAPTER XXXVI.

Of the Sale, &c.. of Firewood, Hay, Straw, Lime and Coal.

CHAPTER XXXVII.

Of Carts and Cartmen, Dirt Carts, Public Porters and Garbage Carts.

CHAPTER XXXVIII.

CHAPTER XXXIX.

Of Stages or Accommodation Coaches.

CHAPTER XL.

Of Hackney Coaches and Cabs.

CHAPTER XLVI.

CHAPTER XLVII.

CHAPTER XLVIII.

CHAPTER XLXIX.

CHAPTER L.

CHAPTER LI.

CHAPTER LII.

CHAPTER LIII.

CHAPTER LIV.

CONTENTS OF THE APPENDIX.

OF THE CITY DEBT.

CITY RAILROADS.

CONTRACTS WITH GASLIGHT COMPANIES.

EXTRACTS FROM THE STATE LAWS,

Note by the Reviser of the Ordinances. — The following analysis was prepared for the purpose of affording a more ready reference to the provisions of the Charter, while the ordinances were in course of revision. After consultation with the Mayor and Committee on Ordinances, it was thought that it might form a convenient appendage to the volume of Ordinances.

ANALYSIS

OF THE

AMENDED CHARTER OF APRIL 14, 1857.

General Powers of the Corporation.

The Corporation known as "the Mayor, Aldermen and Commonalty of the city of New York," shall continue as a body politic and corporate, with the enjoyment of former grants, powers and privileges. (§ 1.)

The Legislative and Executive Powers of the Corporation.

The legislative power of the Corporation is vested in a Board of Aldermen and a Board of Councilmen, who together form the Common Council. (§ 1 and 2.)

The executive power of the Corporation is vested in the Mayor and in the executive departments. (§ 16.)

The legislative acts of the Common Council shall be by ordinance, act, or resolution, which, before becoming final, shall be submitted to the Mayor for his approval. If approved by him, the same shall become a law. If the Mayor do not approve thereof, he shall return the same within ten days to the Board in which the same originated, (or if not in session then, at its next regular meeting,) with his objections. The objections of the Mayor shall be entered at large in the minutes of proceedings of the Board, and shall be published as required by the Charter. After not less than ten days from the return thereof, the Board shall proceed to reconsider the subject. The votes upon the same shall be by yeas and nays, which shall be entered on the journals of the Board. If at least two-thirds of all the members elected to the Board agree to pass the same, the act, together with the objections of the Mayor, shall be sent to the other Board for concurrence. If approved by at least two-thirds of the other Board, it shall become a law. (§ 12.)

If the Mayor do not return the act within the time limited, it shall take effect as if he had approved it. (§ 13.)

Legislative acts may originate in either Board, and may be rejected or amended by the other. (§ 14.)

No legislative act shall be passed by either Board, except by the vote of a majority of all the members elected to such Board. (§ 14.)

No legislative act shall be valid unless it shall have passed both Boards within the same year. (§ 11.)

The Common Council shall make annual and occasional appropriations for every branch and object of city expenditure, and no money shall be drawn from the city treasury, except the same shall have been previously appropriated to the purpose for which it was drawn. (§ 31.)

The Common Council shall provide for the accountability of all officers and others in receipt or expenditure of city funds, by requiring adequate security from such persons. (§ 30.)

The Common Council shall fix the number of clerks to the departments, and shall also fix the terms of office of all officers created by them under authority of law. (§ 21.)

The Common Council may establish such other bureaux in the departments, besides those fixed by the Charter, as they may deem the public interest may require. (§ 28.)

The Common Council may assign to the executive departments and the bureaux created by the Charter such duties as they may direct, not inconsistent with the Charter. (§ 28.)

The members of the Common Council are prohibited from having any interest in matters connected with public affairs. (§ 28.)

No member shall receive compensation for his services as such member. (§ 44.)

The Common Council shall not have authority to borrow money, except in anticipation of the revenue of the year in which such loan shall be made, unless authorized by a special act of the legislature. (§ 32.)

The votes of two-thirds of all the members elected to each Board of the Common Council shall be necessary to authorize an expenditure for any celebration, procession, or entertainment of any kind, or on any occasion. (§ 42.)

The Common Council shall, by ordinance, passed and approved in the same manner as in the case of ordinances for raising and appropriating the money or disposing of the property of the city, prescribe the salaries of officers under the Charter of 1857. (§ 44.)

Of the Mayor.

The Mayor shall, with the advice and consent of the Board of Aldermen, appoint all heads of departments, except the Counsel to the Corporation and the Comptroller of the city of New York, and in case of the removal from office of the incumbents of either of the two last mentioned offices, the vacancy shall be supplied as in the case of other departments (§ 19.)

If any person nominated to office by the Mayor be rejected by the Board of Aldermen, the Mayor shall immediately nominate another person. (§ 19.)

(The legislative acts of the Common Council, submitted to the Mayor for approval, shall be subject to the provisions before recited under "legislative acts.")

It shall be the duty of the Mayor to communicate to the Common Council the situation and condition of the city affairs. (§ 18 subd. 1.)

Also—To recommend to the Common Council measures for the government of the city. (§ 18 subd. 2.)

Also—To be vigilant in causing the city ordinances to be enforced. (§ 18 subd. 3.)

Also—To exercise supervision over the conduct and acts of all subordinate officers, and to receive and examine into complaints against such officers for violation or neglect of duty. (§ 18 subd. 4.)

Also—Generally to perform such duties as may be prescribed by the Charter and ordinances, and the state and United States laws. (§ 18 subd. 5.)

The Mayor may require the opinion in writing, or information of the head of any department, upon any subject relating to his department. (§ 29.)

The Mayor shall be ex-officio member of a board, to whom appropriations for the Alms-house Department and the Board of Education are to be submitted, before being finally made. (§ 25.)

In case of vacancy in the office of Mayor, or of his absence from the city, or of his being prevented by sickness, or other cause, from attending to the duties of his office, the President of the Board of Aldermen shall act as Mayor. (§ 17.)

The Mayor shall have power to appoint such clerks as may be authorized by the Common Council and required in his office. (§ 18 subd. 5.)

He shall countersign warrants drawn by the Comptroller. (§ 22.)

Of the Board of Aldermen.

A majority of the members of the Board shall constitute a quorum for the transaction of business.

The Board shall meet in a chamber separate from that of the Councilmen.

It shall choose a president from its own body.

It shall choose its clerk and other officers.

It shall determine its own rules.

It shall be the judge of the election returns and qualification of its own members.

It shall cause to be kept a journal of its proceedings.

The doors of the Chamber of the Board shall be open during its times of meeting, except when secrecy is required.

Resolutions and reports recommending improvements involving expenditures of money, or taxation, or assessment, shall, before being passed in the Board, be published at least two days; and on every vote in relation thereto, the ayes and noes shall be called and published. (§ 7.)

The Board of Aldermen shall have power, without the consent of the Mayor, by a vote of two-thirds of all the members elected, to remove any of the heads of departments other than the Comptroller and Counsel to the Corporation. (§ 21.)

The Board of Aldermen shall have power to confirm or reject all nominations of officers made by the Mayor. (§ 22.)

The Board shall have power to compel the attendance of absent members ; to punish its members for disorderly behavior ; to expel a member by a vote of two-thirds of its members elected. (§ 8.)

The Board may require the opinion in writing, or information of the head of any department, upon any subject relating to his department. (§ 29.)

The Board shall not act upon any ordinance on the same day on which it shall have passed the other Board, unless by unanimous consent, except in case of invasion, insurrection, riot or pestilence. (§ 37.)

The members of the Board shall not be questioned in any other place for any speech or vote in the Board. (§ 8.)

The stated and occasional meetings of the Board shall be regulated by its own ordinances, and it may meet on the same day with the Councilmen, or on a different day, as judged expedient. (§ 9.)

The Board shall sit as a Board of City Canvassers to canvass the returns of the district canvassers of the Charter elections, in the manner designated by § 53 of Amended Charter of 1857. (§ 53.)

The Board may direct a special election to fill vacancies of their members. (§ 6.)

Of the President of the Board of Aldermen.

The President of the Board of Aldermen shall act as Mayor in case of a vacancy in that office, or in case of the absence of the Mayor from the city, or in case of the Mayor being prevented from attending to the duties of his office. (§ 17.)

The President shall be ex-officio a member of a board to whom appropriations for the Alms-house Department, and for the Board of Education shall, in pursuance of § 25 of the Amended Charter of 1857, be submitted before being finally made. (§ 25.)

Of the Board of Councilmen.

A majority of the members of the Board shall constitute a quorum for the transaction of business.

The Board shall meet in a chamber separate from that of the Aldermen.

It shall choose a president from its own body.

It shall choose its clerk and other officers.

It shall determine its own rules.

It shall be the judge of the election returns and qualification of its own members.

It shall cause to be kept a journal of its proceedings.

The doors of the Chamber of the Board shall be open during its sittings, except when secrecy is required.

Resolutions and reports recommending improvements involving expenditures of money, or taxation, or assessment, shall, before being passed in the Board, be published at least two days, and on every vote in relation thereto, the ayes and noes shall be called and published. (§ 7.)

The Board shall have power to compel the attendance of absent members; to punish its members for disorderly behavior; to expel a member by a vote of two-thirds of its members elected. (§ 8.)

The Board may require the opinion in writing, or information of the head of any department upon any subject relating to his department. (§ 29.)

The Board shall not act upon any ordinance on the same day on which it shall have passed the other Board, unless by unanimous consent, except in case of invasion, insurrection, riot, or pestilence. (§ 37.)

The members of the Board shall not be questioned in any other place for any speech or vote in the Board. (§ 8.)

The stated and occasional meetings of the Board shall be regulated by its own ordinances, and it may meet on the same day with the Aldermen, or on a different day, as judged expedient. (§ 9.)

The Board may direct a special election to fill vacancies of their numbers. (§ 6.)

Of the President of the Board of Councilmen.

The President of the Board of Councilmen shall be ex-officio a member of a board, to whom appropriations for the Alms-house Department and for the Board of Education shall, in pursuance of section 25 of the Amended Charter of 1857, be submitted, before being finally made. (§25.)

Of the Aldermen.

The city shall be divided into seventeen Aldermanic districts, the boundaries of which are defined by § 50.

The Aldermen must be resident of the district from which they are chosen. (§ 5.)

The Aldermen may be compelled by the Board to attend meetings; they may be punished by the Board for disorderly behavior; they may be expelled by a vote of two-thirds of the members elected to the Board. When expelled they shall forfeit all rights as Aldermen. They shall not be questioned in any other place for any speech or vote in the Board. (§ 8.)

They are prohibited from sitting or acting as judges of the Court of

Oyer and Terminer, or in the Courts of General or Special Sessions. But this section shall not prevent their exercising the power of magistrates in the arrest, commitment or bailing of offenders, except that they cannot let to bail or discharge a person arrested or committed by another magistrate. (§ 48.)

For the provisions respecting bribery, see § 52 of the Amended Charter.

Of the Councilmen.

There shall be six Councilmen elected from each senatorial district, as the same now are, or hereafter may be constituted. (§ 4.)

They shall be elected by general ticket in each of said districts, and together shall form the Board of Councilmen. (§ 4.)

They shall be chosen for one year. (§ 4.)

They must be resident of the district from which they are chosen. (§ 4).

They may be compelled by their Board to attend meetings; they may be punished by the Board for disorderly behavior; they may be expelled by a vote of two-thirds of the elected members of their Board. When expelled they forfeit all rights as Councilmen. They shall not be questioned in any other place for any speech or vote in the Board. (§ 8.)

See "Officers under the Charter."

Of the Clerk of the Common Council.

The Clerk of the Board of Aldermen shall be Clerk of the Common Council. (§ 36.)

He shall keep open for inspection the records and minutes of proceedings of the Common Council, except as otherwise ordered. (§ 36.)

He shall appoint and remove at pleasure deputy clerks in his department to the number authorized by ordinance. (§ 36.)

He shall keep the seal of the city. (§ 36.)

His signature shall be necessary to all leases, grants and other documents, as under existing laws. (§ 36.)

He shall publish the proceedings of the Board of Aldermen, except such as require secrecy, in the newspapers employed by the Corporation. (§ 37.)

Whenever a vote shall be taken in the Board upon the passage of an ordinance which shall contemplate any specific improvement, or involve the sale, disposition or appropriation of public property, or the expenditure of public moneys, or income therefrom, or lay any tax or assessment, such ordinance shall, before being sent to the other Board, and immediately after the adjournment of the Board, be published with the yeas and nays, and with the names of the persons voting for or against the same, in the newspapers employed by the Corporation, as part of the proceedings. (§37.)

He shall publish ordinances and parts of ordinances which shall be passed in the Board of Aldermen. (§ 37.)

He shall be clerk of the Board of City Canvassers, and shall within five days from the filing in his office of the statement by the Board of the result of the Charter election, give notice to the persons declared elected. (§ 53.)

He shall countersign warrants drawn by the Comptroller. (§ 22.)

Of the Clerk of the Board of Councilmen.

He shall publish the proceedings (except such as require secrecy) in the Corporation newspapers. (§ 37.)

Whenever a vote shall be taken in the Board upon the passage of an ordinance which shall contemplate any specific improvement, or involve the sale, disposition or appropriation of public property, or the expenditure of public money, or income therefrom, or lay any tax or assessment, such ordinance shall, before being sent to the other Board, and immediately after the adjournment of the Board, be published with the yeas and nays, and with the names of the persons voting for or against the same, in the newspapers employed by the Corporation, as part of the proceedings. (§ 37.)

He shall publish ordinances and amendments of ordinances which shall be passed. (§ 37.)

He shall appoint and remove at pleasure deputy clerks in his department to the number authorized by ordinance. (§ 36.)

Provisions relating generally to Officers of the City Government.

Officers holding under the Charter of 1857, shall be deemed to have vacated their offices when they shall, during their term of office, hold or accept any other civil office under the United States Government, or under the Charter, or when they shall receive any fees or emoluments directed to be paid by any ordinance of the Common Council, except as provided in the Charter. (§ 10.)

Officers of departments cannot incur expense unless an appropriation shall have been made covering the expense, whether the object of expenditure shall have been ordered by the Common Council or not. (§ 28.)

Officers of the Corporation are prohibited in general from having any personal interest in matters connected with the interests of the city. (§ 28.)

The accountability of disbursing and receiving officers shall be provided for by the Common Council, by requiring of them adequate security; such security to be annually renewed; but the security first taken to remain until new security is provided. (§§ 30-45.)

Officers under the city government (whether appointed or elected) shall, on or before the first day of January next succeeding each election, or within five days after receiving notice of such appointment, subscribe an oath or affirmation faithfully to perform the duties of their office, which oath or affirmation shall be filed in the Mayor's office. (§ 39.)

Any person swearing falsely to an oath or affirmation required under this Charter, shall be guilty of perjury. (§ 40.)

Provisions respecting the retention of office of those elected under former laws, until their successors are chosen under the Charter of 1857 shall take office, are specifically set forth in § 51.

Any officer of the city government, or person employed in its service, who shall wilfully violate any of the provisions of the Amended Charter; or

Who shall evade any of said provisions; or

Who shall commit any fraud upon the city; or

Who shall convert any of the public property to his own use; or

Who shall knowingly permit any other person so to convert it, shall be deemed guilty of a misdemeanor; and in addition to the penalties imposed by law, such officer shall forfeit his office and be excluded forever after from receiving or holding any office under the City Charter. (§ 40.)

No officer under the Charter of 1857, except the Collector of the City Revenue, the Collector of Assessments, the Clerk of Arrears, the Counsel to the Corporation, the Inspector of Vessels, (and the City Inspector, from certain sources detailed under his department,) shall receive from the Corporation any perquisites, compensation or commission, except a salary. (§ 44.)

Officers created by or holding office under the Amended Charter of 1857, other than the Mayor, Counsel to the Corporation or Comptroller, may be presented by the Grand Jury, but only upon testimony of witnesses personally cognizant of the facts, and after the person so charged shall have had a reasonable opportunity to appear before said Grand Jury in person in explanation thereof. (See further § 49.)

Persons guilty of bribery of members or officers of the Corporation shall, upon conviction, be imprisoned in a penitentiary for a term not exceeding two years, or shall be fined not exceeding five thousand dollars, or both, in the discretion of the court. (§ 52.)

Any members or officer of the Corporation accepting bribes, shall, upon conviction, be disqualified from holding any public office, trust, or appointment under the Charter of the city of New York, and shall forfeit his office, and shall be punished by imprisonment in the penitentiary not exceeding two years, or by a fine not exceeding five thousand dollars, or both, in the discretion of the court. (§ 52.)

Persons proffering or accepting bribes, shall be competent witnesses against any other person offending in the same transaction, and may be compelled to appear and give evidence before any Grand Jury, or in any court, in the same manner as other persons; but the testimony so given shall not be used in any prosecution or proceeding, civil or criminal, against the person so testifying. (§ 52.)

Officers receiving fees (except those who are by charter allowed to retain them) are required, on receipt thereof, to pay the same into the city treasury. (§ 44.)

The salaries of officers under the Charter of 1857, shall be prescribed by ordinance of the Common Council, to be approved in the same manner as in the case of ordinances for raising and appropriating the money or disposing of the property of the city. (§ 44.)

Provisions applicable to all Executive Departments.

Executive power is vested in them. (§ 16.)

The Common Council may assign to them any duties not inconsistent with the Charter. (§ 28.)

The departments or the officers thereof cannot incur expense unless an appropriation shall have been made covering the expense, whether the object of expenditure shall have been ordered by the Common Council or not. (§ 28.)

All accounts rendered to, or kept in any of them, are subject to the inspection and revision of the Department of Finance. (§ 22.)

Until the Common Council shall otherwise direct, the existing ordinances shall apply to the departments so far as the same are applicable, and are not inconsistent with the Amended Charter. (§ 32.)

1. *As to Clerks to the Departments*—Their number shall be as fixed by the Common Council. (§ 21.)

They shall be appointed and removed by the heads of the different departments. (§ 21.)

2. *As to Clerks in the Departments and Bureaux*—They shall hold office during the same term enjoyed by the heads of departments, unless sooner removed. (§ 21.)

Of Contracts.

All contracts shall be entered into by the appropriate heads of departments. (§ 38.)

Whenever any work is necessary to complete a particular job for the Corporation, and the several parts of said work shall together involve the expenditure of more than two hundred and fifty dollars, the same shall be by contract under regulations established by ordinances of the Common Council, unless by a vote of three-fourths of the members elected to each Board it shall be ordered otherwise. (§ 38.)

Such as are to be made or let by authority of the Common Council for work to be done, or supplies to be furnished, shall be made by the appropriate heads of departments. (§ 38.)

When any supply is needful to be furnished by the Corporation for any particular purpose, and the several parts of such supply shall together involve the expenditure of more than two hundred and fifty dollars, the same shall be by contract under regulations established by ordinance of the Common Council, unless by a vote of three-fourths of the members elected to each Board it shall be ordered otherwise. (§ 38.)

Contracts shall all be founded on sealed bids or proposals made in compliance with public notice, advertised in such newspapers as may be employed by the Corporation for the purpose. (§ 38.)

Such notice shall be published at least ten days in each of such newspapers. (§ 38.)

Such contracts, when given, shall be given to the lowest bidder, the terms of whose contract shall be settled by the Corporation Counsel as an act of preliminary specification to the bid or proposal, and who shall give security for the faithful performance of his contract in the manner prescribed and required by ordinance, and the sufficiency of this security shall, in addition to the justification and acknowledgment, be approved by the Comptroller. (§ 38.)

If the lowest bidder shall neglect or refuse to accept the contract within forty-eight hours after written notice that the same has been awarded to his bid or proposal, it shall be re-advertised and re-let, as above provided. (§ 38.)

When made as directed by the Charter, the contract shall be executed in duplicate and filed in the Department of Finance. (§ 38.)

For each payment made on contracts, a receipt shall be endorsed on the contract by the party receiving the warrant. (§ 38.)

Warrants for payments on contracts shall only be given to the person interested in the same, or to his authorized representative. (§ 38.)

No additional allowance beyond the legal claim under any contract with the Corporation, or for any service on its account, or in its employment, shall ever be allowed. (§ 46.)

No contract shall be awarded to, nor any bid be accepted from, any person who is in arrears to the Corporation upon debt or contract, or who is a defaulter as surety or otherwise upon any obligation to the Corporation. (§ 47.)

Provisions applicable to all the Heads of Executive Departments.

The heads of departments, other than the Counsel to the Corporation and the Comptroller, shall be appointed by the Mayor, with the advice and consent of the Board of Aldermen. (§ 19.)

The heads of executive departments (except the Croton Aqueduct Board, the Counsel to the Corporation and the Comptroller,) shall hold their offices for two years, and until the appointment of their successors. (§ 21.)

The heads of departments (except the Comptroller and the Counsel to the Corporation) may be suspended by the Mayor for cause during any recess of the Common Council. (§ 21.)

The cause of such suspension shall be communicated to the Common Council at the first meeting thereof. (§ 21.)

The heads of departments (except the Comptroller and Counsel) may be removed by the Mayor, by and with the consent of the Board of Aldermen. (§ 21.)

Or they may be removed for cause by the Board of Aldermen, without the consent of the Mayor, by a vote of two-thirds of all the members elected. (§ 21.)

The heads of departments have power to appoint and remove the chiefs of bureaux and clerks in their respective departments, except the City Chamberlain. (§ 21.)

They may severally be required by the Mayor or either Board of the Common Council, to give an opinion in writing, or information upon any subject relating to their several departments. (§ 29.)

They are prohibited from having any private interest in matters connected with public interests. (§ 28.)

They must, in cases where work has been done, or supplies furnished for their department, in cases where from the amount involved no contract is required to be made, certify the necessity thereof, before any expenditure shall be made thereon; such work or supplies must also have been authorized by the Common Council to justify an expenditure on account thereof. (§ 38.)

They shall report in writing to the Common Council quarterly the state of their several departments, with such suggestions in relation to the improvement thereof, and to the public business connected therewith, as they shall deem advisable. (§ 29.)

The heads of the appropriate departments shall superintend the sale of all property sold under authority of the Common Council. (§ 38.)

They shall make all sales of personal property in the custody of their several departments or bureaux, under such regulations as shall be established by ordinances of the Common Council. (§ 38.)

In case of sales of property under authority of the Common Council under their respective superintendence, they shall immediately deposit the proceeds with the City Chamberlain. and immediately cause to be filed an account of sales verified by them in the office of the Comptroller. (§ 38.)

The heads of the appropriate departments shall make all contracts. (§ 38.)

They shall make, in the appropriate departments, all contracts to be made or let by authority of the Common Council for work to be done or supplies to be furnished. (§ 38.)

Provisions relating generally to all Bureaux and Heads of Bureaux in the Executive Departments.

Such others, in addition to those provided by charter, as may be deemed requisite for the public interest, may be established by the Common Council, and duties not inconsistent with the Charter may be assigned them. (§ 28.)

The chiefs of bureaux, except the City Chamberlain and Chief Engineer of the Fire Department, shall be appointed and removed by the heads of their respective departments. (§ 21.)

They shall hold office during the same term enjoyed by the heads of departments, unless sooner removed. (§ 21.)

They are prohibited in general from having any private interest in matters connected with public interests. (§ 28.)

The bureaux established in the *Street Department* are those of the "Superintendent of Wharves," "Superintendent of Repairs and Supplies," Superintendent of Lamps and Gas," "Chief Engineer of the Fire Department," Superintendent of Roads," "Collector of Assessments," "Superintendent of Street Improvements."

The bureaux established in the *Department of Finance* are those of the "Collector of the City Revenue," "Receiver of Taxes," "Clerk of Arrears," "Chamberlain of the city of New York," "Auditor of Accounts."

The bureaux established in the *Croton Aqueduct Board* are those of the "Water Registrar" and "Water Purveyor."

The bureaux established in the *Law Department* are those of the "Corporation Attorney" and the "Public Administrator."

The bureaux established in the *City Inspector's Department* are those of "Sanitary Inspection and Street Cleaning," of "Statistics and Records," of the "Superintendent of Markets."

Of the Department of Finance generally.

It is constituted an executive department. (§ 22.)

It has control of all the fiscal concerns of the Corporation. (§ 22)

It shall prescribe the forms of keeping and rendering all city accounts. (§ 22.)

All accounts rendered to or kept in the other departments of the city government, shall be subject to the inspection and revision of this department. (§ 22.)

The following bureaux are established in this department, viz:

For the collection of the city revenue, the chief officer of which shall be called "the Collector of the City Revenue."

For the collection of taxes, the chief officer of which shall be called "the Receiver of Taxes."

For the collection of arrears of taxes, the chief officer of which shall be called "the Clerk of Arrears."

For the reception of all moneys paid into the treasury of the city, and for the payment of moneys on the warrant drawn by the Comptroller and countersigned by the Mayor and Clerk of the Common Council; the chief officer of which shall be called "the Chamberlain of the city of New York."

An Auditing Bureau, the chief officer of which shall be called "the Auditor of Accounts. (§ 22.)

This department shall settle and adjust all claims in favor of or against the Corporation, and all accounts in which the Corporation is concerned either as debtor or creditor. (§ 22.)

The chief officer of this department is called the Comptroller of the city of New York. (§ 22.)

All contracts, when made as directed by the Charter, shall be executed in duplicate and filed in this department. (§ 38.)

For each payment made on contracts a receipt shall be endorsed on the contract by the party receiving the warrant. (§ 38.)

Warrants for payments on contracts shall only be given to the person interested in such contract or his authorized representative. (§ 38.)

All moneys drawn from the city treasury shall be upon vouchers for the expenditure thereof, examined and allowed by the Auditor, approved by the Comptroller and filed in his office. (§ 22.)

The leases, deeds and other papers connected with this department, shall be drawn by the Law Department. (§ 25.)

Of the Comptroller.

He is constituted the chief officer of the Department of Finance. (§22).

It is provided that the person filling the office at the passage of the Charter should remain until the expiration of his term, and not to be removed, except by the Governor, or after indictment, as provided in sections 20 and 49. (§ 51.)

He shall be elected by the electors of the city for the term of four years, and shall be voted for on a separate ballot. (§ 19.)

He may be removed by the Governor for cause, in the manner provided by law in the case of sheriffs. (§ 20.)

In case of his removal, the vacancy until the next annual election of Charter officers, is to be filled by the Mayor, with the advice and consent of the Board of Aldermen. (§ 20.)

He shall report to the Common Council once in ninety days the name of every person in whose favor an account has been audited, with the decision of the Auditor upon the same, together with the final action of the Comptroller thereon. (§ 22.)

All moneys drawn from the city treasury shall be upon vouchers for the expenditure thereof, examined and allowed by the Auditor and approved by the Comptroller and filed in his office. (§ 22.)

It shall be his duty to publish, two months before the annual Charter election, a full statement of receipts and expenditures during the previous year, with the different sources of revenue, and the amount received from each ; the appropriations made, their objects, and the amount expended under each ; the moneys borrowed, the authority under which the loan was made, and the terms on which it was obtained. (§ 34.)

He is ex-officio a member of a board to whom appropriations for the Alms-house Department and Board of Education are to be submitted before being finally made. (§ 25.)

He shall judge of the adequacy and sufficiency of securities offered by bidders on Corporation contracts, and their justification and acknowledgment must also be approved by him. (§ 38.)

Sales of public property and franchises (other than grants of land under water to which the owners of the upland shall have a preëmptive right), shall be made by public auction and to the highest bidder who will give adequate security. Previous notice of sales under this section shall be given, under direction of the Comptroller in the Corporation newspapers, for thirty days in each paper. (§ 41.)

Of the City Chamberlain.

The Chamberlain shall be appointed by the Mayor, with the consent of the Board of Aldermen, and may be removed in the same manner as the heads of departments. (§ 21.)

He constitutes the chief of a bureau in the Department of Finance, for the reception of all moneys paid into the treasury of the city, and for the payment of moneys on warrants drawn by the Comptroller and countersigned by the Mayor and Clerk of the Common Council. (§ 22.)

He shall keep books showing the amounts paid on account of the several appropriations, and no warrants shall be paid on account of any appropriation after the amount authorized by tax for that specific purpose shall have been expended. (§ 22.)

Of the Receiver of Taxes.

He is constituted the chief of a bureau in the Department of Finance, for the collection of taxes. (§ 22.)

He has all the powers and shall perform all the duties now prescribed by law for the Receiver of Taxes, and the provisions of law relating to him are hereby modified so as to conform to the provisions of this Charter. (§ 22.)

Of the Clerk of Arrears.

He is constituted the chief of a bureau in the Department of Finance for the collection of arrears of taxes, arrears of assessments and arrears of water rents. (§ 22.)

He is excepted from the general rule confining officers under the Charter of 1857 to a salary. (§ 44.)

Of the Auditor of Accounts.

The Auditor of Accounts is constituted the chief of a bureau, to revise, audit and settle all accounts in which the city is concerned as debtor or creditor; to keep an account of each claim for or against the Corporation, and of the sums allowed upon each, and to certify the same, with the reasons for the allowance, to the Comptroller. (§ 22.)

Of the Collector of the City Revenue.

He is constituted the chief of a bureau in the Finance Department for the collection of the revenue arising from rents and interest on bonds and mortgages, and all revenues arising from the use or sale of property belonging to or managed by the city. (§ 22.)

Other duties than those prescribed by the Charter may be assigned to him by the Common Council. (§ 22.)

He is excepted from the general rule confining officers under the Charter of 1857 to a salary. (§ 44.)

Of the Street Department generally.

It is constituted an Executive Department. (§ 23.)

It has cognizance of opening, altering, regulating, grading, flagging, curbing, guttering and lighting streets, roads, places and avenues. (§23.)

It has cognizance of building, repairing and lighting wharves, piers and slips. (§ 23.)

It has cognizance of the care of public buildings and places. (§ 23.)

It has cognizance of the construction and repairing of the public roads. (§ 23.)

It has cognizance of the filling up of sunken lots under the ordinances of the Common Council. (§ 23.)

The chief officer of this department is called the Street Commissioner. [§ 23.]

The following bureaux are established in this department :

The Superintendent of Wharves.

The Bureau of Repairs and Supplies, the chief officer of which shall be called the Superintendent of Repairs and Supplies.

The Bureau of Lamps and Gas, the chief officer of which shall be called the Superintendent of Lamps and Gas.

The Chief Engineer of the Fire Department.

The Superintendent of Roads.

A bureau for the collection of assessments, the chief of which shall be called the Collector of Assessments.

A bureau for grading, flagging, curbing and guttering streets, the chief officer of which shall be called the Superintendent of Street Improvements. (§ 23.)

Of the Street Commissioner.

He is constituted the chief officer of the Street Department. (§ 23.)

The person filling the office at the passage of the Charter shall remain in office until the expiration of his term, and not be removed, except by the Governor, as provided in § 20, or after indictment, as provided in § 49. (§ 51.)

Of the Superintendent of Repairs and Supplies.

The office of Commissioner of Repairs and Supplies, as established before the passage of that Charter, is abolished. (§ 51.)

The Superintendent of Repairs and Supplies is constituted the head of a bureau in the Street Department. (§ 23.)

Of the Superintendent of Street Improvements.

He is constituted the chief of a bureau in the Street Department, for grading, flagging, curbing and guttering the streets. (§ 23.)

Of the Superintendent of Lamps and Gas.

He is constituted chief of a bureau in the Street Department. (§ 23.)

Of the Superintendent of Wharves.

He is constituted the chief of a bureau in the Street Department. (§ 23.)

Of the Collector of Assessments.

He is established as chief of a bureau in the Street Department, for the collection of assessments. (§ 23.)

He is exempted from the general rule confining officers under the Charter of 1857 to a salary. (§ 44.)

Of the Chief Engineer.

He shall be elected in the same manner as is now, or may hereafter be prescribed by law. (§ 21.)

He has charge of repairing fire engines and fire apparatus. (§ 23.)

He is constituted chief of a bureau in the Street Department. (§ 23.)

Of the Superintendent of Roads.

He is constituted the chief of a bureau in the Street Department. (§ 23.)

Of Public Buildings.

The care of them is within the cognizance of the Street Department. (§ 23.)

Of Public Places.

The care of them is within the cognizance of the Street Department. (§ 23.)

The opening, altering, regulating, grading, flagging, curbing, guttering and lighting of them is within the cognizance of the Street Department. (§ 23.)

Of the Law Department generally.

It is constituted an Executive Department of the city government. (§26.)

It shall have charge of, and shall conduct all the law business of the Corporation and of the departments, and all other law business in which the city shall be interested, when so ordered by the Corporation. (§ 26.)

It shall have the charge of, and shall conduct the legal proceedings necessary in opening, widening or altering streets. (§ 26.)

It shall draw the leases, deeds and other papers connected with the Finance Department. (§ 26.)

The chief officer shall be called the Counsel to the Corporation. (§ 26.)

The following bureaux are established in this department, viz:

The "Corporation Attorney," the "Public Administrator." (§ 26.)

Of the Counsel to the Corporation.

He is made the chief officer of the Law Department. (§ 26.)

The person filling the office at the passage of the Charter shall remain in office until the expiration of his term, and not be removed, unless by the Governor, or after indictment, as provided by sections 20 and 49. (§ 51.)

He shall be elected by the electors of the city for the term of three years. (§ 19.)

He may be removed by the Governor for cause, in the manner provided by law in the case of sheriffs. (§ 20.)

In case of his removal, the vacancy until the next annual election of

Charter officers, is to be filled by the Mayor, with the advice and consent of the Board of Aldermen. (§ 20.)

He shall settle the terms of contracts with the Corporation, as an act of preliminary specification to bids, or proposals therefor. (§ 38.)

He is excepted from the general rule confining officers under the Charter of 1857 to a salary. (§ 44.)

Of the Corporation Attorney.

He is constituted the head of a bureau in the Law Department. (§26.)

Of the Public Administrator.

He is constituted the head of a bureau in the Law Department. (§ 26.)

Of the City Inspector's Department generally.

It is established as an Executive Department. (§ 27.)

Its chief officer shall be called the City Inspector. (§ 27.)

It has cognizance of all matters affecting the public health, pursuant to ordinances of the Common Council and the lawful requirements of the Commissioners of Health and the Board of Health. (§ 27.)

The following bureaux are established in this department, viz:

Of "Sanitary Inspection and Street Cleaning," under an officer named Superintendent of Sanitary Inspection; of "Records and Statistics," which shall be under the charge of the Registrar of Records; for the inspection, regulation and management of the "Public Markets," the chief officer of which shall be called the "Superintendent of Markets." (§27.)

The coroners shall make returns to this department of inquisitions taken by them, excepting those charging homicide or felonious assault. (§27.)

Of the City Inspector.

He is constituted the chief officer in the City Inspector's Department. (§ 27.)

The person filling the office at the time of the passage of the Charter shall remain in office until the expiration of his term, and not be removed, except by the Governor, as provided in § 20, or by the court after presentment by the Grand Jury, as provided in § 49. (§ 51.)

He may receive to his own use such portion of the fees allowed for recording births and marriages, as are or may be prescribed by law, and to this extent is excepted from the general rule confining officers under the Charter of 1857 to a salary. (§ 44.)

He shall appoint such number of inspectors and sealers of weights and measures as now or hereafter may exist. (§ 27.)

He may be permitted by the Croton Aqueduct Board to use hydrants for cleaning the streets, under the regulations of that Board. (§ 27.)

Of the Superintendent of Sanitary Inspection.

He is constituted the chief of a bureau in the City Inspector's Department. (§ 27.)

He shall render such services as by ordinance may attach to said bureau in cleaning the streets and in the abatement and removal of nuisances detrimental to the public health in said city. (§ 27.)

Of the Registrar of Records.

He is constituted the chief of the Bureau of Records and Statistics in the City Inspector's Department. (§ 27.)

In this bureau shall be kept all records which by law or ordinance may be required to be kept in the City Inspector's Department. (§ 27.)

Of the Superintendent of Markets.

He is constituted the chief officer in the City Inspector's Department. (§ 27.)

Of Inspectors of Weights and Measures.

They shall be appointed by the City Inspector. (§ 27.)

When so appointed, they succeed to all the powers and duties, and receive the compensation now prescribed by law. (§ 27.)

They hold office on the same terms as chiefs of bureaux. (§ 27.)

Of Coroners.

They shall make returns to the City Inspector of their inquisitions, except those charging homicide or felonious assault. (§ 27.)

Their inquisitions charging homicide or felonious assault shall be filed with the Clerk of the General Sessions. (§ 27.)

Of the Croton Aqueduct Board.

It is continued as an Executive Department.

It shall have charge of the Croton Aqueduct and all the structures and property connected with the supply and distribution of Croton water in the city of New York.

And of the under-drainage of the same.

And of the public sewers of said city.

And of permits for street vaults.

And of paving, re-paving and repairing streets.

And of digging and constructing wells.

And of the collection of the revenue arising from the sale of Croton water.

With such other powers and duties as are, or may be, prescribed by law. (§ 24.)

The chief officers thereof shall be called the President, Engineer and Assistant Commissioner, who together form the Croton Aqueduct Board, and hold their offices for five years. (§ 24.)

The officers at the time of the passage of the Charter shall remain in office until the expiration of their terms, and not be removed, except by the Governor, or after indictment, as provided by sections 20 and 49. (§51.)

The bureaux established in this department are as follows:

For the collection of the revenue derived from the sale of the water, and the chief officer thereof shall be called the "Water Registrar."

For the laying of water pipes; the construction and repairs of sewers, wells and hydrants, and the paving, repaving and repairing of streets, the chief officer of which shall be called the "Water Purveyor."

This department shall, at all times (when the general supply is not endangered,) permit the City Inspector to order the hydrants to be used for cleaning the streets, under their regulations. (§ 27.)

Of the Water Purveyor.

He is constituted as chief of a bureau under the Croton Aqueduct Board, for the laying of water pipes and the construction and repair of sewers, wells and hydrants, the paving, re-paving and repairing of streets. (§ 24.)

Of the Water Registrar.

He is constituted the chief of a bureau in the department of the Croton

Aqueduct Board, for the collection of the revenues derived from the sale of Croton water. (§ 24.)

Of the Alms-house Department

It is constituted an Executive Department. (§ 25.)

It has cognizance of all matters relating to the Alms-house and prisons. (§ 25.)

Its chief officers are called "Governors of the Alms-house." (§25.)

The "Governors" take and hold office and exercise duties, as prescribed by "an act to provide for the government of the Alms-house and Penitentiary in the city and county of New York." (§ 25.)

Ordinary appropriations for the Alms-house, proposed by the Governors, shall, before being finally made, be submitted to a board consisting of the President of the Board of Aldermen, the President of the Board of Councilmen, the Mayor and Comptroller, which Board, if it approve the appropriation, shall report the same to the Supervisors. If it disapprove, it shall return the same with objections to the Governors. If the Governors on reconsideration adhere by a vote of two-thirds of their number then in office, they shall return the appropriation to the said board, who shall report to the Supervisors. (§ 25.)

The annual election of the Governors shall be held on the first Tuesday of December. (§ 53.)

Of the Election of Charter Officers.

The Common Council are authorized and directed to make all necessary arrangements for the conduct and regulation of the election of officers under the Charter of 1857, in conformity as far as may be to the general election law, except as the Charter otherwise provides. (§ 43.)

The annual election for Charter Officers, School Officers and Governors of the Alms-house shall be held on the first Tuesday in December, and the officers shall take office on the first Monday of January next succeeding. (§ 53.)

The provisions of law in force at the time of the passage of the Charter of 1857 in regard to the notification, duration, conduct of election and canvassing of votes at general elections, shall apply thereto, except that the return of all elections provided for by this act, shall be filed by the district canvassers in the several districts with the Clerk of the Common Council, within twenty-four hours after the polls are closed. (§ 53.)

The returns shall be canvassed by the Board of Aldermen, sitting as a Board of City Canvassers. The Clerk of the Common Council shall be Clerk of the said Board of City Canvassers. Said Board shall meet on the Thursday next succeeding such election, and shall, within ten days thereafter, wholly complete such canvass, and file within the same time duplicate statements of the result in the respective offices of the Clerk of the Common Council and the County Clerk. (§ 53.)

The Clerk of the Common Council, within five days succeeding the filing of the said statement, shall give to each person declared elected a certificate thereof. (§ 53.)

Provision relating to Grants from the City.

All persons acquiring grants from the Corporation, under the Charter of 1857, shall be required to purchase, at a fair appraised valuation, the property of the former grantees, or lessees, actually necessary for the purposes of such grant. (§ 41.)

Provision relating to the Sale of Wholesome Food.

No tax or penalty shall hereafter be imposed upon or collected of any person, nor license required for selling or exposing for sale upon his, her, or their own premises, in said city, any wholesome article of food; nor for selling such articles in such parts of the streets of said city, as may be designated by the Common Council for that purpose. (§ 35.)

Provision relating to Ferries.

Ferries shall all be leased. (§ 41.)

Ferry leases shall be revocable by the Common Council for mismanagement or neglect to provide adequate accommodations. (§ 41.)

All persons acquiring ferry leases under the provisions of the Charter shall be required to purchase, at a fair appraised valuation, the boats, buildings, and other property of the former lessees or grantees, actually necessary for the purposes of such ferry. (§ 41.)

The Inspector of Vessels.

He is excepted from the general rule confining officers under the Charter of 1857 to a salary. (§ 44)

Repealing Provisions.

The Amended Charter of 1857 was passed April 14, 1857, and took effect by its terms on the first day of May, 1857.

It repealed specifically the act to amend the Charter passed April 7, 1830; also, the act to amend the Charter passed April 2, 1849, together with the act to amend the same, passed July 11, 1851; also, the act to amend the Charter passed April 12, 1853, together with the act supplementary thereto, passed June 14, 1853.

It also repealed generally all laws inconsistent with its provisions.

But the Charters known as the Dongan and Montgomerie Charters, so far as the same are in force, should so continue, and not be construed as repealed, modified, or in any manner affected. See section 54 of Amended Charter.

REVISED ORDINANCES

OF THE

CITY OF NEW YORK.

REVISED ORDINANCES.

The Mayor, Aldermen and Commonalty of the City of New York, in Common Council convened, do ordain as follows :

CHAPTER I.

OF THE MAYOR AND THE OFFICERS APPERTAINING TO THE MAYOR'S OFFICE.

ARTICLE I.

OF THE MAYOR.

§ 1. The Mayor shall continue to possess the powers and execute the duties conferred and imposed upon him by the charter of the city and the various acts amending the same, by the laws of the state, and by the ordinances and resolutions of the Common Council not inconsistent therewith. Powers and duties of the Mayor.

§ 2. The Mayor may, whenever he shall deem it necessary, issue his proclamation for the apprehension of any person who may have committed a crime within the city of New York, and may, in such proclamation, offer a reward not exceeding five hundred dollars, to be paid out of the city treasury upon the certificate of the Mayor that the service required has been performed. May offer rewards.

§ 3. The Mayor shall receive an annual salary of five thousand dollars. Salary.

ARTICLE II.

OF THE CLERKS IN THE MAYOR'S OFFICE.

Chief Clerk.

§ 4. There shall be an officer, to be denominated the Chief Clerk, in the Mayor's office, who shall be appointed by, and hold his office during the pleasure of, the Mayor.

Bond.

§ 5. Before entering upon the duties of his office, the said Chief Clerk shall execute a bond to the Corporation, with one or more sufficient sureties, to be approved by the Comptroller, in the penal sum of one thousand dollars, conditioned for the the faithful performance of the duties of his office.

Duties of Mayor's Clerk.

§ 6. It shall be the duty of the Mayor's Clerk—

1. To prepare and file in the Mayor's office all oaths of office required to be taken before the Mayor.

2. To take the bonds of such officers as are required to give security before the Mayor, and to transmit them to the Comptroller to be approved and filed.

3. To prepare all such proofs or acknowledgments of deeds or other instruments as require the official attestation of the Mayor.

4. To preserve and keep in the Mayor's office all books and papers which are usually filed, or which are required by law to be filed therein.

5. To collect and receive all fees which are incident to, or payable for, the services performed by the Mayor and mentioned in this section.

6. To deliver to the respective Boards all messages from the Mayor in writing.

7. To attend in the Mayor's office during the usual office hours, and to perform such other services as may be required by the Mayor.

§ 7. He shall enter in a book to be provided for that purpose, and kept in the Mayor's office, open at all convenient times to public inspection, the names of all persons from whom he may receive money as authorized by the last section, the amounts received, and on what account and when paid, and shall render an account thereof, under oath, item by item, to the Comptroller, on Thursday of each week; and shall thereupon pay over the amount so received to the Chamberlain. He shall also thereupon receive from the Chamberlain a voucher for the payment thereof, which he shall forthwith on the same day exhibit to the Comptroller, and shall at the same time leave with him a copy thereof. Duties of the Mayor's clerk

§ 8. The Chief Clerk in the Mayor's office shall receive an annual salary of one thousand five hundred dollars. Salary.

§ 9. There shall be three Assistant Clerks in the Mayor's office, who shall be severally denominated the First Assistant Clerk, the Second Assistant Clerk, and the Third Assistant Clerk, who shall be appointed by the Mayor, and whose several duties it shall be to attend daily at the Mayor's office, and to perform such duties as may be required by the Mayor. Assistant clerks.

§ 10. The First Assistant Clerk in the Mayor's office shall receive an annual salary of one thousand five hundred dollars. First Assistant clerk.

§ 11. The Second Assistant Clerk in the Mayor's office shall receive an annual salary of one thousand two hundred dollars. Second Assistant clerk.

Third Assistant clerk.

§ 12. The Third Assistant Clerk in the Mayor's office shall receive an annual salary of one thousand dollars.

ARTICLE III.

OF THE MARSHALS IN THE MAYOR'S OFFICE.

First Marshal

§ 13. There shall be an officer to be called the First Marshal, who shall be appointed by, and hold his office during the pleasure of, the Mayor.

Bond.

§ 14. Before entering on the duties of his office, the First Marshal shall execute a bond to the Corporation, with one or more sureties to be approved by the Comptroller, in the penal sum of five thousand dollars, conditioned for the faithful performance of the duties of his office.

Duties of First Marshal

§ 15. It shall be the duty of the First Marshal—

1. To issue, and cause to be delivered or published, all notices or requisitions to the different departments or officers of the Corporation, or others, as the Mayor may direct.
2. To superintend, under the direction of the Mayor, the granting of all licenses requiring the Mayor's signature, and to receive the fees therefor, and to collect all fines which the Mayor may be authorized to impose.

Ibid.

§ 16. He shall enter in a book to be provided for that purpose, and kept in the Mayor's office, open at all convenient times to public inspection, the names of all persons from whom he may receive money as authorized by the last section; the amounts received, and on what account and when paid; and shall daily render an account thereof, under oath, item by item, to the Comptroller, and shall thereupon daily pay over the amount so received to the

Chamberlain. He shall also thereupon receive from the Chamberlain a voucher for the payment thereof, which he shall forthwith, on the same day, exhibit to the Comptroller, and shall at the same time leave with him a copy thereof.

§ 17. The First Marshal shall receive an annual salary of one thousand five hundred dollars. Salary.

§ 18. There shall be an officer to be denominated the Second Marshal, who shall be appointed by, and hold his office during the pleasure of, the Mayor. Second Marshal.

§ 19. Before entering upon the duties of his office, the Second Marshal shall execute a bond to the Corporation, with one or more sureties to be approved by the Comptroller, in the penal sum of two thousand dollars, conditioned for the faithful performance of the duties of his office. Bond.

§ 20. It shall be the duty of the Second Marshal to assist the First Marshal and Chief Clerk in the performance of their duties, and, during the absence of either, to perform his duties and such other duties as may be required by the Mayor. Duties of Second Marshal.

§ 21. The Second Marshal shall receive an annual salary of one thousand three hundred dollars. Salary.

CHAPTER II.

OF THE LEGISLATIVE DEPARTMENT.

ARTICLE I.

OF THE COMMON COUNCIL AND ITS POWERS AND DUTIES.

Method of transacting business.

§ 1. The Board of Aldermen and the Board of Councilmen, composing the Common Council, shall sit in separate chambers, and shall transact the Legislative business of the Corporation, as prescribed by the charter of the city of New York, and the various acts amending the same.

As to transaction of Executive business.

§ 2. Neither the Common Council, nor any member thereof, can perform any Executive business whatever, except such as is or shall be specially imposed on them by the laws of this state.

As to Committees with Executive powers.

§ 3. All ordinances and resolutions heretofore adopted, and now in force, authorizing the appointment of committees of the Common Council, with Executive powers, or conferring such powers on any committee, or authorizing a committee to do any act other than to report the facts in relation to the subject referred, with their opinion, for the consideration of the Board, are repealed.

§ 4. No joint committee shall hereafter be created or appointed by the Common Council, except a Joint Committee on Accounts, consisting of three members of each Board, who shall, once in three months, examine the accounts of the several executive departments, and report any delinquencies or errors therein, to the Common Council; and except the Joint Croton Aqueduct Committee of the Common Council, to be appointed according to, and exercise the powers conferred by the act of April 11, 1849, to create the Croton Aqueduct Department in the city of New York. As to Join Committees.

§ 5. No committee shall hereafter be created or appointed by either Board of the Common Council, who shall have power to do any act other than to report the facts in relation to the subject referred, with their opinion thereon, for the consideration of the Board, except as provided in the last section. As to the powers of Committees, generally.

§ 6. A committee of either Board, in reporting upon a subject referred to them, must attach to their report all resolutions, petitions, remonstrances, and other papers in their possession, relative to the matters referred. Committees to attach papers to their reports.

§ 7. No report of a committee of either Board shall be printed, unless by the express direction of the Board in which it is presented, or to which it is sent, specifying the number of copies to be printed. As to printing of reports of Committees.

§ 8. Each Board shall transmit to the other, every ordinance or resolution requiring a concurrent action, together with all papers on which it was founded. As to transmission of papers.

§ 9. When an ordinance or resolution which shall have passed one Board, is rejected in the other, it shall be returned to the Board in which it originated, together with all papers on which it was founded, with notice of its rejection. As to ordinances, &c., rejected by one Board.

As to the messages between the Boards.

§ 10. Messages from one Board to the other shall be communicated by their respective Clerks, unless the Board transmitting the message shall specially direct otherwise.

As to amendments.

§ 11. Either Board may amend any amendment made by the other, to an ordinance or resolution.

As to Committees of Conference.

§ 12. In case of a difference between the two Boards upon any subject of legislation, either Board may request a conference and appoint a committee for that purpose; and the other shall also appoint a committee to confer. The committee shall meet at a time and place to be appointed by the chairman of the committee on the part of the Board requesting the conference. The committee of each Board shall report in writing to the Board appointing them, and may report such modifications or amendments as they think proper. When either Board shall have acted thereon, they shall transmit the same, and the papers relating thereto, to the other, with a message certifying their action thereon.

As to receding from previous action.

§ 13. Either Board may recede from its action on any subject matter of difference between the two Boards, at any time previous to a conference, whether the papers on which the difference arose, are before the Board receding, formally or informally.

As to cases where the Boards adhere to their action.

§ 14. If both Boards adhere to their disagreement, the ordinance or resolution shall be deemed lost, and shall not be again revived during the same session.

As to Committees of Conference.

§ 15. All committees of conference shall consist of three members of each Board, unless otherwise specially ordered by concurrent resolution.

ARTICLE II.

OF THE CLERK OF THE COMMON COUNCIL, AND HIS DEPUTY AND ASSISTANTS.

§ 16. The Board of Aldermen shall appoint a Clerk, who shall hold his office during the continuance of the Board by which he is appointed, and until his successor shall be duly appointed and qualified. He may, however, at any time be removed by that Board, and another clerk be appointed in his stead, who shall hold his office during the unexpired term of the clerk so removed. Clerk of Common Council, how appointed and removed.

§ 17. The clerk so appointed shall, by virtue of his office, be Clerk of the Common Council, and of the Board of Health. The title of his office shall be Clerk of the Common Council, and he shall receive an annual salary of three thousand dollars. Salary, &c.

§ 18. Before entering upon the duties of his office, he shall execute a bond to the Corporation, with one or more sureties, to be approved by the Comptroller, in the penal sum of five thousand dollars, conditioned for the faithful performance of the duties of his office. Shall give bond.

§ 19. He shall attend all the meetings of the Board of Aldermen, and of the Board of Health; and shall keep the minutes thereof; proper records of which he shall cause to be made and kept in his office, in books to be provided for that purpose. His duties.

§ 20. He shall publish all ordinances, and amendments of ordinances which shall be passed, and also the proceedings, in the newspapers which may be employed by the Corporation, except such parts as may require secrecy; and whenever a vote shall be taken in either Board, upon the passage of an ordinance which shall contemplate any Ibid.

specific improvement, or involve the sale, disposition or appropriation of public property, or the expenditure of public moneys or income therefrom, or lay any tax or assessment, such ordinance shall, before the same shall be sent to the other Board, and immediately after the adjournment of the Board at which the same shall have been passed, be published, with the yeas and nays, and with the names of the persons voting for and against the same, in the newspapers employed by the Corporation, as part of the proceedings.

His duties.

§ 21. He shall, in all cases, when required by the Chairman, or a majority of any Committee of the Board of Aldermen, issue, and cause to be served upon persons whose attendance may be required before such Committee, subpœnas, as provided by the law of the state, passed February 8, 1855, accompanied with the usual fee of twenty-five cents ; and shall be entitled to reimbursement therefor by the Comptroller, upon a certificate thereof.

He shall keep the seal of the Corporation.

§ 22. He shall keep the common seal of the Corporation, and cause it to be affixed to all instruments in writing, made or executed by order of the Common Council, pursuant to the charter of the city, or any law of the state.

He shall keep the Mayoralty seal.

§ 23. He shall keep the seal of Mayoralty, and cause the same to be affixed to such instruments as the Mayor shall, from time to time, direct.

He shall issue notices of meetings.

§ 24. He shall issue notices to the members of the Board of Aldermen, and of the Board of Health, when directed by those Boards respectively, and to the members of the different committees of those Boards, and all persons whose attendance will be required before any such committee, when directed by the chairman thereof.

§ 25. He shall, without delay, deliver to all officers of the Corporation, or of the Board of Health, and to all committees of that Board, or of the Board of Aldermen, all resolutions and communications referred to those officers or committees by those Boards respectively.

He shall transmit papers.

§ 26. He shall, without delay, deliver to the Mayor all ordinances or resolutions under his charge, which may require to be approved or otherwise acted upon by the Mayor, with all papers on which the same were founded.

He shall deliver papers to the Mayor.

§ 27. He shall, on the day succeeding the approval by the Mayor of any ordinance or resolution, or on the day succeeding its return by the Mayor, without approval or objection, by which the payment of any sum of money out of the public treasury is directed, deliver to the Comptroller a certified copy of the same.

He shall deliver copies of certain papers to the Comptroller.

§ 28. He shall receive and collect:

He shall collect certain fees.

1. All fees, profits, revenues and emoluments granted by the charter to the Mayor, or which, by virtue of the charter, the Mayor is entitled to receive, except such fees and perquisites as the Mayor is legally entitled to.
2. All fees for licenses to owners and drivers of hackney coaches, carriages and accommodation stages, and to pawnbrokers, dealers in second-hand articles, keepers of junk shops and keepers of intelligence offices.

§ 29. He shall enter in a book, to be provided for that purpose and kept in his office, open at all convenient times to public inspection, the names of all persons from whom he may receive money for the Corporation, the amounts received, and on what account, and when paid, and shall

He shall keep and render an account of moneys received.

render an account thereof, under oath, item by item, to the Comptroller, on Thursday of each week, and shall thereupon pay over the amount, so received, to the Chamberlain. He shall, also, thereupon, receive from the Chamberlain a voucher for the payment thereof, which he shall forthwith, on the same day, exhibit to the Comptroller, and shall, at the same time, leave with him a copy thereof.

Deputy Clerk of the Board of Aldermen.

§ 30. There shall be a Deputy to the Clerk of the Board of Aldermen, who shall assist the Clerk of the Common Council in the performance of the duties of his office, and shall attend to such branches thereof as may be assigned to him by the Clerk, under his direction, and shall receive an annual salary of two thousand dollars.

Powers of the Deputy clerk.

§ 31. In case of a vacancy in the office of the Clerk of the Common Council, the Deputy Clerk of the Board of Aldermen shall act as clerk until the vacancy shall be filled by a new appointment, and until the person appointed shall be duly qualified.

The Deputy clerk shall give bond.

§ 32. Before entering upon the duties of his office, the Deputy Clerk of the Board of Aldermen shall execute a bond to the Corporation, with one or more sufficient sureties, to be approved by the Comptroller, in the penal sum of one thousand dollars, conditioned for the faithful performance of the duties of his office.

Of his Assistant Clerks.

§ 33. There shall be five Assistant Clerks in the office of the Clerk of the Common Council, to be denominated, respectively, the First, Second, Third, Fourth and Fifth Clerks, and who shall perform such duties as shall be assigned to them by the Clerk, and under his direction; the First Clerk shall receive an annual salary of twelve hundred dollars; the Second Clerk shall receive an annual salary of twelve hundred dollars; the Third Clerk shall receive an annual salary of one thousand dollars; the Fourth Clerk shall receive an annual salary of one thousand dollars; the Fifth Clerk shall receive an annual salary of nine hundred dollars.

Of the Messengers, Librarian and Engrossing Clerks.

§ 34. There shall be a Messenger and an Assistant Messenger to the Board of Aldermen, who shall serve all subpœnas, notices, and all other official papers, which shall be delivered to them for that purpose by the Clerk or under his direction, and shall be officially subject to the Clerk; the Messenger shall receive an annual salary of nine hundred dollars; the Assistant Messenger an annual salary of seven hundred and fifty dollars. There shall also be a Librarian and Engrossing Clerk, who shall have charge of the City Library, under the entire supervision of the Clerk of the Common Council, and who shall receive for his services an annual salary of nine hundred dollars. There shall also be an Engrossing Clerk, to engross the proceedings of the Board of Aldermen, who shall be paid for such service at the rate of eight cents per folio.

Of the appointment & removal of these officers

§ 35. All the officers hereinbefore mentioned, except the Clerk of the Board of Aldermen, shall be subject to appointment and removal, as provided in section 36 of the charter of 1857.

ARTICLE III.

OF THE CLERK OF THE BOARD OF COUNCILMEN, HIS DEPUTY AND ASSISTANTS.

His appointment and removal.

§ 36. The Board of Councilmen shall appoint a Clerk, who shall hold his office during the continuance of the Board by which he is appointed, and until his successor shall be duly appointed and qualified. He may, however, at any time, be removed by that Board, and another Clerk be appointed in his stead, who shall hold his office during the unexpired term of the Clerk so removed.

Bond.

§ 37. Before entering upon the duties of his office, he shall execute a bond to the Corporation, with one or more sureties, to be approved by the Comptroller, in the penal sum of one thousand dollars, conditioned for the faithful performance of the duties of his office.

His duties.

§ 38. He shall attend all the meetings of the Board of Councilmen, and shall keep the minutes thereof, proper records of which he shall cause to be made, copied and kept in his office, in books to be provided for that purpose.

Ibid.

§ 39. He shall publish all ordinances and amendments of ordinances which shall be passed, and also the proceedings in the newspapers which may be employed by the Corporation, except such parts as may require secrecy; and whenever a vote shall be taken in the Board, upon the passage of an ordinance which shall contemplate any specific improvement, or involve the sale, disposition or appropriation of public property, or the expenditure of public moneys, or income therefrom, or lay any tax or assessment, such ordinance shall, before the same shall be sent to the other Board, and immediately after the adjournment of the Board at which the same shall have been passed, be published, with the yeas and nays, and with the names of the persons voting for and against the same, in the newspapers employed by the Corporation, as part of the proceedings.

He shall issue notices of meetings.

§ 40. He shall issue notices to the members of the Board of Councilmen, when directed by the Board, and to the members of the different Committees of the Board, and all persons whose attendance will be required before any such Committee, when directed by the chairman, or a majority thereof.

§ 41. He shall, in all cases, when required by the Chairman, or a majority of any Committee of the Board of Councilmen, issue, and cause to be served upon persons whose attendance may be required before such Committee, subpœnas, as provided by the law of the state, passed February 8, 1855, accompanied with the usual fee of twenty-five cents, and shall be entitled to reimbursement therefor by the Comptroller upon a certificate thereof.

He shall notify persons to attend meetings of Committees.

§ 42. He shall, without delay, deliver to all officers of the Corporation, and to all Committees of the Board of Councilmen, all resolutions, communications and other official papers referred to those officers or Committees respectively, by that Board.

He shall transmit papers, &c.

§ 43. He shall, without delay, deliver to the Mayor all ordinances and resolutions passed by the Board of Aldermen, and concurred in by the Board of Councilmen, which may require to be approved, or otherwise acted upon by the Mayor, with all papers on which the same were founded.

He shall deliver papers to the Mayor.

§ 44. There shall be a Deputy to the Clerk of the Board of Councilmen, who shall perform such duties in the office and attend to such branches thereof, as may be assigned to him by the Clerk, and under his direction, who shall receive for his services an annual salary of twelve hundred dollars.

The Deputy Clerk.

§ 45. In case of a vacancy in the office of Clerk of the Board of Councilmen, the Deputy Clerk shall act as Clerk until the vacancy shall be filled by a new appointment, and until the person appointed shall be duly qualified.

The powers of the Deputy Clerk.

§ 46. There shall be an Assistant Clerk in the office of the Clerk of the Board of Councilmen, who shall perform such duties as shall be assigned to him by the Clerk, and

Assistant Clerk.

under his direction, who shall receive for his services an annual salary of one thousand dollars.

Engrossing Clerk. § 47. There shall also be an Engrossing Clerk, to engross the proceedings of the Board of Councilmen, and to perform such other duties as he may be directed by the Clerk of this Board, who shall be paid for such services the sum of nine hundred dollars per annum.

Messenger. § 48. There shall be a Messenger to the Clerk of the Board of Councilmen, who shall serve all subpœnas, notices and other official papers, which shall be delivered to him for that purpose by the Clerk, who shall be officially subject to the Clerk, and shall perform such other business as shall be assigned to him in the general care of the office, and who shall receive for his services an annual salary of nine hundred dollars.

Assistant Messenger. § 49. There shall be an Assistant to the Messenger, who shall aid and assist the Messenger in the general discharge of his duty, and who shall receive for his services an annual salary of five hundred dollars.

Appointment and removal. § 50. All the officers of the Councilmen hereinbefore mentioned, except the Clerk of the Board of Councilmen, shall be subject to appointment and removal, as provided in section 36 of the charter of 1857.

ARTICLE IV.

OF THE OTHER OFFICERS OF THE COMMON COUNCIL.

Readers. § 51. A Reader to each Board shall be appointed by the President thereof, and shall hold his office during the pleasure of the President by whom he is appointed, and shall receive, annually, five hundred dollars each.

§ 52. The Reader of each Board shall aid the President in reading the various ordinances, resolutions, communications and reports which shall come before the Board. Duties of Readers.

§ 53. Each Board shall appoint a Sergeant-at-arms, who shall hold his office during the continuance of the Board by which he is appointed, and until his successor shall be duly appointed and qualified. He may, however, at any time be removed by the Board appointing him, and another Sergeant-at-arms be appointed in his stead, who shall hold his office during the unexpired term of the one so removed. Sergeants-at-arms.

§ 54. The Sergeant-at-arms of each Board shall attend all the meetings of the Board, and shall execute all lawful orders directed to him by the Board, or the President thereof, and they shall receive annually for their services eight hundred dollars each. Duties of Sergeants-at-arms.

§ 55. The Board of Councilmen shall appoint a Door-keeper, who shall hold his office during the pleasure of that Board. Door-keeper to Councilmen.

CHAPTER III.

OF THE DEPARTMENT OF FINANCE.

ARTICLE I.

OF THE DEPARTMENT OF FINANCE AND ITS BUREAUX GENERALLY.

General functions of the Department.

§ 1. The Department of Finance shall have control of all the fiscal concerns of the Corporation, and shall prescribe the forms of keeping and rendering all city accounts, not inconsistent with this ordinance; and all accounts rendered to or kept in the several departments of the city government, shall be subject to the inspection and revision of the officers of this department.

Ibid.

§ 2. It shall also settle and adjust all claims by the Corporation or against them, and all accounts in which the Corporation is concerned, either as debtor or creditor not otherwise provided for by law.

§ 3. There shall be five bureaux in the Department of Finance: Bureaux.

1. A bureau for the collection of the revenue accruing from rents and interest on bonds and mortgages, and for the collection of all revenues arising from the use or sale of property belonging to, or managed by, the city, and for the performance of such duties as may be directed by the Common Council, the chief officer of which shall be called the "Collector of City Revenue."

2. A bureau for the collection of taxes; the chief officer thereof shall be called the "Receiver of Taxes," who shall have all the powers and perform all the duties now prescribed by law for the Receiver of Taxes.

3. A bureau for the collection of arrears of taxes, arrears of assessments and arrears of water rents, the chief officer of which shall be called the "Clerk of Arrears."

4. A bureau for the reception of all moneys paid into the treasury of the city, and for the payment of moneys on warrants drawn by the Comptroller, and countersigned by the Mayor and Clerk of the Common Council; and the chief officer thereof shall be called the "Chamberlain of the city of New York."

5. A bureau, to be called the "Auditing Bureau;" the chief officer thereof shall be called the "Auditor of Accounts."

ARTICLE II.

OF THE COMPTROLLER.

The Comptroller and his salary.

§ 4. The chief officer of the Department of Finance shall be called the Comptroller of the city of New York, who shall be paid monthly for his services at the rate of five thousand dollars per annum.

Bond of the Comptroller.

§ 5. Before entering upon the duties of his office, the Comptroller shall execute to the Corporation a bond, with at least two sufficient sureties, to be approved by the Mayor, and filed in the Mayor's offiee, in the penal sum of twenty thousand dollars, conditioned for the faithful performance of the duties of his office.

Comptrollers duties.

§ 6. The Comptroller shall superintend the fiscal concerns of the Corporation, and manage the same in the manner required by the charter of the city, and the various acts amending the same, by the laws of this state, and by the ordinances or resolutions of the Common Council, not inconsistent with this ordinance.

Ibid.

§ 7. He shall, from time to time, and as often as he may deem necessary, suggest to the Common Council plans for the improvement and management of the city revenue.

Ibid.

§ 8. He shall superintend all the real estate of the Corporation, and report to the Common Council all encroachments thereon.

Ibid.

§ 9. He shall keep and file in his office all title deeds, leases, mortgages, or other assurances of title, and all evidences of debt, contracts, bonds of indemnity, and official bonds, except such as are directed, by this ordinance, to be deposited elsewhere.

§ 10. He shall cause all grants, leases and counterparts of leases or deeds, executed by the Corporation, to be recorded in proper books, to be kept in his office. Comptrollers duties.

§ 11. He shall cause a proper map or survey of all lands or premises granted, conveyed or leased by the Corporation, to be annexed to the grant, deed or lease thereof, and to be therein referred to, before the execution thereof. Ibid.

§ 12. He shall cause a proper map or survey of all lands or premises, ceded, granted, conveyed or leased to the Corporation, to be annexed to the cession, grant, deed, or lease thereof, and to be therein referred to before execution or acceptance thereof. Ibid.

§ 13. He shall direct and superintend the collection of all rents, or other moneys due to the Corporation, and at least once in each month, furnish to the Collector of the City Revenue, accurate accounts of all such rents or moneys as shall remain unpaid. Ibid.

§ 14. He shall revise, audit and settle all accounts in which the Corporation is concerned, either as debtor or creditor, where provision for the settlement thereof is not otherwise provided for by law, and the settlement of which is not especially committed by ordinance to some other authority; and where no such provision, or an insufficient provision has been made, he shall examine such accounts, and report to the Common Council the facts relating thereto, with his opinion thereon. Ibid.

§ 15. He shall draw and sign all warrants on the Chamberlain, for moneys which he is authorized to draw from the treasury, and present the same with the vouchers to the Mayor, to be countersigned by him and the Clerk of Ibid.

the Common Council, respectively. But no such warrant shall be drawn, unless the sum specified therein is embraced in an appropriation previously made for that purpose by the Common Council.

Comptroller's duties. § 16. He shall supervise the fiscal concerns of all departments, bureaux and officers of the Corporation, who shall receive or disburse the public moneys, or who are charged with the management or custody thereof; and may require, at any time, from those departments, bureaux or officers, an account, in writing, of any moneys or property of the Corporation in their hands or under their control.

Ibid. § 17. He shall report to the Common Council immediately upon its discovery, any default or delinquency in any of the departments, bureaux or offices of the Corporation, in respect to the matters mentioned in the last section.

Ibid. § 18. He shall compare the quarterly accounts of the Chamberlain with the vouchers relating to the same, and with the books of the department, and report those accounts, with such information in respect thereto as may be proper, to the Common Council, or to either Board thereof, at its next meeting.

Ibid. § 19. He shall keep true and accurate accounts of all matters appertaining to the department, and submit to the Joint Committee of Accounts, or the Common Council for their examination, when required, a full and detailed statement of all the accounts of the department, together with the accompanying vouchers.

Ibid. § 20. He shall submit to the Common Council, on or before the first day of November, in each year, a detailed estimate of the receipts and expenditures for the year, commencing on the first of January following, in order that the annual appropriations may then be made; and also an estimate of the probable amount of tax that may be required for the year, commencing on the first of January following, with the draft of an act authorizing the raising of such tax, in order that an application may be made to the legislature for authority to levy the same.

§ 21. He shall report to the Common Council, within thirty days after their organization in each year, a statement of all contracts made by the Corporation, or directed or authorized by the Common Council; and not performed or completed, or upon which any money remains unpaid, with the amount of money so remaining unpaid on each. **Comptrollers duties.**

§ 22. He shall report forthwith to the Common Council every case in which an appropriation is exhausted, the object of which is not completed, and accompany such report with a statement of the moneys which have been drawn on such appropriation, the particular purposes for which they were drawn, and the cause of the deficiency, and an estimate of the amount that will be necessary to complete the object of the appropriation. **Ibid.**

§ 23. He shall publish, in the newspapers employed by the Common Council, two months before the annual election of charter officers, in each year, for the general information of the citizens of the city of New York, a full and detailed statement, setting forth : **Ibid.**

1. The receipts and expenditures of the Corporation during the preceding year, and the different sources of the city revenue, and the amount received from each.

2. The several appropriations made by the Common Council, the objects for which they were made, and the amount of moneys expended under each appropriation.

3. The moneys borrowed on the credit of the Corporation, the authority for each loan, and the terms upon which it was obtained.

Comptroller's duties. § 24. He shall direct legal proceedings to be taken, when necessary, to enforce payment of rents or other debts due to the Corporation, or to obtain possession of premises to which the Corporation is entitled.

Ibid. § 25. He shall, as often as the state of the Sinking Fund shall render it necessary, advertise and sell at auction or private sale, as in his judgment may be most expedient, the water lot quit-rents belonging to the Corporation, in such parcels, and on such terms, as the Common Council or the Commissioners of the Sinking Fund may prescribe, and cause proper conveyances to be executed to the purchasers; the avails of which shall be deposited in the treasury to the credit of the Sinking Fund.

Ibid. § 26. He may consent, in the name and on behalf of the Corporation, that the lessee or assignee of a lease made by the Corporation, may assign the same, or underlet the demised premises, where provision is made by the lease that it shall not be assigned, or the premises underlet, without the consent of the Corporation; but he shall not so consent, unless all arrears of rent, and all taxes or assessments upon the premises be paid.

Ibid. § 27. When provision shall be made by a lease, to which the Corporation is a party, or in which it is interested, that appraisers on behalf of the Corporation to determine the rent on renewal of the lease or the value of buildings to be paid for on the expiration thereof, shall be appointed; the appraiser or appraisers on the part of the Corporation may be appointed by the Mayor and the Comptroller.

Ibid. § 28. The Comptroller may accept the cession of streets or avenues, or parts thereof, not ceded or opened, on receiving a sufficient conveyance thereof to the Corporation, with a map of the ceded premises annexed thereto, and a certificate of the Counsel to the Corporation, approving the same. But, in all cases, the expense of the cession must be paid by the party by whom it is made.

§ 29. When several lots or parcels of land belonging to different persons, are assessed for taxes in one parcel, the Comptroller may make the proper apportionment of the tax among the different owners, or may, in cases of difficulty, report the facts to the Common Council, to the end that the apportionment may be made by them. Comptrollers duties.

§ 30. The Comptroller shall preserve, in a book to be kept in his office for that purpose, to be called the Record of Quit-rents, maps of all grants of land, now or hereafter made by the Corporation, on which quit-rents are payable, showing the original grants, and the subdivisions of the same, as near as they can be ascertained. Ibid.

§ 31. He shall enter, in the record of quit-rents, immediately following each map, the names of the owners of the different lots described thereon, with the portion of the quit-rent to which each is subject; and he may receive the sums proportionably due from each owner in payment of his portion of the moneys payable under the original grant, as the same shall, from time to time, become payable. Ibid.

§ 32. He shall, on receiving written notice from the grantee of the Corporation, or his assignee, of the sale of any portion of land subject to quit-rent, enter in the record of quit-rents the name of the purchaser, with the date of the sale, and the portion of the land sold; and he may thereafter receive the sum proportionably due from such purchaser, in payment of his portion of the moneys paya- Ibid.

ble under the original grant, as the same shall, from time to time, become payable.

Comptroller's duties. § 33. He shall cause to be inserted, in all grants of land subject to a quit-rent, a covenant requiring the grantee or his legal representatives, when he or they shall sell the whole or a portion of the land granted, to give to the Comptroller a written notice of the sale, within thirty days after it is made, specifying therein the name of the purchaser, the quantity and location of the land sold, the amount of quit-rent to be paid thereon, and the day of the sale.

Ibid. § 34. Upon receiving the notice mentioned in the last section, the Comptroller shall enter the same in the record of quit-rents, and from that time he may receive from the owner of the lot or parcel mentioned in the notice, or his legal representatives, the sum proportionably due from him in payment of his proportion of the moneys payable under the original grant.

Ibid. § 35. When land, heretofore granted by the Corporation, subject to a quit-rent, portions of which have been assigned by the grantee, shall be re-entered by the Corporation for non-payment of the quit-rent, the Comptroller may grant releases in severalty to such of the assignees of portions of the land granted, as shall, within six months from the re-entry, pay their respective apportionments of commutation money, and the expenses of re-entry and conveyance, with such portions of the rent as may be justly due from the respective assignees for the land held by them, and which shall be apportioned by the Comptroller.

Ibid. § 36. The releases and apportionments mentioned in the last section, shall not, however, be granted or made, unless the assignee, requiring the same, or his legal representatives, shall comply with the terms and conditions prescribed in that section, within thirty days after notice from the Comptroller requiring such compliance.

§ 37. The Comptroller may, from time to time, with the sanction of the Common Council, borrow on the credit of the Corporation, in anticipation of its revenues, such sum or sums, not exceeding in the whole the amount of such revenues, as may be necessary to meet expenditures under appropriations for the current year. Loans to the city.

§ 38. Every loan to be effected, as authorized by the last section, shall be secured by the bonds of the Corporation, payable in not exceeding one year, in such sums as the Comptroller may deem proper, which shall be signed by the Comptroller, countersigned by the Mayor, and sealed with the common seal. City Loans.

§ 39. If the Comptroller shall become disqualified from performing the duties of his office, or shall be absent from or resign the same, the Mayor shall appoint a suitable person to perform the duties during such disqualification or vacancy, subject to confirmation by the Board of Aldermen. Vacancy in office of comptroller.

ARTICLE III.

OF THE DEPUTY COMPTROLLER.

§ 40. There shall be an officer in the Department of Finance, who shall be called the Deputy Comptroller of the city of New York, who shall be paid monthly for his services at the rate of two thousand five hundred dollars per annum. Deputy Comptroller and salary.

§ 41. The Deputy Comptroller shall, before entering upon the duties of his office, execute a bond to the Corporation, with one or more sureties, to be approved by the Bond of Deputy Comptroller.

Comptroller, in the penal sum of ten thousand dollars, conditioned for the faithful performance of the duties of his office.

Duties of the Deputy Comptroller.

§ 42. He shall assist the Comptroller in the performance of the duties appertaining to his office, and shall be competent, under the direction and by the authority of the Comptroller, to perform any of the duties assigned to the Comptroller, except to sign warrants on the Chamberlain. And in case of the absence of the Comptroller, by reason of sickness or other cause, from the office for more than one day at any one time, the Deputy Comptroller shall act as Comptroller, in all matters not inconsistent with the charter, during such absence; and in case of vacancy in the office of Comptroller, the Deputy shall act as Comptroller until the vacancy shall be supplied, as provided by section twenty of the act entitled "An act to amend the charter of the city of New York," passed April 14, 1857.

ARTICLE IV.

OF THE CLERKS IN THE OFFICE OF THE COMPTROLLER.

Clerks in Department of Finance.

§ 43. There shall be sixteen clerks in the Department of Finance, to be denominated respectively the Book-keeper, two Assistant Book-keepers, the Stock Clerk, the First Auditor, the Second Auditor, the Redemption Clerk, the Assistant Auditor, the Clerk to the Comptroller, and seven general clerks. There shall likewise be two Messengers in said office.

Duties of Book-keeper.

§ 44. The Book-keeper shall, under the direction of the Deputy Comptroller, keep a regular set of books by double entry, in which shall be opened and kept as many accounts, under appropriate titles, as may be necessary to show distinctly and separately all the receipts and expenditures of the Corporation; all debts due to and by the

Corporation, and all appropriations made by the Common Council, and the sums expended under the same respectively, and shall perform such other duties as may be directed by the Comptroller.

Duties and salaries of Assistant book keepers

The Assistant Book-keepers under the direction of the Comptroller shall perform such services as may be required in the Department of Finance, or in any bureaux connected with said department. They shall each receive for their services twelve hundred dollars per annum.

Duties of Stock Clerk.

§ 45. The Stock Clerk shall, under the direction of the Comptroller, have charge of the various stocks and loans of the Corporation; prepare certificates for all new stocks or loans, and all transfers of stocks; make out the quarterly and semi-annual dividends on all stocks and loans; receive all temporary loans, and prepare bonds for the payment thereof; prepare warrants for the payment of all stocks and loans falling due, and enter in books, to be provided for that purpose, the certificates, transfers, payments and bonds mentioned in this section, and shall perform such other duties as may be directed by the Comptroller.

Duties of First Auditor.

§ 46. The First Auditor shall audit and prepare warrants for the payment of all bills presented for payment on city account, including the salaries of officers of the Corporation, and enter the same in books provided for that purpose, and shall perform such other duties as may be directed by the Comptroller.

Duties of Second Auditor.

§ 47. The Second Auditor shall audit and prepare warrants for the payment of all claims on trust account, and enter the same in books provided for that purpose, distributing the various accounts under appropriate heads, and shall also have charge of and keep the books of account of the Commissioners of the Sinking Fund, and shall perform such other duties as may be directed by the Comptroller.

Duties of Redemption Clerk.

§ 48. The Redemption Clerk shall prepare lists of property liable to be sold for unpaid taxes, assessments and Croton water rents, and shall enter the same in books to be provided for that purpose, and shall perform such other duties as may be directed by the Comptroller.

Duties of Assistant Auditor.

§ 49. The Assistant Auditor shall have charge of, and make all entries in the proper books, showing the receipts and expenditures in relation to assessments for opening, regulating and paving streets, building and repairing wharves and piers, digging and building wells, constructing public roads, when done by assessment, and filling up sunken lots under ordinances of the Common Council. He shall also have charge of the books in reference to intestate estates, and shall file all returns, documents and vouchers appertaining to the Department of Finance, and shall perform such other duties as may be directed by the Comptroller.

Duties of Clerk to Comptroller.

§ 50. The Clerk to the Comptroller shall enter, in a book to to be provided for that purpose, and kept in the Comptroller's office, all deeds, leases and mortgages of real estate in which the Corporation is interested.

Ibid.

§ 51. He shall also enter in books provided for that purpose, all resolutions of the Common Council and of the Board of Health, and Board of Supervisors, relating to the Department of Finance, the official correspondence of the department, and all contracts or other documents appertaining thereto, and shall perform such other duties as may be directed by the Comptroller.

Salary.

§ 52. The Clerk to the Comptroller shall be paid

monthly for his services at the rate of two thousand dollars per annum.

§ 53. The General Clerks shall perform such services appertaining to the Department of Finance, or in any bureaux connected therewith, as may be required by the Comptroller. The seven General Clerks shall receive for their services the following compensation, five at one thousand dollars each per annum, and two at eight hundred dollars per annum. Duties & salaries of General Clerks.

§ 54. The two Messengers shall perform such duties as may be required by the Comptroller, and shall receive seven hundred dollars per annum for their services. Duties & salaries of Messengers.

ARTICLE V.

OF THE BUREAU OF CITY REVENUE.

§ 55. This bureau, the chief officer of which shall be called the Collector of City Revenue, is charged with the duty of collecting all moneys accruing to the Corporation for rents, market fees, interest and principal on bonds and mortgages; and all revenues arising from the use or sale of manure, and of property belonging to, or managed by, the city, and all other debts due to the Corporation, which may be placed in his hands by the Comptroller, and for the performance of such other duties as may be directed by the Common Council. General functions of the Bureau.

§ 56. The Collector of the City Revenue shall, before entering upon the duties of his office, execute a bond to the Corporation, with one or more sureties, to be approved by the Comptroller, in the penal sum of fifteen thousand dollars, conditioned for the faithful performance of the duties of his office. Bond of the Collector of City revenue.

Duties of Collector of City revenue.

§ 57. He shall enter in a book, to be provided for that purpose, and kept in the office of the Comptroller, open at all convenient times to public inspection, the names of all persons from whom he may receive money for the Corporation; the amounts received, and on what account, and when paid; and shall daily render an account thereof under oath, item by item, to the Comptroller, and shall thereupon daily pay over the amount so received to the Chamberlain. He shall also thereupon receive, from the Chamberlain, a voucher for the payment thereof, which he shall, on the same day, exhibit to the Comptroller, and shall, at the same time, leave with him a copy thereof.

Ibid.

§ 58. He shall report to the Comptroller, all cases in which he shall be unable to collect a debt due to the Corporation, with the reason thereof, to the end that proper measures may be directed by the Comptroller in ascertaining the fair rent of property belonging to the Corporation, and in renting the same.

Ibid.

§ 59. He shall attend daily at the office of the Comptroller, from eleven o'clock in the forenoon to one o'clock in the afternoon, for the purpose of performing such duties as are incident to his office.

Compensation.

§ 60. The Collector of City Revenue shall receive monthly, three quarters of one per cent. upon all moneys received or collected by him, by virtue of the authority contained in this ordinance, in full, for all services performed by him.

Superintendent of Market rents & fees, duties, salary and bond.

§ 61. There shall be in the Bureau for the Collection of the City Revenue, an officer to be styled "the Superintendent of Market Rents and Fees," and for the sale of manure and for the collection of the revenue arising from the sale of manure, whose duty it shall be to grant permits for stands, and also of transferring butcher's stalls within the limits of the several public markets, with power at any time to annul such permits, and also for the sale of manure, and for collecting the revenues arising from the sale of manure, who shall receive annually for his services, the sum of two thousand dollars. Said Superintendent of Market Rents and Fees shall, before entering on the duties of office, execute a bond to the Corporation with surety to be approved by the Comptroller, in the penal sum of five thousand dollars, conditioned for the faithful performance of the duties of his office.

§ 62. The said Superintendent shall have power to fix and determine the rents and fees of all persons holding or occupying streets, sheds or stands in the public markets or within the limits of said markets, and also the fees to be charged for the market wagons or vehicles bringing produce thereto. He shall also sell all the manure and collect the revenue arising from such sale or sales, and pay over the proceeds to the Collector of the City Revenue. Superintendent of Market Rents & Fees.

§ 63. Said Superintendent shall also appoint competent persons to act as inspectors of manure, whose duty it shall be to attend at the various dumping grounds, or at such place or places as said Superintendent shall direct, who shall each receive a compensation of three dollars per day, for such service. Inspector of Manure.

§ 64. There shall be one clerk in this bureau, to be called the Clerk to the Collector of City Revenue, who shall keep the accounts of this bureau, and prepare such papers and perform such other duties appertaining thereto, as shall be directed by the Collector of City Revenue, and he shall receive annually for his services twelve hundred dollars, payable monthly. Clerk to Collector of City Revenue.

Bond of the Clerk.

§ 65. Before entering upon the duties of his office, the Clerk to the Collector of the City Revenue shall execute a bond to the Corporation, with one or more sureties, to be approved by the Comptroller, in the penal sum of five thousand dollars, conditioned for the faithful performance of the duties of his office.

Deputy Collectors of city revenue.

§ 66. There shall be in this bureau, six assistants to the Collector of City Revenue, who shall be called Deputy Collectors of City Revenue; they shall collect daily the market fees and rents as fixed by the Superintendent of Market Rents and Fees, which shall become due in the respective markets, and shall, on Thursday in each week, render an account thereof, under oath, containing the amounts received; and when paid, and shall thereupon pay over the amount so received to the Collector of the City Revenue, and shall generally perform such other duties as may be directed by the Collector of City Revenue; they shall also respectively receive from the Collector of City Revenue, a voucher for the payment thereof, which they shall forthwith, on the same day, exhibit to the Comptroller, and shall, at the same time, leave with him a copy thereof; the Deputy Collectors shall receive an annual salary of one thousand dollars, excepting the Deputy Collectors of Washington and Fulton markets, who shall receive an annual salary of one thousand two hundred dollars each.

Ibid.

§ 67. There shall be two additional Deputy Collectors of City Revenue, who shall perform all the duties now prescribed by ordinance of the Common Council, and shall each receive the sum of twelve hundred dollars per annum for their services.

Bond of Deputy collectors

§ 68. The Deputy Collectors of City Revenue, shall respectively, before entering upon the duties of their office, execute a bond to the Corporation, with one or more sureties, to be approved by the Comptroller, in the penal sum of two thousand dollars.

ARTICLE VI.

OF THE BUREAU OF RECEIVER OF TAXES.

§ 69. The provisions of the act of April 18, 1843, for the collection of taxes in the city of New York, and of the several acts amending the same, shall apply to and govern the Bureau of Taxes, and the officers thereby created shall continue to be the officers of this bureau. Receiver of Taxes.

§ 70. The office for the collection of taxes, in the city of New York, heretofore established by the Common Council, in pursuance of the acts mentioned in the last section, shall continue to be kept in the City Hall. Office where kept.

§ 71. There shall be six Clerks in this bureau, who shall respectively be known as the First, Second, Third, Fourth, Fifth and Sixth Clerks to the Receiver of Taxes, and shall perform such services as may be assigned them respectively by the Receiver of Taxes. Clerks.

§ 72. The Receiver of Taxes may, with the consent of the Common Council, from time to time, appoint as many additional Clerks as may be necessary, not exceeding eight, and for a period not exceeding six months from the date of such appointment, at a rate of compensation not exceeding three dollars for each day. Additional Clerks.

§ 73. There shall be an officer in this bureau, to be called the Messenger to the Receiver of Taxes, who shall serve the notices required by law, and perform such other duties as may be directed by the Receiver of Taxes. Messenger.

ARTICLE VII.

THE BUREAU OF CLERK OF ARREARS.

Duties of Clerk of Arrears.

§ 74. This bureau, the chief officer of which shall be called the Clerk of Arrears, is charged with the duty of collecting all arrears due to the city for taxes on real estate, and assessments on the same, and for "regular rents" of Croton water, which have been returned to him, and for redemption of property sold or leased for any arrears on the same.

Bond.

§ 75. The Clerk of Arrears, before entering upon the duties of his office, shall execute a bond to the Corporation, with at least two sureties, to be approved by the Comptroller, and filed in his office, in the penal sum of twenty thousand dollars, conditioned for the faithful performance of the duties of his office.

Duties of Clerk of Arrears.

§ 76. He shall enter in a book, to be provided for that purpose, and open at all convenient times to the public inspection, the names of all persons from whom he may receive money for the Corporation; the amounts received, on what specific account, and when paid, and shall daily deposit the same with the Chamberlain. He shall, once in each week, distribute the moneys received by him to the several appropriate accounts, and render a statement thereof, under oath, to the Comptroller, and leave with him a copy of the receipt of the Chamberlain therefor.

Ibid.

§ 77. He shall keep in his office, an exhibit of all taxes on real estate, and of regular rents of Croton water which have been added thereto, remaining unpaid, which have been returned to him, on the first day of June, in each year; also, of all arrears unpaid, of every assessment which has been due twelve months or over, and returned to him.

§ 78. He shall keep a record of the titles of assessments confirmed, with the date of confirmation, and date of entry, as the same may be returned to him by the Street Commissioner. Duties of Clerk of Arrears.

§ 79. He shall perform all the duties heretofore required by law to be performed by the Street Commissioner and Comptroller, in relation to advertising, selling and leasing for assessments, taxes and "regular rents" of Croton water, and the redemption of property sold therefor, under the direction of the Comptroller. Ibid.

§ 80. There shall be five clerks in the Bureau of Arrears, and shall respectively be known as the First, Second, Third, Fourth and Fifth Assistant Clerks; and shall perform such duties in the office as may be required by the Clerk of Arrears or the Comptroller. There shall also be a Messenger, who shall perform such duties as the Clerk of Arrears shall designate. Clerks in Bureau of Arrears.

§ 81. Each of the Assistant Clerks shall give bond to the Corporation, in the penal sum of five thousand dollars, with two sufficient sureties, to be approved by the Comptroller, for the faithful performance of their duties. Bond of Assistant clerks

§ 82. The compensation of the Clerk of Arrears, the Assistant Clerks and the Messenger in the Bureau of Arrears, shall be respectively at the rates following, viz: Clerk of Arrears, two thousand dollars per annum; First and Second Assistant Clerks, twelve hundred dollars per annum; Third, Fourth and Fifth Assistant Clerks, each one thousand dollars per annum; and Messenger, eight hundred dollars per annum. Compensation.

§ 83. There shall be paid to, and collected by, the Clerk of Arrears, for the benefit of the city treasury, on his fur- Fees for Searches.

nishing a bill of arrears, or making searches upon a requisition for searches on each lot or piece of property mentioned or referred to therein; in respect to Croton water rents, fifty cents; in respect to taxes, fifty cents; in respect to assessments, fifty cents, and for his certificate upon any such bill or search, when requested, ten cents.

Duties of Clerk of Arrears.

§ 84. All bills for arrears of assessments, taxes and "regular rents" for Croton water, and for redemption and all certificates of the Clerk of Arrears, that no liens remain on any lot for which search has been required, shall be copied, before delivery, into a diary to be kept for that purpose, which copy, after having been compared with the original, by the Clerk of Arrears, shall be signed, respectively, by the Clerk making the search, the Clerk of Arrears and the Comptroller.

ARTICLE VIII.

OF THE BUREAU OF DEPOSIT AND DISBURSEMENT.

Duties of Chamberlain

§ 85. This bureau, the chief officer of which shall be called the Chamberlain of the City of New York, is charged with the duty of receiving moneys paid into the treasury of the city, and the payment of moneys therefrom.

Bond of Chamberlain

§ 86. Before entering upon the duties of his office, the Chamberlain shall execute a bond to the Corporation, with one or more sureties, to be approved by the Comptroller, in the penal sum of two hundred thousand dollars, conditioned for the faithful performance of the duties of his office.

Duties of Chamberlain

§ 87. The Chamberlain shall forthwith deposit all moneys which he may, from time to time, receive, in one or more of the banks in the city of New York, and credit the same to the appropriate accounts, and the various appropriations.

§ 88. He shall, on Thursday in each week, report to the Comptroller the amount deposited by him, as required by the last section; the persons respectively, from whom it was received, and on what account, and the bank or banks in which it is deposited, and to what account credited. Duties of Chamberlain

§ 89. He shall, on the first Monday in January, April, July and October, in each year, render to the Comptroller an account current of the moneys received and paid by him on account of the Corporation, during the preceding quarter, and at the same time deliver to the Comptroller his vouchers for the same, with a certificate of the cashier of the bank in which his deposits are made, showing the amount standing to the credit of the treasury, and of the Commissioners of the Sinking Fund. Ibid.

§ 90. He shall not pay any warrant drawn upon the treasury, unless it be drawn, signed and countersigned, as prescribed by section 15. Ibid.

§ 91. No money received by the Chamberlain, on account of the Corporation, and by him deposited as prescribed by section 87, shall be drawn from the bank or banks in which it is deposited, except on the warrant of the Comptroller, drawn, signed and countersigned, and containing a distinct reference to the appropriation under which it is drawn, as prescribed in section 15, except where otherwise provided by law, and in no case shall the Chamberlain pay any warrant drawn on him without having a sufficient sum to the credit of such appropriation as the warrant designates. Ibid.

§ 92. The Chamberlain may employ two Clerks in this bureau, to be denominated First and Second Clerks, who shall keep the accounts of this bureau, and also a complete set of books, showing the amounts paid on account of the Clerks of Chamberlain several appropriations according to the provisions of the charter and this ordinance. The First Clerk shall receive for his services fifteen hundred dollars annually; the Second Clerk shall receive for his services twelve hundred dollars annually; and the Chamberlain shall charge the same in his account with the Corporation.

ARTICLE IX.

OF THE AUDITING BUREAU.

Duties of Auditor.

§ 93. This bureau, the chief officer of which shall be called "Auditor of Accounts," is charged with the duty of revising, auditing and settling all accounts in which the city is concerned, as debtor or creditor; and the Auditor of Accounts shall keep an account of each claim for or against the Corporation, and the sums allowed upon each, and certify the same, with reasons therefor, to the Comptroller.

Ibid.

§ 94. He shall, once in ninety days, make out a list of the names, and his decision on each claim referred to in the preceding section, to accompany the report to the Common Council, which the Comptroller is required to make, with his final action thereon.

Ibid.

§ 95. He shall prepare warrants on the treasury, as provided by this ordinance; and, after obtaining the approval of the Comptroller to the audit of the claim, and his signature to the warrant, shall cause the same to be presented, with the vouchers, to the Mayor and Clerk, for their signatures, respectively.

Assistant Auditors & their duties.

§ 96. There shall be two Assistant Auditors, who shall perform the duties prescribed by the next section of these ordinances, in relation to the Finance Department, and such other services as may be required of them, as assistants to the Auditor of Accounts.

§ 97. The Assistant Auditors shall have charge of, and make all entries in the proper books, showing the receipts and expenditures in relation to assessments for opening, regulating and paving streets, building and repairing wharves and piers, digging and building wells, constructing public roads, when done by assessment, and filling up sunken lots, under ordinances of the Common Council. They shall also have charge of the books in reference to intestate estates, and shall file all returns, documents and vouchers appertaining to the Department of Finance, and shall perform such other duties as may be directed by the Comptroller.

Assistant Auditors & their duties.

CHAPTER IV.

OF THE STREET DEPARTMENT.

ARTICLE I.

OF THE STREET DEPARTMENT AND ITS BUREAUX GENERALLY.

General cognizances of the Street Department.

§ 1. The Street Department shall have cognizance of opening, altering, regulating, grading, flagging, curbing, guttering and lighting streets, roads, places and avenues; of building, repairing and lighting wharves and piers, and filling up and cleaning out slips and basins; the construction and repairing of public roads; the care and improvement of public lands and places; the filling up of sunken lots; the construction, repairing, lighting and care of the buildings, offices, rooms and public yards of the Corporation; the supplying the public buildings and offices and rooms of the Corporation, the court-rooms for which supplies are furnished by the Corporation, the police station-houses, the engine and other houses of the Fire Department, and the public markets, with fuel, stationery, printing and all other things necessary therefor; the construction, altering and repairing of fire engines, hose, and all other machines and apparatus for the use of the Fire Department; the removing incumbrances from streets, roads, places, wharves, piers and slips; the doing and furnishing of all other necessary work, repairs and supplies not provided for in other departments; and the collecting of all assessments.

§ 2. There shall be eight bureaux in the Street Department, viz: Bureaux.

1. A bureau for opening, altering, regulating, grading, flagging, curbing and guttering streets, roads, places and avenues, and for filling up sunken lots, to be called the "Bureau of Street Improvements."
2. A bureau for the construction, repairing and care of the public wharves and piers, and the filling up and clearing out of slips and basins, to be called the "Bureau of Wharves."
3. A bureau for making and repairing the public roads, to be called the "Bureau of Roads."
4. A bureau for the care and regulation of the public grounds and parks, to be called the "Bureau of Lands and Places."
5. A bureau for lighting the public streets, roads, places, avenues, wharves, piers and markets, and for

doing all work, and procuring all supplies and fixtures necessary for that purpose, to be called the "Bureau of Lamps and Gas."

6. A bureau for constructing and repairing public buildings, and for procuring all necessary supplies for the Corporation, to be called the "Bureau of Repairs and Supplies."

7. A bureau for repairing fire engines and fire apparatus, under the charge of the Chief Engineer of the Fire Department, and for the construction of all new fire engines and fire apparatus, to be called the "Bureau of the Chief Engineer of the Fire Department."

8. A bureau for the collection of assessments, to be called the "Bureau of the Collection of Assessments."

ARTICLE II.

OF THE STREET COMMISSIONER.

Street Commissioner.

§ 3. The chief officer of the Street Department shall be denominated the "Street Commissioner," who shall have general charge and direction of all matters entrusted to the Street Department. He shall, by virtue of his office, be one of the Surveyors of the city of New York.

Bond of the Street Commissioner.

§ 4. The Street Commissioner, before entering upon the duties of his office, shall execute a bond to the Corporation, with at least two sureties, to be approved by the Mayor, and filed in the office of the Comptroller, in the penal sum of ten thousand dollars, conditioned for the faithful performance of the duties of his office.

Duties of the Street Commissioner.

§ 5. All contracts for work, materials or supplies, relating to any of the matters under the cognizance of the

Street Department, shall be made by the Street Commissioner, and bonds, to be approved by the Comptroller, shall be taken for the faithful performance thereof; all such contracts shall be executed in triplicate, by the Street Commissioner, on the part of the Corporation, and by the contractor. One original copy, so executed, shall be kept and filed in the office of the Street Commissioner; one shall be filed in the office of the Comptroller, and the third shall be given to the contractor.

§ 6. No expenditure shall be made for any work or supplies relating to any of the matters within the cognizance of the Street Department, unless such work or supplies shall have been authorized by the Common Council, except that whenever any such work or supplies shall be necessary, and the total cost thereof shall not, in any one case, exceed two hundred and fifty dollars, the Street Commissioner may cause the same to be done, or furnished, under the supervision of the appropriate officer of the department; but no such expenditure shall be made, without the written order of the Street Commissioner, and a certificate by him, of the necessity thereof, in each case; and a copy of all such orders and certificates shall be filed in the office of the Street Commissioner, and of the bureau by which the expenditure is made. A detailed statement of all such expenditures shall be made quarterly to the Common Council.

Work & Supplies under Street Department.

§ 7. No payment shall be made on any work or job done by contract, for any extra work thereon not specified in the contract, unless such extra work shall have been done by the written order of the Street Commissioner, directing the same, and stating that such work is not included in the contract, nor until the Street Commissioner shall have communicated the facts in the case to the Com-

Extra work.

mon Council. And no such expenditure shall, in any case, be made, the total amount of which, on any one work, shall exceed two hundred and fifty dollars, unless the same be authorized by the Common Council.

Payment for work under Street Department.

§ 8. All moneys payable by the Corporation, for work done, or supplies furnished, by contract or otherwise, under the Street Department, shall be paid by the Comptroller, by warrant drawn in favor of the person or persons to whom payments are due, except as provided in section 23 of this chapter, and except that in the case of a pay-roll for labor performed, under the supervision of the Street Department, the Comptroller may draw a warrant for the total amount of such pay-roll, in favor of the Chamberlain, who shall make the payments therein specified.

Ibid.

§ 9. No payments shall be made for any work or supplies, within the cognizance of the Street Department, except upon the requisition of the Street Commissioner, upon triplicate vouchers duly certified. Receipts shall be taken upon each of such vouchers, at the time of payment, one of which shall be filed in the office of the Comptroller, one in the office of the Street Commissioner, and one in the office of the bureau under whose superintendence the expenditure was incurred.

Duties of Street Commissioner.

§ 10. The Street Commissioner shall, when required by the Common Council, inquire into and report upon any of the matters within the cognizance of the Street Department; and shall, from time to time, communicate to the Common Council any information or suggestion which he may deem important in relation thereto.

Ibid.

§ 11. He shall issue proposals, and advertise for bids for all contracts connected with his department; and whenever a survey or plans shall be necessary for any work authorized by the Common Council, or for the purpose of reporting any necessary information to the Common Council, he shall cause such survey or plans to be made by a competent surveyor, architect or engineer, as the nature of the work may require.

§ 12. He shall control and direct all expenditures to be made by the Street Department; shall countersign and draw his requisition upon the Comptroller for the payment of all bills and accounts therefor, which, in his judgment are correct, and which may be duly certified by the superintendent of the bureau under whose supervision the expenditure was incurred; except that all bills and accounts for expenditures under the supervision of the Deputy Superintendent of Repairs and Supplies shall be certified by him; and no requisition shall be drawn by the Street Commissioner for the payment of any bills or accounts until the same shall have been duly certified as aforesaid, or if not so certified, until the facts in the case shall have been communicated to the Common Council, except that the bills and accounts for expenditures for the removal of incumbrances, or for other expenditures authorized by ordinance but not under the immediate supervision of any bureau of the Street Department, shall be certified by the Street Commissioner. Duties of the Street Commissioner.

§ 13. He shall, on the first Tuesday in each month, render to the Comptroller a full statement, under oath, of all the moneys paid by him on account of the Street Department. Ibid.

§ 14. The Street Commissioner shall present and report to the Counsel or Attorney of Corporation, all encroachments on the streets or avenues in the city of New York which may be brought to his notice, or take such Ibid.

other action thereon as may be prescribed by ordinance in relation thereto.

Inspectors of contract work.

§ 15. He shall appoint a competent inspector of contract work connected with his department, in all cases where he may deem the public interests require such inspector, or the Common Council shall direct the same. Each inspector so appointed shall receive as compensation for his services a sum not to exceed two dollars per day; and in all cases where an assessment shall be levied for any improvement, the amount paid for inspection on any contract work connected therewith shall be assessed and collected, with the other expenses of such improvements, except where the inspectors' wages are legally chargeable to the contractor.

Duties of Street Commissioner.

§ 16. In all cases where provision is made by ordinance that the consent of the Street Commissioner may be obtained to authorize any act to be done, he may grant permits therefor, subject to the restrictions of the ordinances in relation thereto.

Ibid.

§ 17. The Street Commissioner shall report to the Common Council all assessments made against the Corporation, or awards for any proposed opening or widening of any street or avenue, with the amount of such assessment or award in each case, and the circumstances connected therewith.

Ibid.

§ 18. He shall cause such books and accounts to be kept in the Street Department, and in the several bureaux thereof, as may be necessary at all times to exhibit a full and complete record of all the transactions and expenditures of the department.

Ibid.

§ 19. He shall cause to be entered in books, to be provided for the purpose, and kept in his office, open at all convenient times to public inspection, the names of all persons from whom he may receive money for the Corporation on trust account, or otherwise; the amounts received, on what account, and when paid; and shall render a certified account thereof, under oath, item by item, to the Comptroller, on Thursday of each week, and shall thereupon pay over the amount so received to the Chamberlain. He shall thereupon receive, from the Chamberlain duplicate vouchers for the payment thereof, one of which he shall, on the same day, file in the office of the Comptroller.

§ 20. He shall make to the Common Council, on the first meeting in the months of January, April, July and October, a detailed statement of all the expenditures of the Street Department, on all work or supplies done or furnished by contract or otherwise. Duties of the Street Commissioner.

§ 21. He may direct the removal of any article or thing whatsoever which may encumber or obstruct a street or avenue, wharf or pier, in the city of New York, under the penalties prescribed by law. Removal of Incumbrances.

§ 22. He is hereby authorized and directed to employ, under his direction, four competent persons, at a salary of three dollars per diem, the duty of two of whom it shall be to report to the Street Commissioner any article or thing whatsoever which may encumber or obstruct a street, avenue or place, and, with his consent, to order the same to be removed; and, if not removed within twenty-four hours thereafter, to order the same to be removed to the yard, under the care of the Deputy Superintendent of Repairs and Supplies, or other suitable place. Ibid.

It shall be the duty of the other two persons to report to the Street Commissioner any article or thing whatsoever which may encumber or obstruct any wharf, pier or slip, and, with his consent, to order the same to be removed; and if not removed within twenty-four hours thereafter, to cause the same to be removed to the yard, under the care of the Deputy Superintendent of Repairs and Supplies, or other suitable place.

And in case there shall be placed in any slip any permanent obstruction, without due authority, and the same shall not be removed within one week after notice to remove the same shall be given to the owner or occupant thereof, or shall have been posted conspicuously thereon, the Street Commissioner may cause the same to be removed, and after advertisement of ten days, sell the materials so removed at public auction, unless the expenses of such removal shall have been previously repaid; and he shall account for and pay over the proceeds of such sales, as provided in sections 27 and 28 of this chapter.

Expenses, how defrayed.

§ 23. For the purpose of defraying any expense which may be incurred in pursuance of the last section, or such other minor incidental expenses of the department as cannot be conveniently accounted for on separate vouchers, the Street Commissioner may, by a requisition, draw upon the Comptroller. for a sum not exceeding one hundred dollars.

He may, in like manner, renew the draft as often as may be necessary; but no such renewal shall be made until the money paid upon the previous draft shall be accounted for to the Comptroller by satisfactory vouchers for the expenditure of the money paid thereon.

Ibid.

§ 24. When a draft shall be made upon the Comptroller, in conformity with the last section, he shall draw his warrant in favor of the Street Commissioner, for the amount thereof.

§ 25. All articles removed, as provided in section 22 of this chapter, may be redeemed by the owner, upon his paying to the Street Commissioner, for the use of the Corporation, the necessary expenses of removal, together with six cents per day for every cart-load thereof, during the time it shall remain unclaimed. Removal of Incumbrances.

§ 26. The Street Commissioner shall enter in a book, to be provided for that purpose, a list of all articles so removed, with the time of removal and the expenses thereof; and when the same shall be redeemed, he shall likewise enter therein the name of the person redeeming the same, and the amount received therefor, and shall render a certified account thereof to the Comptroller, on Thursday of each week, and shall thereupon pay over the amount so received to the Chamberlain. He shall also thereupon receive from the Chamberlain duplicate vouchers for the payment thereof, one of which he shall, on the same day, file in the office of the Comptroller. Ibid.

§ 27. He shall, between the first and tenth days of February, May, August and November, in each year, advertise and sell at public auction all such articles so removed as shall have been in the public yard, or other suitable place, one month prior to the time of advertising; and he shall, immediately after such sale, account for and pay the proceeds thereof into the city treasury, in the manner provided in the last section. Ibid.

§ 28. Should the proceeds of such sale exceed the expenses of transportation and sale, together with the amount charged for storage, the excess shall be paid to such person or persons as shall exhibit to the Street Commissioner satisfactory proof of the ownership of the articles to which the same relates; and the Comptroller, Ibid.

on the certificate of the Street Commissioner, is authorized to draw his warrant in favor of such person, for the amount which may be due to them.

Public clocks

§ 29. The Street Commissioner shall also appoint a suitable person, at the salary of five hundred dollars per year, whose duty it shall be to attend to and regulate the public clocks.

Apportionment of Assessments.

§ 30. The Street Commissioner, in all cases of assessments where an aggregate sum is assessed upon any number of lots belonging to several owners, shall cause apportionments to be made among the lots, as they may be respectively owned; provided that, in the judgment of the said Street Commissioner, no difficulty is presented, requiring the intervention of the Common Council; but no apportionment made by the Street Commissioner shall be valid, until the same shall be communicated to the Common Council, and entered in a book to be kept for that purpose in the Bureau of Collection of Assessments.

ARTICLE III.

OF THE DEPUTY STREET COMMISSIONER.

The Deputy Street Commissioner.

§ 31. There shall be an officer in the Street Department who shall be called the Deputy Street Commissioner.

Bond.

§ 32. The Deputy Street Commissioner shall, before entering upon the duties of his office, execute a bond to the Corporation, with one or more sureties, to be approved by the Comptroller, in the penal sum of five thousand dollars, conditioned for the faithful performance of the duties of his office.

His duties

§ 33. He shall assist the Street Commissioner in the performance of the duties appertaining to his office, and shall be competent, under the direction and by the authority of the Street Commissioner, to perform any of the duties assigned by this ordinance to the Street Commissioner, except to sign contracts and requisitions on the Comptroller. And in case of the absence of the Street Commissioner, by reason of sickness or other cause, from the office for more than one day at any one time, the Deputy shall act as Street Commissioner during such absence; and in case of a vacancy in the office of Street Commissioner, the Deputy shall act as Street Commissioner, until the vacancy shall be supplied by a new appointment, and until the person appointed shall be duly qualified.

ARTICLE IV.

OF THE CLERKS IN THE OFFICE OF THE STREET COMMISSIONER.

§ 34. There shall be ten clerks in the office of the Street Commissioner, viz: one Chief Clerk, one Contract Clerk, two Book-keepers, one Map Clerk, and five general clerks. Clerks in office of Street Commissioner.

§ 35. The Chief Clerk shall, under the Street Commissioner, have general charge of the papers and records of the office, and shall perform such duties appertaining to the Street Department as may be assigned to him by the Street Commissioner. He shall be paid monthly for his services at the rate of two thousand dollars per annum. Chief Clerk.

§ 36. The Contract Clerk shall prepare all contracts for work done under the authority of the Street Department, and shall keep, in books to be provided for that purpose, suitable records thereof, and shall enter on the original contract all payments made on any contract under the Street Department, and shall perform such other duties as may be directed by the Street Commissioner. He shall be paid monthly for his services at the rate of two thousand dollars per annum. Contract Clerk.

Book keepers § 37. The Book-keepers shall have charge of the books of account of the Street Department, under the direction of the Street Commissioner, and shall perform such other services appertaining to the Street Department, as may be required by him. They shall be paid monthly for their services; theFirst Book-keeper at the rate of two thousand dollars per annum, and the Second Book-keeper at the rate of one thousand five hundred dollars per annum.

Map Clerk. § 38. The Map Clerk shall have charge of the maps, plans and profiles belonging to the Street Department, and shall perform such other duties as may be required by the Street Commissioner, and shall be paid for his services monthly at the rate of twelve hundred dollars per annum.

General Clerks. § 39. The General Clerks shall perform such services appertaining to the Street Department as may be required by the Street Commissioner, and shall be paid monthly for their services at the following rates of compensation, viz: one at the rate of one thousand five hundred dollars per annum; two at the rate of one thousand two hundred dollars each per annum, and two at the rate of one thousand dollars each per annum.

Messengers. § 40. There shall be in the office of the Street Commissioner one Messenger and two Assistant Messengers, who shall perform such duties appertaining to the Street Department, as may be required by the Street Commissioner. The Messengers shall be paid monthly for their services at the following rates, viz: the Messenger at the rate of one thousand dollars per annum; one Assistant Messenger at the rate of seven hundred and fifty dollars per annum, and one Assistant Messenger at the rate of five hundred dollars per annum.

ARTICLE V.

OF THE BUREAU OF STREET IMPROVEMENTS.

§ 41. This bureau, the chief officer of which shall be denominated the "Superintendent of Street Improvements," shall have charge of the opening, altering, regulating, grading, flagging, curbing and guttering of streets and avenues, and the filling up of sunken lots. He shall receive payment monthly for his services at the rate of two thousand dollars per annum. Superintendent of Street Improvements.

§ 42. The Superintendent of Street Improvements, shall, before entering upon the duties of his office, execute a bond to the Corporation, with one or more sureties, to be approved by the Comptroller, in the penal sum of two thousand dollars, conditioned for the faithful performance of the duties of his office. His Bond.

§ 43. He shall take charge of the making of all estimates and surveys connected with the opening, altering, regulating, grading, flagging, curbing and guttering streets and avenues, and the filling up of sunken lots, and oversee and superintend the execution of all ordinances of the Common Council, and of all contracts relative thereto. Duties of Superintendent of Street Improvements.

§ 44. He shall cause to be kept in his bureau accounts of the time of all persons to be paid by wages for work under the supervision of his bureau, and of the work upon which they are engaged, and of all other expenditures of his bureau, and of the expense of each particular work or job with the items thereof. Ibid.

§ 45. He shall examine and audit all pay-rolls and all accounts for work done or materials furnished under the supervision of his bureau, and if found correct, shall certify them in writing, and shall deliver them with proper vouchers to the Street Commissioner; and in all cases of Ibid.

contract work under his supervision, he shall examine and inspect the works, from time to time, and report to the Street Commissioner as to the fulfillment or breach of the contract therefor; and he shall certify on every voucher for payment thereon, that such payment is due in accordance with the terms of the contract.

Duties of Superintendent of Street Improvements.

§ 46. He shall in all matters connected with his bureau, be under the control, direction and supervision of the Street Commissioner, who may approve or disapprove all accounts certified by him, and by whom alone all requisitions upon the Comptroller, for payment thereof, shall be drawn.

Clerks in Bureau of Street Improvements.

§ 47. There shall be four Clerks in this bureau, to be called the First, Second, Third and Fourth Clerks to the Superintendent of Street Improvements, who shall keep the accounts of this bureau, and prepare such papers and perform such other duties appertaining thereto as shall be directed by the Superintendent of Street Improvements. They shall be paid monthly at the following rates : the First Clerk at the rate of one thousand five hundred dollars per annum ; the Second Clerk at the rate of one thousand two hundred dollars per annum, and the Third and Fourth Clerks each at the rate of one thousand dollars per annum.

Inspector of Side-walks.

§ 48. The Street Commissioner shall appoint in this bureau a suitable person to act as Inspector of Sidewalks, and whose duty it shall be to perform, under the supervision of the Superintendent of Street Improvements, all the duties now prescribed by ordinance of the Common Council for the Inspector of Sidewalks, and who shall receive the same compensation as now allowed to said inspector. He shall also, in addition to the duties now prescribed by ordinance, attend to the numbering and renumbering of streets and avenues and places, and the putting up of Street signs, under the direction of the Superintendent of Street Improvements.

§ 49. The Superintendent of Street Improvements is specially charged with the duty of attending to the enforcement of all laws of this state, and ordinances and resolutions of the Common Council, relating to the subjects enumerated in sections 41 to 48 inclusive of this chapter, and is required, from time to time, to report to the Corporation Attorney all violations thereof. Duties of Superintendent

ARTICLE VI.

OF THE BUREAU OF WHARVES.

§ 50. This bureau, the chief officer of which shall be called the Superintendent of Wharves, is charged with the duty of inspecting the condition of the public wharves and piers, and superintending the erection and repairing of the same, and the filling up and cleaning out of slips and basins. He shall be paid monthly for his services, at the rate of two thousand dollars per annum. Superintendent of Wharves.

§ 51. The superintendent of Wharves shall, before entering upon the duties of his office, execute a bond to the Corporation, with one or more sureties, to be approved by the Comptroller, in the penal sum of five thousand dollars, conditioned for the faithful performance of the duties of his office. His Bond.

§ 52. He shall exercise a constant inspection and supervision of the condition of the public wharves, piers and slips, and of the erection and repairing of the public wharves and piers, and the excavating of slips; and shall, from time to time, suggest and report to the Street Commissioner such improvements and alterations thereof as he Duties of Superintendent of Wharves.

may deem necessary or proper, with estimates of the expense thereof. If the Street Commissioner approve thereof, he shall report the same to the Common Council, except where the expenditure for repairs shall not exceed two hundred and fifty dollars, when he may direct the same to be done under the supervision of the Superintendent of Wharves; but no such expenditure shall be made by the Superintendent of Wharves, except upon the written order and certificate of the Street Commissioner, as provided in section 6 of this chapter.

Duties of Superintendent of Wharves.

§ 53. He shall cause to be kept in his bureau accounts of the time of all persons to be paid by wages for work done under the supervision of his bureau, and of the work upon which they are engaged, and of all the other expenditures of his bureau, and of the expense of each particular work or job, with the items thereof.

Ibid.

§ 54. He shall examine and audit all pay-rolls, and all accounts for work done or materials furnished under the supervision of his bureau, and if found correct, shall certify them in writing, and shall deliver them, with proper vouchers, to the Street Commissioner; and in all cases of contract work under his supervision, he shall examine and report to the Street Commissioner as to the fulfillment or breach of the contract therefor; and he shall certify, on every voucher for payment thereon, that such payment is due, in accordance with the terms of the contract.

Ibid.

§ 55. He shall, in all matters connected with his bureau, be under the control, direction and supervision of the Street Commissioner, who may approve or disapprove all accounts certified by him, and by whom alone all requisitions upon the Comptroller for payment thereof shall be drawn.

Ibid.

§ 56. The Superintendent of Wharves is especially

charged with the duty of attending to the enforcement of all laws of this state and ordinances and resolutions of the Common Council, relating to the wharves and piers in the city of New York; and is required, from time to time, to report to the Corporation Attorney all violations thereof.

§ 57. There shall be one clerk in this bureau, to be called the "Clerk of the Bureau of Wharves," who shall keep the books and accounts of this bureau, and perform such other services appertaining to the Street Department as may be required by the Street Commissioner or the Superintendent of Wharves. He shall receive payment monthly for his services, at the rate of twelve hundred dollars per annum. Clerk of Bureau of Wharves.

§ 58. The Street Commissioner may appoint a general foreman in this bureau, who shall have charge, under the Superintendent of Wharves, of all work not done by contract, and whose compensation therefor shall not exceed three dollars per day. Foreman in Bureau of Wharves.

ARTICLE VII.

OF THE BUREAU OF ROADS.

§ 59. This bureau, the chief officer of which shall be called the "Superintendent of Roads," is charged with the duty of making and repairing the public roads. Superintendent of Roads.

§ 60. The Superintendent of Roads shall, before entering upon the duties of his office, execute a bond to the Corporation, with one or more sureties, to be approved by the Comptroller, in the penal sum of two thousand dollars, conditioned for the faithful performance of the duties of his office. He shall receive payment monthly for his services, at the rate of two thousand dollars per annum. His Bond.

Duties of Superintendent of Roads.

§ 61. He shall be the overseer of roads and highways, and shall take charge of, oversee and superintend the making and repairing of the public roads, and inspect all work done thereon, by contract or otherwise.

Ibid.

§ 62. He shall make all estimates necessary to, or connected with, the making and repairing of the public roads, when required by the Street Commissioner.

Ibid.

§ 63. He shall, from time to time, examine the state of the public roads, and report all the repairs thereof, which, in his judgment, may be necessary, to the Street Commissioner.

Ibid.

§ 64. He shall cause to be kept in his bureau accounts of the time of all persons to be paid by wages, for work under the supervision of his bureau, and of the work upon which they are engaged, and of all the other expenditures of his bureau, and of the expense of each particular work or job, with the items thereof.

Ibid.

§ 65. He shall examine and audit all pay-rolls, and all accounts for work done or materials furnished under the supervision of his bureau, and, if found correct, shall certify them in writing, and shall deliver them, with proper vouchers, to the Street Commissioner; and in all cases of contract work under his supervision, he shall examine and report to the Street Commissioner as to the fulfillment or breach of the contract therefor, and he shall certify on every voucher for payment thereon, that such payment is due, in accordance with the terms of the contract.

Ibid.

§ 66. He shall, in all matters connected with his bureau, be under the control, direction and supervision of the Street Commissioner, who may approve or disapprove of all accounts certified by him, and by whom alone all requisitions upon the Comptroller for the payment thereof shall be drawn.

§ 67. The Superintendent of Roads is specially charged with the duty of attending to the enforcement of all laws of this state, and ordinances and resolutions of the Common Council, relating to the public roads in the city of New York, and is required, from time to time, to report to the Corporation Attorney all violations thereof. Duties of Superintendent of Roads.

§ 68. The Street Commissioner may employ, when required, a clerk in this bureau, to be called the Clerk of the Bureau of Roads, who shall be paid monthly for his services, at the rate of eight hundred dollars per annum. Clerk in Bureau of Roads.

ARTICLE VIII

OF THE BUREAU OF LANDS AND PLACES.

§ 69. This bureau, the chief officer of which shall be called the Superintendent of Lands and Places, is charged with the duty of inspecting the condition of, and superintending and keeping in order the public grounds and places belonging to the Corporation. The Superintendent of Lands and Places shall receive payment monthly for his services, at the rate of two thousand dollars per annum. Superintendent of Lands and Places.

§ 70. The Superintendent of Lands and Places shall, before entering upon the duties of his office, execute a bond to the Corporation, with one or more sureties, to be approved by the Comptroller, in the penal sum of two thousand dollars, conditioned for the faithful performance of the duties of his office. His Bond.

§ 71. He shall exercise a constant inspection and supervision of the public grounds and parks, and of keeping the same in proper order, and shall, from time to time, suggest Duties of Superintendent of Lands and Places.

and report to the Street Commissioner such improvements therein as may be necessary and proper, with estimates of the expense thereof, if the Street Commissioner approve.

Duties of Superintendent of Lands and Places.

§ 72. He shall cause to be kept in his bureau accounts of the time of all persons to be paid by wages for work under the supervision of his bureau, and of the work upon which they are engaged, and of all the other expenditures of his bureau, and of the expense of each particular work or job, with the items thereof.

Ibid.

§ 73. He shall examine and audit all pay-rolls and all accounts for work done, or materials furnished, under the supervision of his bureau, and, if found correct, shall certify them in writing, and shall deliver them, with proper vouchers, to the Street Commissioner; and, in all cases of contract work, under his supervision, he shall examine and report to the Street Commissioner as to the fulfillment or breach of the contract therefor, and he shall certify on every voucher for payment thereon, that such payment is due in accordance with the terms of the contract.

Ibid.

§ 74. He shall, in all matters connected with his bureau, be under the control, direction and supervision of the Street Commissioner, who may approve or disapprove all accounts certified by him, and by whom alone all requisitions upon the Comptroller for the payment thereof shall be drawn.

Ibid.

§ 75. The Superintendent of Lands and Places is specially charged with the duty of attending to the enforcement of the laws of this state, and ordinances and resolutions of the Common Council, relating to public grounds and parks in the city of New York, and is required, from time to time, to report to the Corporation Attorney all violations thereof.

Foreman in Bureau.

§ 76. The Superintendent of Lands and Places may appoint a foreman in the Bureau of Lands and Places, who shall receive for his services two dollars and a half per day; and two keepers in each of the following parks, who shall each receive for their services one dollar and a half per day, viz: the Battery, the City Hall park, Washington Parade ground, Union square, Stuyvesant parks, Madison square and Tompkins square. The Superintendent of Lands and Places may, with the consent of the Street Commissioner, employ, from time to time, such additional labor as may be necessary, to keep the public parks and grounds in proper order.

Keepers of Parks and laborers.

ARTICLE IX.

OF THE BUREAU OF LAMPS AND GAS.

Superintendent of Lamps and Gas.

§ 77. This bureau, the chief officer of which shall be called the Superintendent of Lamps and Gas, is charged with the duty of superintending the lighting of the public streets, roads, places, avenues, wharves, piers and markets; the construction and repairs of the public lamps, and the procuring all necessary supplies and fixtures therefor. He shall receive payment monthly for his services, at the rate of two thousand dollars per annum.

His Bond.

§ 78. The Superintendent of Lamps and Gas shall, before entering upon the duties of his office, execute a bond to the Corporation, with one or more sureties, to be approved by the Comptroller, in the penal sum of two housand dollars, conditioned for the faithful performance of the duties of his office.

Duties of Superintendent of Lamps and Gas.

§ 79. He shall make all estimates necessary to or connected with any of the matters referred to in section 77 of this chapter.

Ibid.

§ 80. He shall take charge of, oversee and superintend he construction, repairing, cleaning, trimming and lighting of public lamps; and shall preserve and keep in such place as may be prescribed by the Street Commissioner, the oil and other supplies appertaining to his bureau.

Duties of Superintendent of Lamps and Gas.

§ 81. He shall, from time to time, inspect the public lamps, and, with the consent of the Street Commissioner, shall cause the same to be repaired forthwith, when any repairs are necessary.

Ibid.

§ 82. He shall, forthwith, report to the Street Commissioner all violations of any contracts for supplying the city with oil or gas for the lighting of the public lamps, and every omission or neglect on the part of any person whose duty it is to clean, trim or light the same.

Ibid.

§ 83. He shall subject all oil which may delivered upon any contract, to a thorough examination, before emptying it from the original vessel in which it may be delivered; and if it be found, in any respect, inferior, either in quantity or quality to that required by the contract, he shall forthwith report the same to the Street Commissioner.

Ibid.

§ 84. He shall cause all lamps to be hereafter placed in the streets and avenues, in conformity with the ordinances or resolutions of the Common Council, now in force or hereafter to be adopted.

Ibid.

§ 85. He shall cause to be kept in his bureau accounts of the time of all persons to be paid by wages for work under the supervision of his bureau, and of the work upon which they are engaged, and of all the other expenditures of his bureau, and of the expense of each particular work or job, with the items thereof.

Ibid.

§ 86. He shall examine and audit all pay-rolls and all accounts for work done or materials furnished, under the supervision of his bureau; and, if found correct, shall certify them in writing, and shall deliver them, with proper vouchers, to the Street Commissioner; and in all cases of contract work under his supervision, he shall examine and report to the Street Commissioner as to the fulfillment or breach of the contract therefor; and he shall certify, on every voucher for payment thereon, that such payment is due, in accordance with the terms of the contract.

§ 87. He shall, in all matters connected with his bureau, be under the control, direction and supervision of the Street Commissioner, who may approve or disapprove all accounts certified by him, and by whom alone all requisitions upon the Comptroller for payment thereof shall be drawn. Duties of Superintendent of Lamps and Gas.

§ 88. The Superintendent of Lamps and Gas is specially charged with the enforcement of all ordinances and resolutions of the Common Council, for the protection of public lamps, and shall report all violations thereof to the Corporation Attorney. Ibid.

§ 89. The Superintendent of Lamps and Gas shall have authority to appoint in this bureau, to assist the Superintendent of Lamps and Gas in the performance of the duties thereof an Inspector of Oil, and not to exceed six competent persons, to be called Inspectors of Lamps, whose daily pay shall not exceed two dollars each. Inspector of Oil, and Inspector of Lamps.

§ 90. There shall be one clerk in this bureau, to be called the Clerk of the Superintendent of Lamps and Gas, who shall keep the accounts thereof, and prepare all the estimates and other papers appertaining thereto; and who shall perform such other duties as may be directed by the Superintendent of Lamps and Gas. He shall be paid monthly for his services at the rate of one thousand two hundred dollars per annum. Clerk to Superintendent of Lamps & Gas.

ARTICLE X.

OF THE BUREAU OF REPAIRS AND SUPPLIES.

Superintendent of Repairs and Supplies.

§ 91. This bureau, the chief officer of which shall be called the "Superintendent of Repairs and Supplies," is charged with the duty of superintending the construction and repairing of public buildings.

His Bond.

§ 92. The Superintendent of Repairs and Supplies shall, before entering upon the duties of his office, execute a bond to the Corporation, with one or more sureties, to be approved by the Comptroller, in the penal sum of two thousand dollars, conditioned for the faithful performance of the duties of his office. He shall be paid monthly for his services, at the rate of two thousand dollars per annum.

Duties of Superintendent of Repairs & Supplies.

§ 93. He shall take charge of, oversee and superintend the constructing and repairing of the public buildings, and the inspection of all work done thereon, by contract or otherwise, and have general superintendence over the Deputy Superintendent of Repairs and Supplies.

Ibid.

§ 94. He shall make all estimates necessary to or connected with the constructing and repairing of the public buildings, when required by the Street Commissioner.

Ibid.

§ 95. He shall cause to be kept in his bureau correct accounts of the time of all persons to be paid by wages for work on the construction or repairs of public buildings, and of the work upon which they are engaged, and of all expenditures relating thereto, and of the expense of each particular work or job, with the items thereof.

Ibid.

§ 96. He shall examine and audit all pay-rolls and all accounts for work done or materials furnished for the construction or repairs of public buildings; and if found correct, shall certify them in writing, and shall deliver them, with the proper vouchers, to the Street Commissioner. In all cases of contract work under his supervision, he shall examine, and report to the Street Commissioner, as to the fulfillment or breach of the contract therefor; and he shall certify, on every voucher for payment thereon, that such payment is due, in accordance with the terms of the contract.

Duties of Superintendent of Repairs & Supplies.

§ 97. He shall examine the state of the public buildings from time to time; and whenever any requisition for repairs thereto shall be referred to him by the Street Commissioner, he shall report all repairs thereof which, in his judgment, may be necessary, to the Street Commissioner, who shall lay the same before the Common Council, except where the expense thereof shall not in any case exceed two hundred and fifty dollars, in which case the Street Commissioner may cause the repairs to be made under the supervision of the Superintendent of Repairs and Supplies; but no expenditure shall be made by the Superintendent of Repairs and Supplies, except upon the written order and certificate of the Street Commissioner, in accordance with section 6 of this chapter.

Assistant to Superintendent of Repairs and Supplies, and Inspector of work.

§ 98. The Superintendent of Repairs and Supplies may employ, whenever the same shall be necessary, a competent person to assist the Superintendent of Repairs and Supplies in the performance of the duties of his office, whose monthly pay shall not exceed one hundred dollars; and not to exceed two competent persons, to inspect and estimate the value of all work not done by contract, the daily pay of each of whom shall not exceed two dollars and a half; and no account shall be allowed for any such work, until such inspection and estimate shall have been made.

Duties of Superintendent of Repairs & Supplies.

§ 99. He shall, in all matters connected with his bureau, be under the control, direction and supervision of the

Street Commissioner, who may approve or disapprove of all accounts certified by him, and by whom alone all requisitions upon the Comptroller for the payment thereof shall be drawn.

Clerks in Bureau of Repairs & Supplies.

§ 100. There shall be two clerks in this bureau, to be called the First and Second Clerks to the Superintendent of Repairs and Supplies, who shall keep the accounts of this bureau, and prepare such papers, and perform such other duties appertaining thereto, as shall be directed by the Superintendent of Repairs and Supplies. They shall be paid monthly for their services, as follows: the First Clerk at the rate of one thousand two hundred dollars per annum, and the Second Clerk at the rate of eight hundred per annum.

ARTICLE XI.

OF THE DEPUTY SUPERINTENDENT OF REPAIRS AND SUPPLIES.

Deputy Superintendent of Repairs & Supplies.

§ 101. There shall be in the Bureau of Repairs and Supplies, an officer who shall be called the Deputy Superintendent of Repairs and Supplies, who is charged with the duty of superintending the supplying the public rooms and offices and court-rooms of the Corporation, the police station-houses, the engine and other houses of the Fire Department, and the public markets, with fuel, stationery, printing, and all other things necessary therefor, and of superintending the furnishing of all other necessary supplies for the Corporation, except in cases where other provision is made therefor. He shall receive payment monthly for his services, at the rate of two thousand dollars per annum.

His Bond

§ 102. The Deputy Superintendent of Repairs and Supplies shall, before entering upon the duties of his office, execute a bond to the Corporation, with one or more sureties, to be approved by the Comptroller, in the penal sum of two thousand dollars, conditioned for the faithful performance of the duties of his office.

§ 103. He shall take charge of, and superintend the delivery and preservation of all supplies to be furnished under his supervision, and shall have charge of keeping clean and in proper order the public rooms, offices and court-rooms of the Corporation, and of the warming and lighting of the same; and for that purpose he may, with the written consent of the Street Commissioner, employ so many and such persons as may be necessary therefor, and at such compensation, not to exceed one dollar and a half per day, in any case, as may be allowed by the Street Commissioner. A statement of all persons so employed, with the rate of compensation allowed to each, and of his occupation, shall be submitted quarterly to the Common Council. Duties of Deputy Superintendent of Repairs and Supplies.

§ 104. He shall make all estimates necessary to or connected with the furnishing the supplies mentioned in this chapter, when required by the Street Commissioner; and, with the consent of the Street Commissioner, shall purchase all such supplies not furnished by contract, when the expense thereof shall not exceed two hundred and fifty dollars in any one case; but no expenditure shall be incurred by the Deputy Superintendent of Repairs and Supplies, except upon the written order and certificate of the Street Commissioner, in accordance with section 6 of this chapter. Ibid.

§ 105. He shall have the care of the public yards and store-houses of the Corporation and of all things that may be stored therein, and may, with the consent of the Street Commissioner, employ not to exceed two keepers for each Ibid.

of the public yards, whose pay shall not exceed two dollars per day.

Duties of Deputy Superintendent of Repairs and Supplies.

§ 106. He shall cause to be kept in his office correct accounts of the time of all persons employed by him, in accordance with section 103 of this chapter, and of all expenditures incurred under his supervision, with the items thereof, and shall keep a separate account of all supplies furnished to each of the several departments, bureaux and courts, and shall furnish each of them at the time of the delivery of any supplies, or at least once in each month, a statement of the articles supplied upon their requisition, with the quantities and prices; he shall take receipts for all articles delivered, which shall be filed in his office.

Ibid.

§ 107. He shall examine and audit all accounts for work done and for supplies of fuel, stationery, printing and other necessary things under his supervision, and, if found correct, shall certify them in writing, and deliver them, with the proper vouchers, to the Street Commissioner; and in all cases of supplies furnished by contract under his supervision, he shall examine and report to the Street Commissioner as to the fulfillment or breach of the contract therefor, and shall certify on every voucher for payment thereon that such payment is due in accordance with the terms of the contract.

Ibid.

§ 108. He shall, in all matters connected with his duties, be under the control, direction and supervision of the Street Commissioner, who may approve or disapprove all accounts certified by him, and by whom alone all requisitions upon the Comptroller for the payment thereof shall be drawn.

Clerks in Bureau of Repairs & Supplies.

§ 109. There shall be three clerks, in this bureau, to be called First, Second and Third Clerks to the Deputy Superintendent of Repairs and Supplies, who shall keep the accounts of this bureau, and perform such other duties as may be directed by the Deputy Superintendent of Repairs and Supplies. The First Clerk shall be paid monthly for his services, at the rate of one thousand two hundred dollars per annum; the Second Clerk shall be paid monthly for his services, at the rate of one thousand dollars per annum; the Third Clerk shall be paid monthly for his services, at the rate of eight hundred dollars per annum.

§ 110. The term City Hall, as used in this ordinance, includes all the public buildings in the Park. There shall be in the Bureau of Repairs and Supplies an officer, who shall be known as the Keeper of the City Hall, and who shall be paid monthly for his services, at the rate of one thousand two hundred and fifty dollars per annum. Keeper of City Hall.

§ 111. The Keeper of the City Hall shall have charge, under the supervision of the Deputy Superintendent of Repairs and Supplies, of keeping the City Hall, and shall superintend the keeping clean and in proper order the rooms in the City Hall. He shall, when necessary, cause fires to be made therein, except in the rooms occupied by the courts or offices of the United States, the Commissioners of Emigration, the Governors of the Alms-house, the Croton Aqueduct Board, the Board of Education, and the Law Institute. His duties.

§ 112. He shall also provide for the meetings of the respective Boards of the Common Council, and their committees, and shall preserve and take care of the furniture used in, and the fuel or other articles supplied for the use of, the City Hall, except as provided in the last section, and perform such other duties connected with his office as may be assigned him by the Street Commissioner. Ibid.

May reside in City Hall. § 113. He may occupy for himself and his family such rooms in the City Hall as may be assigned him by the Street Commissioner.

Duties of Keeper of City Hall. § 114. He shall superintend and keep an account of the time of all persons appointed by the Deputy Superintendent of Repairs and Supplies, to assist him in the performance of his duties, in pursuance of section 103 of this chapter, and shall prepare and certify all accounts and payrolls therefor, and shall deliver them to the Deputy Superintendent of Repairs and Supplies, by whom, if found correct, they shall also be certified, and be delivered to the Street Commissioner.

ARTICLE XII.

OF THE BUREAU OF THE CHIEF ENGINEER OF THE FIRE DEPARTMENT.

Chief Engineer of Fire Department. § 115. This bureau, of which the Chief Engineer of the Fire Department shall be the chief officer, is charged with the duty of repairing fire engines, hose-carts, hooks and ladders, hose, and other machines and apparatus, for the use of the Fire Department.

His duties. § 116. The Chief Engineer of the Fire Department shall oversee and superintend the repairing of fire engines, hose-carts, hooks and ladders, hose, and other machines and apparatus, for the use of the Fire Department.

Ibid. § 117. He shall make all estimates necessary to, or connected with, the performance of the duties of his bureau, when required by the Street Commissioner.

Ibid. § 118. He shall, from time to time, inspect the fire engines, hose-carts, hooks and ladders, hose, and other machines and apparatus, for the use of the Fire Department; and shall report to the Street Commissioner any repairs which may be required thereon. If the Street Commissioner approve thereof, he shall report the same to the Common Council, except that when the expenditure shall not exceed seventy-five dollars in any one case, he may direct the same to be done.

§ 119. The Chief Engineer may, with the consent of the Street Commissioner, make small repairs in the Corporation yard, to the hose and hooks and ladders of the Fire Department. Duties of Chief Engineer.

§ 120. He shall cause to be kept in his bureau accounts of the time of all persons to be paid by wages for work, under the supervision of his bureau, and of the work upon which they are engaged, and of all the other expenditures of his bureau, and of the expense of each particular work or job, with the items thereof. Ibid.

§ 121. He shall examine and audit all pay-rolls and all accounts for work done, or materials furnished, under the supervision of his bureau, and, if found correct, shall certify them in writing, and shall deliver them, with proper vouchers, to the Street Commissioner; and in all cases of contract work under his supervision, he shall examine and report to the Street Commissioner as to the fulfillment or breach of the contract therefor; and he shall certify on every voucher for payment thereon that such payment is due, in accordance with the terms of the contract. Ibid.

§ 122. He shall, in all matters connected with his bureau, be under the control, direction and supervision of the Street Commissioner, who may approve or disapprove all accounts certified by him, and by whom alone all requisitions upon the Comptroller for the payment thereof shall be made. Ibid.

§ 123. No new fire engine, hose, or hook and ladder Construction of Fire Engines, &c.

carriage, shall be constructed for the Fire Department, unless the same shall be authorized by the Common Council.

Superintendent of Fire Apparatus. § 124. There shall be in this bureau, a Superintendent of Fire Apparatus, to be appointed by the Street Commissioner, who shall be a practical machinist, and fire engine builder, and who shall be an exempt fireman, whose duty it shall be to superintend the construction and proper working and keeping of fire apparatus, and such other duties as may be required in the direction of the Fire Department, which shall not interfere with any existing ordinance, or conflict with the firemen in the discharge of their duties. The Superintendent of Fire Apparatus shall receive payment for his services monthly, at the rate of one thousand dollars per annum.

Foreman of Corporation Yard. § 125. There shall be a Foreman of the Corporation Yard, in this bureau, to be appointed by the Chief Engineer, whose duty it shall be to superintend the repairing and cleaning of hose, and take charge of the same, and to perform all such other duties as may be assignd to him by the Chief Engineer, and shall receive a salary of one thousand dollars per annum, payable monthly. There shall also be two clerks in this bureau, to be appointed by the Chief Engineer, who shall keep the accounts of this bureau, and perform such other duties as shall be directed by the Chief Engineer, at a salary of one thousand dollars each per annum, payable monthly. The Chief Engineer shall also have authority to employ laborers in the Corporation Yard, not to exceed eight in number, at a compensation of two dollars per day.

ARTICLE XIII.

OF THE BUREAU OF COLLECTION OF ASSESSMENTS.

§ 126. This bureau, the chief officer of which shall be called the "Collector of Assessments," is charged with the duty of collecting all assessments which are confirmed according to law. Collector of Assessments

§ 127. The Collector of Assessments shall, before entering upon the duties of his office, execute a bond to the Corporation, with at least two sureties, to be approved by the Comptroller, in the penal sum of twenty-five thousand dollars, conditioned for the faithful performance of the duties of his office. His Bond.

§ 128. The Collector of Assessments may appoint, not to exceed four Deputy Collectors of Assessments, who shall assist the Collector of Assessments in the performance of the duties of the bureau. Each of the Deputy Collectors shall, before entering upon the duties of his office, execute a bond to the Corporation, with at least two sureties, to be approved by the Comptroller, in the penal sum of ten thousand dollars, conditioned for the faithful performance of the duties of his office. Deputy Collectors of Assessments.

§ 129. Upon receiving an assessment list for collection, the Street Commissioner shall charge the amount thereof on the books in his office, to the account of the Collector of Assessments, and shall thereupon transmit the same to the Collector of Assessments, for collection. Collection of Assessments

§ 130. Immediately after receiving such assessment list, the collector shall cause to be entered in a book to be kept for that purpose, and to be called "the Record of Titles of Assessments Confirmed," the title and amount of such assessment, the date of its confirmation, and the date of such entry. Ibid.

Collection of Assessments

§ 131. The Collector of Assessments shall, also, cause to be entered in books to be kept for that purpose, and to be called the "Records of Assessments," under the title of each assessment, the name of the street on which each lot assessed is situated, with the ward, and the assessment map, or the block number of each lot; the name of the person to whom it is assessed; the dimensions of the lot; the amount of the assessment, and the time of its confirmation; and in such books shall also be entered, before the expiration of one week from the time of the payment of any assessment, by the Collector or Deputy Collector receiving the same, opposite each item on which payment has been made, the fact of such payment, and the date thereof, and every such entry shall be verified by the signature of the Collector or Deputy Collector making the same.

Ibid.

§ 132. The Collector of Assessments shall thereupon deliver the assessment list to one of the Deputy Collectors for collection, and shall immediately notify the Street Commissioner of the deputy to whom it has been delivered. He shall apportion the lists between the deputies in such manner, as that the collections of the bureau may be divided as nearly as may be, equally between them.

Ibid.

§ 133. Immediately upon receiving an assessment list, the Deputy Collector shall prepare, in suitable books to be kept for that purpose, under the title of The Assessment, a condensed recapitulation thereof, containing, under the name of each person assessed, the ward and the map or the block number of each lot assessed in his name, and the amount of the assessment thereon; and on such books shall also be entered, at the time of the payment of any assessment, in such manner as to identify the items on which each payment is made, the date of the payment and by whom made, and the amount of the assessment, and the amount of interest paid in each case.

§ 134. The Deputy Collector shall, thereupon, prepare and cause to be sent to each of the persons named in such assessment list, if such persons can be found, a notice of such assessment, specifying therein the title of the assessment, the date of its confirmation, the ward and the map or the block number of each lot assessed in his name, and the amount so assessed. Collection of Assessments

§ 135. If any assessment duly confirmed, or any part thereof, remain unpaid for sixty days after the entry thereof in the Records of Titles of Assessments Confirmed, the Deputy Collector may, with the consent of the Street Commissioner, make application for a warrant to levy the same, according to law. Ibid.

§ 136. The Deputy Collector shall, after the expiration of the respective periods of sixty days mentioned in the last section, receive and collect interest upon all unpaid assessments; except that in case of assessment and award to the same person, he shall receive and collect interest only upon the excess of the assessment over the award. Ibid.

§ 137. The Deputy Collector, having any assessment list in charge for collection shall, before the expiration of one year from the date of confirmation thereof, unless the same has previously been done and recorded, as next hereinafter provided, personally demand, at two several times, of each of the persons required by law to pay any part of said assessment, the payment thereof; except where such persons do not reside in the city of New York, or where, after diligent search and inquiry, they cannot be determined or found. It shall be the duty of the Deputy Collector, within one week after making any such demand, to make an entry thereof in books to be kept for that purpose, and to be called "The Records of Demands for Payment of Assessments;" and every such entry shall be made in such man- Ibid.

ner as to identify each item of the assessment for which payment was demanded, and the name of the person on whom, and the place where the demand was made, and the date thereof; and shall be verified by the signature and the affidavit of the Collector or Deputy Collector by whom such demand was made.

Duties of Deputy Collectors of Assessments.

§ 138. Each of the Deputy Collectors shall, on Tuesday of each week, or oftener, if required, furnish to the Collector of Assessments, and to the Street Commissioner, an account in writing, item by item, of all moneys collected by him, stating the amount of assessment, and the interest thereon, paid on each lot, with the ward and the map, or the block number thereof, and upon what assessment, the name of the person making each payment, and the date thereof; and such account shall be verified by the signature and the affidavit of the Deputy Collector making the same. He shall thereupon pay over to the Collector of Assessments all moneys collected by him on such assessments, and shall receive from him triplicate vouchers therefor, one of which shall immediately thereafter be filed with the Comptroller, and one with the Street Commissioner.

Duties of Collector of Assessments.

§ 139. The Collector of Assessments shall cause the returns so made by the Deputy Collectors to be filed in books to be provided for that purpose, and shall, on Monday of each week, pay over to the Chamberlain all moneys received from the Deputy Collectors, and shall also thereupon receive from the Chamberlain triplicate vouchers for the payment thereof, on which vouchers shall be specified the amount paid on each assessment. He shall forthwith, on the same day, file one of such triplicate vouchers with the Comptroller, and one with the Street Commissioner.

List of Delinquents.

§ 140. Each of the Deputy Collectors shall, on being required, furnish to the Street Commissioner or to the

Collector of Assessments, a list of all delinquents, with the amounts uncollected upon any assessment list delivered to him for collection.

§ 141. The Collector of Assessments shall, on the expiration of one year from the date of confirmation of any assessment list, return each list to the Street Commissioner, with an account of all items remaining unpaid thereon, stating the name of the street on which each lot on which the assessment remains unpaid is situated, with the ward and the map or the block number of each lot; the name of the person to whom it is assessed, the dimensions of the lot and the amount of the assessment thereon; and such account shall be accompanied by a statement in writing, specifying for each item thereof that two personal demands for payment have been made by a Collector or a Deputy Collector of Assessments of the person or persons required by law to pay for the same; or that such person or persons do not reside in the city of New York, or that, after diligent search and inquiry, such person or persons cannot bè determined or found; and such statement shall be verified by the signature and affidavits of the Collector or Deputy Collector having the knowledge thereof; and no collections shall be made by any Collector or Deputy Collector of Assessments, on any assessment so returned. Unpaid Assessments.

§ 142. Upon receiving such returns, and an examination thereof, the Street Commissioner shall, if they be found correct, credit the amount thereof to the account of the Collector of Assessments, and charge the same to the Bureau of Arrears; and shall thereupon transmit the assessment list, the returns, and the affidavits relating thereto, to the Comptroller, and receive from him a voucher therefor. Ibid.

§ 143. It shall be the duty of the Comptroller, if in Ibid.

case of any assessment, so returned, he shall have reason to believe that items have been returned as unpaid on which payments have been made, or that the demands for payment have not been made as provided by law, to notify the Street Commissioner thereof; and it shall be the duty of the Street Commissioner thereupon, with the consent of the Comptroller, to cause notices to be served upon each of the person or persons required by law to pay such items returned as arrears, that payment is due thereon, and that the property so returned is liable to sale; and the Street Commissioner shall make the Comptroller a detailed report of all such cases in which notices are served.

Duties of Collector of Assessments.

§ 144. The Collector of Assessments shall cause to be kept a ledger, on which shall be entered, under the title of each assessment received for collection, the amount thereof, the date of the confirmation, the name of the deputy having it in charge for collection, the amount of principal and interest returned by the deputy as collector thereon, and when returned, and the amounts paid to the Chamberlain by the collector, and when paid. Accounts shall also be kept in such ledger, with each of the Deputy Collectors, in which they shall be severally charged with the amounts of the assessment lists placed in their hands for collection; and accredited with the amounts paid to the Collector of Assessments, and the amount of unpaid assessments returned in accordance with section 141, as arrears.

Collection of Assessments

§ 145. Each of the Deputy Collectors shall keep a cash book, on which shall be entered, immediately on the receipt of each payment on any assessment, the ward, and the map, or the block number of each lot on which payment is made, the name of the person making the same, and the date thereof, and the amount of the assessment paid, and the interest collected thereon.

§ 146. If any collections shall be made on any assessment by the Collector of Assessments, all the provisions of this ordinance in respect to the books to be kept, and the entries, returns and affidavits to be made by the Deputy Collectors, shall also be applicable to the Collector of Assessments in regard to all collections made by him. Duties of Collector of Assessments.

§ 147. All the records, books, accounts and vouchers hereinbefore provided to be kept in this bureau, shall be held as appertaining thereto, and as the property of the Corporation; except that each Deputy Collector may retain one of the triplicate vouchers for payments made by him to the Collector of Assessments, and the Collector of Assessments may retain one of the triplicate vouchers for payments made by him to the Chamberlain. Records, Vouchers, &c for Assessments.

§ 148. A receipt shall be given by the Collector or Deputy Collector, receiving any payment on account of any assessment, to the person making the same; on which shall be stated the name of the person making the payment, and the date and amount thereof; the title of the assessment, and the ward, and the map or block number of each lot, on which payment is made; and every such receipt shall have printed conspicuously thereon, the following words : Ibid.

NOTICE.

"The liens for which payment has been made, may be discharged of record, in the office of the Comptroller, on the presentation of this receipt to the Clerk of Arrears."

§ 149. It shall be the duty of the Clerk of Arrears on presentation of any such receipt, to countersign the same; and to enter, in books to be kept in his bureau for that purpose, the title of the assessment for which such receipt was given, the ward, and the map, or the block number of Ibid.

each lot, on which payment was made, as specified in such receipt; the name of the person making such payment, and the date and amount thereof; and the date of the presentation of such receipt to the Clerk of Arrears, and the name of the person by whom presented. And it shall be the duty of the Clerk of Arrears, once in each week, to cause the entries so made, to be compared with the accounts of the Collector of Assessments, of moneys paid to the Chamberlain, filed in the office of the Comptroller.

Compensation of Collectors of Assessments.

§ 150. The Collector and the Deputy Collector shall each receive, as compensation for their services, an equal part of two and one-half per cent. on all items of assessments collected by the bureau during their term of office, and of two per cent. on all unpaid items of assessments returned during their term of office, to the Bureau of Arrears, for which two personal demands for payment have been made by the Collector or Deputy Collectors on the persons required by law to pay the same. No moneys, however collected on any assessment, shall be retained on account of such fees or compensation; but the amount of fees thereon shall be paid monthly, on the requisition of the Street Commissioner, to the extent of any moneys which may have been collected, and paid into the city treasury, upon such assessment, or interest moneys accruing thereon. No moneys collected on any assessment shall be retained on account of the compensation herein provided; but such compensation shall be paid by warrant of the Comptroller, on the requisition of the Street Commissioner.

Amount of Assessments

§ 151. No assessment for a less amount than five dollars, shall hereafter be made on any lot, for any improvement; the assessment for which is required by law to be confirmed by the Common Council.

ARTICLE XIV.

OF SURVEYING.

§ 152. Whenever in the proper administration of the duties of his office, the Street Commissioner may require the services of the City Surveyor, he shall have authority to employ such one of the City Surveyors, as he may approve, for that purpose. Employment of City Surveyors.

§ 153. No City Surveyor employed by the Street Department, shall receive compensation therefor, at a greater rate than as follows; nor shall any surveyor's bill be paid, unless the same be first certified to by the Street Commissioner: for a preliminary survey, in regulating a street or avenue, or for making a country road, for the first line of level, three cents per lineal foot, measuring through the centre of the street, avenue or road; and for every additional line of levels, one cent per lineal foot, to be measured in the same manner. For a preliminary survey in filling sunken lots, one dollar and fifty cents per lot, of two thousand five hundred square feet. Compensation of Surveyors employed by Street Department.

For grading, when done alone, five cents per lineal foot; measuring through the centre of the street or avenue.

For grading, and setting curb and gutter, when done under the same contract, eight cents per lineal foot; measuring through the centre of the street or avenue.

For grading, setting curb and gutter and flagging, when done under the same contract, eleven cents per lineal foot; measuring through the centre of the street or avenue.

For setting curb and gutter alone, three cents per lineal foot; along the line of the work done.

For setting curb and gutter and flagging, when done under the same contract, but not in connection with grading, four and one-half cents per lineal foot, along the line of curb.

For flagging, when done alone, three cents per lineal foot; along the line of work done.

For setting stakes, making final survey, &c., in the filling of sunken lots, one dollar and fifty cents per lot of two thousand five hundred square feet.

For fencing, including the priliminary survey, three cents per foot.

For making a country road, ten cents per lineal foot; measuring through the centre of the road.

For establishing a new grade line, one cent per lineal foot; measuring along the line.

For assessment list and maps, three cents per lineal foot of map front; it being understood that the Surveyor shall, in every case, furnish a duplicate list and map, without additional charge.

A surveyor, employed by the Street Commissioner to make a survey for public slips, or other purposes, the compensation for which is not otherwise provided for, shall receive such compensation as shall be certified by the Street Commissioner.

Compensation of Surveyors employed by Street Department.

§ 154. In all cases, when the same is required, a protraction, or profile, and such drawings and calculations, shall be furnished to the Street Commissioner, as may be required by him, without extra compensation. A Surveyor shall be entitled to receive payment for a preliminary survey, on the completion of the same to the satisfaction of the Street Commissioner. He shall receive payment for the other services mentioned in this paragraph, on the completion of the work, and its acceptance by the Street Department.

§ 155. The amount paid for any of the services mentioned in the last section, whenever the same shall have been rendered in relation to any improvement, or work, for which an assessment may afterwards be made, shall be included in such assessment. Fees of City Surveyors.

§ 156. A surveyor shall be entitled to receive ten dollars for every certificate to a contractor, which shall be paid by the Street Commissioner: the amount so paid for such certificate shall be deducted from the payment to be made to the contractor, on account of the work certified to be done. Ibid.

CHAPTER V.

OF THE LAW DEPARTMENT.

ARTICLE I.

OF THE LAW DEPARTMENT AND ITS BUREAUX GENERALLY.

General cognizance of the Law Department.

§ 1. The Law Department shall have the charge of, and conduct all the law business of the Corporation, and of the departments thereof, and all other law business in which the city shall be interested, when so ordered by the Corporation; and shall have the charge of, and conduct the legal proceedings necessary in opening, widening or altering streets; and draw the leases, deeds and other papers, connected with the Finance Department.

Bureaux.

§ 2. There shall be two bureaux in the Law Department.

1. A bureau for the prosecution of all actions for violations of the ordinances of the Common Council, or arising under the charter of the city, or under the laws of this State, where a penalty is given to the Corporation, or to the Overseers of the Poor, or to the Alms-house Department, and for the conducting of all proceedings before justices, or upon appeal, in relation to bastardy cases and prosecutions upon bastardy and abandonment bonds; to be called the Bureau of the Corporation Attorney.

2. A bureau for the administration of the estates of persons dying intestate, where no other administrator is appointed, to be called the Bureau of the Public Administrator.

ARTICLE II.

OF THE COUNSEL TO THE CORPORATION AND HIS CLERKS.

§ 3. The chief officer of the Law Department shall be denominated the Counsel to the Corporation. Counsel.

§ 4. The Counsel to the Corporation shall, before entering upon the duties of his office, execute a bond to the Corporation, with two sufficient sureties, to be approved by the Mayor, and filed in the office of the Comptroller, in the penal sum of five thousand dollars, conditioned for the faithful performance of the duties of his office. Bond of Counsel.

§ 5. He shall, from time to time, when required, advise the Common Council, the Board of Supervisors and the Board of Health, and their committees and officers respectively, and the head of any department or bureau of the Corporation, upon all matters which may be submitted to him for his opinion. Duties of the Counsel.

§ 6. He shall draw such ordinances as may be required of him by either Board of the Common Council, or by any committee thereof. Ibid.

§ 7. He shall, when required by the Common Council, prepare the draft of any bill to be presented by the Corporation of the city to the Legislature, for passage, with a proper memorial for the passage thereof. Ibid.

§ 8. He shall draw the leases, deeds and other papers connected with the Finance Department, and all contracts for any of the other departments of the Corporation, when so required by the head of the department. Ibid.

Duties of the Counsel.

§ 9. He shall prosecute and defend, as the Attorney and Counsel to the Corporation, all actions which may be brought by or against them, or any of the heads of department, or bureaux, or any officer thereof, for or by reason of any matter or duty connected with or growing out of their respective offices, or in which the Corporation are interested, in any court in this state, except actions by or against the Public Administrator, as provided in section 40, and actions for violations of the ordinances of the Common Council, or arising under the charter of the city, or under the laws of this state, where a penalty is given to the Corporation, or to the Overseers of the Poor, or to the Alms-house Department, and except proceedings before Justices, or upon appeal, in relation to bastardy cases and prosecutions upon bastardy and abandonment bonds.

Ibid.

§ 10. When he shall recover a debt due to the Corporation, which may have been placed in his hands for collection, he shall forthwith render an account thereof, under oath, to the Comptroller, stating the nature of the debt, the person against whom it was recovered, and the amount and time of the recovery, and shall immediately thereupon pay over the amount so received to the Chamberlain. He shall also thereupon receive from the Chamberlain a voucher for the payment thereof, which he shall forthwith, on the same day, exhibit to the Comptroller, and shall, at the same time, leave with him a copy thereof.

Ibid.

§ 11. He shall, on the twentieth day of December, in each year, report to the Common Council the titles of all actions in his hands, prosecuted or defended by him, as provided in section 9 of this chapter, and then pending and undetermined, with such other information in respect thereto as he may deem necessary or proper.

Ibid.

§ 12. He shall keep, in proper books, to be provided for

that purpose, a register of all actions prosecuted or defended by him, as provided in section 9 of this chapter, and all proceedings had therein.

Duties of the Counsel.

§ 13. He shall, on the first Monday of January, April, July and October, in each year, furnish to the Comptroller an account, under oath, of all disbursements which he may have made in conducting the actions prosecuted or defended by him, as provided in section 9 of this chapter; and upon being satisfied of the correctness thereof, the Comptroller shall draw his warrant in favor of the Counsel for the amount so disbursed.

Compensation of the Counsel.

§ 14. The compensation to be paid to the Counsel to the Corporation, for all the services he may be required to render, shall be as fixed by law. He shall, nevertheless, be entitled to receive, in addition, from parties other than the Corporation, his proper fees and necessary disbursements, and the taxable costs in all actions and proceedings which may be conducted, prosecuted or defended by him as such counsel, as provided in section 9 of this chapter.

Duties of the Counsel.

§ 15. Upon the expiration of his term of office, or his resignation thereof, or removal therefrom, the Counsel to the Corporation shall forthwith, on demand, deliver to his successor in office all deeds, leases, contracts and other papers in his hands, belonging to the Corporation, or delivered to him by the Corporation, or any of its officers, and all papers in actions prosecuted or defended by him, as provided in section 9 of this chapter, then pending and undetermined, together with his register thereof, and of the proceedings therein, and a written consent of substitution of his successor, in all such actions then pending and undetermined.

Ibid.

§ 16. He shall, from time to time, report to the Common Council the condition of the Law Department, and shall suggest such improvements and alterations, in respect thereto, as he shall deem necessary or proper.

Clerks in the Law Department.

§ 17. There shall be two clerks in the Law Department, to be denominated respectively the First and Second Clerks of the Counsel to the Corporation, who shall prepare and copy such papers relating to the department, and perform such other services in relation thereto, as the Counsel to the Corporation shall direct.

Additional Counsel.

§ 18. The Counsel to the Corporation is authorized to employ additional counsel to aid in the trial or argument of causes or proceedings of importance in which the city may be a party interested.

Compensation in lieu of clerk hire.

§ 19. The Comptroller of the city of New York is hereby authorized and directed to allow and pay to the Counsel to the Corporation, in monthly payments, the annual sum of eight thousand dollars, in lieu of all charges against the Corporation for clerical assistance and clerk hire in the conduct of his business.

ARTICLE III.

OF THE BUREAU OF THE CORPORATION ATTORNEY.

General cognizances of the Bureau of Corporation Attorney

§ 20. This bureau, the chief officer of which shall be called the Corporation Attorney, is charged with the prosecution of all actions for violations of the ordinances of the Common Council, or arising under the charter of the city, or under the laws of this state, where a penalty is given to the Corporation, or to the Overseers of the Poor, or to the Alms-house Department, and with the conducting of all proceedings before Justices, or upon appeal, in relation to bastardy cases, and the prosecution of bastardy and abandonment bonds.

Bond of the Corporation Attorney.

§ 21. The Corporation Attorney shall, before entering upon the duties of his office, execute a bond to the Co rpo ration, with one or more sureties, to be approved by the Comptroller, in the penal sum of two thousand dollars, conditioned for the faithful performance of the duties of his office.

§ 22. He shall institute an action in any of the cases mentioned in section 20 of this chapter, when instructed to do so by the Common Council, or the chief officer of any department or bureau, or upon the complaint of any other person, when in his judgment the public interest requires that the same shall be prosecuted. Duties of the Corporation Attorney.

§ 23. He may compromise with the party complained of either before or after an action shall have been brought for any violation of an ordinance of the Common Council, where the penalty does not exceed twenty-five dollars, and where, in his judgment, the public interest does not require that an action should be prosecuted therefor. Ibid.

§ 24. In all actions which he is required by section 20 of this ordinance to prosecute, he shall appear as the Attorney and Counsel of the Corporation. Ibid.

§ 25. He shall not bring an appeal in any action in which judgment shall have been given against the Corporation, except with the consent of the Counsel to the Corporation, or by direction of the Common Council. Ibid.

§ 26. He shall, on the first Thursday in each month, report to the Comptroller a statement, under oath, of the actions instituted by him, and settled before judgment; of the complaints compromised by him, in which no action shall have been commenced, and of all actions prosecuted to judgment, with the result thereof, whether for or against the Corporation, and whether an execution has been issued thereon; and, if so, whether it has been collected; and shall include therein a particular account, item by item, of all Ibid.

penalties or other moneys which he may have received for the Corporation, and from whom they were received respectively, and on what account and when paid. He shall also state therein, item by item, an account of officers' or court fees paid by him, and on what account and when they were respectively paid, and shall exhibit at the foot of the account the balance thereof, whether for or against the Corporation.

Duties of the Corporation Attorney.

§ 27. If the account shall exhibit a balance in his hands in favor of the Corporation, he shall forthwith pay over such balance to the Chamberlain, and shall thereupon receive from the Chamberlain a voucher for the payment thereof, which he shall forthwith, on the same day, exhibit to the Comptroller, and shall, at the same time, leave with him a copy thereof.

Ibid.

§ 28. If the account exhibit a balance against the Corporation, the Comptroller, upon being satisfied of the correctness thereof, shall draw a warrant in favor of the Corporation Attorney for the amount of such balance; but in every such case he shall report the fact, with the account so rendered to the Common Council.

Ibid.

§ 29. Every officer employed by the Corporation Attorney to serve process in an action brought by him, in the name of the Corporation, shall pay to the Corporation Attorney all moneys which he may receive, both for penalty and costs, upon a judgment; and the Corporation Attorney shall, at least once in each month, pay every officer so employed by him his legal costs and fees.

Ibid.

§ 30. He shall, on the twentieth day of December in each year, report to the Common Council the titles of all the actions in his hands, which he is authorized, by section 20 of this ordinance, to prosecute on behalf of the Corporation, then pending and undetermined, with the state thereof, and with such other information, in respect thereto, as he may deem necessary or proper.

§ 31. He shall keep, in proper books, to be provided for that purpose, a register of all actions prosecuted by him, pursuant to section 20, of this chapter, and of all proceedings had therein.

Duties of Corporation Attorney.

§ 32. The salary to be paid to the Corporation Attorney shall be a full compensation, as between him and the Corporation, for all the services he may be required to render by this chapter; but he shall nevertheless be entitled to receive from adverse parties the taxable costs in all actions in which he may recover judgment against them.

Compensation.

§ 33. Upon the expiration of his term of office, or his resignation thereof, or removal therefrom, the Corporation Attorney shall forthwith, on demand, deliver to his successor in office all papers in his hands belonging to, or delivered to him by the Corporation or the Alms-house Depart ment, or any of their officers, and all papers in actions prosecuted by him, as authorized by section 20 of this chapter, and which are then pending and undetermined, together with his register thereof, and of the proceedings therein, and a written consent of substitution of his successor in all such actions then pending and undetermined.

Duties of Corporation Attoruey.

§ 34. There shall be two clerks in this bureau, to be denominated respectively the First and Second Clerks of the Corporation Attorney, who shall prepare and copy such papers relating to this bureau, and perform such other services, in relation thereto, as the Corporation Attorney shall direct. The First Clerk shall receive an annual salary of twelve hundred and fifty dollars, and the Second Clerk shall receive an annual salary of one thousand dollars. There shall be a Messenger in this bureau, who shall receive an annual salary of two-hundred and fifty dollars.

Clerks and Messengers in Bureau of Corporation Attorney

Compensation of Corporation Attorney.

§ 35. In lieu of all salary, allowance or compensation paid to the Corporation Attorney, there shall be paid to said Attorney an annual salary of five thousand dollars, and no more, which shall be in full compensation to him for all services he is required to render under the charter of the city, or the ordinances of the Common Council of the city of New York, or the laws of this state, or for any other duty he may discharge, or service he may render.

ARTICLE IV.

OF THE BUREAU OF THE PUBLIC ADMINISTRATOR.

General cognizance of Bureau.

§ 36. This bureau, the chief officer of which, shall be called the Public Administrator, is charged with the administration of the estates of persons dying intestate, where no other administrator is appointed.

Bond of Public Administrator.

§ 37. The Public Administrator shall, before entering upon the duties of his office, execute a bond to the Corporation, with such sureties as shall be approved by the Mayor or Recorder of the city of New York, in the penal sum of ten thousand dollars, conditioned for the faithful discharge of all duties enjoined on him by law, and particularly that he will account for and pay over all moneys and property which may come to his hands as such administrator, according to law.

Duties of Public Administrator,

§ 38. He shall possess the powers and perform the duties conferred and imposed upon him by the laws of this state.

Ibid.

§ 39. He shall furnish the Comptroller with copies of all letters of administration which shall be granted by him, within three days after the granting thereof.

May employ Counsel.

§ 40. He may employ an attorney or counsel in any action commenced by or against him, where the creditors, or persons interested in the distribution of the estate, shall advise or assent to the prosecution or defence thereof, and where the funds belonging to the estate are sufficient to pay the costs and fees incurred therein. But in no such case shall a charge for costs or fees be made against the Corporation by the Public Administrator, or by the attorney or counsel employed by him.

§ 41. He shall, on the 20th day of December in each year, report to the Common Council the titles of all actions prosecuted by or against him, and then pending and undetermined, with such other information in respect thereto as he may deem necessary or proper. Duties of Public Administrator.

§ 42. He shall report to the Comptroller, on the first Thursday in each month, and oftener, if required, the amount of money received by him since his last return, on account of any estate upon which he shall have administered. Ibid.

§ 43. He shall render to the Common Council, on the first day of January in each year, or within fourteen days after that day, a statement, on oath, and in a tabular form, of the following particulars in each case in which he shall have taken charge of and collected any effects, or in which he shall have administered on any estate during the preceding year. Ibid.

1. The name of the deceased;
2. His occupation;
3. The place of his residence at the time of his death;
4. The country or place from which he came, if he were not a resident of this state at the time of his death;
5. The moneys received for commissions and expenses;
6. The total amount of his receipts and expenditures;
7. The total amount of debts ascertained and allowed;

8. The amount of costs;
9. The amount distributed;
10. The date of the letters of administration.

Duties of Public Administrator.

§ 44. He shall, at the same time, report to the Common Council a transcript of such of his accounts as have been closed or finally settled, and of those on which any money has been received by him as part of the proceeds of any estates on which he has administered ; he shall deposit all moneys by him collected and received, as required by law, in such bank as the Counsel to the Corporation shall designate.

Ibid.

§ 45. The Public Administrator must deposit all moneys by him collected and received, within two days after the receipt thereof, in the bank designated in the last section, to the joint credit of himself and the Comptroller, except so much as may be necessary to pay the current expenses of any proceedings authorized by law, to be allowed by the Surrogate, and which shall not exceed twenty dollars in any one case.

Ibid.

§ 46. He shall, whenever required, exhibit to the Comptroller the bank book showing such deposits, and all other vouchers and documents relating to his office.

Moneys how drawn out.

§ 47. The money so deposited can be drawn out only on the joint check of the Public Administrator and the Comptroller, in the cases where, by law, the Public Administrator is required to pay out moneys; and the Comptroller must preserve a register of all checks signed by him, as a part of the documents of his office.

Ibid.

§ 48. The Comptroller, before signing any check for money so deposited, shall examine the bank book showing the deposit, and the vouchers on which the check is required to be drawn, and shall satisfy himself fully as to the correctness thereof; and in case of doubt or difficulty, he shall report the case to the Common Council for their direction.

§ 49. The Comptroller may distribute and pay any unadministered balance of an intestate's estate, remaining in the city treasury, to the persons legally entitled thereto, whenever he and the Public Administrator shall be satisfied that the person claiming the same is legally entitled thereto; but if they be not satisfied thereof, they shall report the case to the Common Council for their direction. Moneys, how distributed.

CHAPTER VI.

OF THE CROTON AQUEDUCT BOARD.

ARTICLE I.

OF THE CROTON AQUEDUCT BOARD AND ITS BUREAUX GENERALLY.

Powers and duties of the Board.

§ 1. The Executive Department called the Croton Aqueduct Board, is invested, by the laws of this State, with the following powers and duties:

1. With the direction and settlement of all suits, claims and demands against the Corporation, or against the Water Commissioners of the city of New York, created by the act for the appointment of Water Commissioners by the Governor and Senate for the city of New York, passed May 2, 1834.

2. With the charge of the Croton Aqueduct, and all structures and works and property connected with the supply and distribution of water to the city of New York, and the underground drainage of the same; and of the public sewers of the city; and of permits for street vaults; and of paving, repaving and repairing streets, and digging and constructing wells; and the collection of the revenues arising from the sale of the Cro-

ton water; with such other powers and duties as shall or may be prescribed by law. Powers and Duties of the Board.

3. With the preservation of the Croton lake and waters; with the preservation of the banks of the Croton river from injuries or nuisances; with the execution of such measures as may be necessary to preserve and increase the quantity of water and keep it pure; with the management, preservation and repairs of the dam, gates, aqueduct, high bridge, reservoirs, mains, pipes, pipe-yard, and property of every description, belonging to the Water Works; and they shall have the construction of such new works, and the purchase and laying down of such mains and pipes as the Common Council may authorize; and also the construction, repairs and cleansing of all the sewers and underground drains, but subject to the orders and directions of the Common Council, as to the times and places of building new sewers, and to the general plan which has been or may be adopted for the sewerage and drainage of the city. They shall be responsible for the supply of water, and the good order and security of all the works from the Croton lake to the city inclusive, for the exactness and durability of the structures which may be erected, and of the daily work to be performed, and for the sufficiency of the supply in the pipe-yard to meet every casualty, and for the fidelity, care and attention of all persons employed by the Department in watching the works, and in making constructions and repairs; and shall inspect thoroughly the interior of the aqueduct, and make the necessary repairs, at least twice in each year.

Bureaux. § 2. There shall be two bureaux in the Croton Aqueduct Department.

1. A bureau for the collection of the revenue derived from the sale of the Croton water ; and the chief officer thereof shall be called the Water Registrar.
2. A bureau for the laying of water pipes and the construction and repairs of sewers, wells and hydrants, and the paving, repaving and repairing of streets: the chief officer of which shall be called the Water Purveyor.

ARTICLE II.

OF THE CROTON AQUEDUCT BOARD.

Officers composing the Board. § 3. The chief officers of the Croton Aqueduct Board shall be called the President, Engineer, and Assistant Commissioner; who, together, shall form the Croton Aqueduct Board, and shall hold their offices for five years.

Salaries. § 4. The salaries of the officers composing the Croton Aqueduct Board shall be as follows: For the President-Commissioner, three thousand dollars per annum ; for the Commissioner-Engineer, five thousand dollars per annum; for the Assistant Commissioner, three thousand dollars per annum.

Contracts. § 5. All contracts for materials or work for the Croton Aqueduct, or for the construction, repair or cleaning of sewers and underground drains, shall be made by the Croton Aqueduct Board; and bonds, for the faithful performance thereof, shall be approved and taken by them.

Payment of Moneys. § 6. All moneys payable by the Corporation for the performance of the contracts mentioned in the last section, or for work done by authority of the Croton Aqueduct Board, and all bills or accounts for the salaries of the officers and men attached thereto, and for blank books, paper, and contingencies of the Department, shall be paid by the warrant of the Comptroller, upon the requisition of the Croton Aqueduct Board, against the appropriation applicable thereto, and all such contracts and accounts shall be kept and filed in the office of the Croton Aqueduct Board.

§ 7. No new works connected with the Croton Aqueduct shall be constructed, nor shall any mains or pipes be purchased or laid down, or new sewers constructed, except with the authority of the Common Council; and except also, that in case of any unexpected casualty or damage to the pipes, reservoirs or other structures connected with the aqueduct, the Croton Aqueduct Board shall take immediate measures for the preservation and repair of the same; the expense of which shall be paid on their requisition by the warrant of the Comptroller. Work, how authorized.

§ 8. All sewers and drains in any of the streets, avenues or public places in the city, shall be under the charge of the Croton Aqueduct Board, who shall keep the same in good order and condition, and clean and free from obstructions, and shall cause such repairs to be made to them and to the receiving basins, culverts and openings connected therewith, as may from time to time become necessary. Such sewer culverts shall be cleaned at night and not in the day time. Sewers and Drains.

§ 9. The Croton Aqueduct Board shall prescribe the mode of piercing or opening any of the sewers or drains, and the form, size and material of which connections made therewith shall be composed. Ibid.

§ 10. They may, with the consent of the Street Commissioner, grant permission to persons to construct, at Private Drains, Sewers, &c.

their own expense, sewers or drains, or to lay pipes to connect with any sewers or drains built in any of the streets or avenues in the city, on being furnished with the written consent of the owners of a majority of the property upon the street through which such sewer, drain or pipe is to pass; but such permission shall not be granted except upon the agreement, in writing, of the persons applying therefor, that they shall comply with the ordinances in relation to excavating the streets; that they will indemnify the Corporation for any damages or costs to which they may be put, by reason of injuries resulting from neglect or carelessness in performing the work so permitted, and that no claim will be made by them or their successors in interest against the Corporation, if the work so permitted be taken up by authority of the Common Council, or for exemption from an assessment lawfully imposed for constructing sewers or drains in the same vicinity; and upon the further condition that the Common Council may, at any time, revoke such permission, and direct such sewers, drains or pipes to be taken up or removed.

Private Drains, Sewers, &c.

§ 11. If any connection or opening be made into any sewer or drain without the permission authorized in the last section, or in a mode different from that prescribed therefor, the person making such connection or opening, and the owner directing it, shall respectively be liable to a penalty of fifty dollars.

Ibid.

§ 12. All openings into sewers or drains for the purpose of making a connection therewith from any house, cellar, vault, yard or other premises, shall be made by persons licensed, or to be licensed, in writing, for that purpose, by the Croton Aqueduct Board.

Ibid.

§ 13. Every person who now is or who shall be licensed as provided in the last section, shall, before performing any work authorized thereby, execute and deposit in the Croton Aqueduct Department a bond to the Corporation, in the sum of one thousand dollars, with one or more sufficient sureties, to be approved by the President of the Board, conditioned that he will faithfully make the opening into such sewers or drains; that he will leave no obstructions, of any description whatever, therein; that he will properly close up the sewers or drains so opened; that he will make no opening into the arch of any sewer or drain; that he will comply with the ordinances in relation to excavating the streets, and that he will indemnify the Corporation of and from all accidents and damage consequent thereupon, for or by reason of any opening in any street, lane or avenue made by him, or by those in his employment, for the purpose of putting down any service pipe or pipes for the introduction of the Croton water, or for making any connection with any public or private sewer, or for any other purpose or object whatever; and that he will also replace and restore the street pavement over such opening, to as good state and condition as he found it, and keep and maintain the same in good order, to the satisfaction of the Water Purveyor, for the period of six months next thereafter.

§ 14. There shall be paid to the President of the Croton Aqueduct Board, for the use of the Corporation, for every permit to connect with a sewer or drain from any house, store or building, the sum of ten dollars; and for every hotel, boarding-house, or public building covering more than twenty-five by fifty feet, an additional sum in that proportion. Private Sewers, Drains, &c.

§ 15. There shall be paid to the President of the Croton Aqueduct Board, for the use of the Corporation, for every permit to connect with a sewer or drain from a manufactory, brewery, distillery, or the like, for the purpose of Ibid.

carrying off water or fluid which shall not deposit sediment or obstruction, such sum as shall be fixed by the Croton Aqueduct Board.

Private Sewers, Drains, &c.

§ 16. Any person obtaining a permit as provided in the last section, who shall permit any substance which shall form a deposit or obstruction in a sewer, drain or receiving basin, to flow into the same, shall be liable to a penalty of fifty dollars for each offense.

Ibid.

§ 17. The President of the Croton Aqueduct Board shall keep a record of all permits granted by that Board for connections with sewers or drains, in which he shall enter the names of all persons from whom he may receive money for such permits, with the amount received from each person, and the time when it was received. He shall render an account thereof, under oath, item by item, to the Comptroller, on Thursday of each week, and shall thereupon pay over the amount so received to the Chamberlain. He shall also thereupon receive from the Chamberlain a voucher for the payment thereof, which he shall forthwith, on the same day, exhibit to the Comptroller, and shall at the same time leave with him a copy thereof. In case the President shall be temporarily absent, the Assistant Commissioner shall act in his stead.

Trespasses.

§ 18. The Croton Aqueduct Board is requested to abate all trespasses on the Croton Aqueduct property, and prevent lands of the Croton Aqueduct being used for roads except at crossings; also to enclose the Croton Aqueduct lands through all the villages, and at such other places as, in their opinion, the proper preservation of the work and the city title to the lands may require.

Repairs to Streets.

§ 19. The Croton Aqueduct Board shall ascertain, and report to the Common Council, from time to time, what repairs are necessary to any of the streets; and when required by the Common Council, the said Board shall inquire into and report upon all applications to the Common Council, in relation to paving, repaving, or repairing streets or digging wells. The said Board shall advertise for estimates and contract for wells and pumps, and for paving, repaving and repairing the streets.

§ 20. There shall be in the office of the Croton Aqueduct Board the following officers, who shall be appointed in the manner directed by the charter: — One Assistant Engineer, who shall receive an annual salary of one thousand four hundred and fifty dollars; one Clerk to the Croton Aqueduct Board, who shall receive an annual salary of one thousand four hundred dollars; one Messenger to the Croton Aqueduct Board, who shall receive an annual salary of seven hundred dollars. Officers in the office of the Board.

ARTICLE III.

OF THE BUREAU OF THE WATER REGISTRAR, AND THE SCALE OF WATER RENTS.

§ 21. This bureau, of which the Water Registrar is the chief officer, is charged with the duty of collecting the revenues derived from the sale of the Croton water, and has the especial charge and superintendence of the accounts of the departments, under the direction of the Croton Aqueduct Board. Cognizance of the Bureau.

§ 32. The Water Registrar, before entering upon the duties of his office, shall execute a bond to the Corporation, with two sufficient sureties, to be approved by the Comptroller, in the penal sum of fifteen thousand dollars, conditioned for the faithful performance of the duties of his office. Bond of Registrar.

Duties of Registrar.

§ 23. He shall, on Thursday of each week, render to the Comptroller an account, under oath, item by item, of all moneys received by him, containing the names of the persons from whom they were received, the amounts received, and on what account, and when paid; and shall thereupon pay over the amount so received to the Chamberlain.

Deputy and Clerks.

§ 24. There shall be in this bureau a Deputy Registrar, an Accountant, and five Clerks, who shall severally receive for their services an annual salary of one thousand dollars.

Deputy Registrar.

§ 25. The Deputy Registrar shall superintend, under the direction of the Registrar, the keeping of the accounts, the receiving of the water rents, and the issuing of permits for the use of the water, and shall generally assist the Registrar in the performance of his duties. He shall, before entering on the duties of his office, execute a bond to the Corporation, with two sureties, to be approved by the Comptroller, in the penal sum of ten thousand dollars, conditioned for the faithful performance of the duties of his office.

Accountant.

§ 26. The Accountant shall keep the accounts of the Bureau of the Water Registrar, under the direction of the Registrar, and in such manner as shall be prescribed by the Croton Aqueduct Board.

Clerks.

§ 27. The Clerks shall, respectively, prepare and copy such papers appertaining to this bureau, as may be directed by the Water Registrar, and shall generally perform such other duties connected therewith, as may be assigned them by that officer.

Salary of Registrar.

§ 28. The Water Registrar shall receive an annual salary of one thousand five hundred dollars.

Scale of Water Rents.

§ 29. The annual regular rents to be collected by the Croton Aqueduct Board shall be as follows, to wit:— Scale of Water Rents.

1. On all tenements coming within the provisions of the law of April 11, 1849, having a front width of sixteen feet and under, and of not more than one story high, the sum of four dollars; of not more than two stories high, the sum of five dollars; of not more than three stories high, the sum of six dollars; of not more than four stories high, the sum of seven dollars; and five stories high and over, the sum of eight dollars.

2. On all tenements having a front width of not more than eighteen feet and over sixteen, and of not more than one story high, the sum of five dollars; of not more than two stories high, the sum of six dollars; of not more than three stories high, the sum of seven dollars; of not more than four stories high, the sum of eight dollars; and of five stories high and over, the sum of nine dollars.

3. On all tenements having a front width of not more than twenty feet and over eighteen, and of not more than one story high, the sum of six dollars; of not more than two stories high, the sum of seven dollars; of not more than three stories high, the sum of eight dollars; of not more than four stories high, the sum of nine dollars; and of five stories high and over, the sum of ten dollars.

4. On all tenements having a front width of not more than twenty-two feet six inches, and over twenty feet, and of not more than one story high, the

Scale of Water Rents.

sum of seven dollars; of not more than two stories high, the sum of eight dollars; of not more than three stories high, the sum of nine dollars; of not more than four stories high, the sum of ten dollars; and of five stories high and over, the sum of eleven dollars.

5. On all tenements having a front width of not more than twenty-five feet, and over twenty-two feet and six inches, and of not more than one story high, the sum of eight dollars; of not more than two stories high, the sum of nine dollars; of not more than three stories high, the sum of ten dollars; of not more than four stories high, the sum of eleven dollars; and of five stories high and over, the sum of twelve dollars.

6. On all tenements having a front width of not more than thirty feet, and over twenty-five feet, and of not more than one story high, the sum of ten dollars; of not more than two stories high, the sum of eleven dollars; of not more than three stories high, the sum of twelve dollars; of not more than four stories high, the sum of thirteen dollars; and of five stories high and over, the sum of fourteen dollars.

7. On all tenements having a front width of not more than thirty-seven feet six inches, and over thirty feet, and of not more than one story high, the sum of twelve dollars; of not more than two stories high, the sum of thirteen dollars; of not more than three stories high, the sum of fourteen dollars; of not more than four stories high, the sum of fifteen dollars; and of five stories high and over, the sum of sixteen dollars.

8. On all tenements having a front width of not more than fifty feet, and over thirty-seven feet six inches, and of not more than one story high, the sum of fourteen dollars; of not more than two stories high, the sum of fifteen dollars; of not more than three stories high, the sum of sixteen dollars; of not more than four stories high, the sum of seventeen dollars; and of five stories high and over, the sum of eighteen dollars. Scale of Water Rents.

9. In the apportionment of regular rents upon a dwelling-house, the family or families occupying the same to number not more than fifteen persons; for every ten persons beyond that number, an additional rent of two dollars and fifty cents per year shall be charged.

10. The rents of all tenements which shall exceed in width fifty feet, shall be the subjects of special contract with the Croton Aqueduct Board.

11. The extra and miscellaneous rates shall be as follows, to wit:—

Bakeries.—In the average daily use of flour, for each barrel the sum of three dollars per annum.

Bathing Tubs, in private houses, beyond one, at three dollars per annum each; and five dollars per annum each on public houses, boarding-houses, bathing establishments, and barbers' shops.

Boarding Schools shall be charged at the rate of from fifteen to fifty dollars each; and *School Houses* at the rate of from ten to twenty dollars each per annum.

Building Purposes.—For each one thousand bricks laid, the sum of ten cents per thousand.

Scale of Water Rents.

Cow Stables.—For each and every cow, the sum of seventy-five cents per annum.

Fountains.—Ordinarily used three hours per day, for a period of not more than four months in the year, shall be charged as follows:—A one-sixteenth of an inch jet, the sum of seven dollars per annum; for a one-eighth of an inch jet, the sum of fifteen dollars per annum; for a one-quarter of an inch jet, the sum of forty dollars per annum; for a one-half of an inch jet, the sum of ninety dollars per annum; and for an inch jet, the sum of two hundred dollars per annum. No fountain shall be permitted on any premises where the water is not taken for other purposes, and to an extent sufficient for those purposes; and if the water from the jet or fountain be permitted to flow into premises adjacent to or in the neighborhood where it may be used for other purposes, the supply shall be stopped, and the amount of payment forfeited.

Horses, Private.—For two horses there shall be charged the sum of six dollars per annum; and for each additional horse, the sum of two dollars.

Horses, Livery.—For each horse, up to and not exceeding thirty in number, the sum of one dollar and fifty cents each per annum; and for each additional horse, the sum of one dollar.

Horses, Omnibus and Cart.—For each horse, the sum of one dollar per annum.

Horse Troughs.—For each trough on sidewalks, the sum of five dollars per annum.

Hotels and Boarding-houses shall, in addition to the regular rate for private families, be charged for each lodging room, at the discretion of the Croton Aqueduct Board. Scale of Water Rents.

Porter-houses, Taverns and Groceries shall be charged an extra rate of from three to thirty dollars.

Printing Offices shall be charged at such rates as may be determined, in the discretion of the Croton Aqueduct Board.

Refectories shall be charged at such rates as may be determined, in the discretion of the Croton Aqueduct Board.

Slaughter-houses shall be charged at the rate of from ten to twenty dollars per annum each.

Steam Engines shall be charged, by the horse power, as follows: For each horse power up to and not exceeding ten, the sum of ten dollars per annum; for each exceeding ten and not over fifteen, the sum of seven dollars and fifty cents each; and for each horse power over fifteen, the sum of five dollars.

Street Washers.—For each street washer on the side-walk, the sum of two dollars per annum.

Water Closets.—For every water closet beyond one, the sum of two dollars per annnm.

All manufacturing and other business requiring a large supply of water, are to be charged therefor, per one hundred gallons, on the average estimated quantity during the year; the year to be estimated at three hundred days, as follows :—

Scale of Water Rents. When the quantity used averages two hundred gallons per day, or less, at the rate of five cents per one hundred gallons.

When the quantity used averages from two hundred to three hundred gallons per day, at the rate of four cents per hundred gallons.

Where the quantity used averages from three hundred to one thousand gallons per day, at the rate of three and a half cents per one hundred gallons.

Where the quantity used averages from one thousand to two thousand gallons per day, at the rate of three cents per one hundred gallons.

Where the quantity used averages from two thousand to ten thousand gallons per day, at the rate of two cents per one hundred gallons.

Where the quantity used exceeds ten thousand gallons per day, the price shall be fixed by the Croton Aqueduct Board; but in no case at less than one cent per one hundred gallons.

12. All matters not hereinbefore embraced, are reserved for special contract by and with the Croton Aqueduct Board.

ARTICLE IV.

OF THE BUREAU OF THE WATER PURVEYOR.

Cognizance of Bureau. § 30. This bureau, of which the Water Purveyor shall be the chief officer, is charged with the superintendence of the laying of water pipes, and the construction and repairs of sewers, wells and hydrants, and paving, repaving and repairing the streets.

Bond of Water Purveyor § 31. The Water Purveyor shall, before entering upon the duties of his office, execute a bond to the Corporation, with one or more sureties, to be approved by the Comptroller, in the penal sum of two thousand dollars, conditioned for the faithful performance of the duties of his office.

§ 32. He shall make all estimates necessary to the laying of water pipes and the construction and repairs of sewers, wells and hydrants, and the paving, repaving and repairing of streets, when required by the Croton Aqueduct Board. Duties of Water Purveyor.

§ 33. He shall keep correct accounts of the time of the men employed, and the work upon which they are engaged, and the expense attending the same, when it is not done by contract, and shall report the same, under oath, once in each week, to the Croton Aqueduct Board. Ibid.

§ 34. He shall examine, audit and certify to the Croton Aqueduct Board, all accounts for supplies furnished or work done under his supervision, and as to the fulfillment or breach of any contract to be performed under his direction. Ibid.

§ 35. He shall, from time to time, examine the state of the water pipes, sewers and underground drains, wells, pumps, hydrants and street pavements, and report all repairs thereof, which, in his judgment, may be necessary, to the Croton Aqueduct Board. Ibid.

§ 36. He shall, with the consent of the Croton Aqueduct Board, employ a competent person to inspect the paving of any street, when done under a contract with the Corporation, whose daily pay shall not exceed one dollar and fifty cents, and which shall be assessed and collected with the other expenses of such paving.

§ 37. He shall, with the consent of said Board, employ, Ibid.

on daily pay, as many competent persons as may be necessary, with carts and other implements, to repair the pavements.

Duties of Water Purveyor

§ 38. He shall, in all matters connected with his bureau, be under the control, direction and supervision of the Croton Aqueduct Board; and in addition to the duties prescribed by this article, shall perform such other duties appertaining to the Croton Aqueduct Department as may be required of him by that Board.

Contract Clerk.

§ 39. There shall be in the Bureau of the Water Purveyor, a Contract Clerk, who shall receive an annual salary of one thousand two hundred dollars; and two other clerks, who shall severally receive an annual salary of one thousand dollars.

Salary of Purveyor.

§ 40. The Water Purveyor shall receive an annual salary of one thousand five hundred dollars.

ARTICLE V.

GENERAL PROVISIONS.

Repairs, &c.

§ 41. The Croton Aqueduct Board may, from time to time, make such rules and regulations in respect to service and conduit pipes, tapping, paving and repairing the streets, and other matters affecting the distribution of the Croton water, as they may deem proper.

Contracts.

§ 42. All work to be done and all materials to be purchased on account of or for the Croton Aqueduct Works, exceeding one hundred dollars, except when such work or materials are rendered immediately necessary by some sudden and unforeseen cause, shall be by contract, after due notice.

Proposals for contracts.

§ 43. Public notice shall be given of the time and place at which sealed proposals shall be received for contracts for or on account of the Croton Aqueduct Works, which notice shall be published at least one week in the papers designated by the Corporation. No alternative or indefinite condition or limitation as to price in a proposal shall be received or acted on; nor shall more than one proposition from any one person for the same contract be received. All the propositions, when more than one is offered, from the same person, for the same object, shall be rejected.

§ 44. Every person who shall enter into any contract for work to be done on the Croton Aqueduct Works, shall give satisfactory security for the faithful performance of his contract according to its terms; and if any person shall neglect or refuse to perform his contract, he shall be excluded from any interest in any future contract in relation to the Croton Aqueduct Works. Security of Contractors.

§ 45. No extra allowance over and above the contract price shall be made to any contractor, unless such extra allowance be directed by the Common Council. Extra allowance.

§ 46. All persons contracting for a supply of water, shall pay the cost of the materials and labor used and expended on the streets, necessary to make the connection with the conduit pipes, or pay such annual interest thereon as required by the rules and regulations of the Croton Aqueduct Board. No street shall be opened, nor pipes bored, or connection made, unless under the direction of the Croton Aqueduct Board, under the penalty of fifty dollars for each offense. Manner of supplying Water, &c.

§ 47. All persons are forbid to open any street pavement and bore any water pipe for the purpose of conducting the water into any dwelling or other edifice, or any other use, under the penalty of fifty dollars for each Ibid.

offense, unless with the written permission of the President of the Croton Aqueduct Board.

Water rents, how payable. § 48. All rents for the use of the water shall be paid in advance, at the time of applying for the water, and before any permit is issued; to be calculated up to the first day of May succeeding; and all rents shall continue to be collected in advance on the first day of May annually, so long as the contract exists; and no contract for the supply of the water shall be binding for a longer period than until the second succeeding first day of May after such contract is entered into.

Rents, unpaid. § 49. The supply of water shall be cut off in all cases where the rent is behind, and unpaid, ten days.

Rents, how applied. § 50. All rents and other emoluments which may accrue from the use and application of the water, shall, in the first instance, be applied to meet the current expenses and repairs of the Croton Aqueduct Works, next, to the payment of the interest on the Water Stock, and lastly, to the redemption of said stock.

Sprinkling the Streets. § 51. The Croton Aqueduct Board shall continue to grant licenses to such persons as it may deem proper, and who will comply with the conditions of this ordinance, for permission to use Croton water from such of the public hydrants as may be designated by said Board, for the purpose of sprinkling the public streets of the city.

Ibid. § 52. Every person who shall thus obtain a license, shall pay to the Croton Aqueduct Board at the rate of one and a half cents for every hundred gallons that shall be respectively used by them for such purpose; the payments to be made monthly under oath.

Ibid. § 53. The sprinklers used by every such person shall conform, in every respect, to a pattern kept in the office of the Croton Aqueduct Board, which shall be in form and shape as follows, that is to say: A tin cylinder six feet in length, curved, so as to give a versed sine of seven inches; of a diameter not to exceed two and one-half inches at the inlet, tapering thence at each end to a diameter of not more than two inches; the four centre sheets or feet of which shall each be pierced with three rows of holes, and the end feet or sheets each with four rows; said holes to be in parallel rows, and at least one-half of an inch apart, and of a size not to exceed number sixteen wire. The first or bottom row of holes shall be at right angles to the inlet, and the sprinkler, when in use, shall be so hung as to throw the water directly on the street; the ends of the cylinder shall be without holes.

§ 54. Every cart used for sprinkling streets, under the provisions of this ordinance, shall have painted on each side of the cask, and exposed to public view, in black letters of not less than two inches in length, and on a white ground, the name and residence of the person under whose license the work is performed. Sprinkling of streets.

§ 55. Any person licensed to use Croton water for the purpose of sprinkling the streets as aforesaid, who shall violate the provisions of this ordinance, shall, in the discretion of the Croton Aqueduct Board, have his license revoked. Ibid.

§ 56. If any person shall bathe, go into the Croton water at either of the reservoirs or any part of the Croton Aqueduct, or shall throw any stones, chips or dirt, or any other material, substance or thing whatever, into the reservoirs or into the water, or gate-houses, or into the ventilators or aqueduct, or fountain basins, or shall in any manner injure or disfigure any part of the Croton Injuring the works, &c.

Aqueduct Works, he shall be subject to a fine not to exceed fifty dollars, to be imposed by any Police Justice or any magistrate, either on his view, or in a summary manner. And in default of payment of any fine so imposed, such Police Justice, or magistrate, shall commit such offender to the city prison for a period not to exceed thirty days, unless such fine is sooner paid.

Trespasses, &c.

§ 57. In case any person shall tresspass on any part of the embankment of the Croton Aqueduct reservoirs, or go or remain on the same, without permission of the proper persons having charge of the same; or in case any person does not comply with the regulations of the Croton Aqueduct Board, as to the times they shall leave the embankments of said reservoirs, or the grounds or buildings attached to said reservoirs, that then and in that case such person shall be subject to a fine of twenty-five dollars, to be levied and collected in the manner prescribed in the last section; and in default of payment, imprisonment, as in like manner, not to exceed twenty days, in the city prison.

Hydrants.

§ 58. No person or persons, except the Mayor, Aldermen and Councilmen of the respective districts shall, without previous permission in writing from the Croton Aqueduct Board, unscrew or open any hydrant belonging or attached to the Croton Aqueduct Works, erected for the extinguishment of fires, except in cases of fires in the neighborhood; nor shall leave said fire hydrant open for a longer time than shall be limited in said permission; nor shall use the water for other purposes than may be mentioned in said permission; under the penalty of not less than five dollars nor more than twenty-five dollars for each offense, in the discretion of the magistrate before whom the complaint shall be made.

§ 59. No person or persons, except such as may be licensed by the Croton Aqueduct Board, to sell water to shipping, shall take the water from any hydrant erected or to be erected in the city of New York, and attached to the Croton water pipes, for the purpose of selling the said water or offering it for sale, under the penalty of twenty-five dollars. Taking water from hydrant

§ 60. The Water Purveyor is instructed to cause the hydrants to be kept closed, and report all violations of the law to the Corporation Attorney. Hydrants.

§ 61. The Croton Aqueduct Board shall at all times, when the general supply of water is not thereby endangered, permit the City Inspector to order the hydrants to be used for cleaning the streets under the regulations of said Board. Street Cleaning.

§ 62. No person or persons shall use the Croton water for washing streets, sidewalks, steps or buildings, from the first day of May to the first day of November following, in each year, after 8 A. M.; and from the first day of November to the first day of May following, after 9 A. M., under the penalty of five dollars for each offense. Washing the Streets.

§ 63. Any person or persons who shall obstruct the access to the different stop cocks connected with the water pipes, by placing thereon stone, brick, lumber, dirt, or any other materials, or who shall permit any such materials to be placed thereon by those in his or their employ, shall be subject to the penalty of fifty dollars for each offense, with an additional sum of twenty-five dollars for each day the same shall be continued after notice of removal shall have been served. Obstructing Stop Cocks.

Penalties. § 64. The penalties prescribed in sections 58, 59 and 63 of this ordinance, shall be imposed on the offender in like manner as is provided in section 56 of this ordinance in respect to the penalty therein prescribed; and in default of the payment, the offender shall be subject to the like punishment by imprisonment as in the said section prescribed.

CHAPTER VII.

OF THE CITY INSPECTOR'S DEPARTMENT.

ARTICLE I.

OF THE CITY INSPECTOR'S DEPARTMENT AND ITS BUREAUX GENERALLY.

§ 1. The City Inspector's department shall have cognizance of all matters affecting the public health pursuant to the ordinances of the Common Council and the lawful requirements of the Commissioners of Health, and of the Board of Health; of cleaning the public streets; of the superintending, inspection, regulation and management of the public markets; of the inspection and sealing of weights and measures; and of the location and control of the public pounds, *General cognizance of the Department.*

§ 2. There shall be four bureaux in the City Inspector's Department, as follows: *Bureaux.*

1. The bureau of Sanitary Inspection and Street Cleaning.
2. The bureau of Records and Statistics.
3. The bureau of Markets.
4. The bureau of Weights and Measures.

ARTICLE II.

OF THE CITY INSPECTOR AND HIS CLERKS AND MESSENGERS.

City Inspector. § 3. The chief officer of the City Inspector's Department shall be denominated the City Inspector.

Bond. § 4. The City Inspector, before entering upon the duties of his office, shall execute a bond to the Corporation with at least two sureties, to be approved by the Mayor and filed in the office of the Comptroller, in the penal sum of ten thousand dollars, conditioned for the faithful performance of the duties of his office.

Salary of City Inspector. § 5. The City Inspector shall receive an annual salary of five thousand dollars.

Duties of City Inspector § 6. The City Inspector shall take all necessary measures to ascertain every nuisance which may exist in the city of New York, and to cause it to be forthwith removed.

Ibid. § 7. He shall cause all putrid and unsound beef, pork, fish, hides or skins, all dead animals, and every putrid, offensive, unsound or unwholesome substance found in any street or other place in the city, to be forthwith removed and disposed of by removal beyond the limits of the city or otherwise, so as most effectually to secure the public health.

Ibid. § 8. He shall inspect or cause to be inspected all privies, sinks and cesspools in the city of New York, and see that the same are built according to law.

Ibid. § 9. He shall license such persons as may be proper, to act as night-scavengers, all or any of whom he may at any time displace and appoint others in their stead, and he shall make such rules and regulations for their government as he may deem proper.

Ibid. § 10. He shall keep a register in which he shall enter the situation of all such sinks and privies as he shall au thorize to be emptied, and the days on which the emptying thereof shall be required.

§ 11. He shall cause all such boarding and lodging houses as the Board of Health shall direct, to be examined, and shall report to that Board the number of each house, and the name of the street on which it is situated; the name of the tenant or occupant, the number of lodgers or boarders therein, with their names and occupations, the number of apartments therein and the apartments used as lodging rooms. Duties of City Inspector.

§ 12. He shall inspect or cause to be inspected all houses reported as mentioned in the last section, as often as he shall deem necessary, and at least once in each week between the first day of May and the first day of November in each year. Ibid.

§ 13. He shall obey all orders and instructions given by the Board of Health, pertaining to the performance of all or any of his duties. Ibid.

§ 14. He shall receive and file in his office all reports directed to be made to him by measurers, weighmasters and inspectors, and shall make an aggregate report thereof to the Common Council during the month of January in each year. Ibid.

§ 15. He shall, from time to time, report to the Common Council respecting all lots, yards, buildings, cellars, alleys, sinks, vaults, cesspools, privies, public and private docks and slips, and common sewers which shall require cleaning, altering or repairing, in order to preserve the health of the city. Ibid.

§ 16. He shall report to the Common Council and to the Board of Health all circumstances which shall come to his knowledge, endangering the health of the city or prejudicial thereto. Ibid

Duties of City Inspector.

§ 17. He shall report to the Common Council suitable ordinances for the correction and removal of nuisances, and when the same shall be passed shall record them in his office, and cause copies thereof to be served on the persons whose duty it shall be to correct, abate or remove such nuisances.

Ibid.

§ 18. He shall keep a register of the names of all persons returned as dead, which shall be open at all convenient times to public inspection.

Ibid.

§ 19. He shall publish on Tuesday of each week, in the Corporation papers, a list of the deaths occurring in the preceding week, specifying the number of deaths in each ward, with the sexes, ages and diseases of the persons so dying; and during the month of January in each year he shall report to the Common Council and publish in like manner the whole number of deaths in the city during the preceding year, with the sexes, ages and diseases of the persons so dying.

Ibid.

§ 20. All moneys payable by the Corporation for the performance of contracts or for work done under or by direction of this department, shall be paid by the Comptroller in pursuance of the provisions of the charter; and the City Inspector shall, on the first Thursday of each month, render to the Comptroller a full statement, under oath, of the receipts and expenditures of his department, and all the accounts, vouchers and certificates relating thereto shall be kept and filed in the office of the City Inspector; and he shall superintend the enforcement of all ordinances relating to his department, and have power to employ all necessary assistance for that purpose, and shall report to the Common Council all delinquencies therein, and shall, from time to time, suggest to the Common Council such alterations or improvements in the ordinances connected with the department or any branch thereof, as he may deem proper.

§ 21. He may enter into any premises at any time between sunrise and sunset, and examine any building, cellar, vault, sink, cesspool, privy, lot, yard or alley in the city. Duties of City Inspector.

§ 22. He may, by an order in writing, direct any nuisance to be abated, or unwholesome matter or substance to be removed, and may prescribe the time and mode of doing so, and the place to which such offensive or unwholesome matter or substance shall be removed. Ibid

§ 23. He may cause the nuisance to be abated, or the matter or substance to be removed in case of a neglect or refusal to comply with such order by the person whose duty it is to comply therewith, after he shall have been personally served with a copy of the order. Ibid.

§ 24. He shall have a slate with the names of the Street Inspector and Health Warden of each ward placed in every station-house in the city for the information of the public, and for the purpose of receiving such complaints as may be made in case of neglect on the part of the contractors for cleaning the streets, in performing their work. Ibid.

§ 25. He shall be permitted by the Croton Aqueduct Board to use hydrants for cleaning the streets, under the regulations of that Board. Ibid.

§ 26. He may grant permission to empty any sink, privy or cesspool which may, in his judgment, require to be emptied, when the public health will not be endangered thereby. Ibid.

§ 27. He may, with the written consent of the Mayor, grant a permit for the removal of the remains of any person interred within the city, to a place without the same, on the application of a relative or friend of such person, when there shall appear no just objection to the same. Ibid.

Duties of City Inspector.

§ 28. He shall have such powers and duties as were heretofore imposed on the late Commissioner of Streets and Lamps, relative to the bureau of "Cleaning Streets," and "the Inspection, Regulation and Management of the Public Markets," and "the Inspection of Weights and Measures," and "the Keeping of the Public Pounds," so far as the same are not conflicting with other ordinances.

Clerks in City Inspector's office.

§ 29. There shall be two clerks in the City Inspector's office, who shall be denominated First and Second Clerks, and who shall perform such duties connected therewith as may be required by the City Inspector. The salary of the First Clerk shall be fifteen hundred dollars per annum. The salary of the Second Clerk shall be twelve hundred dollars per annum.

Messengers in City Inspector's office.

§ 30. There shall be a Messenger in the City Inspector's office at an annual salary of eight hundred dollars, and an Assistant Messenger at an annual salary of seven hundred dollars.

ARTICLE III.

OF THE BUREAU OF SANITARY INSPECTION AND STREET CLEANING.

Superintendent of Sanitary Inspection, and his salary.

§ 31. This bureau shall be under the control of an officer to be called the "Superintendent of Sanitary Inspection," who shall receive an annual salary of two thousand five hundred dollars, which shall be inclusive of allowance for a horse and wagon.

His Bond.

§ 32. The Superintendent of Sanitary Inspection, before entering upon the duties of his office, shall execute a bond to the Corporation with one or more sureties, to be approved by the Comptroller, in the penal sum of five thousand dollars, conditioned for the faithful performance of the duties of his office.

§ 33. The Superintendent of Sanitary Inspection shall have cognizance and charge of the cleaning of the public streets, and the control and management of the Corporation yard. It shall be his duty to cause to be made annually an inspection of the sanitary condition of the city between the first day of November and the first day of June following, and such inspection shall be made in such manner, and returns of the same be prepared and made in such form, as the City Inspector shall direct. He shall also cause the investigation of all nuisances endangering the public health, and their abatement or removal in such manner as the City Inspector may direct. He shall supervise all the inspections which are now, or shall hereafter be ordered, to be made by the City Inspector's Department, such inspection to be in accordance with, and returns to be made in such forms as the City Inspector may direct. He shall, from time to time, report to the City Inspector all facts within his knowledge relating to or affecting the public health. Duties of Superintendent of Sanitary Inspection.

§ 34. The Superintendent of Sanitary Inspection shall make estimates necessary to, or connected with, the cleaning of streets when required by the City Inspector. Ibid.

§ 35. He shall keep correct accounts of the time of men employed in his bureau, and of the work upon which they are engaged, and the expense attending the same when it is not done by contract, and shall report the same once in each week to the City Inspector. Ibid.

§ 36. He shall forthwith report to the City Inspector all violations of any agreement for cleaning the streets, and every omission or neglect on the part of any person whose duty it is by any law of the State, or by any ordinance or resolution of the Common Council to inspect the streets or roads, or to prevent any incumbrance thereof, and if such Ibid.

neglect shall occur on the part of any policeman or officer of the police, he shall, in like manner, report the same forthwith to the Police Commissioners.

Duties of Superintendent of Sanitary Inspection.

§ 37. The Superintendent of Sanitary Inspection shall render such services relative to the duties of the City Inspector's Department, as he may be required by the City Inspector, and for that purpose he shall have, exercise and possess, all the powers and duties by law or ordinance conferred upon the City Inspector, whilst acting under the direction of the City Inspector. He shall examine, audit, and certify to the City Inspector, all accounts for work done under his supervision, and no requisition shall be drawn for any bills, accounts or contracts for cleaning the streets, unless certified by the Superintendent of Sanitary Inspection, and the Comptroller shall not pay any bill or money for the work of street cleaning, either by contract or otherwise, unless the same shall be audited and approved, as herein provided, and approved by the City Inspector, and paid upon his requisition; and no payments chargeable to any appropriation to be disbursed or expended by the City Inspector's Department, shall be made, by the Comptroller, unless so approved by the City Inspector.

Ibid.

§ 38. The "Superintendent of Sanitary Inspection" shall, in all matters be under the direction, control and supervision of the City Inspector, and the "City Inspector" may approve or disapprove all accounts certified by him, and by whom alone all requisitions upon the "Comptroller" for payment thereof, shall be drawn.

Clerks in Bureau of Sanitary Inspection, &c.

§ 39. There shall be two clerks in this bureau, to be denominated First and Second Clerks to the "Superintendent of Sanitary Inspection," who shall keep the accounts thereof, and prepare all estimates and other papers appertaining thereto, and who shall perform such other duties connected therewith as shall be directed by the Superintendent of Sanitary Inspection. The First Clerk shall receive annually for his services twelve hundred and fifty dollars, and the Second Clerk shall receive an annual salary of one thousand dollars. There shall also be a "Ticket and a Complaint Clerk" in said bureau, who each shall receive an annual salary of eight hundred and fifty dollars.

§ 40. There shall be an "Inspector" in each ward of the city, to be called the "Street Inspectors," whose duty it shall be, under the direction of the "Superintendent of Sanitary Inspection," to attend to the condition of the streets in the various wards for which they were appointed, and to report to the "Superintendent of Sanitary Inspection" the condition of the streets, and all violations of any contract for street cleaning, and shall each receive for his services the sum of three dollars per day.

Street Inspectors.

§ 41. There shall be in said bureau of "Sanitary Inspection and Street Cleaning" an "Inspector, and seven assistant inspectors of meats and articles of food and provision," whose duty it shall be, under the direction of the "City Inspector" and the "Superintendent of Sanitary Inspection" to visit and inspect all "slaughter houses," "meat shops," "butcher shops," poultry and fish stands, stores or other places kept for the sale or exposure for sale, of any kind of meats, poultry, fish or any articles of provision or food, in any place in the city other than the "public markets," and seize and remove any and all unsound, unhealthy, putrid or unwholesome veal, beef, pork, fish, poultry, or any article of food, and to take all measures for the detection and prevention of the sale of all such unsound, unwholesome articles of food, and to secure a strict enforcement of the laws and ordinances relative thereto; and make

Inspectors of meats, and articles of food and provision.

full report, of the same to the said Superintendent. The salary of the "Inspector" shall be the sum of one thousand dollars per annum; the salary of each Assistant shall be nine hundred dollars per annum.

Complaint & Pay-roll cl'k.

§ 42. There shall be a clerk in this bureau, who shall be called the "Complaint and Pay-roll Clerk to the Superintendent of Sanitary Inspection," and perform such duties relative to the complaints and pay-rolls of the street cleaning branch of the said bureau, as said Superintendent may direct, who shall receive an annual salary of six hundred dollars.

Superintendent of Scavengers, carts, &c.

§ 43. There shall also be an officer in this bureau, to be called the "Superintendent of Night Scavengers' carts and dumping piers," whose duty it shall be to inspect all night scavengers' carts, and superintend the removal of night soil at the several piers set apart for that purpose, who shall receive the sum of three dollars per day.

Health Wardens.

§ 44. The Health Wardens of the city shall perform such services in the investigation, abatement and removal of nuisances as the City Inspector or the Superintendent of Sanitary Inspection shall or may direct, and they shall be appointed as by law provided, and shall each receive the sum of three dollars per day.

ARTICLE IV.

OF THE BUREAU OF MARKETS.

Superintendent of Markets.

§ 45. This bureau, the chief officer of which shall be called the "Superintendent of Markets," is charged with the duty of superintending the public markets, the inspection, regulation and management thereof, and of the transferring stalls and stands, and all other stalls and stands therein, and shall receive an annual salary of two thousand dollars.

§ 46. The Superintendent of Markets shall, before entering upon the duties of his office, execute a bond to the Corporation, with one or more sureties, to be approved by the Comptroller, in the penal sum of two thousand dollars, conditioned for the faithful performance of the duties of his office. His Bond.

§ 47. He shall, from time to time, visit the several markets, and examine the condition thereof; shall advise and direct the Clerks thereof concerning the regulation of the same; shall examine the provisions, vegetables, and other articles of food exposed for sale in the markets or other places, and when he has reason to suspect them to be unwholesome or unfit to be exposed for sale, shall order or cause them to be removed. Duties of Superintendent of Markets.

§ 48. He shall, with the consent of the City Inspector, from time to time, recommend for license as butchers, such persons as may be proper; and upon such recommendation, the Mayor may, from time to time, issue licenses, under his hand and seal, to the persons named therein, to exercise and carry on the trade and business of a butcher, in such places as may be designated in the license, but not elsewhere. Ibid.

§ 49. He may, with the consent of the City Inspector, grant permits, in writing, to such persons as may be proper, to sell meat by the quarter, in such part of the public markets, respectively, as may be designated for that purpose, and which persons shall be known as Permit Butchers; and he may, at any time, with the like consent, annul such permits; but no such permit shall be granted to a person who holds a license from the Mayor, to exercise the trade or business of a butcher. Ibid.

§ 50. He may, with the consent of the City Inspector, grant permits, in writing, to such persons as may be proper, Ibid.

at a daily rate, to be mentioned therein, to occupy stands in the public markets, and may, at any time, with the like consent, annul such permits.

Duties of Superintendent of Markets.

§ 51. He may, with the consent of the City Inspector, appoint proper persons to remove dirt and filth from the public markets, and to perform such other services about the public markets as are necessary to cleanse the same, at a specified compensation, and may, with the like consent, at any time remove them, or appoint others in their stead.

Ibid.

§ 52. For the purpose of defraying the expenses to be incurred in pursuance of the last section, the Superintendent of Markets may, by a requisition, to be countersigned by the City Inspector, draw upon the Comptroller for a sum not exceeding two hundred dollars.

Ibid.

§ 53. He may, in like manner, renew the draft as often as may be necessary, but no such renewal shall be made until the money paid upon the previous draft shall be accounted for to the Comptroller, by satisfactory vouchers for the expenditure of the money paid thereon.

Ibid.

§ 54. When a draft shall be made upon the Comptroller, in conformity with the last two sections, he shall draw his warrant in favor of the Superintendent of Markets for the amount thereof.

Ibid.

§ 55. The Superintendent of Markets is specially charged with the enforcement of all laws of this state, and all ordinances and resolutions of the Common Council, regulating the Markets, and is required forthwith to report to the Corporation Attorney all violations of the same.

Ibid.

§ 56. He shall, from time to time, report to the City Inspector, the condition of the several markets, and shall, at all times, be under the direction and control of that officer.

§ 57. It shall be the duty of the Superintendent of Markets to prepare a register or list of all permanent stalls or stands of the several markets; the name of those occupying, and the fee or rent per week or month paid for the same; and the Superintendent, under the direction of the City Inspector, for that purpose, shall have the power to arrange and re-number the stands or stalls in the several markets, and equalize the rents or fees thereof; and the occupants of such stands or stalls shall immediately, at their own expense, cause numbers to be placed thereon. A copy of such register or list shall immediately after the same has been prepared, be filed by said Superintendent with the Comptroller, and all returns of market rents or fees shall be made in accordance with such register or list.

Duties of Superintendent of Markets.

§ 58. No transfer or assignment of any stall or stand in any of the public markets shall be made without written permission of the City Inspector and the Superintendent of Markets, and such transfer duly entered upon such register or list, and notice thereof given to the Comptroller, who shall consent to such transfer before any removal can be made of such transfer. In case of any person being removed, or any permit being annulled, the party or parties in interest shall have the privilege of making an appeal to the Common Council on any decision made by the City Inspector concerning such removal.

Transfer of Stalls.

§ 59. There shall be a Clerk to the Superintendent of Markets, to keep the books of said bureau, under the direction of the City Inspector and Superintendent of Markets, at an annual salary of eight hundred dollars, who shall render such services as may be required by the head of the Department or the chief officer of the bureau.

Clerk to Superintendent of Markets.

§ 60. There shall be a Clerk to each of the public markets in the city of New York and a Deputy to the Clerks

Clerks of Markets.

of Washington and Fulton markets, respectively, each of which Clerks and Deputy Clerks shall be an officer of the Bureau of Markets, and shall perform such duties as now are, or may hereafter by ordinance or resolution be conferred upon them.

Bond of Clerks of Markets.

§ 61 The Clerks of Markets shall, respectively, before entering upon the duties of their office, execute a bond to the Comptroller, in the penal sum of one thousand dollars, conditioned for the faithful performance of the duties of their respective offices.

Duties of clerks of Markets.

§ 62. The Clerks of Markets shall collect daily the market fees and rents which shall have become due in their respective markets, and shall, on Thursday in each week, render an account thereof, under oath, to the Comptroller, containing the amounts received, and when paid, and shall thereupon pay over the amount so received to the Chamberlain.

Ibid.

§ 63. They shall also thereupon, respectively, receive from the Chamberlain a voucher for the payment thereof, which they shall forthwith, on the same day, exhibit to the Comptroller, and shall at the same time leave with him a copy thereof.

Ibid.

§ 64. They shall cause all the dirt and filth which shall accumulate in the public markets, and the limits thereof, to be removed daily by the persons appointed for that purpose, as prescribed by section 51.

Ibid.

§ 65. They may suspend any person having a stated stall or stand in a public market, to which they are respectively attached, or occupying a part thereof, or of the street adjoining the same, from occupying or using any part of such market or street, whether he be a licensed butcher or not.

§ 66. Immediately upon such suspension, the Clerk making the same shall report the facts thereof, with the reasons for the suspension, to the City Inspector, who shall hear the same upon sufficient notice to the person suspended, and an opportunity afforded him to be heard in his defense, and whose decision upon the matter shall be final, provided the Mayor shall approve the same. Duties of Clerks of Markets.

§ 67. The Clerks, and Deputy Clerks created by this chapter, shall be subject to the control and supervision of the City Inspector, and shall, from time to time, report to him such matters as may be necessary or proper, respecting the condition of the markets. Duties of Clerks.

§ 68. They are also charged with the enforcement of all ordinances and resolutions of the Common Council appertaining to their duties, respectively, and are required forthwith to report to the Corporation Attorney all violations thereof. Ibid.

§ 69. The Clerk of Washington market shall receive an annual salary of one thousand dollars; the Deputy Clerk of Washington market an annual salary of eight hundred dollars; the Clerk of Fulton market an annual salary of nine hundred dollars; the Deputy Clerk of Fulton market an annual salary of seven hundred and fifty dollars. Salaries of Clerks of Markets.

§ 70. The Clerks of Catherine, Essex, Union, Jefferson, Tompkins, Clinton and Centre markets shall each receive the sum of two dollars per day. The Clerks of Franklin and Gouverneur markets the sum of one dollar and fifty cents per day. Ibid.

ARTICLE V.

OF THE BUREAU OF RECORDS AND STATISTICS.

Registrar of Records, his duties and salary.

§ 71. The chief officer of this bureau shall be called the "Registrar of Records," and is charged with the duty of keeping all returns of inquisitions taken by the Coroners of the city and county of New York, which shall be made or returned, as by law provided, and the records of births, marriages and deaths, and such other records as may be by law or ordinance required to be kept in this department; the granting and recording all burial permits, and permits for the disinterment of the remains of deceased persons, and the preparation of all documents, or reports of said department, relating to said bureau; and the keeping of all such books, accounts or records, and perform such other duties as the City Inspector may, from time to time, direct; and he shall assist the City Inspector in the performance of the duties imposed upon that office, and for that purpose he shall possess, in relation to the duties of his bureau, all the powers which are now, or may hereafter be conferred by ordinance upon the City Inspector, relative thereto, and shall receive an annual salary of twelve hundred dollars.

Bond and duties.

§ 72. The Registrar of Records before entering upon the duties of his office, shall execute a bond to the Corporation, with one or more sureties, to be approved by the Mayor, in the penal sum of two thousand dollars, conditioned for the faithful performance of the duties of his office. He shall keep or cause to be kept, under the direction and supervision of the City Inspector, all records herein mentioned, and prepare all reports, documents and papers, and keep all books and accounts appertaining to said bureau, and he shall perform such other duties connected with the department as may be required by that officer. There shall be a Clerk in this bureau, to be called the Clerk to the Registrar of Records, who shall perform such duties appertaining thereto, as shall be directed by said Registrar of Records, who shall receive an annual salary of one thousand dollars; there shall also be one Burial Permit Clerk and one Recording Clerk, each at an annual salary of eight hundred dollars.

ARTICLE VI.

OF THE BUREAU OF WEIGHTS AND MEASURES.

§ 73. There shall be a bureau in the City Inspector's Department denominated the Bureau of Weights and Measures, which shall have cognizance of and perform all the duties and possess all the powers and receive compensation as now by law prescribed.* Cognizance of Bureau.

§ 74. There shall be appointed by the City Inspector four Inspectors of Weights and Measures and two Sealers of Weights and Measures, who shall hold office upon the same terms as chiefs of bureaux. Inspectors & Sealers of Weights and Measures.

§ 75. Each of said Inspectors of Weights and Measures shall, before entering upon the duties of his office, execute to the Mayor, Aldermen and Commonalty of the city of New York a bond in the penal sum of two thousand dollars, with one or more sufficient sureties, conditioned for the faithful performance of the duties of his office. Bond.

* For duties and compensation of Inspectors and Sealers, see chapter entitled "Of Weights and Measures."

CHAPTER VIII.

MISCELLANEOUS PROVISIONS RESPECTING THE EXECUTIVE DEPARTMENTS AND THEIR OFFICERS.

ARTICLE I.

OF THE OFFICERS OF THE DEPARTMENTS AND BUREAUX, AND THEIR ACCOUNTABILITY.

Terms of office.

§ 1. The terms of office of the several officers not herein provided for, shall be as provided by the laws of this state.

Appointment of officers.

§ 2. The Mayor shall appoint, by and with the advice and consent of the Board of Aldermen, all officers whose appointment is not, by the laws of the state, or herein otherwise provided for.

Oath of office.

§ 3. All officers of the Executive Departments shall, before they enter on the duties of their respective offices, take and subscribe before the Mayor, and file in his office, the following oath or affirmation.

"I do solemnly swear, (or affirm, as the case may be), that I will support the Constitution of the United States, and the Constitution of the State of New York; and that I will faithfully discharge the duties of the office of ——, according to the best of my ability."

Eligibility of Corporation officers.

§ 4. No person or persons shall be eligible to any appointment under the Common Council of the city of New York, unless he or they shall, at the time of such appointment, be actual residents of the city and county of New York.

§ 5. In all cases, except where this ordinance otherwise provides, the heads of departments and other persons applying to the Comptroller for warrants for money to be by them disbursed, shall furnish that officer with the following vouchers: Vouchers for money.

1. When a payment shall have been completed by the signing of a pay-roll, the pay-roll, or a copy thereof, signed by the party receiving money, shall be filed with the Comptroller.
2. When a demand shall have been settled by giving a receipt, the receipt, or a copy thereof, signed by the party receiving the money mentioned therein, shall be filed with the Comptroller.
3. When payments are made for supplies furnished for the use of the Corporation, the original bill, or a copy thereof, with a receipt thereon, signed by the party receiving the money mentioned therein, shall be filed with the Comptroller.
4. When supplies have been furnished, or work done, not coming within any particular department, and which, in their nature, are not subject to any general regulation, the account therefor shall be accompanied by an affidavit that the supplies have been furnished or work done, and that the charge therefor is in all respects just, which shall be filed with the Comptroller.

§ 6. All officers, or other persons, to whom the collection or receipt of public moneys is intrusted, and who are required by the laws of this state, or by any ordinance of the Common Council, to pay the same to the Chamberlain, or to make a report thereof to the Comptroller, shall fur- Collection or receipt of moneys.

nish the account or report, under oath, at the time, and in the manner required by such law or ordinance.

Collection or receipt of moneys.

§ 7. In case of any neglect or refusal to make such payment or report, the Comptroller shall forthwith report the same to the Common Council.

Ibid.

§ 8. If such delinquency shall occur during a recess of the Common Council, the Comptroller shall forthwith report the same to the Mayor.

Vouchers.

§ 9. Every officer of the Corporation intrusted with the receipt or disbursement of the public moneys, shall exhibit the books and vouchers of his office to the Mayor, the Comptroller, the head of his department, or any member of the Common Council, at all reasonable times, when so required.

Collection & receipt of moneys.

§ 10. If any officers of the city government, or other persons receiving a salary from the Comptroller, who shall be and are intrusted with the collection or receipt of public moneys, and who are required by any law of the state or any ordinance of the Common Council, to pay such moneys to the Chamberlain, or to make a report thereof to the Comptroller, shall fail to furnish such account, or report at the time and in the manner required by such law or ordinance, the Comptroller shall be authorized, in addition to his other powers, to withhold the payment of any salary.

Quarterly Reports.

§ 11. The Street Commissioner, the City Inspector, and the Croton Aqueduct Department, are, and each of them is hereby directed to report, in writing, to the Common Council, quarterly, the state of the department under their charge, and a full and particular statement of the receipts and expenditures of such department, showing fully how and in what way or manner the expenditures are made; to whom and for what purpose; naming such person or persons, and for what particular work or service such expenditure has been made; and also a full and particular statement of the receipts of such department, showing fully how and to whom such receipts are made.

§ 12. No officer of the Corporation, who shall receive a fixed salary, or rate of compensation for his services, shall be entitled to extra compensation for any service which he may render to the Corporation, or which may be required of him by an ordinance or resolution of the Common Council, the Board of Supervisors, or the Board of Health, unless provision be expressly made for such extra compensation by the ordinance or resolution requiring the service. Extra compensation of officers.

ARTICLE II.

OF CONTRACTS FOR SUPPLIES AND WORK FOR THE CORPORATION.

§ 13. All supplies to be furnished, or work to be done for the Corporation, whether they are to be paid for out of the city treasury, or out of trust moneys under the control of, or to be assessed or collected by the Corporation, shall be furnished or performed by contract, except for printing, and where provision is otherwise made by this ordinance. Contracts, when necessary.

§ 14. All contracts to be entered into on the part of the Corporation, for the purposes mentioned in the last section, must be authorized by the Common Council, and when so authorized, shall be made by the department under whose direction the supplies are to be furnished, or the work performed, except that contracts for stationery for the Common Council, the Board of Supervisors, the Board of Health, and the departments, bureaux and officers of the Corporation; and for fuel for the public buildings and offices other than those attached to the Alms-house Department, shall be made by the Comptroller. Contracts, how authorized.

Proposals & Estimates. § 15. No contract shall be made, signed or executed until proposals therefor have been advertised, and estimates received and decided upon, as provided by this ordinance, except when otherwise provided by law, nor shall any contract be made, signed or executed for a sum exceeding two hundred and fifty dollars, until all the proposals, estimates, contracts and papers relating thereto shall have been laid before the Common Council, and confirmed by them, and an appropriation made therefor.

Ibid. § 16. The several departments empowered by section 14 to make contracts on the part of the Corporation, shall issue proposals for estimates therefor, and advertise the same in the Corporation papers for at least ten days before the day on which the estimates are to be opened. There shall be kept in each of said departments an appropriate box to be designated "Estimate Box," with a proper opening in the top thereof to receive estimates for which proposals have been issued. Such box shall be kept locked, except at such times as it may be necessary to open the same to examine and decide upon said estimates, and the key thereof shall be retained by the head of the department. It shall be the duty of the head of the department to deposit in said box all estimates duly presented to him, for work to be done under the direction of the department, immediately on the receipt thereof by him.

Ibid. § 17. The proposals for estimates shall be in such form as may be prescribed by the department making the same, and shall contain the following particulars:

1. They shall require that the person making the estimate shall furnish the same in a sealed envelope, to the head of the appropriate department at his office, on or before a day and hour therein named, not less than ten days from the first publication thereof.

2. They shall state the quantity and quality of the supplies, or the nature and extent, as near as possible, of the work required.
3. They shall state that the estimates received will be publicly opened by the head of the department issuing the proposals, at his office, at a day and hour therein mentioned.
4. They shall state the amount in which security is required for the performance of the contract.
5. They shall state, briefly, the several matters required by the next four sections, to be contained in or to accompany the estimates.

§ 18. Each estimate shall contain:

Estimates on contracts.

1. The name and place of residence of the person making the same.
2. The names of all persons interested with him therein, and if no other person be so interested, it shall distinctly state that fact.
3. That it is made without any connection with any other person making an estimate for the same purpose, and is in all respects fair, and without collusion or fraud.
4. That no member of the Common Council, head of a department, chief of a bureau, deputy thereof, or clerk therein, or other officer of the Corporation, is directly or indirectly interested therein, or in the supplies or work to which it relates, or in any portion of the profits thereof.

Ibid.

§ 19. The estimate shall be verified by the oath, in writing, of the party making the estimate, that the several matters stated therein are in all respects true.

Sureties with estimates.

§ 20. It shall be accompanied by the consent, in writing, of two householders or freeholders in the city of New York, to the effect that if the contract be awarded to the person making the estimate, they will, upon its being so awarded, become bound as his sureties for its faithful performance, and that if he shall omit or refuse to execute the same, they will pay to the Corporation any difference between the sum to which he would be entitled upon its completion, and that which the Corporation may be obliged to pay to the person to whom the contract shall be awarded at any subsequent letting; the amount in each case to be calculated upon the estimated amount of the work by which the bids are tested.

Sureties with estimates.

§ 21. The consent mentioned in the last section shall be accompanied by the oath or affirmation, in writing, of each of the persons signing the same, to be taken before any judge of any court of record in this county, that he is a householder or freeholder in the city of New York, and is worth the amount of the security required for the completion of the contract, and stated in the proposals as prescribed by section 17 of this chapter, over and above all his debts of every nature, and over and above his liabilities as bail, surety or otherwise, and that he has offered himself as a surety, in good faith, and with an intention to execute the bond required by section 27 of this chapter, if the contract shall be awarded to the person or persons for whom he consents to become surety.

Estimates for contracts, how presented & opened.

§ 22. The envelope containing the estimate shall be indorsed with the name or names of the person or persons presenting the same, the date of its presentation, and a statement of the work to which it relates; and no estimate shall be taken from the "Estimate Box," or the envelope thereof opened by any one, except at the time and in the manner herein designated for deciding upon such estimates. At the time and place appointed for that purpose in the proposals as prescribed in this chapter, the head of the department, in the presence of the Comptroller, and such of the parties making them as may desire to be present, shall then and there open the said estimate box, and the estimates to be examined at that time, as may appear from the indorsements thereon, shall be taken from said box. The said head of department shall then and there publicly open and read all estimates which he may have received for the contract mentioned in such proposals, and shall reject all estimates not furnished in conformity with this chapter, and shall thereupon award the contract as prescribed by section 38 of the City Charter of 1857. In the event of the Comptroller not attending at said time and place, such estimates shall not be opened, and the said head of department shall adjourn the opening of said estimates to another time, not exceeding five days, and shall publicly announce to those present the time and place of such adjournment. At such adjourned day, the Comptroller bring present, he shall proceed to open the same in manner aforesaid.

Samples with estimates for contracts.

§ 23. When proposals are issued for a contract to furnish any article of which a sample can conveniently be furnished, the head of the department issuing the same may require that such sample be delivered at his office, or at the office of the head of the appropriate bureau in his department, within such time before the opening of the estimates as he may prescribe, and if it be not so furnished or do not conform to the quality required by the proposals, the estimate delivered by the person furnishing or omitting to furnish the same, as the case may be, shall be rejected. The samples of articles furnished, as aforesaid, shall be at all times subject to the inspection and examination of the members of the Common Council, or any committee thereof.

Reservation of 10 per cent on contracts.

§ 24. In all contracts for work for the Corporation, where provision is made for the payment of the contract, price by installments, a provision shall be inserted that the contractor shall allow ten per cent. of the contract price of the work actually done, to remain as security, till the whole work shall be completed, according to the contract.

Retention of last installment on contracts.

§ 25. In all contracts for work done by or for the Corporation, the head of the department having charge thereof shall cause to be inserted a provision that the payment of the last installment due in pursuance thereof, shall be retained until such head of department shall have satisfactory evidence that all persons who have done work or furnished materials under any such contract, and who may have given written notice to such head of department, at any time within ten days after the completion of said work, that any balance for such work or materials is still due and unpaid, have been fully paid or secured such balance. And if any person so having done work or furnished materials, and giving such notice as aforesaid, shall furnish satisfactory evidence to the department that money is due to him by the contractor under such contract, such head of department shall retain such last installment, or such portion thereof as may be necessary, until such liability shall be discharged or secured. And in all such contracts the time for the completion and finishing of such work shall be inserted.

Clause in contracts to prevent accidents.

§ 26. In all contracts for work for the Corporation, upon any public building, or in any public street or place, in the performance of which accidents or injuries may happen to the person or property of another, a provision shall be inserted that the contractor shall place proper guards for the prevention of accidents, and shall put up and keep, at night, suitable and sufficient lights during the performance of the work, and that he will indemnify the

Corporation for any damages or costs to which they may be put by reason of injury to the person or property of another, resulting from negligence or carelessness in the performance of the work.

§ 27. Every contract for supplies or work by the Corporation shall be executed by the contractor or contractors to whom the same may be awarded, and shall be accompanied by a bond, in the penalty mentioned in the proposals therefor, executed by the persons consenting to become bound as sureties, as provided in section twenty, or by such other persons as shall be substituted therefor, with the consent of the head of the department making such contract, conditioned for the faithful performance of the contract, and every provision therein contained, and which bond shall be accompanied by the oath, in writing, of the person signing the same, that each is a householder or freeholder in the city of New York, and is worth the amount of the security required for the completion of the contract, and stated in the proposals, as hereinbefore prescribed. And the several departments of the city government, by which every and each contract for work to be done for the Corporation, shall be made in pursuance of the authority of these ordinances, shall have power, and it shall be their duty to require and enforce the faithful execution of each and every contract so made by them; and in case the contractor or contractors shall fail in any respect, to perform the work which he or they have contracted to render or perform, within the time limited for the performance of the same, then it shall be the duty of such department, having charge of such work, to do and complete the same, in the manner provided for the performance of the same in the contract, and the cost of the same shall be a charge against such delinquent contractor or contractors, provided, however, that the head of any department by whom any such

Form of contracts.

contract shall be made, may, on good and sufficient cause, extend, for a reasonable time, the period fixed for the completion thereof; but he shall report to the Common Council, at the next meeting thereafter of either Board of the same, the cause or causes of such extension, together with his reasons therefor, and the Common Council may, on such report being made to them, either diminish or enlarge the period of such extension as may be deemed proper.

Ten per cent. to be paid on contracts to be reimbursed by assessments.

§ 28. Whenever any contract shall be made hereafter, by any of the departments of the Corporation, the amount whereof is to be afterward collected by assessments from the property benefited by the work to be done under said contract, it shall be the duty of the head of department making such contracts, to cause to be inserted therein a clause, that as the work progresses, payments will be made to the contractors, by monthly installments of seventy per cent. on the work performed, and the head of department making such contracts shall forthwith file a copy thereof with the Comptroller.

Provision for raising money to pay contracts.

§ 29. The amount due contractors on all contracts now confirmed by the Common Council, and on work now in progress, under contracts on account of regulating and paving streets, building sewers, and all other work ordered to be done by contract, by virtue of ordinances of the Common Council, shall be paid by the Comptroller, from the proceeds of Assessment Bonds, issued in accordance with the act of the legislature, passed April 16, 1852; but no moneys shall be paid on account of said assessments or contracts until a copy of the original contracts has been filed with the Comptroller of the city by the head of department having such work in charge, with a certificate, in writing, from the head of such department, stating the amount of work that has been completed, and the amount due the contractor for such work, acording to the terms of the original contract; upon the amount thus certified and ascertained to be due to the contractor, the Comptroller shall pay *seventy per cent.* — the remaining thirty per cent. to be reserved until the final completion of the contract.

§ 30. For the purpose of providing for the payments contemplated under this ordinance, it shall be the duty of the Comptroller, from time to time, to borrow such sums as may be necessary, (as provided in the act entitled "An act to authorize the Mayor, Aldermen and Commonalty of the city of New York to issue Assessment Bonds," passed April 16, 1852,) upon bonds to be known as "Assessment Bonds," at a rate of interest not to exceed seven per cent. per annum; and the bonds so issued shall be paid from the collections made on the assesment lists, when confirmed by the Common Council, and which are hereby specifically pledged for such purpose; and the contractors to whom payments shall have been made, in accordance with the provisions of sections 28 and 29 of this chapter, shall, upon the final payment of the amount due upon their several contracts, be charged at the rate of seven per cent. per annum, for all sums that may have been advanced to them, as provided in the foregoing sections of this ordinance; and it shall be the duty of the Comptroller to deduct from the amount due on each contract, the interest money so charged.

Provision for raising money to pay contracts.

§ 31. Whenever any payment shall become due upon any contract, according to the provisions thereof, or in accordance with any of the provisions of these ordinances, it shall be the duty of the head of department having such work in charge, to furnish to the person or persons en-

Certificate of amount due on contract.

titled to such payments, a certificate, in writing, signed by the head of such department, specifying the contract upon which such payment is due, and the amount due upon such contract.

Payment on certificate of amount due.

§ 32. It shall be the duty of the Comptroller, on the presentation of such certificate being made to him, to pay the amount thereof, and indorse such payment upon the contract upon which said payment is made; but no payment shall be made upon such contract beyond the amount thereof, and the final payment thereon shall not be made until the head of department having such work in charge, shall furnish the Comptroller, who shall file the same in his office, a certificate, signed by the head of such department, that the work mentioned in such contract has been completed according to the terms of said contract, and to the satisfaction of the head of department giving such certificate. The final payment upon any such contract shall be at least thirty per cent. on the amount thereof, and the certificate of such final payment shall not be given until the assessment for said work shall be confirmed by the Common Council.

Record of Assessment Bonds.

§ 33. The Comptroller shall keep a record of all bonds so issued, specifying the particular work on account of which the same may be issued, and all moneys collected on account of any work, for the payment of which said bonds were issued, shall be faithfully applied as aforesaid; and all sums thus received by the Comptroller, for interest, from the contractors beyond the amount paid as interest, upon the assessment bonds, contemplated by this ordinance, shall be paid into the Sinking Fund pledged for the redemption of the city debt.

Contracts, less than ten thousand dollars, how paid.

§ 34. Sections 28 to 34 shall apply only to contracts of ten thousand dollars and over. Contracts involving an expenditure of less amount than ten thousand dollars may be paid by the Comptroller, with assessment bonds, issued in accordance with the state law of April 16, 1852, in the manner prescribed by these ordinances, only upon the confirmation of the assessment by the Common Council. And it is also hereby expressly provided that, hereafter, when the Street Commissioner and Comptroller, or either of them, have reason to believe that the assessable property is insufficient to provide for its full payment by an assessment made in compliance with the laws of the state, and the ordinances of the Common Council, it shall be the duty of the Comptroller to have a certified copy of the valuation of the property fronting on the avenues or streets embraced in the ordinance, and if the sum required to complete the work is greater than the sum which can be assessed and collected from the property, the work shall not be put under contract, but all the facts, with the opinions of the Street Commissioner and the Comptroller, in relation to the matter, shall be reported to the Common Council, to the end that the payment of all assessment bonds issued under this chapter for the payment of contractors may be amply provided for by the property benefited by the improvement.

Contracts not to exceed appropriations.

§ 35. It shall not be lawful for the several departments of the city, and those having charge of expenditures, to make contracts or incur expenditures authorized by the Common Council, to an amount exceeding the several appropriations made, unless an appropriation sufficient to cover such excess shall have been made by the Common Council.

Appropriations.

§ 36. All resolutions authorizing expenditures to be hereafter made, shall provide for defraying the same from the general appropriations for the year; but in case any special appropriation shall be made for any object of expenditure under any of the several heads of accounts, the same shall be considered as forming a part of the several heads of accounts and of the general appropriation.

Proof of the work done.

§ 37. Each and every contractor shall be required to have an affidavit from the Surveyor, setting forth the amount of work done of every description, that may be charged in each bill or assessment list of said contract, and that said affidavit be attached to said assessment list; also, that the Inspector be requested to furnish an affidavit attached to each contract, that the said work is done according to the plan and specifications; said affidavit to be attached to each assessment list before presented for confirmation.

Repairs on Roads.

§ 38. The Street Commissioner is authorized and directed to purchase the materials necessary to make the repairs required to the roads; the said materials to be delivered at points on the roads where the repairs are required; and is authorized and directed to employ such labor as may be necessary, to distribute such materials, and make such repairs without contract.

Notice to parties to be assessed.

§ 39. It shall be the duty of heads of appropriate departments, on application being made to the Common Council for any object or measure, the expense of effecting which is by law directed to be assessed upon the property benefited, or for any change or alteration of the established grade or height of any street or avenue, to give notice in the newspapers employed by the Corporation of such application, requesting such as may object to such application, to present the same in writing, at the office of said department, on or before the expiration of ten days from the date of such notice.

Payment of interest to contractors.

§ 40. In all cases of delinquency in the payment of any assessment for work done, under a contract made by any contractor with the Corporation, in respect to any street or road, and in respect to the building of wharves, piers, slips and sewers in this city, and in all such like contracts, on a final settlement with every such contractor, there shall be allowed and paid to such contractor all interest money which shall have been collected on his account or contract, first deducting the collector's commissions on so much of the said interest as shall have been collected and received by him.

§ 41. In all contracts for work done at the expense, and by the said the Mayor, Aldermen and Commonalty, for the more speedy execution of any by-laws, ordinances, orders or directions of the said Mayor, Aldermen and Commonalty, and which, by any law the said Mayor, Aldermen and Commonalty are authorized to collect, by assessment or otherwise, from the owners or occupants, lessees or parties interested in any property deemed benefited thereby, provision shall be made for the payment of the amount of said contract, on the completion of the work to the satisfaction of the department making such contract.

Full payment may be made to contractors in certain cases.

§ 42. It shall be lawful for the department making any contract, of the character mentioned in the preceding section of this chapter, to make provision for the payment to any contractor of installments on account of such work, as the same progresses, reserving ten per cent. of the contract price of the work actually done, to remain as security till the whole work be completed according to the contract.

Reservation of 10 per cent.

§ 43. The Street Commissioner shall hereafter insert a clause in all contracts for building piers and bulkheads, or repairing the same, that no more timber or other materials shall be deposited in the slips or basins than is necessary for the completion of the work specified in the contract.

Contract building piers, &c.

CHAPTER IX.

OF THE SINKING FUND.

ARTICLE I *

OF THE SINKING FUND FOR THE REDEMPTION OF THE CITY DEBT.

Sources of the fund for the redemption of city debt.

§ 1. All moneys heretofore received, and hereafter to be received, from the following sources, are hereby pledged, appropriated to, and constitute and form, a fund called "The Sinking Fund of the City of New York, for the redemption of the City Debt," until the whole of the stocks of the city of New York shall be finally and fully redeemed, namely:

* The following note is taken from the edition of the Corporation Ordinances revised and published in 1845.

On the 9th of August, 1813, the Common Council passed the first ordinance creating the Sinking Fund. (See MSS. Book of Ord. March 9, 1812, p. 293.) This ordinance does not appear in any printed edition of the Corporation Ordinances, but with some slight variations, is the same as those appearing in the revisions of 1817, 1821, 1823, 1827 and 1834, p. 219.

The Revision of 1839, p. 140-145, contained the same ordinance with some variations. The whole subject has, however, been revised in the present ordinance, the general objects of which are thus stated in the report of the Finance Committees of both Boards, presented to the Board of Aldermen, December 29, 1843. (Doc. Board of Aldermen, vol. 10, p. 593.) Speaking of the present ordinance, the Committee observe:

"The present ordinance aggregates, with some amendments, the propriety of which

1st. For commutation of quit-rents on grants.

2d. For quit-rents arising from such grants as were issued prior to the year one thousand eight hundred and four.

3d. The net proceeds of all sales of real estate belonging to the Corporation, when sold.

4th. The net proceeds of all bonds and mortgages payable to the Corporation, when collected.

5th. For licenses to pawnbrokers, and dealers in the purchase or sale of second-hand furniture, metals or clothes.

6th. For hackney coach licenses, and street vaults.

7th. For exclusive occupation of private wharves, basins and piers.

8th. For market fees and market rents.

9th. The proceeds of all bonds and mortgages which may have, or shall become, the property of the Corporation, in pursuance of the ordinance creating "The Fire Loan Stock of the City of New York."

---

experience has suggested, all ordinances of the city relating to the Sinking Fund. Existing ordinances provide only for the administration of the fund as it comes into the Commissioners' hands, in cash. The proposed ordinance, in addition to this, is intended to establish a permanent policy in the management and sale of the unconverted property of the city, pledged to the Sinking Fund. The objects to which this fund ought to be devoted are two-fold: one, for the liquidation of the *principal* of the city debt; and the other, the payment of *interest*, as it accrues. This has already been legislated upon by the State Government. It is enacted that the revenues assigned by the Corporation for the extinguishment of the debt, be permanently pledged for that purpose. The ordinances of the Corporation fully respond to this. It has likewise been enacted, that all other revenues of the Corporation, be pledged to the payment of the interest thereon; and in the same law, the State pledged themselves to pass all other necessary laws to levy a proper tax, in case these revenues should at any time prove insufficient. These revenues were sufficient, until the creation of the Water Debt, and thereupon, the legislature, in conformity with its pledge, passed a permanent law for the levying of this deficiency annually. The Corporation, although it has paid the interest, has never passed, in the form of an ordinance, a provision in conformity with the State pledge; and this is proposed in the ordinance now submitted by your Committee."

10th. The buildings included in the establishment called the Alms-house, at Bellevue, together with the lots of land and water rights attached thereto, when sold, and the rents, when leased.

11th. Such portions thereof of the annual taxes levied in the city and county of New York, as may be collected for the redemption of the "Floating Debt Stock of the City of New York," and "The Fire Indemnity Stock of the City of New York."

12th. All such other sources of revenue or sums of money as the said Corporation shall hereafter think proper to appropriate to said fund.

ARTICLE II.

OF THE SINKING FUND FOR THE PAYMENT OF INTEREST ON THE CITY DEBT.

Sources of the fund for payment of interest.

§ 2. All moneys hereafter to be received from the following sources, are pledged, appropriated and applied to, and constitute and form a fund, to be called "The Sinking Fund of the City of New York," for the payment of the interest accruing and to accrue upon the stocks of the city of New York, until the same shall be fully and finally redeemed, namely:

1st. For interest on all bonds and mortgages owned by the Corporation.

2d. For commutation of alien passengers.

3d. For Mayoralty fees.

4th. For fines and penalties.

5th. For fees and fines collected by the Clerks of Courts for the Corporation.

6th. For rents from all sources not already pledged.

7th. For tavern and excise licenses.

8th. For sales of all property of the Corporation other than real estate.

9th. Such portion of the annual taxes levied in the Water District of the city of New York as may be collected to supply the deficiency of interest accruing on the Water Stocks of the city of New York.

10th. Nothing in this chapter shall be so construed as to impair or affect any pledge heretofore made and now existing, of any property or its proceeds embraced in this chapter, or in the ordinances relating to the city debt.

ARTICLE III.

OF THE OFFICERS OF THE SINKING FUND.

§ 3. The Mayor, Recorder, Comptroller and Treasurer of the said city, and the Chairman of the Finance Committee of the Board of Aldermen, and the Chairman of the Finance Committee of the Board of Councilmen, for the time being, shall constitute and be denominated "The Commissioners of the Sinking Fund of the City of New York." Commissioners of the Sinking fund.

§ 4. Any four or more of the persons named in the third section of this article, of whom the Comptroller shall be one, shall be and are hereby authorized to discharge the trusts and duties vested in them by this chapter. Ibid.

§ 5. All purchases to be made of the city stocks, shall be made by, or under the direction of the Commissioners of the Sinking Fund as herein and hereby constituted. Duties of the Commissioners.

§ 6. The said Commissioners shall, from time to time, invest the moneys which shall constitute the Sinking Fund, for the redemption of the city debt, or as much as they Ibid.

can in the purchase of stocks created by the Corporation of the city of New York, at the market price, not exceeding the par value thereof; and if, at any time, such investments cannot be made at par, then the said Commissioners shall be authorized to invest the said moneys, or such part thereof as they may see fit, either in the purchase of the said stock or the stock of the State of New York, or the stock of the United States, notwithstanding such stock may be above the par value thereof.

Duties of the Commissioners. § 7. The powers conferred on the said Commissioners in the preceding section of this article, shall be so construed as to render it imperative on the said Commissioners, at all times, to give preference to the purchase of City Stock, if the same can be procured at a reasonable rate.

Ibid. § 8. Whenever the said Commissioners shall have invested any part of the said fund in the purchase of the stocks of this state, or of the United States, and shall at any time thereafter be enabled to purchase any of the city stocks at such prices as they may judge best for the public interest, they shall forthwith sell and dispose of the same, and invest the said stocks of the state, or of the United States, or the net proceeds thereof, in the City Stock, if, in their opinion, such disposition would be beneficial to the public interest.

Ibid. § 9. Whenever the said Commissioners shall have invested any part of the said fund in the purchase of city stock, and shall at any time thereafter be enabled to purchase any of the city stock, which shall be by its terms redeemable at an earlier day, they may forthwith sell the same, and invest the net proceeds in such other city stock, if, in their opinion, such exchange shall be desirable and beneficial to the public interest.

Ibid. § 10. Whenever any of the moneys constituting "The

Sinking Fund" for the redemption of the city debt shall be required for any such purchases or investments as are in this article before-mentioned, or for the redemption of any of the city stocks at their maturity, the amount of money respectively required shall be paid from the treasury, by warrant signed by the said Commissioners, or any four of them, the Comptroller being one.

§ 11. All stocks and securities which shall be purchased by the said Commissioners, shall be transferred to the said Commissioners; and all transfers thereof, when disposed of pursuant to the provisions of this chapter, shall be made by the said Commissioners, or any four of them, of whom the Comptroller shall be one. Duties of the Commissioners.

§ 12. The City Stock which shall be purchased by the Commissioners, shall not be canceled by them until the final redemption of the said stock, and all interest accruing thereon, shall regularly be carried to the said Sinking Fund for the redemption of the city debt. Ibid.

§ 13. The revenues herein assigned for the redemption of the city debt, shall be kept distinct from all other revenues belonging to the said Commissioners. Ibid.

§ 14. All moneys constituting the fund for the payment of the interest on the city debt, whenever required to meet such interest, shall be drawn from the treasury in the manner prescribed in section 10 contained in this chapter. Ibid.

§ 15. Nothing in this ordinanee shall be so construed as to prevent the said Commissioners from temporarily investing the unemployed moneys belonging to the Sinking Fund in the temporary bonds of the Corporation. Ibid.

§ 16. It shall be the duty of the Comptroller to keep a correct journal of the proceedings of the said Commissioners, to be verified by any four of them, himself being Journal and report of Commissioners.

one, and once in each year, or oftener if required, to render unto the Common Council a full and detailed report of the proceedings of the said Commissioners.

Report of Commissioners.

§ 17. The said report shall specify the disbursements, purchases, exchanges and sales, made by the said Commissioners, the prices at which, and the parties from whom such purchases, with whom such exchanges, and to whom such sales shall have been made, the amounts and description of the stocks of this city purchased by the said Commissioners, the amounts and description of the stocks of this state, and of the United States then held by them; the amounts paid for interest on the City Stocks, with a detailed statement of the receipts and the unemployed moneys in the City Treasury to the credit of each division of the Sinking Fund.

Construction.

§ 18. The terms " City Debt," and " City Stock " used in this article, shall be construed to mean any stock or fund created by the Corporation of the city of New York.

ARTICLE IV.

OF THE DISPOSITION OF REAL ESTATES.

Comptroller shall take charge of real estate.

§ 19. It shall be the duty of said Comptroller to take charge of all the real estate belonging to the Corporation, and to prevent all encroachments thereon.

Also, of deeds &c., and Certificates of Stock.

§ 20. It shall be the duty of said Comptroller to keep all title deeds, leases, bonds and mortgages, and other assurances of title, and all certificates of stock belonging to the Sinking Fund.

Collection of Revenues.

§ 21. It shall be the duty of said Comptroller to superintend the collection of all rents, interests and demands, due the said Sinking Fund, and to direct all necessary measures to compel the payment of them, and report the condition of the same to the Common Council quarterly.

§ 22. It shall be the duty of the said Comptroller to consent, in the name, and behalf of the Corporation, whenever he deems it proper, that the lessee or assignee of any lease made by the Corporation, may assign such lease or underlet the demised premises; but no such consent shall be given unless all arrears of rent be paid in full, and all taxes and assessments due thereon. Assignment of Leases, &c.

§ 23. It shall be the duty of the said Comptroller, under the sanction of the Commissioners of the Sinking Fund, to appoint appraisers on behalf of the Corporation, to settle the rent on renewal of any leases, or the value of the building to be paid for on the expiration of any lease in which the Corporation is, or shall be interested, whenever by the provisions of such lease the appointment of such appraisers is required. Appraisers of rent & buildings.

§ 24. The said Comptroller is hereby authorized, with the sanction of the said Commissioners, to assign any bond or mortgage held by the Commissioners of the Sinking Fund, to any person or persons who may elect to take such assignment, upon the payment in full of the principal and interest due on said bond and mortgage; and the Mayor and Clerk of the Common Council are hereby authorized and directed to execute, under their hands and seal of the city, any such assignment, upon evidence being exhibited to them, showing that the principal and interest of such bond and mortgage has been paid into the treasury of said city to the credit of the Commissioners of the Sinking Fund. Assignment of Bonds and Mortgages.

§ 25. Upon the payment of any bond and mortgage in full, it shall be the duty of the said Comptroller to prepare and cause to be executed, a proper satisfaction of such bond and mortgage, and the said Mayor and Clerk of the Payment of Bonds and Mortgages.

Common Council are hereby authorized to execute the same, upon the production of evidence that the same has been paid, as provided in the preceding section of this article. But no release of any part of the premises contained in such mortgage, from the lien created by such mortgage thereon, shall be made or executed by them.

Commutation of Quit rents.

§ 26. Whenever any person or persons may desire to commute any quit-rent due the Corporation, it shall be the duty of the said Comptroller to calculate such commutation at the rate of six per cent., and upon the production of evidence that the same and all arrears of rent have been paidinto the treasury, as provided in section 24, of this chapter, it shall be the duty of the Mayor and Clerk to execute a release of such quit-rent.

Unproductive property

§ 27. Whenever any property belonging to the Corporation is unproductive, or the term for which it may have been leased or let shall have expired, or be about expiring, it shall be the duty of the said Comptroller, to let the same for a term not exceeding one year, as provided in the next succeeding section, if, in his judgment, it will be beneficial to the public interest to do so.

Leasing of Property.

§ 28. Whenever, in the judgment of the said Comptroller, it shall be more advisable to lease property belonging to the Corporation, it shall be his duty to communicate the same, with his reasons therefor, to the Commissioners of the Sinking Fund, and if they concur with him, they are hereby authorized and empowered to lease the same in such manner as they may deem most fit for the interest of the city, conforming in such leasing to the provisions of the act, entitled "An act further to amend the charter of the city of New York," passed April 14, 1857, and upon the production of a certificate signed by a majority of said Commissioners, of whom the Comptroller shall be one, it shall be the duty of the said Mayor and Clerk of the Common Council to execute such leases under their hands and seal of the city; said lease to be submitted to the Common Council for their sanction before being executed.

§ 29. In all cases of grants hereafter to be made, of lands under water on the shores of the island of New York, or on the shores of Long Island, and within the limits of the various charters of the city of New York, and in all cases of extensions of grants previously made, it shall be the duty of the Comptroller and the Street Commissioner of the said city of New York, to report to the Commissioners of the Sinking Fund, what sum of money shall, in their judgment, be charged as consideration for such grant, and if the said Commissioners, or a majority of them, shall agree to the terms reported by the said Comptroller and Street Commissioner, then the said Comptroller shall be, and he is hereby authorized to cause such grants to be issued to the parties who may legally be entitled to the same.

Grants of Lands under water.

§ 30. The preceding section shall not apply to grants to be made on the North or Hudson river, between Hammond and Thirtieth streets; so far as the consideration money is concerned; but the rates to be charged for grants between said Hammond and Thirtieth streets, shall be as follows :

Reservation grants on certain parts of Hudson river

For each running foot along the exterior lines of the present grants (excluding the width of streets), and along the westerly line of the Eleventh avenue (excluding the width of streets) when not granted, viz:

For grants between		Hammond and Bank streets....	$20
"	"	Bank and Bethune streets......	19
"	"	Bethune and Troy streets......	18
"	"	Troy and Jane streets.........	17
"	"	Jane and Horatio streets.......	16

For grants between	Horatio and Gansevoort streets.	15
" "	Gansevoort and Twelfth streets.	14
" "	Twelfth street and centre of the block, between Thirteenth and Fourteenth streets	13
" "	The centre of the block, between Thirteenth, Fourteenth and Nineteenth streets...........	10
" "	Between Nineteenth and Twenty-fourth streets.............	12
" "	Twenty-fourth and Thirtieth streets, west of the Eleventh avenue	10

Payment for grants.

§ 31. No grant shall be made by virtue of this ordinance, except for a specific consideration, to be paid in cash, or in five annual installments, secured by bond and mortgage on the premises granted, with annual interest, at the rate of seven per cent. per annum. The first installment to be paid on the issuing of the grants.

Covenants in grants.

§ 32. All grants made by virtue of this ordinance, shall contain the usual covenants, including those in relation to streets or avenues passing through them, and also in relation to bulkheads and wharfage.

Bulkheads or piers.

§ 33. No grant made by virtue of this ordinance, shall authorize the grantee to construct bulkheads or piers, or make land in conformity thereto, without permission so to do is first had and obtained from the Common Council, and the grantees shall be bound to make such land, piers or bulkheads, at such times and in such manner as the Common Council shall direct, under penalty of forfeiture of such grant, for non-compliance with such directions of the Common Council.

§ 34. Nothing contained in the two next preceding sections, shall be construed as applying to water grants, to be made on the shores of Long Island. Grants on L. Island shore.

§ 35. The Commissioners of the Sinking Fund are hereby authorized to sell and dispose of all real estate belonging to the Corporation, and not in use for or reserved for public purposes, at public auction, at such times and on such terms as they may deem most advantageous for the public interest, in conformity with the provisions of the statute in this article before referred to, provided, however, that no property shall be disposed of for a smaller sum than that affixed to the description of said property under article fifth of this chapter, and at least thirty days' previous notice of the time and place of such sale, including a description of the property to be sold, be published in each of the newspapers employed by the Corporation. Sale of Real Estate.

ARTICLE V.

OF THE VALUATION AT WHICH REAL ESTATE BELONGING TO THE SINKING FUND SHALL BE SOLD.

§ 36. Real estate, under lease, without covenants of renewal, shall not be sold for a less sum than the same may be appraised at by the Commissioners of the Sinking Fund and the Street Commissioner, or a majority of them, at a meeting to be held and an appraisement made, within one month prior to the date of the sale. Ibid.

§ 37. Real estate, under lease, with covenants of renewal, shall not be sold for a less sum than an amount equal to a commutation on the present rents reserved, calculated at six per cent. Ibid.

§ 38. Real estate, not embraced in the last two preceding sections, shall not be sold for a less sum than the same Ibid.

may be appraised at, pursuant to section 36 of this chapter.

Sales of Real Estates.

§ 39. Whenever any real estate shall have been sold pursuant to the preceding sections of this chapter, it shall be the duty of the Commissioners of the Sinking Fund, or a majority of them, to give a certificate under their hands that the same has been sold pursuant to the provisions of this chapter, and upon the production of such certificate and the evidence that the proceeds of such sale have been paid into the treasury to the credit of the Sinking Fund, for the redemption of the city debt, it shall be the duty of the Mayor of the city and the Clerk of the Common Council to execute proper conveyances of such real estate under their hands and the seal of the City Corporation.

CHAPTER X.

OF THE FIRE DEPARTMENT.

ARTICLE I.

OF THE DEPARTMENT GENERALLY.

General privileges and duties.

§ 1. The Fire Department shall exercise the powers, perform the duties, and enjoy the privileges imposed and conferred on it by the charters of the city and the various acts amending the same; by the laws of this state and by the ordinances of the Common Council.

Department, of whom to consist.

§ 2. The Fire Department shall consist of a Chief Engineer, thirteen assistant engineers, twelve fire wardens, and such number of fire engine men, hose men, hook and ladder men, and hydrant men, who shall be citizens of the United States, of the age of twenty-one years and upwards, as now are or hereafter may be, from time to time, appointed, in the manner required by law, and who shall be respectively distinguished by the several appellations aforesaid.

ARTICLE II.

OF THE CHIEF ENGINEER, ASSISTANT ENGINEERS AND FIRE WARDENS.

Chief Engineer, how appointed.

§ 3. The Chief Engineer of the Fire Department shall be elected every three years by the members of the Fire Department, by ballot, and the person receiving the greatest number of votes for the office shall thereupon be entitled to a nomination to the Common Council for appointment.

Time of election.

§ 4. The election for the selection of Chief Engineer, under this ordinance, shall take place on the first Tuesday after the first Monday in February, 1860, and thereafter every succeeding three years.

Powers and duties of Chf. Engineer.

§ 5. The Chief Engineer shall, in all cases of fire, have the sole and absolute control and command over all the assistant engineers and other persons connected with the Fire Department. It shall be his duty to direct the other engineers to take proper measures to arrange the several fire engines in the most advantageous manner, and to cause them to be duly worked for the effectual extinguishment of fires. It shall also be his duty to examine, twice in every year, into the condition and number of the fire engines, and other fire apparatus and fire engine houses, and report the same once a year to the Common Council, together with the names of all the members of the Fire Department, and the respective associations to which they belong. He shall also report in writing to the Common Council all accidents by fire that may take place in this city, with the causes thereof, as well as they can be ascertained, and the number of and description of the buildings destroyed or injured, together with the names of the owners or occupants. He shall, whenever any of the fire engines, hose carts, trucks and hooks and ladders or other apparatus shall require to be repaired, report the same forthwith to the proper officer, and under his direction, superintend the repairs thereof. He shall report all violations or disobedience of orders to the Commissioners of the Fire Department. He is authorized, under the direction of the Common Council, to sell for cash any old and condemned fire engines and hose, deposited at the public yard, and shall pay the money received therefor to the City Chamberlain, and deposit the receipt for such money with the Comptroller. He shall also have such further powers and perform such other duties as are provided in this ordinance.

§ 6. The Chief Engineer shall receive for his salary the yearly sum of five thousand dollars. Salary of Chf. Engineer.

§ 7. The nomination of the assistant engineers shall be made by the firemen by ballot, every three years, and the persons receiving the greatest number of votes, shall be respectively entitled to a nomination to the Common Council for appointment to such office. Assistant Engineers, how appointed.

§ 8. The Common Council may, at their pleasure, or when a new election shall be asked for by a majority of the firemen, order a new election for one or more of such assistant engineers, and the person or persons nominated at such new election shall, when duly confirmed, serve only for and during the remainder of the term or terms of the person or persons in whose place or places he or they may respectively be elected. New election for Assistant Engineers.

§ 9. At least one of the Assistant Engineers to be elected pursuant to the foregoing provisions, shall reside at Harlem; at least one shall reside east of the Sixth avenue, and between Twenty-second and Eighty-sixth streets; and at least one shall reside west of the Sixth ave- Residence of Assistant Engineers.

nue and between Twenty-second and Eighty-sixth streets. There shall be in all thirteen assistant engineers, and as many more as may, from time to time, be designated by the Common Council.

Assistant Engineers, to whom subject.

§ 10. The Assistant Engineers, when attending fires, are subject to the directions of the Chief Engineer.

Engineer's cap & trumpet.

§ 11. The Chief Engineer and Assistant Engineers shall respectively wear at fires a leathern cap, painted white, with a gilded front thereto, and a fire engine blazoned thereon, and shall also carry a speaking trumpet, painted black, with the words "Chief Engineer," "Engineer No. 1," (as the case may be,) in white, and the same designations shall also be painted on their caps, respectively.

Vacancy of Engineers.

§ 12. Whenever a vacancy shall occur in the offices of Chief Engineer or Assistant Engineers, the engineers and the foremen of the fire companies, collectively, shall have power, and it shall be their duty to call a special election and designate the time for holding the same, to the end that a nomination to the Common Council may be made pursuant to these ordinances to supply such vacancy or vacancies.

Ibid.

§ 13. In case of vacancy in the office of Chief Engineer, the senior Assistant Engineer shall discharge the duties of Chief Engineer until the vacancy shall be filled.

Certificate of election of Assistant Engineers.

§ 14. It shall be the duty of the Chief Engineer or the senior Assistant Engineer, to certify under his hand to the Common Council, the names of the persons who may from time to time, be designated, pursuant to the provisions of the 7th section of this ordinance, for the respective offices for which they may have been nominated, to the end that if approved of by the Common Council, they may be appointed.

§ 15. The engineers and the foremen and assistant foremen of the fire companies shall have power, and it shall be their duty to establish and provide regulations for holding and conducting the elections authorized to be held as aforesaid, and rules for the qualifications of electors thereat. Regulation of elections.

§ 16. Every fireman, whose appointment as a member of the Fire Department shall have been confirmed three months next preceding the nomination at which he may offer to vote, pursuant to these ordinances, and who shall then be, and for the said three months shall have been, an acting and actual member of the Fire Department, shall be entitled to one vote upon such nomination. Who qualified to vote at elections.

§ 17. The Comptroller is directed to pay no bill of expenses of any election for Chief Engineer or other engineers of the Fire Department, which, including advertising, inspectors' expenses, room-hire, stationery, &c., shall exceed the sum of twenty-five dollars. Expenses of elections limited.

§ 18. The Fire Wardens shall be appointed in pursuance of the statutes of the state, and when attending fires shall be subject to the direction of the Chief Engineer and the Assistant Engineers of the Fire Department. Fire Wardens.

§ 19. It shall be the duty of the said Fire Wardens immediately on the alarm of fire, to repair to the place where it may be, and aid and assist in procuring supplies of water to the fire engines, as the chief or assistant engineers may direct, to prevent the hose from being trodden upon, and to keep all idle and suspected persons at a proper distance from the fire and from the vicinity; and the citizens are hereby enjoined to comply with the orders and directions of the said Fire Wardens in the premises. Duties of Fire Wardens.

§ 20. It shall be the duty of said Fire Wardens twice in every year, viz: in the months of June and December, Ibid.

Duties of Fire Wardens.

and as much oftener as they may think proper, to examine the dwelling-houses and other buildings in their respective wards, for the purpose of ascertaining all violations of any act in force, for the more effectual prevention of fires in New York; and also, to examine the fire-places, hearths, chimneys, stoves and the pipes thereto; ovens, boilers, kettles, and also all chemical apparatus which, in their opinion, may be dangerous in causing or promoting fires, and also, the places where ashes may be deposited, and upon finding any of them defective or dangerous, they, or either of them, shall direct the owner or occupant, either by a printed or written notice, to alter, remove or amend the same, in such manner and within such reasonable time as they, or either of them, may deem necessary; and in case of neglect or refusal so to do, the party offending shall forfeit and pay twenty-five dollars, and for every day after the time allotted as aforesaid, to alter, remove or amend the same, in conformity with the direction aforesaid, the party so offending shall forfeit and pay the further sum of five dollars; and all the expenses of any removal, alteration or amendment as aforesaid, shall be paid in the first instance by the occupant, but shall be chargeable against the owner of such dwelling-house or other building, and shall be deducted from the rent of the same, unless such expense be rendered necessary by the act or default of such occupant, or unless there be a special agreement to the contrary between the parties. And it shall moreover be the duty of the Fire Wardens, or either of them, at such times as aforesaid, to enter into and examine all buildings, livery or other stables, hay-boats or vessels, and places where any gunpowder, hemp, flax, tow, hay, rushes, firewood, boards, shingles, shavings, or other combustible materials may be lodged, and give such directions in writing in the premises, as may be deemed necessary by them, or him, relative to the removal thereof. And in case of neglect or refusal on the part of the possessor of such combustible materials, or any of them, to remove or secure the same within the time and in the manner directed by the said Fire Wardens, or either of them, the party offending shall forfeit and pay twenty-five dollars, and the further sum of five dollars for every day's neglect to remove or secure the same, after being so notified.

Fire Wardens' cap & trumpet.

§ 21. Each of the Fire Wardens shall, when attending at fires, wear a leathern hat, with the brim black, the crown painted white, and the city arms blazoned on the front, and shall also carry a speaking trumpet painted white, with the word "Warden," painted in black thereon.

Salaries of Fire Wardens

§ 22. The Fire Wardens shall receive severally, the salary fixed by the Legislature, viz: five hundred dollars per annum. The Clerk of the Board of Fire Wardens, shall receive an annual salary of eight hundred dollars per annum.

ARTICLE III.

OF THE FIREMEN AND FIRE COMPANIES, AND HEREIN OF FIRE APPARATUS AND THE MANAGEMENT AND CARE THEREOF, AND THE REGULATIONS TO BE OBSERVED AT FIRES.

Organization of Fire companies, and duties of firemen.

§ 23. The firemen shall be divided into companies, to consist of as many members as the Common Council shall, from time to time direct,* to attend to the fire engines,

* BY RESOLUTION.—The complement of men allowed to the different engine, hose and hook and ladder companies, shall be as follows :

	Men.
First class engines	70
Second class engines	60
Third class engines	50
Hose companies	30

Organization of Fire companies, and duties of firemen.

hydrants, hose-wagons and hooks and ladders belonging, or that may hereafter belong to the Corporation of the city, or to such hydrants, fire engines, hose-wagons and hooks and ladders as the Common Council shall direct, and each of the companies shall, and may choose out of their own number, a foreman, assistant foreman and clerk, in such manner, and at such times, as they think proper; and it shall be the duty of the said firemen, as often as any fire shall break out in the said city, to repair immediately upon the alarm thereof to their respective engines, hose-wagons, hooks and ladders, and convey them to, or near, the place where such fire shall happen, unless otherwise directed by the Chief or other Engineer; and there, in conformity with the directions given by the Chief Engineer or other Engineers, to work and manage the said engines or apparatus and implements, with all their skill and power; and when the fire is extinguished, they shall not remove therefrom but by the direction of an engineer, and on such direction they shall return their respective hose-wagons, hooks and ladders, engines and apparatus, well washed and cleansed, to their several places of deposit. If any firemen shall neglect to attend to any fire as aforesaid, or leave his fire engine or other apparatus while at any fire without permission, or shall neglect to do his duty on such occasions without reasonable excuse, he shall, for every default, forfeit and pay the sum of three dollars, and may, on request of the company to which he belongs, be removed from his station as foreman.

Hydrant companies to remain as they are.

And the Chief Engineer is hereby directed not to receive any more returns of members elected to the various fire companies until the membership of each conforms to the before-mentioned standard.

Resolution, November 10, 1854.

Amended by resolution, January 5, 1857.

Amended by resolution, January 7, 1857.

§ 24. It shall be the duty of each and every fire company in going to, or returning from any fire or alarm of fire, or removing their apparatus from their respective places of deposit, to obey the orders of the Chief or other Engineer. Companies to obey Engineers.

§ 25. And in case any foreman or assistant foreman, or any other fireman, having charge of any fire company, disobeying or refusing to obey any order or direction given by the Chief or other Engineer, he shall, for such offense, be suspended or expelled from the Fire Department. Officers to obey Engineers.

§ 26. It shall be the duty of all members of the Fire Department, to prevent all persons not belonging to the department, from entering any house or handling any apparatus belonging to the department. Strangers not to be permitted in engine houses.

§ 27. It shall be the duty of each and every fireman, to prevent boys or disorderly characters from congregating in or about the place of deposit of their various apparatus, and not to allow the said place of deposit to be used for any other purposes than those directly connected with the performance of their duty as firemen. No persons other than members and exempt members of the company, or of the Fire Department, in good standing, shall be allowed to sleep in any engine, hose, or hook and ladder house; neither shall the street doors of the said houses be kept open except while persons are passing in and out, or while any necessary repairs or cleaning are being performed. It shall also be the duty of the said firemen to see that good order is preserved in and about the houses occupied by their respective companies, and to prevent any persons from habitually congregating on the walks in front of the houses of their said apparatus. Engine houses, regulations concerning.

Regulations in going to & returning from fires.

§ 28. In going to or returning from a fire, the drag-rope shall be the proper place for the firemen, except the officers in command, and it shall be their duty to prevent all boys, and noisy and improper persons, from taking hold of the rope. On no account shall a person, other than a member of the company, or a member or exempt member of the Fire Department, known to at least two of the members of the company present, be allowed to manage, or have any control of the tongue or tiller of any apparatus, in going to or returning from a fire. It shall also be the duty of the officers and members of each and every company when returning with their apparatus from a fire, or alarm of fire, to prevent any racing of their company with any other company, and to abstain from any conduct that would be likely to cause a breach of the peace, or reflect discredit on the Fire Department. It shall further be their duty to use all endeavors to cultivate good feeling among the members of the Fire Department.

Officers to be responsible for neglect.

§ 29. Each and every officer or member in command of a company shall be held responsible for his actions, while exercising command over any fire apparatus, or for any willful neglect or violation of any of the duties incumbent upon him.

Regulations concerning suspended or expelled firemen.

§ 30. No fireman, while under suspension for any violation of the ordinances relative to the Fire Department, shall be permitted to wear a fire-cap bearing the frontispiece of the company to which he is attached, nor be allowed to vote at any election held by the company; neither shall he be permitted to take part in any of the meetings, or to frequent the house occupied by his company. And no person suspended or expelled from the Fire Department shall be allowed to take command or exercise control over any fire apparatus while he remains under such sentence of suspension or expulsion.

§ 31. It shall be the duty of each and every company on an alarm of fire being given for the district or districts in which the said company does duty, to proceed with all due diligence and by the most convenient route to the fire, or to the place from whence the said alarm originated, unless otherwise directed by an Engineer; avoiding all lying in wait, or any departure from their usual route, for the purpose of racing with any other company. Duties of companies on alarm of fire.

§ 32. Any Engineer, officer of a company or member of the Fire Department, who shall violate any of the ordinances relative to the Fire Department, or who shall knowingly or willfully consent to or assist in any violation of the same, shall be liable to suspension or expulsion from the Fire Department. And any company so found guilty of a violation of any of the ordinances of the Fire Department, shall be liable to be disbanded. Penalties for violation of any of these ordinances.

§ 33. All persons who may in future be elected to fill vacancies in fire companies, shall present to the Chief Engineer a certificate of such election, signed by the foreman and secretary of the company in which he has been elected; and said candidate, before the Chief Engineer presents his name to the Commissioners of the Fire Department, shall make affidavit that he is a citizen of the United States; is twenty-one years of age; that it is his intention to perform active duty as a fireman in the company in which his name is enrolled; and that he will promote subordination in the Department. Election of members of fire companies.

§ 34. No boys or other persons, known as volunteers, shall be permitted to assume the garb of firemen; or have access to any places of deposit of the fire engines, hose, hook and ladder, or other apparatus of the Fire Department; or run as members with any such engine, hose-cart or hook and ladder truck; or form any association similar Volunteers prohibited.

in any way to those known as "volunteer associations." And any fire company in the city of New York, which shall consent to any violation of the provisions of this section, shall be forthwith disbanded.

Numbers of the companies.

§ 35. The numbers of the members of the engine, hook and ladder, hose and hydrant companies, and the numbers and locations of the fire apparatus of the city, shall remain as at present existing, subject to be varied and modified by the Common Council.

Appointment of firemen.

§ 36. Whenever any fireman is appointed to supply any vacancy in any company, it shall be his duty to call on the Treasurer of the Fire Department, and procure a certificate, within one month from the date of his appointment, specifying the name and number of the company to which such fireman shall be elected; and each fireman, after being re-elected, shall obtain a new certificate as aforesaid; and it shall be the duty of the Chief Engineer to certify, on every return, whether a vacancy exists in the company.

Expulsion of firemen.

§ 37. If a fire company shall vote for the expulsion of a fireman belonging thereto, the same shall be forthwith reported by the Chief Engineer to the Commissioners of the Fire Department.

Complaints against firemen.

§ 38. All complaints by the Chief Engineer or Assistant Engineers against firemen for misconduct in the performance of their duties, shall be forthwith reported to the Commissioners of the Fire Department.

Offenses by firemen, how reported.

§ 39. In case of any breach of the peace, or other violation of good order, on the part of any of the firemen while on duty, the officer in command of the party offending shall forthwith report the name of the person or persons so offending to the Commissioners of the Fire Department; and in case of his neglect to do so, he shall be held responsible for the same.

§ 40. It shall be the especial duty of the foreman and assistant foreman of each engine, hose, hook and ladder and hydrant company, to see that the provisions of the last preceding section are fully and strictly enforced so far as regards the company to which such foreman or assistant foreman may be attached; and if either or both of them aid or consent to the violation of the provisions of such section, they or either of them so offending shall be immediately expelled from the department. Offenses by firemen, how reported.

§ 41. The foremen of engine companies and the firemen shall, when on duty, wear leathern caps, in the form heretofore used; and the said caps shall be painted and distinguished in the manner following, viz: the cap of each foreman shall be painted black, with a white frontispiece, and the word "foreman," with the initials of the name of the foreman, and the number of the engine to which he belongs, painted thereon in black. The cap of each fireman shall be painted black, with the initials of the name of the fireman, and the number of the engine to which he belongs, painted in front thereof in white. The foremen of each of the hook and ladder companies shall wear a cap painted black, with a white frontispiece, and the word "foreman" and the initials of his name, and the number of the company to which he belongs, and a hook and ladder painted thereon in black; and each member of the hook and ladder companies shall wear a cap painted black, with the initials of his name and the number of the company to which he belongs, with a hook and ladder painted in front thereof in white; and each foreman of the fire hose companies shall wear a cap painted black, with a white frontispiece, and the word "foreman," and the initials of his name and the number of the company to which he belongs, and a coil of hose painted thereon in black; and each member of the said fire hose companies shall wear a cap painted black, Caps.

with the initials of his name and the number of the company to which he belongs, with a coil of hose painted thereon in white; and the assistant to each respective company shall wear a cap painted in the same manner as that of the foreman of the company, with the word "assistant," in lieu of the word "foreman." And it shall be the duty of the Chief Engineer to report to the Commissioners of the Fire Department the name of every person who shall neglect or refuse to comply with the foregoing requisitions, which said person shall thereupon be removed from his office.

Caps and Badges. § 42. All members of the New York Fire Department, and such exempt members as are authorized by the Commissioners of the Fire Department, shall hereafter, when on duty as firemen, or at fires, wear the leathern cap, as heretofore used, or a badge, as hereinafter provided, which said badge shall be worn in a plain, conspicuous manner on the breast, and shall be worn and visible during the whole time that such member or exempt member shall remain at the fire; and any fireman neglecting or refusing to wear his badge, as above specified, shall be subject to a suspension or expulsion from the department, and any exempt fireman so refusing or neglecting, shall be subject to a fine of not less than twenty-five, or over two hundred and fifty dollars, and imprisonment not less than ten days; and all fines so collected shall be paid over to the Treasurer of the Fire Department fund.

Badges. § 43. The badge mentioned in the preceding sections shall be made of Princes' metal, bearing the letters, "N. Y. F. D." and each badge shall bear a distinct number, in raised figures thereon, of white metal; the same to represent the number of each company, and also a register number, in small figures, stamped thereon; and the badge to be worn by exempt firemen, as provided for in section 42, of this chapter, shall be composed of white metal, with the figures thereon of Princes' metal; but in all other respects to conform to the badge herein described for the use of the active members of the Department; said badges shall be struck from dies, which shall be exclusively the property of the Corporation of the city of New York, and shall be placed in the custody of the Clerk of the Common Council; and all of such badges shall be numbered, as the Commissioners of the New York Fire Department may direct.

§ 44. The said badges shall be deposited with the Commissioners of the New York Fire Department, who shall have sole charge of the distribution of the same; and it shall be the duty of the said Commissioners to keep a register of the names of all persons who now are, or who may hereafter become members of the New York Fire Department, and of the number of the company to which said persons are attached, and also of the names of such exempt firemen, as may in writing be permitted by said Commissioners to wear the badges aforesaid, and of the number of the badge delivered to each of said firemen or exempt firemen. Badges.

§ 45. It shall be the duty of the Commissioners of the New York Fire Department to deliver to each fireman, one of the badges aforesaid; and the said Commissioners shall also deliver one of the aforesaid badges to each of such exempt firemen as may, by virtue of section 16, of an act of the Legislature of the State of New York, entitled "An act for the better regulation of the firemen in the city of New York," passed March 29th, 1855, be permitted by said Commissioners to wear the same. Ibid.

§ 46. The badges herein named shall be the exclusive property of the city of New York, and when any member Ibid.

of the Fire Department shall resign or be suspended or expelled therefrom, it shall be the duty of the foreman and secretary of the company to which such member was attached, to make a return of such suspension, expulsion or resignation forthwith to the Chief Engineer, together with the badge formerly worn by such member, and the Chief Engineer shall report weekly to the Commissioners aforesaid the names of such members of the Fire Department as shall have resigned or been suspended or expelled therefrom since his last report, and shall, with said report, return to the said Commissioners the badges worn by such members.

Badges. § 47. If the foreman and secretary of any company, or either of them, shall fail to comply with the provisions of the preceding section in relation to the return of badges, no return of members elected by such company shall be received therefrom, unless good and satisfactory cause shall be shown to the Commissioners why said badges are not returned; and should any member of the Fire Department lose his badge, it shall be his duty to report said loss within two weeks to the said Commissioners, and it shall be their duty to inquire into the circumstances of the case, and unless they are satisfied that such loss was without fault on the part of said member, they shall have power to suspend or expel said member from the Department, in their discretion; but should the loss be satisfactorily accounted for to the said Commissioners, then they shall grant a new badge to said member, who shall pay one dollar, upon receiving the same, as a penalty for said loss (which money shall be paid to the Treasurer of the Fire Department Fund by said Commissioners, they taking his receipt for the same), and any member of the Department not complying with the above provision shall be expelled.

Ibid. § 48. Every exempt fireman receiving a badge, shall have the permission to wear the same renewed some time during the month of May in each year, otherwise such permission shall be deemed revoked, and the said Commissioners may, at any time, revoke any permission so granted by them; but in case such permission is not renewed, or is revoked, it shall be the duty of such exempt fireman to restore the badge previously worn by him to the said Commissioners.

§ 49. Any member of the New York Fire Department, or exempt fireman, who shall loan his badge to any person, shall be liable to the penalties as set forth in section 42 of this chapter; and if any badge shall become broken or the figures be displaced while in the possession of such member or exempt fireman, he shall return the same forthwith to the said Commissioners, and in default of the same, said member may be expelled or suspended, and such exempt fireman shall have the permission to wear the same revoked. Badges.

§ 50. Any member of the New York Fire Department, or exempt fireman, who shall violate any of the foregoing provisions of this chapter contained in sections 42, 43, 44, 45, 46, 47, 48 and 49, shall be subject to a fine of not less than twenty-five, or over two hundred and fifty dollars and to imprisonment for the term of ten days, and all fines so collected shall be paid over to the Treasurer of the New York Fire Department Fund. Penalties.

§ 51. It shall be the duty of the police, when a fire occurs, to form a line, at least two hundred feet distant from the said fire on each side thereof; and they shall not, under any circumstances, permit any person to pass said line, unless said person shall wear the uniform or badge of the Fire Department, the uniform of the Insurance Patrol, or be a member of the Common Council, a member of the Police Department, an owner of property within, or resident in, the prescribed lines. Regulations at fires.

Regulation at fires. § 52. It shall be the duty of the police to promptly remove, from within the said lines, all persons not designated in the last preceding section; and all persons refusing to retire, at the request of a policeman, from within the said lines, shall be deemed guilty of a misdemeanor, and forthwith arrested.

Regulations in going to or returning from fires. § 53. No fire engine, nor hook and ladder, nor hose cart, shall, in going to, or returning from any fire, or at any other time, be run, driven, wheeled, or placed upon any sidewalk, except by the special order of one of the engineers, under the penalty of twenty-five dollars for each offense, to be forfeited and paid by every person aiding or assisting in, or consenting to the violation of any one of the provisions of this section, to be recovered by the Attorney of the Corporation, for the use of the Corporation; and also under the further penalty of the expulsion of the foreman, assistant foreman, and all the members of the company.

Regulations as to engines, &c. § 54. No such fire engine, hook and ladder, or hose cart, during any fire in this city, or any report of fire, or at any time under any pretense whatever, shall be taken or removed out of its house, unless the foreman or assistant foreman, or at least two of the firemen of the company to which the same shall belong, shall be present, and consent thereto, under the penalty of ten dollars for every such offense, to be forfeited and paid by, and recovered from any and every person aiding and assisting in, or consenting to, the violation of any of the provisions of this section.

Ibid. § 55. It shall be the duty of the several engineers, and of every foreman and assistant foreman of every fire company, to report all violations of the last preceding section, to the Treasurer of the Fire Department.

Letting out engines. § 56. No fire engine shall be let out for hire, or lent, in any case, without permission from the Alderman and Councilman of the district wherein it is wanted to be used, and the Chief Engineer; and in default thereof, the firemen so offending shall be removed from the Fire Department.

§ 57. The Commissioners of the Fire Department, under the advice of the Chief Engineer, shall be authorized and empowered to take any fire engine, hook and ladder, or hose truck, from the company, and place the same in the public yard, or give the same to some other company. Taking engines, &c., from companies.

§ 58. All firemen attached to any fire engine, hose, or hook and ladder company, whose machine and implements shall have been ordered to the public yard, for want of a sufficient complement of men to manage the same, shall be attached by the Commissioners of the Fire Department to any other company they may designate; and in case of their refusal to designate such company to which they wish to be attached, they shall be liable to expulsion. Trasfer of firemen.

§ 59. Each company shall be allowed, for expense of gas, the annual sum of seventy-five dollars. Gas.

§ 60. It shall be the duty of the foreman and secretary of the several fire companies, to make an annual return of the members of their respective companies, to the Chief Engineer, as heretofore; such returns shall, however, be made, under the oath of the foreman and secretary, that the persons therein named, as members of their respective companies, are actual and active members thereof; and it shall be the duty of the Clerk of the Common Council, on the said returns being presented by the said Chief Engineer, to correct the register of the firemen, in his office, in accordance with said returns. Returns of members to the Chief Engineer.

§ 61. The Chief Engineer is directed not to receive any Ibid.

annual returns from companies, but such as conform to section first of the ordinance, passed June 22, 1842, relative to the Fire Department, as follows: "The Fire Department of the city of New York shall consist of a Chief Engineer, Assistant Engineers, fire engine men, hose men, hook and ladder and hydrant men, who shall be citizens of the United States, of the age of twenty-one years, and upwards."

Reports of the Fire Commissioners. § 62. It shall be the duty of the Foreman and Secretary of each and every engine, hose and hook and ladder company, to report to the Board of Fire Commissioners, on the second Tuesday in April and October in each year, a list of members, with the number of fires, or alarms of fire, which have occurred during the preceding six months, in the districts in which they perform duty, and the amount of duty performed by each member, which report must be sworn to before the Board of Fire Commissioners; and the Foreman and Secretary of each and every company neglecting to comply with this ordinance shall be expelled.

ARTICLE IV.

OF BELL-RINGERS.

Bell ringers, how appointed. § 63. The Mayor of the city of New York shall appoint three persons, to act as bell-ringers at each of the different alarm districts in the city of New York. Such persons shall be selected from among the exempt firemen of the city, or from such firemen as have been disabled by injuries received in the performance of their duty.

Compensation. § 64. The bell-ringers so appointed, shall receive, as remuneration for their services, the sum of six hundred dollars each, per annum, and shall be subject to removal by the Mayor, for misdemeanor or negligence of duty.

§ 65. The Comptroller is authorized and directed to pay the salaries of the bell-ringers appointed, in accordance with section 63 of this ordinance, out of the appropriation for the Fire Department. Compensation.

§ 66. A person shall be appointed to take charge of the Post-office bell, according to the rules and regulations of fire-alarm bell-ringers, and to ring the same on occasions of fires, and the sum of one hundred dollars per annum shall be allowed as compensation. Post office bill.

§ 67. All bell-ringers, and persons charged with the ringing of bells, in case of fire, shall, on neglect to comply with the requisitions of the ordinances and regulations for the ringing of bells, in cases of fire, be removed from office by the person or authority having power to remove them, on such person or authority being credibly informed of such neglect; and the person so removed shall not be reappointed to that or any other office under the Corporation, within one year after such removal. Removal of Bell-ringers for neglect.

§ 68. Upon the happening of any fire, the several alarm-bells of the district, and all other alarm-bells shall be rung, and the ringing shall be continued until the ringing of the district bell wherein the fire shall occur shall be stopped. Ringing of Fire-bells.

§ 69. The Chief Engineer shall report to the Common Council, all cases of neglect on the part of bell-ringers to churches, to ring their bells in cases of alarms of fire. Report for neglect,

§ 70. The stations for bell-ringers shall be as follows: the cupola of the City Hall; the cupola of Essex Market; the cupola of Union Market; the bell-tower in Twenty-second street; the bell-tower in Thirty-third street; the bell-tower in Macdougal street; the bell-tower at Mount Morris; the bell-tower in Marion street, and Yorkville bell-tower. Stations of bell-ringers.

ARTICLE V.

OF FIRE DISTRICTS.

Fire Districts.

§ 71. The city of New York shall be divided into eight fire districts:

1. The first fire district shall comprise all that part of the city lying north of Twenty-second street, and east of the Sixth avenue.
2. The second fire district shall comprise all that part of the city lying north of Twenty-second street, and west of Sixth avenue.
3. The third fire district shall comprise all that part of the city bounded and containing as follows: beginning at the foot of North Moore street, on the North river, and extending easterly, in a straight line, to the corner of Leonard and Church streets; thence northerly, in a straight line, to the corner of Eighth avenue and Twenty-second street; thence westerly, along Twenty-second street to the North river; thence southerly, along the North river to the place of beginning.
4. The fourth fire district shall comprise all that part of the city bounded and containing as follows: beginning at the corner of Leonard and Church streets; running thence northerly, in a straight line, to the corner of Eighth avenue and Twenty-second street; thence easterly, along Twenty-second street to Lexington avenue; thence southerly, in a straight line, to the corner of Elm and Leonard streets, and thence westerly, in a straight line, to the corner of Church and Leonard streets.
5. The fifth fire district shall comprise all that part of the city bounded and containing as follows:

commencing at the corner of Elm and Leonard streets, and running thence northerly, in a straight line, to the corner of Lexington avenue and Twenty-second street; thence easterly, along Twenty-second street, to the East river; thence southerly, and along the East river to Fourteenth street; thence southwesterly, in a straight line, to the corner of Leonard and Orange streets; thence westerly, in a straight line, to the place of beginning. Fire Districts.

6. The sixth fire district shall comprise all that part of the city bounded and containing as follows: beginning at the corner of Leonard and Orange streets, and running thence easterly, in a straight line, to the foot of Market street, on the East river; thence along the East river to Fourteenth street; thence southwesterly, in a straight line, to the place of beginning.

7. The seventh fire district shall comprise all that part of the city bounded and containing as follows: beginning at the foot of Market street, on the East river, and running thence westerly, in a straight line, to the corner of Leonard and Elm streets; thence southerly, along a straight line, intersecting Wall street, at the junction of Nassau, Wall and Broad streets, and continued through the Battery to the North river.

8. The eighth fire district shall comprise all that part of the city bounded and containing as follows: beginning at the foot of North Moore street, on the North river, and running thence easterly, in a straight line, to the corner of Leonard and Elm streets; thence southerly, along a straight line,

intersecting with Wall street, at the junction of Nassau, Wall and Broad streets, and continued through the Battery to the North river.

Signals.

§ 72. In case of fire in the first fire district, the signal shall be one stroke from the alarm bells.

In the	Second	District,	two	strokes.
"	Third	"	three	"
"	Fourth	"	four	"
"	Fifth	"	five	"
"	Sixth	"	six	"
"	Seventh	"	seven	"
"	Eighth	"	eight	"

Duties in Districts.

§ 73. All fire companies shall do duty in any two fire districts the Chief Engineer may designate, and no company shall be allowed to take their apparatus in any other district, except by his permission or direction, or in case of a general alarm.

Ibid.

§ 74. No fire company shall remove their apparatus out of the district designated by the Chief Engineer, (except as hereinbefore provided) in case of fire or alarm of fire, under penalty of being subject to expulsion or suspension from the Fire Department, unless they shall be permitted by the Chief Engineer, who may, as may also any Assistant Engineer, give the necessary signal, which is hereby declared to be the constant ringing of the alarm bell in the district in which the fire is raging, when the whole department shall proceed to the scene of conflagration.

Signal for assistance.

§ 75. The signal for assistance shall be the continual ringing of all the district bells, except on the Halls of Justice, which will always ring the district in which the fire is raging.

ARTICLE VI.

SPECIAL PROVISIONS.

§ 76. The Mayor, Recorder, Aldermen and Councilmen shall severally bear, when attending at fires, a wand with a gilded frame at the top. Insignia of City Officials at fires.

§ 77. The names and places of abode of the members of the Common Council, Engineers, Fire Wardens and Foremen of the respective companies, and Bell-ringers, shall annually in the month of June, be printed and set up in the several station-houses by the City Inspector; and whenever any fire shall happen in the night, the policemen shall give notice to each of the members of the Common Council, Engineers, FireWardens, foremen and bell-ringers, within their respective precincts; and it is moreover required of every policeman on duty, upon the breaking out of any fire, to alarm the citizens by crying fire, and mentioning the street where it may be, so that the firemen and citizens may thereby be directed where to repair; and if any policeman shall neglect so to do, he shall forfeit and pay the sum of one dollar; and if it shall happen that a chimney only shall be on fire, either by day or by night, the fire bells and the bells of the several churches in the city shall not be rung, but only on occasions where a building shall be proclaimed to be on fire; and it is enjoined on the occupants of dwellings to place a lighted candle at the windows of their respective buildings, when fire may happen at night, in order that the citizens may pass along the streets with the greater safety. List of officers to be placed in Station-houses. Duties of Police.

§ 78. The salary of the Clerk to the Commissioners of the New York Fire Department, shall be eight hundred dollars per annum. Clerk of Commissioners.

Messenger of Commissioners.

§ 79. The Commissioners of the New York Fire Department shall nominate, and the Common Council shall appoint a suitable person to be a Messenger.

Duties of Messenger.

§ 80. The said Messenger shall have charge of the meeting room of the said Commissioners, and keep the same in order; he shall have charge of the door at all meetings, and shall deliver all notices and documents as may be required by said Commissioners, and perform such other duties as they may deem necessary. Said Messenger may be removed at any time, by a majority of said Commissioners, for non-performance or neglect of any of his duties.

Salary of Messenger.

§ 81. The said Messenger shall receive an annual salary of six hundred dollars.

CHAPTER XI.

OF THE PREVENTION OF FIRES.

§ 1. If any chimney, stove pipe, or flue within this city shall take fire, the occupant of the house to which such chimney, stove pipe, or flue appertains, shall forfeit and pay five dollars. Chimneys, stove-pipes & flues.

§ 2. All carpenters, or others, making or using shavings, shall, respectively, at the close of each day, cause the same to be securely stowed in some safe place, remote from danger by means of fire, under the penalty of five dollars for each omission so to do. Shavings.

§ 3. No person shall kindle any fire, nor furnish the materials for any fire, nor in any way authorize or allow any fire to be made in any street, road or lane, or on any pier or bulkhead in this city, except for the purpose of boiling tar, which fire shall not be more than six feet from the bulkhead, or the end of the pier, under the penalty of ten dollars for every such offense. Kindling fires in streets.

§ 4. No person shall have, put, or keep, any hay or straw uncovered in any stack or pile, or in any other way exposed within one hundred yards of any building to the southward of Fourteenth street, or shall have put, or keep to the southward of said line, any hay, straw, hemp, flax, shavings, or rushes, in any building not built of stone or brick and covered with tile or slate or other fire-proof materials, which is, or shall be, within ten feet of any dwelling-house or chimney whatsoever, under the penalty of twenty-five dollars for every such offense, and the further penalty of ten dollars for every twenty-four hours the same shall so remain after a printed or written notice Hay & straw, hemp, flax, shavings and rushes.

has been given to the owner or person having charge thereof, by any Fire Warden, to remove the same.

Stables.

§ 5. No owner or occupant of any stable within this city, or any person in the employment of such owner or occupant, shall use therein any lighted candle or lamp, except the same shall be securely kept within the lantern, under the penalty of ten dollars for every such offense.

Fines, to whom appropriated.

§ 6. All the fines, penalties and forfeitures imposed on the members of the Fire Department, for not attending to fires, shall, when received, be paid to the treasurers of the respective companies aforesaid, in which the delinquencies may happen, for the use and benefit of said companies, and all the other fines, penalties and forfeitures imposed by the ordinance relating to the Fire Department and by this chapter,shall, when recovered, be paid to the Treasurer of the "Fire Department of the city of New York," for the use and benefit of the said Fire Department. The Chief Engineer shall, annually, on the second Monday of December in each year, report to the Common Council the amount of the sums which may be received by the Fire Department of the city of New York, and the application thereof.

Suits for penalties.

§ 7. It shall be lawful for the Fire Department of the city of New York, and for the respective companies thereof, or persons duly authorized by them to receive, sue for, and recover, in the name of the Mayor, Aldermen and Commonalty of the city of New York, all the fines, penalties and forfeitures hereby imposed and appropriated for the respective uses as aforesaid.

CHAPTER XII.

OF THE STORING AND KEEPING OF GUNPOWDER AND FIREWORKS.

§ 1. It shall not be lawful for any person or persons, except as hereinafter provided, to have or keep any quantity of gunpowder in any house, store, building, or other place in the city of New York, to the northward of a line running through the centre of Sixty-second street, from the North to the East river. Gunpowder.

§ 2. It shall be lawful for the Mayor to grant licenses for the erection of magazines for the storage of gunpowder in this city, to the northward of Sixty-second street, but no more than six such magazines shall at any time be licensed or permitted. Such magazines shall be erected in such convenient places as may be designated by the respective licenses therefor, and shall be placed remote from any dwelling, and shall be built in accordance with plans and specifications to be approved by, and under the direction of the Superintendent of Repairs and Supplies, who shall have authority to prescribe the materials of which such magazines shall be composed, and the manner in which the same shall be constructed. Such magazines, shall, at all times, be subject to the authority and direction of the Common Council, who may make all such rules and regulations in respect thereto as they may deem the public interests require, and they may, at any time, revoke any such license, or cause such magazines, or any of them, to be removed from place to place. Licenses for Magazines.

§ 3. Nothing in this ordinance contained shall apply to the storing and keeping of gunpowder in the State Arsenal in Fifth avenue, above Sixty-fourth street. Arsenal.

Penalties.

§ 4. Every person storing any gunpowder in the portion of the city of New York, in the first section of this chapter specified, (except in such licensed magazines,) without the license provided by the second section of this chapter, and any person who shall or may, in pursuance of any license granted under the said last mentioned section, store or keep any gunpowder in any such magazine or place, and shall not in all respects fully comply with the lawful directions of the Superintendent of Repairs and Supplies, or of the Common Council, as provided by this chapter, shall forfeit and pay the sum of one hundred dollars for each day during which any such gunpowder shall be so stored or kept, contrary to the provisions of this chapter ; and when any person or persons shall have obtained any such license as is provided for in the said second section of this chapter, and shall, in any respect, fail to comply with the said directions of the said Superintendent of Repairs and Supplies, or the said Common Council, such person shall, from the time of any such failure to comply therewith, be deemed to have violated the provisions of this chapter, and shall be subject to its penalty, in the same manner as if no such license had been granted.

Fireworks.

§ 5. No person or persons shall store any fireworks, of any kind or description, other than Chinese fire-crackers, within the fire limits of the city of New York, except as is hereinafter provided.

Ibid.

§ 6. Fireworks, excepting colored pot and lance wheels, and other works of brilliant colored fires, not exceeding in value one thousand dollars, may be kept for retailing within the fire limits, from the tenth day of June to the tenth day of July of each year, and no longer, on a written permission; such permission to be granted by the Chief Engineer of the Fire Department.

§ 7. If any fireworks are kept in violation of the provisions of this chapter, the same may be seized or taken by any police officer of the said city, upon the order of the Mayor, of a captain of police, or any one of the fire wardens; and the same shall be kept by such Mayor, captain or fire warden, upon whose order the same were taken, at some suitable place, beyond the fire limits, and sold at public auction, within one week after such taking; three days' notice of the time and place of such sale shall be given to the person or persons from whose possession the same were taken, and the proceeds, after deducting expenses of conveyance, storage and sale, shall, within one one week after the sale, be paid over by the person ordering the seizure, to the Treasurer of the Fire Department Fund, for the use and benefit of the said fund. Seizure.

CHAPTER XIII.

OF THE FIRING OF FIRE-ARMS, CANNONS AND FIREWORKS.

Firing on the Battery.

§ 1. Every cannon or piece of artillery that shall hereafter be discharged or fired off upon the Battery, shall be placed at the easterly end thereof, as near to the flagstaff as practicable, and in the immediate rear of the paved walk fronting the water, and shall be ranged and pointed in the direction and toward Governor's Island.

Ibid.

§ 2. No cannon or piece of artillery shall be discharged or fired off upon the Battery, except at the place, and ranging in the manner provided in the first section of this chapter.

Firing at Castle Garden.

§ 3. No cannon or piece of artillery shall be discharged or fired off upon the premises of Castle Clinton or Garden, except on the westerly side thereof; and the same shall only be discharged or fired off in the direction and toward the westerly shore of the Hudson river.

Firing in the Parks.

§ 4. No cannon or piece of artillery shall be discharged or fired off in the Park (except on the Fourth day of July, and then only cannon not over six pounds calibre) Washington square, or Union square, nor in any street, lane, avenue, or public place in the city of New York, south of Twenty-third street, except as is provided in the foregoing sections of this chapter.

Penalties.

§ 5. Any person or persons, commander or other officer, or private of any artillery or other military company, troop of horse, corps, regiment, battalion, brigade or division, who shall violate any or either of the provisions of this chapter of these ordinances, or shall cause or permit the same to be done, shall severally forfeit and pay the sum of fifty dollars for each discharge or firing off of any piece of artillery, to be paid into the city treasury for the use of the city.

§ 6. No tavern-keeper, keeper of a public house, garden or place of resort, nor any other person, shall suffer or permit any person to practice with or fire off any pistol, gun, fowling-piece or other fire-arms, in or upon his or her premises, nor shall suffer or permit any pistol gallery, erected in his or her house, or upon his or her premises, to be used for the purpose of practicing with any pistol gun, fowling-piece or other fire-arms, upon the first day of the week, called Sunday, under the penalty of fifty dollars for each offense, to be sued for and recovered from the person keeping such public house, tavern, public garden, pistol gallery, place of resort or premises; and also the further penalty of fifty dollars for each offense, to be sued for and recovered from the person firing off or practicing with a pistol, gun, fowling-piece or other fire-arms; and in case such person so offending shall be an apprentice, such penalty shall be sued for and recovered from the master of such apprentice, or in case such person so offending shall be a minor and not an apprentice, the same shall be sued for and recovered from the father of, or in case of the death of the father, then from the mother or guardian of such minor. Firing arms on Sundays.

§ 7. No person shall fire, discharge or set off in the city of New York, any rocket, cracker, torpedo, squib, balloon, or other fireworks, or thing containing any substance in a state of combustion, under the penalty of five dollars for each offense. Firing Fire-works.

§ 8. No person shall sell, or expose for sale, nor fire, discharge or set off, in the city of New York, any fire- Selling and firing certain fire-works.

works called or known by the name of "snakes," or "chasers," or any fireworks called or known by the name of "double-headers," nor any fireworks under any other name, composed of the same material and of the same character of those fireworks specified in this section, under the penalty of fifty dollars for each offense, to be sued for and recovered of the person selling or exposing the same for sale, firing off or discharging the same. And in case such person shall be an apprentice, such penalty shall be sued for, and recovered of and from the master of such apprentice. In case such person shall be a minor, and not an apprentice, the same shall be sued for, and recovered of, and from the father, or in case of the death of the father, then of and from the mother or guardian of such minor.

Firing arms within the city.

§ 9. No person shall fire or discharge any gun, pistol, fowling-piece or other fire-arms in the city of New York, under the penalty of ten dollars for each offense.

CHAPTER XIV.

OF PAVING, REPAVING AND REPAIRING THE CARRIAGE-WAYS OF STEEETS AND AVENUES.

Paving streets.

§ 1. All streets in the city of New York of twenty-two feet in width and upwards, shall be laid or paved in the middle, which part shall remain as a cart-way, and shall have a gutter or kennel on each side next adjoining the foot-path, and shall be paved with sufficient paving stone and arched in such a manner as the Croton Aqueduct Board shall direct.

Expense of paving streets, how borne.

§ 2. Whenever the carriage-way of any of the streets in the city of New York, or part of the same, not less than the space or distance between, and including the intersection of two streets, shall be repaired or newly paved and the crosswalks laid, and the sidewalks extended to the width required by law, at the expense of the individual owners of the lots in the same, and the work approved by the chiefs of bureau having special cognizance thereof, such streets, or parts of streets, shall forever thereafter be paved, repaired and repaved at the expense of the Corporation; but this section shall not be construed to apply to sidewalks, but to the pavement or carriage-way of streets only; and nothing in this section contained shall be construed to apply to any wooden pavement in said city.

Citizens may pave streets.

§ 3. Any citizen, or number of citizens, shall be allowed to pave the street opposite to his or their property, where the same shall extend from the intersection of one cross street to the intersection of another, provided the same be done in conformity to the regulations of the Common Council.

Regulations as to paving.

§ 4. All pavements hereafter to be laid in any of the streets or lanes of this city, by the Water Purveyor or contractors for the construction of sewers, or for the laying of water, gas or other pipes, shall, after the pavement is laid or driven down, have covered over them one inch in thickness of pure sand, and no more.

Ibid.

§ 5. Any and all persons other than the Water Purveyor, who may hereafter pave, or cause to be paved, any street, lane or other thoroughfare, or portion thereof, in this city, shall have the sand, dirt and rubbish cleaned off said street, lane or thoroughfare, or any part thereof, within twelve days after any such pavement shall be completed, except such pavement as shall be laid over pipes, which shall be cleared off within six days after the same shall be laid; this section shall be so construed as to apply to the removal of all sand, dirt or rubbish collected in any part of any and all streets, lanes and thoroughfares covered by any pavement so done or laid, or excavation that may have been made, or other work done in pursuance thereof; and no contract for paving, in pursuance of this section, shall be accepted as completed, unless the Water Purveyor shall certify that this section has been fully complied with.

Ibid.

§ 6. Any person or persons, excepting the Water Purveyor, neglecting or refusing to remove the dirt, sand or rubbish, mentioned in section five of this chapter, within the time specified therein, shall forfeit and pay the sum of twenty-five dollars for each offense; and in addition thereto, the Water Purveyor shall cause the same to be removed at the expense of the party so neglecting or refusing, who shall be liable to repay and refund the same, and which shall be collected and paid into the city treasury.

Spilling dirt from carts.

§ 7. Any contractors, or other person or persons, causing any cart to be loaded and heaped up with manure, sand, earth, mud, clay or rubbish, so that the contents, or any part thereof, shall be scattered in any street, avenue, lane, pier or bulkhead in this city, shall forfeit and pay the sum of five dollars for each offense.

§ 8. It shall not be lawful for either of the gas companies of this city, to break up any of the pavements of this city, without the permission of the Croton Aqueduct Board, and such consent shall not be given until the party applying therefor shall enter into a stipulation, satisfactory to the said Board, to repair and replace the said pavement to the satisfaction of the said Board at his and their own expense, by a day to be named in such permit; and if any person or persons shall neglect and refuse to repair and replace the same, in accordance with such stipulation and permit, they shall forfeit and pay for each offense the sum of fifty dollars; and in addition thereto, shall be liable to pay the expense of repairing and replacing such pavement, and which shall be done by and under the direction of the Water Purveyor.

Breaking pavements by Gas companies.

§ 9. It shall be lawful for the persons employed to pave or repave any street in the city of New York, to place proper obstructions across such street or cart way, for the purpose of preserving the pavement then newly made, or to be made, until the same shall be fit for use; leaving at all times a sufficient passage for foot passengers, and giving at least three days' notice of such obstruction, by written or printed notices, put up in at least three of the most conspicuous places in the street.

Obstructions in paivng streets.

§ 10. No person or persons shall, without the consent of the Water Purveyor, in writing, or without the consent of the person superintending said paving, throw down, displace or remove any such obstruction mentioned in the last preceding section of this chapter, under the penalty of fifteen dollars for every such offense.

Ibid.

Obstructions in paving streets.

§ 11. Nothing contained in this chapter shall be construed to authorize any person or persons to stop up or obstruct more than the space of one block and one intersection at the same time, in any one street, or to keep the same so stopped up for more than two days after the cart-way is finished.

Ibid.

§ 12. Whenever any person or persons shall have authority, under any contract with the Corporation, or any officer thereof, or under any permit authorizing the same, to remove the pavement from, or to excavate, or to occupy or use any part of the public streets and avenues in the city, so as to obstruct the travel in any streets or avenues, and to prevent the same from being used for the time being for the purposes of travel, such person or persons shall erect or cause to be erected, in conspicuous positions, at the several points of intersection of such street or avenue so obstructed, with the cross streets nearest to such obstruction, a suitable notice of such obstruction; which notice shall be in such manner and form as the Croton Aqueduct Board may at any time direct.

Penalty.

§ 13. Every person who shall violate this provision shall be subject to a penalty of ten dollars, to be sued for and recovered in any court of competent jurisdiction.

Record of streets paved

§ 14. The Croton Aqueduct Board shall keep a book, containing an account of all streets, and parts of streets to be paved, repaired and repaved, at the expense of the Corporation.

CHAPTER XV.

OF FLAGGING AND LAYING AND REPAIRING SIDEWALKS, AND CURB AND GUTTER STONES.

§ 1. All streets in the city of New York, of twenty-two feet in width and upward, shall have sidewalks on each side thereof, laid with brown, or gray, or oblong flat stones. Side-walks, with what to be flagged.

§ 2. In all streets in the city of New York, of the width of forty feet and upward, which are paved, or shall hereafter be paved or repaved, the sidewalks or footwalks between the lines of the streets and kennels shall be of the following width, that is to say: Width of side walks.

1. In all streets forty feet wide, ten feet.
2. In all streets fifty feet wide, thirteen feet.
3. In all streets sixty feet wide, fifteen feet.
4. In all streets seventy feet wide, eighteen feet.
5. In all streets eighty feet wide, nineteen feet.
6. In all streets above eighty feet, and not exceeding one hundred feet, twenty feet.
7. In all streets of more than one hundred feet, twentwo feet, and no more.

§ 3. In all streets less than forty feet in width, such proportion thereof as may be directed by the Street Commissioner, shall be used and flagged for sidewalks and footpaths. Ibid.

§ 4. All sidewalks in the city of New York shall be raised from the curb stone in the proportion of two inches on ten feet, under the penalty of ten dollars, to be sued for and recovered from the persons laying and fixing the same, and the owner or owners of the lot fronting on the sidewalk, severally and respectively. Height of side-walks.

§ 5. No person shall extend the sidewalk before his lot beyond that of his neighbor, in any street where the same is not yet extended to the width allowed by law, under Extent of flagging.

the penalty of ten dollars for each offense, to be sued for and recovered from the person or persons so violating, and the owner or owners of the lots fronting on such sidewalk, severally and respectively.

Extent of flagging.

§ 6. The last preceding section of this chapter shall not be construed to prevent the extending of any such sidewalks, when a majority of the owners of property on the same side of the street, and between the two nearest corners, by and with the permission of the Street Commissioner, agree to and do extend the sidewalks in front of their respective lots of ground in like manner.

Removal of flagging.

§ 7. No sidewalk, or any part of a sidewalk, laid with brick or flagging, in any part of the city of New York, shall hereafter be taken up, or the brick or flagging removed therefrom, for any purpose whatever, without the written permission of the Street Commissioner, under the penalty of twenty-five dollars for every such offense.

All sidewalks and private c.rt-ways .o be flagged.

§ 8. All private cart-ways crossing any of the sidewalks of the city of New York, and all sidewalks whatever, to the south of Delancey and Spring streets, including said streets, shall be paved with brown or gray square, oblong or flat stones, hewn and laid closely together; and not with brick or with round or paving stones, under the penalty of ten dollars upon the owner and occupant of the lot in front of which such cart-way or sidewalk shall be, severally and respectively.

Ibid.

§ 9. In case any part of such private cart-way, or any part of such sidewalk shall not be paved, repaved or repaired according to the provisions of the last section, it shall be lawful for the said Street Commissioner, or Superintendent of Street Improvements, to order, in writing, the same to be done, within a time mentioned in such order; at the expiration of which time the same may be done under the direction of the said Commissioner or Superintendent, and the expense thereof collected of the owner or owners, occupant or occupants of the lot fronting thereon.

§ 10. All curb stones which shall hereafter be laid for the purpose of supporting the sidewalks, shall not be less than three feet in length, five inches thick, and twenty inches wide throughout, and shall be of the best hard blue, or gray granite, and cut, prepared and laid in the following manner, that is to say: ten inches of the stone shall be laid below the kennel, and ten inches above it, except where the length of curb stone to be laid or relaid shall be less than the space between the streets crossing that in which it is to be laid; in which case if the curb stone in front of the lots adjoining shall be put eight inches above the gutter stone, the curb to be laid or raised as aforesaid shall not be placed more than eight inches above the gutter stone, unless the person or persons laying or relaying the same, shall, by permission of the owner or owners of the lots adjoining, at his, her or their own expense, raise the adjoining sidewalk or sidewalks, and repave the same in a proper manner, for a space of at least five feet in width, so as to prevent any abrupt irregularity in the pavement of the sidewalk; the top of the stone shall be cut to a bevel of one inch, the front be cut smooth, and to a fair line to the depth of fourteen inches; the ends from top to bottom to be truly squared, so as to form close and even joints; and the front so laid as to present a fair and unbroken line, under the penalty of ten dollars for each or any violation of either of the provisions of this section, to be sued for and recovered from the persons laying and fixing the same, and the owner or owners of the lot fronting on the sidewalk so fixed, severally and respectively. All gutter stones which shall hereafter be laid in this city, shall be of the best hard freestone or granite, at least thir- Curb-stones.

ty inches in length, fourteen inches in width and six inches thick; and shall be cut to a fair and level surface without windings, with true and parallel sides, and the ends squared so as to form tight and close joints, under the penalty of ten dollars, to be sued for and recovered from the person or persons laying the same, and the owner or owners of the lot fronting on the sidewalk or street, severally and respectively.

Ranging of side-walks.

§ 11. If any street, when paved, shall not exactly range, the gutter or outside of the foot-path or sidewalk, shall be laid out and made as nearly in a straight line as the street will permit; and the ascent and descent of the same shall be regulated by the Superintendent of Street Improvements, and a profile thereof, with the regulations distinctly marked thereon, shall be deposited and kept in the office of the Street Commissioner.

Side-walks, when to be flagged.

§ 12. When any carriage-way shall have been paved, and a majority of the owners of lots on the same block shall have regulated and paved their sidewalks, the Street Commissioner shall give notice to the owner or owners, or occupant or occupants, of any lots in front of which the sidewalks shall not be paved, to regulate and pave the same, within a certain time, to be designated in such notice.

Ibid.

§ 13. In case of any neglect or refusal to comply with the requisitions contained in the notice mentioned in the last preceding section, the owner or owners, occupant or occupants, shall forfeit the penalty of twenty-five dollars for each neglect or refusal, severally and respectively.

Who to flag and repair sidewalks.

§ 14. The owner or owners, lessee or lessees, occupant or occupants of any house or other building or vacant lot fronting on any street or avenue, shall, at his, her, or their charge and expense, well and sufficiently pave, according to the ordinances, and keep and maintain in good repair, the sidewalks and curb and gutter of such street or avenue, in front of any such house or other building, or vacant lot.

§ 15. Upon complaint being made to the Street Commissioner, to his satisfaction, that any sidewalk and curb and gutter, or either, are not paved or repaired according to the ordinances, it shall be lawful for the said Commissioners to cause a notice to be served upon the owner or owners, lessee or lessees, occupant or occupants, of any such house or other building, or vacant lot of ground fronting on any street or avenue, to repair or relay, as the case may require, the sidewalk and curb and gutter, or either, in front of the same, within ten days after the service of such notice.

Who to flag and repair Sidewalks.

§ 16. In default of such owner or owners, lessee or lessees, occupant or occupants, repairing or relaying, as the case may require, such sidewalks and curb and gutter, or either, within the time required by said notice, and complying with the said notice, it shall be lawful for the Street Commissioner to order the same to be done, and in case the expense thereof shall not exceed the sum of two hundred and fifty dollars, to appoint such person or persons to do the same as he shall deem proper; and in case such expense shall exceed the aforesaid sum of two hundred and fifty dollars, the same shall be done by contract, according to the ordinances.

Ibid.

§ 17. The expense of such work, together with the expense of surveying the same, and certifying to the work done and materials furnished by one of the city surveyors, shall be paid out of the appropriation for sidewalks.

Ibid.

§ 18. It shall be the duty of the Street Commissioner, immediately upon the completion of such work, and the

Ibid.

payment thereof, to report the same to the Corporation Attorney, who shall recover the amount to be paid, with ten dollars as penalty, from the owner or owners, lessee or lessees, occupant or occupants, of any such house or other building, in front of which the expense was incurred, in any court having jurisdiction thereof, in the name of the Mayor, Aldermen and Commonalty of the city of New York.

Penalties on sidewalks. § 19. It shall be the duty of the Corporation Attorney, in returning to the Comptroller an account of moneys recovered in such suits, to specify that the same were recovered "for penalties on sidewalks," and it shall be the duty of the Comptroller to credit the amount thus paid to the fund appropriated as aforesaid.

CHAPTER XVI.

OF SEWERS AND DRAINS.

§ 1. All sewers or drains in any of the streets, avenues, and public places in the city of New York, shall be in charge of the Croton Aqueduct Board, whose duty it shall be to keep the same in good order and condition, to cause such repairs to be made to them, and to the receiving basins, culverts, openings, or any part connected therewith, as may, from time to time, become necessary, and to cause the same to be well and sufficiently cleansed, and kept free from obstructions. General cognizance over Sewers and Drains.

§ 2. The manner of piercing or opening into any of said sewers or drains shall be prescribed by said Board, which shall also determine the form, size and material of which all connections made therewith shall be composed, and shall have authority to grant permission to make lateral connections with said sewers. Piercing or opening Sewers or Drains

§ 3. The Croton Aqueduct Board shall have authority to grant permission to persons to construct at their own expense, sewers or drains, or to lay pipes, to connect with any sewers or drains built in any of the streets or avenues of the city, which they may deem proper and judicious, on being furnished by the applicants with the written consent of a majority of the owners of property of the street or avenue in front of which said sewer, drain or pipe is to pass: such permission to be conditioned, that the persons applying therefor shall comply with the ordinances of the Corporation in relation to excavating the streets, be responsible for damages or injuries caused to persons, animals or property, by reason of any neglect or carelessness Construction of Sewers & Drains by individuals.

connected with the work permitted; that no claim be made by them, or their successors in interest, if the same be taken up by authority of the Corporation; nor exemption from assessment for building sewers or drains in the vicinity of their property.

Connections with Sewers and Drains.

§ 4. No connection shall be made with any sewer or drain, without the written permission of the Croton Aqueduct Board; and any connection or opening made into any sewer or drain without such permission, or in a manner different from the mode prescribed for such opening by said Board, shall subject the person making the same, and the owner of the premises directing it, respectively, to a penalty of fifty dollars.

Ibid.

§ 5. All permissions given by the said Board, to connect with sewers and drains, and all sewers, drains or pipes constructed and laid by their permission, to connect with any sewers or drains in any of the streets or avenues of the city, shall be upon the express condition that the Mayor, Aldermen and Commonalty of this city may at any time revoke and annul the same; and the persons making such connections, or their successors in interest, shall have no right to demand or claim any damages in consequence of such permission being revoked and annulled.

Ibid.

§ 6. All openings into any streets or drains for the purpose of making connection therewith from any house, cellar, vault, yard or other premises, shall be made by persons to be licensed by the Croton Aqueduct Board, in writing, to perform such work; and the said persons before being so licensed, shall execute a bond to the Mayor, Aldermen and Commonalty of the city of New York, in a sufficient penal sum, with surety, conditioned that they will carefully make the openings into any sewers or drains in the manner prescribed by said Board without injuring them; leave no obstructions of any description whatever in them, and properly close up the sewer or drain around the connection made by them, and make no opening into the arch of any sewer or drain; that they will faithfully comply with the ordinances relating to opening and excavating streets, be responsible for any damages or injuries that may occur to persons, animals or property, by reason of any neglect or carelessness on their part, connected with said work, and that they will properly refill and ram the earth, and suitably restore the pavement taken up for excavating, and repave the same, should it settle or become out of order within three months thereafter; and in case any person so licensed shall neglect to repair the pavement aforesaid within twenty-four hours after being notified, the said Board may cause the same to be done, and charge the expense thereof to the person so neglecting.

Fee for connections with Sewers and Drains.

§ 7. Ten dollars shall be paid to the said Board for permission to connect from each house, store or building, with any sewer or drain. Each hotel, boarding-house, or public building, covering more ground than twenty-five feet by fifty feet, shall pay proportionally for such additional space of ground covered by each respectively. Manufactories, breweries, distilleries and the like, for permission to connect with sewers or drains, for the purpose of carrying off water or fluid that will not deposit sediment or obstruction, shall pay such sums as shall be fixed and determined by said Board; and any manufacturer, brewer, distiller or the like, permitting any substance to flow into any sewer, drain or receiving basin, which shall form a deposit that tends to fill said sewer, drain or basin, shall be subject to a penalty of fifty dollars for each offense.

Moneys received for permits.

§ 8. The Board aforesaid shall keep a record of all permits granted by them for connections with sewers or drains, and shall pay to the treasurer of the city all sums received by them, by virtue of this chapter, and render an account thereof, once in each week, to the Comptroller, verified by oath or affirmation; the sums so paid and accounted for, shall be applied towards repaying the expenditures incurred by the treasury on account of repairs to, and cleaning of, sewers, drains and their appendages; and said Board is authorized to draw upon the Comptroller, from time to time, for such necessary sums as shall be required for the due carrying into effect the provisions of this chapter; and they shall, once in each month, render an account to the Comptroller, with the vouchers thereof, of all moneys expended by them, drawn as aforesaid.

Connections with Sewers or Drains.

§ 9. All connections with sewers or drains, used for the purpose of carrying off animal refuse from water closets or otherwise, and slops of kitchens, shall have fixtures for a sufficiency of Croton water, to be so applied as to properly carry off such matters, under the penalty of five dollars for each day the same are permitted to remain without such fixtures for supplying said water.

Inspection of Sewers.

§ 10. Said Board shall have authority to employ a suitable person, at a compensation not to exceed one dollar and fifty cents per day, to examine the condition of all sewers, receiving basins, culverts and their appendages, and fixtures to connections therewith.

Regulations as to Sewers and Receiving Basins.

§ 11. No butcher's offal, or garbage, dead animals, or obstructions of any kind whatsoever, shall be placed, thrown or deposited in any receiving basin or sewer; and any person so offending or causing any such obstruction or substance to be placed so as to be carried into such basin or sewer, shall be subject to a penalty of ten dollars for each offense; and any person injuring, breaking or removing any portion of any receiving basin, covering-flag, man-hole, vent or any part of any sewer or drain, or obstructing the mouth of any sewer or drain, shall be subject to a penalty of twenty dollars for each offense; nor shall any quantity of marble or other stone, iron, lead, timber, or any other substance, exceeding one ton in weight, be placed or deposited upon any wharf or bulkhead through which any sewer or drain may run ; nor upon or over any sewer or drain where the same shall be within three feet of the surface of the street, under the penalty of fifty dollars for each offense, to be recovered of the person or persons causing or permitting the same.

§ 12. It shall be the duty of the policemen of the several wards to be vigilant in the enforcement of the provisions of this chapter, and report any violations thereof to the Corporation Attorney. The captains of the several police districts shall, on observing or being informed of the opening of, or excavating in, any street or avenue, require the person making such opening or excavation, to exhibit to him the authority or permission for such opening; and if none have been given by the proper officer, or if the exhibition thereof be refused, said captain of police shall, without delay, make complaint to the Attorney of the Corporation, and report the same to the Croton Aqueduct Board. Duties of Police as to violations, &c.

§ 13. It shall be the duty of every person having charge of the sweeping and cleaning of the streets in the several wards, to see that the gutters are properly scraped out before the water is suffered to flow from any hydrant for the purpose of washing the same, in order that no substance or obstruction be carried into any of the receiving basins ; every person violating this section, to be subject to a penalty of five dollars for each offense. Duties of those cleaning streets.

14. In the building of all sewers under ordinances of Connection pipes

the Common Council, it shall be discretionary with the executive department, under whose direction the same are ordered to be built, to lay so many connection pipes from the sewers to the line of curb stones, as the said department may deem necessary, unless otherwise ordered by the Common Council; the expense thereof to be borne by the owners or occupants of the houses and lots intended to be benefited thereby.

Regulations connected with Gas pipes.

§ 15. Whenever a sewer or culvert is to be constructed, altered, or repaired in any street in the city of New York, in which the gas pipes of either the Manhattan or New York Gaslight companies are laid, it shall be the duty of the contractor or contractors thereof to give notice in writing, of the same to the said companies, or to the one whose pipes are laid in the street about being disturbed by the construction, alteration, or repairing of such sewer or culvert, at least twenty-four hours before breaking ground therefor.

Ibid.

§ 16. It shall be the duty of the said gas companies, or the one whose pipes are about being disturbed by the construction, alteration or repairing of any sewer or culvert, on the receipt of the notice provided for in the preceding section, to remove or otherwise protect and replace the main and service-pipes, lamp-posts, and lamps when necessary, under the direction of the Croton Aqueduct Board, and all expenses or damages incurred or sustained by either of the said companies thereby, unless the same shall have been caused by or through the negligence or carelessness of the contractor or contractors, or neglect of said companies, shall form a portion of the expenses of such sewer or culvert, and shall be assessed and collected in the same manner as the other expenses thereof—provided, however, that the company notified in accordance with the preceding section shall comply with such notice, by causing the pipes, lamp-posts and lamps to be protected and replaced when necessary, during the progress of the work; and shall also furnish a bill of such expenses or damages, if any, duly certified by the inspector appointed by the Croton Aqueduct Board, to the assessors of said sewer or culvert, within five days after receipt of notice of the completion thereof.

§ 17. The said inspector, appointed by the Croton Aqueduct Board, shall, in addition to the usual certificate, furnish to the said assessors a certificate, stating whether or not such expenses or damages, or any and what part thereof, have been caused by or through the negligence or carelessness of the contractor or contractors of the sewer or culvert, and any such expenses or damages as shall be so certified to have been caused by the negligence or carelessness of the contractor or contractors, shall be charged to him or them, and shall be deducted from the amount to be paid him or them, and shall be paid to the company by whom such bill shall have been rendered. Regulations connected with Gas pipes.

§ 18. The preceding provisions shall be made part of every contract hereafter made for constructing, altering or repairing any sewer or culvert in any street of this city in which the pipes of either the Manhattan or New York Gaslight companies shall be laid, at the time of making such contract. Ibid.

§ 19. It shall be the duty of the person or persons by whom or for whose benefit any excavation is to be made for constructing, altering, or repairing a vault, waste-pipe or drain, in any street of this city, to give notice, in writing, thereof, to the company whose pipes are laid in the street about to be disturbed by the construction, alteration or repairing of such vault, waste-pipe or drain, at Ibid.

least twenty-four hours before commencing the same; and such person or persons shall, at his or their expense, sustain, secure and protect said pipes from injury, and replace and pack the earth wherever the same shall have been removed, loosened or disturbed, under or around them, so that such pipes shall be well and substantially supported; and if such person or persons shall fail so to sustain, secure and protect said pipes from injury, or to replace and pack the earth under or around them, as by the provisions of this section required, then the same may be done by the company to whom the same may belong, and the cost thereof, and all damages sustained by either of said companies thereby, shall be paid by said person or persons to said company, and the said company may, in default thereof, maintain an action against him or them therefor.

Regulations connected with Gas pipes.

§ 20. The provisions of the last preceding section shall be made part and a condition of every permit that shall be hereafter granted to any person or persons for making any excavation for the construction, alteration or repairing any vault, waste-pipe or drain in any street in which the pipes of either of the said companies shall be laid at the time of granting such permit, provided said company, or either of them, provide said permits, or pay a just proportion therefor.

CHAPTER XVII.

OF THE LIGHTING OF PUBLIC GAS LAMPS.

§ 1. No person, unless authorized by the Manhattan Gaslight Company, shall, at any time, light, or cause to be lighted, any public lamp which said company is or shall be required to light, under their contract made with the Mayor, Aldermen and Commonalty of the city of New York, dated May 5, 1848; and no person, unless authorized by the New York Gaslight Company, shall, at any time, light, or cause to be lighted, any public lamp which the said New York Gaslight Company is or shall be required to light, under their contract, made with the said Mayor, Aldermen and Commonalty of the said city. Any person violating the provisions of this section shall thereby incur and be liable to a penalty of five dollars, payable to the company whose lamps shall be so lighted, or caused to be lighted, for every such violation; and either of said companies shall be liable to a like fine of five dollars, for wilfully neglecting to light any lamp according to contract, said fine to be payable to the city treasury.

CHAPTER XVIII.

OF VAULTS, CISTERNS AND AREAS.

Permission to construct vaults or cisterns.

§ 1. The Croton Aqueduct Board, on application for that purpose, during the recess of the Common Council, is hereby empowered to give permission to construct any vaults or cisterns in the streets, provided, in the opinion of a majority of said Board, no injury will come to the public thereby.

Ibid.

§ 2. No person shall cause or procure any vault or cistern to be constructed or made in any of the streets in the city of New York, without the written permission of the Croton Aqueduct Board, under the penalty of one hundred dollars, to be sued for and recovered from such person and the master builder, or person who made the same, severally and respectively.

Ibid.

§ 3. Every application for permission to erect such vault or cistern shall be in writing, signed by the person making the same, and shall state the number of square feet of ground which is required for the same, and the intended length and width of the same.

Ibid.

§ 4. After obtaining permission to construct or make such vault or cistern, and previous to the commencement thereof, the person so applying shall forthwith pay to the Chamberlain of the city of New York, the sum of fifteen cents for each square foot of ground mentioned as required for such vault or cistern, under the penalty of fifty dollars.

Size of vaults or cisterns.

§ 5. No person shall erect or build, or cause or permit any vault or cistern to be made, which shall extend further than the line of the sidewalk or curb stone of any street under the width of forty feet, under the penalty of two hundred and fifty dollars; and in all streets of forty feet wide and upward, it shall be at the discretion of the Croton Aqueduct Board how far such vault or cistern may be extended, not exceeding two fifths of said street.

§ 6. It shall be the duty of every person for whom any vault or cistern may be constructing, to procure the same to be measured by one of the City Surveyors, and to deliver to the Croton Aqueduct Board a certificate of the said measurement, signed by such surveyor, before the arching of such vault or cistern shall be commenced, under the penalty of one hundred dollars. Regulations of constructing vaults or cisterns.

§ 7. If it shall appear by such certificate or otherwise that such vault or cistern occupies a greater number of square feet than shall have been paid for as aforesaid, the owner of such vault or cistern, and the master builder, by whom or under whose direction such vault or cistern shall be constructed, shall, in addition to the penalty imposed in and by section four of this chapter, severally and respectively forfeit and pay the sum of fifty cents for each square foot of ground occupied by such vault or cistern, over and above the number of square feet paid for as aforesaid. Ibid.

§ 8. All vaults or cisterns shall be constructed of brick or stone, and the outward side of the grating or opening into the street, shall be either within twelve inches of the outside of the curb stone of the sidewalk, or within twelve inches of the coping of the area in front of the house to which such vault shall belong, under the penalty of one hundred dollars, to be paid by the owner or person making or causing the same to be made. Ibid.

§ 9. All grates to vaults shall be made of iron, the bars whereof shall be three-fourths of an inch wide, and one- Grates of Vaults.

half of an inch thick, and not more than three-quarters of an inch apart, under the penalty of twenty-five dollars, to be paid by the owner of the vault or occupant of the house to which the same shall belong, severally and respectively.

Prevention of accidents.

§ 10. Every owner or occupant of any house or lot of ground, within the paved parts of the city of New York, before which any vault, pit, hole, cistern or well, shall be made, and every person making or having charge of such vault, pit, hole, cistern or well, shall, during the whole of every night while such vault, pit, hole, cistern or well, shall be opened or uncovered, cause a lighted lamp or lantern, to be placed and kept at some convenient spot, so as to cast its light upon such vault, pit, hole, cistern or well, under the penalty of ten dollars.

Time for completion of vaults or cisterns.

§ 11. All vaults or cisterns shall be completed, and the ground closed over them, within three weeks after they are commenced, under the penalty of five dollars for every day thereafter, during which the same shall remain uninclosed, to be recovered from the owner or builder of the same, severally and respectively.

Size of area.

§ 12. No area in the front of any building in the city of New York, shall extend more than one-fifteenth part of the width of any street, nor in any case more than five feet, measuring from the inner wall of such area to the building; nor shall the railing of such area be placed more than six inches from the inside of the coping on the wall of such area, under the penalty of two hundred and fifty dollars, to be recovered from the owner and builder thereof, severally and respectively.

Inclosure of areas.

§ 13. Every area shall be inclosed with a railing, the gates of which shall be so constructed as to open inwardly, under the penalty of two hundred and fifty dollars for each offense, to be recovered from the owner or builder thereof, severally and respectively.

§ 14. Every description of opening below the surface of the street, in front of any shop, store, house or other building, whether covered or open, shall be considered and held to be a vault or cistern, within the meaning of this chapter; and the master builder, or owner or person for whom the same shall be made or built, shall be liable to the provisions, payments and penalties of this chapter, severally and respectively. General provisions.

§ 15. The last preceding section of this chapter shall not be construed to refer to those openings which are used exclusively as places for descending to the cellar floor of any building or buildings by means of steps. Ibid.

§ 16. No person shall remove, or cause or procure, or suffer or permit to be removed, or insecurely fixed, so that the same can be moved in its bed, any grate or covering to the opening or aperture of any vault in the city of New York, under the penalty of ten dollars. Grates and other coverings, of openings of.

§ 17. The last preceding section of this chapter shall not be construed to prevent the removal of such grate or covering, provided the aperture to such vault, during the removal of such grate or covering, shall be inclosed with a strong box or curb at least twelve inches high. Ibid.

§ 18. No person shall suffer or permit any grate or covering to any vault to be removed therefrom, or insecurely fixed thereon, so that the same can be moved in its bed, within one hour before sunset on any day, under the penalty of twenty dollars, to be sued for and recovered from the owner and occupant of the house to which such vault shall belong, severally and respectively. Ibid.

§ 19. In all cases where the owners of property in that part of the city, laid out by the Commissioners of Streets Areas.

and Roads, shall, in the erection of dwellings, set the same back from the lines of the streets or avenues, a distance of three feet and upward, for the purpose of ornamental court-yards in front, they shall be permitted to inclose for such purpose, with a neat iron railing, in addition to the space receded from, so much of the sidewalk in front as is allowed by ordinance for stoops; the gates of such inclosures to be so constructed as to open inwardly, under the penalty of two hundred and fifty dollars for each offense.

CHAPTER XIX.

OF PUBLIC WELLS, PUMPS, CISTERNS AND HYDRANTS.

ARTICLE I.

OF BUILDING WELLS AND PUMPS.

§ 1. All applications for wells and pumps, in any part of the city of New York, shall be made to the Croton Aqueduct Board. Applications for Wells and Pumps.

§ 2. It shall be the duty of the said Board, as soon as may be after the receipt of such application, to submit the same to the Alderman and Councilmen of the district of the ward in which the well is to be located, and if approved by them, the said Board shall present to the Common Council the ordinance necessary to carry the application into effect, in the manner provided for by law. Ibid.

§ 3. All public wells hereafter built by order of the Common Council, shall be examined and inspected by the Water Purveyor, and shall be paid for by the Croton Aqueduct Board, in the usual manner, on receiving from the said Water Purveyor a certificate of his approval of the work, and that the same is built in conformity to law, the said work to be done in accordance with the provisions of law and ordinances as to all work done for the Corporation. Inspection of Public Wells.

§ 4. No public well shall hereafter be built in any of the avenues of this city. No Wells in avenues.

§ 5. No person shall build any well in any of the avenues of this city, under the penalty of fifty dollars, and the Croton Aqueduct Board shall cause the same, in all such cases, to be filled up. Ibid.

Removal of Wells and Pumps.

§ 6. The Croton Aqueduct Board is hereby authorized, under the direction of the Alderman and Councilmen of the district of each ward respectively in which any well and pump may be so located as to incumber the carriage-way or sidewalks of any street in the city, to remove the same to some more proper and convenient place in the vicinity.

ARTICLE II.

GENERAL PROVISIONS AS TO PUBLIC WELLS, PUMPS, CISTERNS AND HYDRANTS.

Regulations as to use of water.

§ 7. No person or persons shall take the water from any public well, pump or cistern in the city of New York, for the purpose of selling or offering the same for sale, under the penalty of twenty-five dollars for each offense.

Ibid.

§ 8. No person shall take or use the water from any public cistern or hydrant, except in case of fire, and for the purpose of extinguishing the same, under the penalty of twenty-five dollars for each offense.

Ibid.

§ 9. No person having charge of any public cistern or hydrant, shall suffer or permit any water to be taken therefrom, except for the purpose of extinguishing fire, under the penalty of twenty-five dollars for every such offense.

Protection of Pumps.

§ 10. No person shall willfully do, or cause, or suffer to be done, any damage to any of the public pumps in the city of New York, under the penalty of twenty-five dollars for each offense.

Regulations os to use of water.

§ 11. Every person who shall place, or assist in placing or cause, or procure to be placed, any hogshead, barrel, tub, or other vessel of greater capacity than ten gallons, in any street in the city of New York, within twenty-five feet of any public well or pump, for the purpose of filling the same with water from any such well or pump, or who shall put, or cause to be put, into any such vessel any water from such pump or well, shall forfeit and pay the sum of ten dollars for each offense.

§ 12. The last preceding section shall not be construed to prevent the immediate filling of any vessel therein mentioned, provided the same shall be forthwith removed. Regulations as to use of water.

§ 13. If any person except one of the engineers or foremen of the fire companies, shall unscrew any of the hydrants belonging or attached to the Corporation water works, erected for the extinguishment of fire, or interfere with the same, or any part of the works belonging to the said establishment, whereby the said establishment, or any or either of the pipes, hydrants, stop-cocks, or any part of the works may be injured, or the water taken therefrom or wasted, they shall be liable to a penalty of fifty dollars for each and every such offense. Unscrewing Hydrants.

§ 14. No person shall wash, or cause, or procure or permit to be washed, any horse or carriage within twenty-five feet of any pump, in any street in the city of New York, under the penalty of ten dollars for every such offense. Washing of Horses and Carriages.

§ 15. No person shall water, or suffer or permit any horse to drink or be watered, at or within ten feet of any pump or well in any street of the city of New York, under the penalty of five dollars for each offense, to be paid by the owner or person watering or permitting such horse to water, severally and respectively. Watering Horses.

CHAPTER XX.

OF THE ERECTION OF BARRIERS TO PREVENT ACCIDENTS.

When a fence or railing to be erected.

§ 1. It shall be the duty of every person or persons engaged in digging down any road or street, in paving any street, building any sewer or drain, trench for water pipes, or digging and building a well in any of the public roads, streets or avenues, under contract with the Corporation of this city, made through either or any of the departments of the said Corporation, or by virtue of any permission which may have been granted to them, by the Mayor and Common Council, or either of the said departments, or either of them, where such work, if left exposed, would be dangerous to passengers, to erect a fence or railing at such excavations, or work, in such a manner as to prevent danger to passengers who may be traveling such streets, roads or avenues, and to continue and uphold the said railing or fence, until the work shall be completed or the obstruction or danger removed. And it shall also be the duty of such persons to place upon such railing or fenee, at twilight in the evening, suitable and sufficient lights, and keep them burning through the night, during the performance of said work, under the penalty of two hundred and fifty dollars for every neglect.

Ibid.

§ 2. The provisions of the preceding section shall apply to every person who shall place building materials in any of the public streets or avenues, or be engaged in building any vault, or constructing any lateral drain from any cellar to any public sewer, or who shall do or perform any work causing obstructions in the public streets, by virtue of any permit from any executive department; and also to all public or Corporation officers, engaged in performing any work in behalf of the Corporation, whereby obstruc tions or excavations shall be made in the public streets.

§ 3. The extent to which such railing or fence should be built, in the several cases, is hereby defined as follows, to wit: Extent of fence or railing.

In digging down any street or road, by placing the same along the upper bank of such excavation, or by extending the fence so far across the street or road, as to prevent persons from traveling on such portion as would be dangerous. In paving any street or avenue, by extending it across the carriage-way of such street or avenue, or if but a portion of the width of such carriage-way be obstructed, across such portion, in which case the obstructions shall be so arranged as to leave a passage-way through, as nearly as may be, of uniform width.

In the building of a sewer, by placing it across the carriage-way, at the ends of such excavations as shall be made.

In the building of a well, by inclosing the same, and the obstructions connected therewith, on one or more sides.

In building vaults, by inclosing the ground taken for the vaults.

In placing building materials in the streets, by placing it across so much of the street as shall be occupied by such materials; and the materials shall be so placed as to occupy a space of uniform width, except brick or stone piled solid at least seven feet high. In all cases sufficient lights are to be placed upon such building materials, fences or railings, and kept burning during the night, as provided by the preceding sections.

Parties answerable for damage.

§ 4. In all cases where any person or persons shall perform any of the work mentioned in the preceding sections, either under contracts with the Corporation, or by virtue of permission obtained from the Mayor and Common Council, or either of the departments, such persons shall be answerable for any and every damage which may be occasioned to persons, animals or property, by reason of carelessness in any manner connected with the said work.

Duties of Chiefs of Bureaux in this connection.

§ 5. It shall be the duty of the chiefs of the bureaux having charge of the particular class of improvement, to see that the requirements contained in this chapter, in regard to the erection of fencing, and placing lights, in all cases, be complied with, severally, under the penalty of fifty dollars for each and every neglect.

Ibid.

§ 6. It shall also be the duty of the said chiefs of bureaux, when any of the work referred to in any of the preceding sections shall be performed, whether for digging down streets or roads, paving streets, building sewers and building wells, or digging trenches for water pipes, by persons under contract with the Corporation, or for building vaults, or placing building materials in the streets, or constructing drains, or any other work for forming an obstruction to the said street, by virtue of permission duly obtained, to see that the requirements of this chapter in regard to erecting the necessary fences, and placing the necessary lights, be complied with, and to make the necessary complaint to the Corporation Attorney, for any omission on the part of the person referred to, under the penalty of fifty dollars for every neglect.

Contracts to have a covenant as to this subject.

§ 7. In all contracts for paving streets, constructing sewers, and building wells and pumps, or for doing any other work, whereby accidents or injuries may happen, in consequence of any neglect or carelessness during the performance thereof, it shall be the duty of the departments by whom such contracts are made, to insert a covenant, requiring the contractor or contractors to place proper guards for the prevention of accidents, and to put up and keep suitable and sufficient lights burning at night, during the performance of the work; and that they will keep the Corporation harmless and indemnified against all loss and damage which may be occasioned by reason of any unskillfulness or carelessness, in any manner connected with the execution and completion of the work.

§ 8. In all contracts for digging down any road or street, where such digging, if left exposed, would be dangerous to passengers, the head of the proper department shall insert a covenant, whereby the contractors shall be bound, at their own expense, to erect a fence or railing along or across the street, in such a manner as to prevent danger to passengers, and so to continue and uphold the said fence or railing, until the street is completed.

Contracts to have a covenant as to this subject.

§ 9. A like fence or railing shall be put up and upheld, in all cases in which a road or street is dug out at the cost of the Common Council.

Streets dug by Corporation.

CHAPTER XXI.

OF PRESERVING THE MONUMENTS DESIGNATING THE STREETS AND AVENUES.

Notice of covering or removing monuments.

§ 1. No person or persons shall cover up or remove any of the monument stones for designating the avenues and streets in the city of New York, without first giving the Street Commissioner three days' notice thereof, in writing, under the penalty of fifty dollars.

Street Commissioner's duties.

§ 2. It shall be the duty of the Street Commissioner, on receiving such notice, forthwith to cause one of the City Surveyors to take the necessary measures to raise or lower such monument to the proper grade of the city, and to cause such alteration to be noticed on maps, to be kept in the office of the Street Commissioner for that purpose.

Covenant in contracts.

§ 3. It shall be the duty of the Street Commissioner, in all contracts hereafter made by him, for regulating any of the streets or avenues in which monuments are placed, to insert therein a covenant on the part of the contractors, to give the notice above required, and to replace such stones, under the direction of the said Commissioner.

To be replaced.

§ 4. Whenever the Street Commissioner shall ascertain that any monument stone has been removed, he shall forthwith cause the same to be placed in its proper position, and shall note the same on the map, in the manner before stated.

Expenses, how defrayed.

§ 5. The expenses attending the same shall be paid by the Comptroller, on the certificate of the Street Commissioner.

CHAPTER XXII.

OF NUMBERING THE STREETS.

§ 1. In all cases where the number or numbers of streets have been directed to be changed, or shall hereafter be so directed, either by resolution or ordinance of the Common Council, the said number or numbers shall be so changed within twenty days after a copy of the said ordinance or resolution shall have been served, personally, upon the occupant, owner or lessee, tenant or sub-tenant of the premises. Change of numbers, time for completion.

§ 2. For every neglect to comply with the foregoing section, the owner, occupant, lessee, tenant or sub-tenant, shall forfeit and pay the sum of fifty dollars, and the further penalty of ten dollars for each day, or part of a day such number or numbers shall remain unchanged, to be recovered from the owner, occupant, lessee, tenant or sub-tenant, severally and respectively. Penalties.

§ 3. In the event of non-compliance with the first section of this chapter, it shall be the duty of the Inspector of Sidewalks to cause the number or numbers to be forthwith changed; and the expense thereof to be collected from the parties aforesaid, as an additional penalty. Change of numbers.

§ 4. In all cases of renumbering the streets it shall be the duty of the Inspector of Sidewalks to furnish to the Croton Aqueduct Department a transcript of all changes made, showing in parallel columns, the old and new street numbers. Record of old and new numbers.

§ 5. Whenever any street north of Thirteenth street, inclusive, shall be directed to be numbered, the Inspector Method of numbering north of 13th street.

Method of numbering north of 13th street.

of Sidewalks shall cause the numbers to commence at the Fifth avenue, beginning with number one, and numbering continually to either river; and that said streets shall hereafter be called and known as East Thirteenth street and West Thirteenth street, and so on, the dividing line to be the Fifth avenue.

CHAPTER XXIII.

OF CLEANING THE STREETS AND HEREIN OF THE REMOVAL OF SNOW AND ICE, AND THE SALE AND CARTAGE OF MANURE.

ARTICLE I.

OF CLEANING THE STREETS.

Contract district.

§ 1. The city, with the exception of the Twelfth Ward, shall constitute one contract district.

How often to be swept.

§ 2. The contractor shall cause the surface of all streets, avenues, lanes and alleys, and all gutters, wharves, piers, heads of slips, public lands and places, and the limits of the public markets, to be thoroughly cleaned and swept once each and every week; and all dirt, manure, ashes, garbage and rubbish, so swept up, to be removed immediately therefrom.

Removal of filth, &c., from markets.

§ 3. The said contractor shall cause all dirt, filth and rubbish, of all and every kind, to be removed from each of the public markets, and such other public markets as shall hereafter be erected, and the limits thereof within their respective districts, every Sunday, before the hour of nine o'clock in the morning, and every other day excepting Saturday, before four o'clock in the afternoon.

Removal of Garbage, &c.

§ 4. The said contractor shall cause to be removed from the streets, in tight carts, all ashes, garbage, rubbish, and sweepings of every kind, which may be delivered to them, or that may be placed in vessels upon the sidewalks, or in the front area of, or upon the upper area step of, any dwelling-house, store or public building, between the hours of seven, A. M., and six, P. M., of each and every day, Sundays excepted.

Ash Carts. § 5. The drivers of all carts employed as ash carts shall have a bell attached to their carts or harness, that notice of their approach may be had; and shall receive all ashes, garbage, sweepings and rubbish which shall be delivered them, or that may be placed upon the sidewalk in vessels, or in the area, or upon the upper cellar step of every dwelling-house, store or public building.

Time of sweeping certain streets. § 6. Broadway, from the Battery to Fourteenth street, shall be swept, during the night and before the hour of seven, A. M., once every twenty-four hours; Park row and Chatham street, Bowery to Grand street, Fulton street, east from Broadway; Cortland street, Wall street, Maiden lane, Whitehall street and Grand street, east from Broadway, shall be swept seven times in each month.

Ibid. § 7. All streets, lanes and alleys embraced in the First, Second, Third, Fourth, Fifth and Sixth Wards, together with Canal street, West Broadway, Third and Sixth avenues to Fourteenth street, shall be swept, in like manner, once per week, and all the dirt, manure, ashes, garbage and rubbish of every kind, so swept up, shall be removed immediately therefrom. All streets below Chambers street shall be cleaned, during the night and before the hour of seven, A. M., between the first day of May and the first day of October; and during the night, and before the hour of nine o'clock, A. M., between the first day of October and the first day of May in each year.

When the performance of such work is impracticable from the state of the weather, the City Inspector may, from time to time, in writing, designate a later hour for the work, or dispense with the same temporarily; but said officer shall not grant such dispensation for a period longer than one week from the date thereof.

§ 8. The said contractor shall remove snow, ice and other obstructions from the crosswalk and gutters, and shall also remove snow, hail and ice from the front of all public buildings and places, engine-houses, station-houses and court-rooms, within twenty-four hours after such snow or hail has ceased to fall, and shall keep the streets conveniently passable for vehicles during the winter, and clean all gutters intersecting the same. Removal of snow, ice, & other obstructions.

§ 9. The said contractor shall remove from the city all dirt, manure, garbage, ashes and rubbish of every kind as fast as the same can be collected, and no deposit of any kind shall be made in the city, except such as may be suitable to fill up low ground, or sunken lots, and that may be required for such purpose, with the consent of the owner of such ground or lots, and of the City Inspector. The city will furnish to the contractor the right to use the berths designated by the Common Council for the loading of vessels, but the contractor must protect the right thereto from unlawful infringement. Garbage, rubbish, &c.

§ 10. If the contractor shall fail to perform any duty required by these specifications, for the space of twenty-four hours after he shall have been notified thereof, by notice, in writing, left at his residence or place of business, by the City Inspector, he shall be subject to a fine of five dollars, for each and every street so reported; and should said contractor fail to perform his contract, according to the written specifications, for a further space of twenty-four hours, in regard to the street or streets so reported, he shall be subject to a further fine of twenty-five dollars; Neglect of contractors; Provisions respecting.

Neglect of Contractors; Provisions respecting.

said fine to be deducted from the reserve fund of ten per cent., hereinafter provided for; and if such fund is not sufficient, then such fine or fines shall be deducted from such moneys as may be due, or become due, said contractor from the city. Should the said contractor further fail of performing his contract, as aforesaid, for the space of one week, the City Inspector shall, forthwith, without any delay, communicate the facts in relation thereto to the Common Council, and the said Common Council shall, thereupon, proceed to investigate the alleged non-performance of said contract, by said contractor; and it shall be optional with said Common Council to annul said contract, or compel a specific performance thereof by said contractor, or his sureties. Should the said contract be annulled and declared forfeited, as aforesaid, the said contractor shall not be entitled to claim any moneys for any work performed under said contract, after a resolution, annulling said contract, shall have been approved by the Mayor, and written notice thereof given said contractor, in person, or left at his office or place of business. After said contract shall have been annulled, as aforesaid, it shall be the duty of the City Inspector, forthwith, to advertise for proposals for cleaning the streets uncontracted for, in compliance with the specifications herein, and to cause the work, under said forfeited contracts to be done by other persons, pursuant to law, and the specifications herein; and all charges for such work, over and above the amount that the aforesaid contractor would have been entitled to for the same, together with such other expenses, losses, &c., that would have been incurred by the city, by reason of said forfeiture, shall be charged to said contractor; provided, however, that neither said contractor nor his sureties shall be liable for any expenditure or loss sustained by the city, by reason of said forfeiture or annulment of said contract, after the expiration of thirty days from the date of said annulment, and notice thereof, as aforesaid. Should the payment due, or becoming due to the said contractor be insufficient to reimburse the city for the expense incurred by reason of said annulment, the Comptroller shall then direct such action to be taken in law as may be necessary to recover from the sureties of said contractor any deficiency that may arise by reason thereof.

Filth from Receiving basins & sewers.

§ 11. The said contractor shall receive from the Croton Aqueduct Department, and carry away all dirt, rubbish and filth taken from the receiving basins and sewers, free from any charge or expense to the city, or said Croton Aqueduct Department.

Use of Croton water in cleaning streets.

§ 12. The contractor shall be allowed to use the Croton water from hydrants, for sprinkling streets in advance of the sweepers employed therein, but not more than one hydrant to be open at a time, and this only so far as to enable him, conveniently, to fill his watering-pots, and to be carefully closed when left. The said contractors to pay for repairs, by the Croton Aqueduct Department of hydrants damaged by the said contractors, or the men in their employ.

Security to be given by contractors.

§ 13. The contractor shall give good and sufficient security in an amount or amounts from not more than ten sureties, of two hundred thousand dollars, for the faithful performance of his contract; such security to be approved by the Comptroller; and the Comptroller shall draw his warrant, semi-monthly, for the proportionate amounts of the contract, after having deducted ten per cent. from each payment, except as hereinbefore otherwise provided, until the expiration of each year from the time of the award of his contract, upon a certificate of the City Inspector of the faithful performance of the work. If, at the expiration of each year, as aforesaid, the contracts have been faithfully performed on the part of the contractors, to the satisfaction of the City Inspector, and he shall certify thereto, then the Comptroller shall issue his warrant for the additional ten per cent. deducted from the aforementioned payment.

Proposals to be advertised.

§ 14. The City Inspector is hereby authorized and directed to advertise for proposals, and to contract with the lowest bidder, pursuant to the provisions of the charter, for cleaning the streets and avenues of the city, for a term of five years, in compliance with the specifications herewith accompanying, and that he transmit the said award of contract to the Common Council, for confirmation.

ARTICLE II.

OF THE REMOVAL OF SNOW AND ICE.

Removal from sidewalks and gutters.

§ 15. The owner, or occupant, or person having charge of each house or other building, or lot or lots of ground, in the city of New York shall, within the first four hours after every fall of snow or hail or ra n, which shall freeze on the sidewalks and in the gutters, cause the same to be removed entirely from off the sidewalks opposite such house, building, lot or land, under the penalty of three dollars for every such neglect, to be paid by the said owner, occupant or person having charge, severally and respectively.

Strewing ashes or sand.

§ 16. In case the ice or snow shall be so congealed, that it cannot be removed without injury to the pavement, the owner, occupant or person having charge of any building, lot or land as aforesaid, shall, within the first four hours after every fall thereof, cause the sidewalks opposite his, her or their premises, to be strewed with ashes or sand, under the penalty of one dollar, to be paid by the owner or occupant, or person having charge thereof, severally and respectively.

§ 17. It shall be the duty of the Superintendent of Sanitary Inspection and Street Cleaning, immediately after every fall of snow or hail or rain, which shall freeze on the crosswalks or in the gutters, forthwith to cause the same to be removed from the said crosswalks, and from out of the said gutters to the breadth of one foot, in the several wards respectively, and the said crosswalks and gutters shall be kept clean and free from all obstructions.

Removal from cross-walks.

§ 18. The owners or occupants of all houses and lots in the city of New York, shall level the snow and ice in front of his or their premises, in such a manner as will admit of the convenient passing of horses, sleighs and carriages, under the penalty of one dollar for every neglect, to be recovered from the owner or occupant, or person having charge thereof, severally and respectively.

Leveling snow & ice.

§ 19. In case the owner, occupant or person having charge of any house, lot, building or land, shall neglect to comply with any of the provisions of the previous sections of this chapter, it shall be the duty of Superintendent of Sanitary Inspection and Street Cleaning to cause the same to be done.

To be done by authorities when owners neglect.

§ 20. In addition to the penalties imposed by the preceding sections of this chapter, said owner, occupant or person having charge of any such premises, shall likewise pay to the Superintendent of Sanitary Inspection and Street Cleaning, for causing the snow to be removed, as provided in the last preceding section, the sum of eighteen and three quarter cents for every twenty-five feet in width,

In such case cost to be paid by owners, &c.

which shall have been cleaned by order of the said Superintendent, and so in proportion for any greater or less extent; which said amount the said Superintendent may sue for and recover, in any court having cognizance thereof, in the name of the Mayor, Aldermen and Commonalty of the city of New York; the same being first demanded.

ARTICLE III.

OF THE SALE AND CARTAGE OF MANURE, SAND AND DIRT.

Manure, how to be sold.

§ 21. All manure shall be sold in the city of New York by the cart or wagon load; and every such load shall contain fourteen bushels, heaped measure.

Carting of manure.

§ 22. All manure shall be carted in close boxes, the front and sides of which shall be at least twenty inches in height, and the tail-board at least fifteen inches in height, and the said boxes shall be well secured so as to prevent any part of the load from running out.

Penalties.

§ 23. Every person who shall neglect or violate any of the provisions of this law, shall forfeit and pay for every such offense the sum of five dollars, to be recovered in the name of the Mayor, Aldermen and Commonalty of the city of New York, in any court having cognizance thereof.

Inspectors of Manure.

§ 24. The Superintendent of Sanitary Inspection and Street Cleaning may, whenever he deems the same necessary, employ, not exceeding six persons, to act as inspectors of manure, under his direction, who shall receive at the rate of one dollar and fifty cents per day for every day they may be so employed.

Removal of manure from streets.

§ 25. No person or persons, excepting such as are employed by the Superintendent of Sanitary Inspection and Street Cleaning, or the contractor for street cleaning, shall take up or carry away, or remove any manure, from any street, lane, avenue, head of slip, or public place or wharf in the city of New York, under the penalty of ten dollars for each offense.

§ 26. No person shall, at any time, for himself or for any other person, deposit or keep on his premises, or on the premises of any other person, manure of any kind, dirt, filth or sweepings, exceeding two cart loads, at any place in the city of New York to the southward of Fourteenth street, except for agricultural or horticultural purposes, under the penalty of twenty-five dollars for each offense.

Not more than two loads to be kept in one place.

§ 27. No manure, filth or sweepings other than that removed by authority of the Superintendent of Sanitary Inspection and Street Cleaning, shall at any time between the first day of April and the last day of November, be carted or transported to any wharf to the southward of Fourteenth street, in the city of New York, under the penalty of ten dollars for each offense.

Time of removal of manure, filth, &c

§ 28. No deposit of manure for sale shall be kept at any place in the city of New York, south of Twenty-eighth street, except as hereinafter mentioned, under the penalty of twenty-five dollars, to be paid by the owner or owners thereof, or the occupant of the lot or lots, or other place in which such manure shall be kept, severally and respectively. But it shall and may be lawful for the Aldermen and Councilmen of the several districts to permit, in writing, under their hands, the depositing of manure in any lot or other place in said district, south of Twenty-eighth street, with the written consent of the owner of the ground, between the first day of November and the first day of March in each year, under such regulations, and during such time as they may deem proper, and subject to be removed at any time whatever, on the order of said Aldermen and Councilmen.

Deposit of manure for sale.

CHAPTER XXIV.

OF OBSTRUCTING THE FREE USE OF THE PUBLIC STREETS, WHARVES, AND PIERS.

Prohibition of incumbrances.

§ 1. No person shall incumber or obstruct any street, wharf, or pier in the city of New York, with any article or thing whatsoever, without having first obtained written permission from the Mayor or Street Commissioner, or of the Superintendent of Sanitary Inspection and Street Cleaning, under the penalty of five dollars for each offense, and a further penalty of five dollars for each day, or part of a day, such incumbrance or obstruction shall continue.

Cellar doors.

§ 2. No person or persons shall construct or continue any cellar door, which shall extend more than one twelfth part of any street, nor more than five feet into any street, under the penalty of two hundred and fifty dollars for each offense.

Basement or cellar steps.

§ 3. Every entrance, or flight of steps, projecting beyond the line of the street, and descending into any cellar or basement story of any house or other building, where such entrance or flight of steps shall not be covered, shall be inclosed with a railing on each side permanently put up, from three to three and a half feet high, with a gate to open inwardly, or with two iron chains across the front of the entrance way, one near the top and one in the centre of the railing, to be closed during the night, unless there be a burning light over the steps, to prevent accidents, under the penalty of twenty dollars for every offense, to be recovered from the owner, assigns, or lessee thereof, severally and respectively.

§ 4. This ordinance shall not apply to buildings already erected before the twenty-fifth of March, one thousand eight hundred and thirty-four, until the owners and occupants thereof shall receive twenty days' notice, from the Street Commissioner, directing such railing, with gate or chain to be put up in manner aforesaid. Exception.

§ 5. The owner of any such building shall not be liable for the said penalty, for not keeping any such gate closed, or chains fastened across the front of such entrance or flight of steps, when not the actual occupant thereof, any thing to the contrary, in this chapter contained notwithstanding. Ibid.

§ 6. No person or persons shall construct or continue any bay-window or other window, which shall extend into any street more than one foot from the wall of any house or other building, under the penalty of two hundred and fifty dollars for each offense, to be paid by the owner or owners thereof, or the person or persons who constructed the same severally and respectively. Windows.

§ 7. No person or persons shall hereafter construct any porch over a cellar door, under the penalty of two hundred and fifty dollars. Cellar porch.

§ 8. No person or persons shall construct or continue any platform, stoop or step, in any street in the city of New York, which shall extend more than one tenth part of the width of the street, nor more than seven feet, nor with any other than open backs or sides, or railing; nor of greater width than is necessary for the purpose of a convenient passage-way into the house or building; nor any stoop or step which shall exceed five feet in height; under the penalty of two hundred and fifty dollars. Stoops, platforms, &c.

Exception. § 9. Nothing contained in the preceding sections of this chapter, shall be deemed to prohibit the continuation of any porches, doors, stoops, platforms or steps, which were heretofore erected, unless the same shall be complained of to the Street Commissioner, and he shall have directed their removal or alteration within a reasonable time.

Balustrades. § 10. All persons who wish hereafter to erect balustrades projecting beyond the street line, shall first obtain a written permit from the Street Commissioner.

Ibid. § 11. No balustrade shall hereafter be erected, excepting from the second story of any house, nor shall it project more than one twentieth of the width of the street wherein it may be erected, nor more than three feet in any case whatever.

Ibid. § 12. None but iron braces and railings shall be used for balustrades; the strength and firmness shall be tested by the Street Commissioner; and in case he object to the strength of the same, it shall be made as he shall direct, or removed, under penalty of five dollars per day.

Posts. § 13. No post shall be erected or put up in any of the streets, roads, lanes or highways in the city of New York, unless under the direction of the Street Commissioner, under the penalty of five dollars for every such post.

Awning posts § 14. No person shall place or fix, or continue in any street in this city, any awning post or railing, or any cloth or canvas for an awning, unless under the direction of the Street Commissioner, and made conformably to the next section of this chapter, under the penalty of ten dollars for each offense.

Ibid. § 15. All posts fixed in any street for the purpose of supporting any awning, shall not exceed nine inches in diameter, and the rail crossing the same shall not exceed seven inches in width or height, and four inches in thickness; the said posts shall be placed next to and along the inside of the curb stone, and the upper side of the rail, which is intended to support the awning, shall not be less than eight feet nor over ten feet in height above the sidewalk, and the cross-rail shall be strongly mortised through the upright posts.

§ 16. It shall be the duty of the said Street Commissioner to order and direct any awning post which is erected or continued in any street in the city of New York contrary to the last above section, to be forthwith removed; and any person who shall neglect or refuse to comply with such direction and order, shall forfeit and pay for every such offense the sum of ten dollars. Awning posts

§ 17. The owners or occupants of property in any street of this city, exceeding the width of forty feet, and from which the wooden awning posts have been or may hereafter be directed to be removed, shall be, and they are hereby permitted to erect in front of their respective buildings thereon, iron posts, and none others, for the support of awnings, with an iron cross-rail, which shall be nine feet and no more, from the curb stone to the top of said rail; said posts shall be placed eight inches within the outer side of the curb stone, and shall conform in all respects to a pattern or model now deposited in the office of the Street Commissioner. Ibid.

§ 18. Such iron posts, as well as those which may be at the time of the passage of this ordinance erected in any street of this city, shall be well and securely braced from the building with wrought iron rails or rods, at least one inch in diameter, in the proportion of one brace for each post. Ibid.

Awning posts

§ 19. The owners or occupants of property in any street not exceeding the width of forty feet, shall be, and they are hereby permitted to construct from their respective buildings thereon, wrought iron brackets for the support of awnings; which said brackets shall be firmly secured to the building, and project on a line with the inner side of the curb stone, and shall be eight feet and six inches, and no more in height, from the curb stone to the top of the outer cross-rail.

Ibid.

§ 20. It shall be the duty of the Street Commissioner to order and direct the removal forthwith, of all iron awning posts and brackets which are now, or may be hereafter erected, constructed, or continued in any street of this city, contrary to the preceding provisions of these ordinances, and any person who shall neglect or refuse to comply with such direction or order, shall forfeit and pay for every such offense, the sum of five dollars.

Ibid.

§ 21. The preceding sections relating to awnings and awning posts, shall not apply where the erection of iron awning posts and brackets are permitted by these ordinances.

Awnings.

§ 22. No portion or part of any cloth or canvas used as an awning, shall hang loosely down from the same, over the sidewalk or foot-path, under the penalty of five dollars for each day's offense.

Removal of Obstructions.

§ 23. The Street Commissioner is hereby authorized, whenever he shall deem it proper, to order any step-stone used for entering carriages, any railing or fence, any sign, sign-post, or other post, any area, bay-window, or other window, porch, cellar, door, platform, stoop or step, or any other thing which may incumber or obstruct any street, to be altered or removed therefrom, within such time as shall be limited by the said Commissioner.

§ 24. The order or direction, mentioned in the last preceding section, shall be in writing, and shall be served personally, or by leaving it at the house or place of business of the owner, occupant or person having charge of the house or lot in front of which such step-stone or other incumbrance or obstruction may be; or by posting the said notice or order upon such step-stone or other incumbrance or obstruction. Removal of Obstructions.

§ 25. If any owner, occupant, or person having charge of any such house or lot in the city of New York, shall refuse or neglect to obey or comply with such notice or order, he, she or they shall forfeit and pay the sum of ten dollars; and the further sum of five dollars for each and every day, from and after the time limited and appointed in said order, until the same shall have been complied with. Ibid.

§ 26. No goods, wares, merchandise or manufactures of any description, shall be placed or exposed to show or for sale, upon any balustrade, that now is, or hereafter may be erected in this city, under the penalty of ten dollars for each offense. Goods on balustrades.

§ 27. No person shall hang or place any goods, wares or merchandise, or any other thing, at any greater distance than twelve inches in front of his, her or their house or store, or other building, under the penalty of five dollars for each offense. Hanging goods in front of premises.

§ 28. No person shall place, hang or suspend at any greater distance than twelve inches in front of, and from the wall of any house or store, or other building, any sign, showbill, or showboard, under the penalty of ten dollars, for each offense. Signs, show-bills & show-boards.

§ 29. The said Street Commissioner, with the assent of the Alderman and Councilmen of any district of a ward in Trees.

which any tree may be standing, may cause the same to be cut down and removed from the street, and shall cause so much of the sidewalk or carriage-way as may be injured by the removal of such tree, to be properly repaired.

Trees.

§ 30. No person shall plant, or suffer or permit any tree or shoot to be planted, in any street in the city of New York, under the penalty of fifteen dollars for every such offense.

Ibid.

§ 31. The last preceding section of this chapter shall not be construed, to prevent the planting of trees in any street which is of the width of forty feet and upwards, provided the same be planted upon the sidewalk or foot-path, and within twelve inches of the curb stone.

Ibid.

§ 32. No person shall cut down, destroy, or in any way injure any tree or shoot, standing in any street or public place in the city of New York, under the penalty of fifty dollars for each offense.

Raising of goods outside of buildings.

§ 33. No person or persons in the city of New York, whether agent, owner or employer, shall suffer or permit any cask, bale, bundle, box, crate or any other goods, wares or merchandise, or any boards, planks, joists or other timber, or any thing whatsoever, to be raised from any street on the outside of any building, into any loft, store or room; or to be lowered from the same, on the outside of any building by means of any rope, pulley, tackle or windlass, under the penalty of twenty-five dollars, to be recovered by an action of debt from such person, agent, owner or employer.

Obstructing side-walks.

§ 34. No person shall lead, drive or ride any horse, or drag any wheel or hand-barrow, or saw any wood, or lay or place any wood, coal or other thing, or any goods, wares or merchandise, or any other article whatsoever, upon any foot-path or sidewalk, under the penalty of five dollars for each offense.

§ 35. No person shall drive, or back, or lead any horse or cart, or other wheel carriage, on the foot-path or sidewalk of any street, under the penalty of five dollars for each offense. Horses, carts, &c., on the side-walks.

§ 36. No owner or occupant of any store or house shall permit or suffer any cart or other wheel carriage, to be driven, or otherwise to pass, or go over or upon the foot-path or sidewalk opposite to such house or store, for the purpose of loading or unloading such cart or other wheel carriage, or for any other purpose whatever, under the penalty of five dollars for each offense. Ibid.

§ 37. If any cartman or other person shall break or otherwise injure any foot-path or sidewalk, he or they shall, within twenty-four hours thereafter, cause the same to be well and sufficiently repaired and amended, under the penalty of ten dollars. Injuring sidewalks

§ 38. No person shall obstruct the walks laid across the public streets, or at the head of the public slips in the city of New York, by placing or stopping his horse, cart or other carriage, upon or across any of the said walks, or by placing or putting any other obstruction or thing across or on the same, under the penalty of five dollars for each offense. Cross-walks and heads of Slips.

§ 39. No person, without permission of the Common Council, shall take up, remove, or carry away, or cause or permit to be taken up, removed or carried away, any turf, stone, sand, clay or earth from any street, public place, or highway in the city of New York, under the penalty of twenty-five dollars for each offense. Carrying dirt &c., from the streets.

§ 40. No person shall remove, or cause or permit to be removed, or shall aid or assist in removing any building Moving buildings.

into, along or across any street, lane or alley, or public place in the city of New York, to the southward of Fourteenth street, under the penalty of two hundred and fifty dollars for every such offense.

Removing Pavements. § 41. No pavement in any street in the city of New York, which has been accepted by the Corporation to be kept in repair at the public expense, shall hereafter be taken up, or the paving-stones removed therefrom, for any purpose whatever, without the authority of the Common Council, or the written permission of the Croton Aqueduct Board, under the penalty of two hundred and fifty dollars for every such offense.

Dumping earth, &c., in the streets. § 42. No person, without permission of the Common Council, shall dump or deposit any earth, dirt, rubbish or other article, (except for the purposes of building,) in any street, either upon the cartway, or sidewalks, or any public place, under the penalty of ten dollars for every offense, and if the same shall be dumped or deposited by a dirt cart, the owner or driver thereof shall also be liable to be punished for misdemeanor, pursuant to the provisions of the act of the Legislature, entitled "An act relative to the powers of the Common Council of the city of New York, and the Police and Criminal Courts of the said city," passed January 23d, 1833.

CHAPTER XXV.

OF THE PUBLIC PLACES AND GROUNDS.

§ 1. No person shall play at ball, quoits or any other sport or play whatsoever, in any public place in the city of New York, nor throw stones, nor run foot races in or over or upon the same, under the penalty of five dollars for each offense. Publicplaces.

§ 2. No person shall walk, stand or lie upon any part of the Park, Battery, or any other public square or place which is laid out and appropriated for grass or shrubbery, under the penalty of five dollars for each offense. Grass and Shrubbery.

§ 3. No person shall pull up, break down, trample upon or injure any of the trees, grass or shrubbery in any such public square or place, under the penalty of five dollars for each offense. Trees, grass, &c.

§ 4. The persons exercising the duties of keepers of the public places shall see that the foregoing provisions are observed. Enforcement.

§ 5. The said persons so exercising the office of keepers, are hereby particularly enjoined to have removed to the public pound, all swine and neat cattle which are found within the public places and grounds, and to report to the Attorney of the Board all violations of this law. Swine & cattle.

§ 6. No carriage-horse, or cart shall be allowed to enter the Park, but those having business with some officer located therein. Vehicles in the Parks.

§ 7. No person shall deposit, or cart manure of any kind, dirt, filth, sweepings of streets or rubbish, upon that Battery.

portion of the city known as the Battery, or upon the Battery enlargement, under the penalty of twenty-five dollars for each offense, to be recovered from the owner of any boat, cart or other vehicle, or the person having charge of the same, severally and respectively.

Battery.

§ 8. The Mayor of the city is hereby authorized to enforce the provisions of the last section, until a sea wall is built around the Battery enlargement.

Penalties.

§ 9. The Corporation Attorney is hereby authorized and directed to prosecute for the penalty, all complaints for any violation of section 7 of this chapter.

CHAPTER XXVI.

OF VESSELS, WHARVES, PIERS AND SLIPS.

ARTICLE I.—OF LEASING THE PUBLIC DOCKS, WHARVES, PIERS AND SLIPS.
II.—OF THE LAYING OF VESSELS AT THE WHARVES, AND REGULATIONS OF VESSELS.
III.—OF THE RATES OF WHARFAGE.
IV.—OF INCUMBERING THE SLIPS.
V.—OF THE RINGING OF BOAT BELLS.
VI.—OF THE LUMBER DOCK.

ARTICLE I.

OF LEASING THE PUBLIC DOCKS, WHARVES, PIERS AND SLIPS.

§ 1. The several docks, wharves, piers and slips belonging to the Corporation, and not now leased by private contract, shall, from time to time, be leased singly, at public auction, in the most advantageous manner, to the highest bidder, by the Comptroller, such leases to be for a term of not less than one, nor more than ten years, subject to the reservation or exception of small boats, contained and mentioned in the next section of this chapter, and also subject to the usual covenants contained in the leases of the said public docks, wharves, piers and slips, and such other stipulations as the Comptroller may deem expedient; and such leases shall be made in accordance with the provisions of the act of the Legislature, entitled " An act further to amend the charter of the city of New York," passed April 14, 1857. Leasing Wharves,&c.

§ 2. The rates of fees of wharfage on vessels of not more than five tons burden, accruing in all or any of the Leasing Wharfage of Small boats.

docks, wharves, piers or slips within this city which by law they may use, belonging to the Corporation, shall hereafter be separately leased, and be known as the Small Boat District; and the necessary reservation or exception of such small boats shall be made in the other leases of the docks and slips.

Report of violations.

§ 3. It shall be the duty of the lessee or lessees of the public wharves, piers and slips, for the time being, to report to the Attorney of the Corporation, the names of all persons who shall violate any of the provisions of this chapter.

ARTICLE II.

OF THE LAYING OF VESSELS AT THE WHARVES, AND THE REGULATIONS OF VESSELS.

Laying of Vessels.

§ 4. The Superintendent of Wharves of the city of New York, shall and may order any vessel, steamboat or small craft, to remove from the berths assigned and reserved for the manure boats in the public slips; and any person who has the charge of any vessel, steamboat or small craft, who shall neglect or refuse to obey the order of the said Superintendent in the premises, shall forfeit and pay for every such offense the sum of fifty dollars.

Sea Vessels.

§ 5. If any description of sea vessel shall come into or lay at or within any of the said docks, wharves, piers or slips, or if any coasting vessel, above the burden of one hundred and fifty tons, shall come into or lay within the same, excepting the Old and Coffee-house slips, unless by special permission in writing, obtained therefor from the Mayor or Superintendent of Wharves, agreeably to the provisions of this chapter, the owner, master or person having charge of the same, shall forfeit and pay for every such offense the sum of ten dollars, and the additional sum of ten dollars for every twenty-four hours any such vessel shall lay at or within the same.

§ 6. If any coasting vessel above the burden of one hundred tons shall come into or lay at or within any of the public docks, wharves, piers or slips, situate on the East river, excepting the Old and Coffee-house slips, unless by special permission in writing, obtained therefor from the Mayor, or Superintendent of Wharves, the owner, master or person having charge of the same, shall forfeit and pay for every such offense the sum of ten dollars for every twenty-four hours any such vessel shall lay at or within the same. Coasting vessels.

§ 7. The last preceding section of this chapter shall not be construed to prevent all or any coasting vessel belonging to this State, and navigating the Hudson river, from coming into and laying at and within any of the public wharves, docks, piers and slips of this city, in like manner as if they were under the burden of one hundred tons. Ibid.

§ 8. If any steamboat, safety-barge, tow boat or freight boat, connected with any steamboat establishment shall come into or lay at or within any of the public docks, wharves, piers or slips aforesaid, or shall occupy the water belonging to any such public dock, wharf, pier or slip, unless by special permission, in writing, obtained therefor from the Mayor, or Superintendent of Wharves, the owner or owners, master, agent or person having charge of the same, shall forfeit and pay for every such offense the sum of twenty-five dollars, and the additional sum of twenty-five dollars for every twenty-four hours any such vessel shall lay at or within the same. Steamboats, barges, &c.

§ 9. The private wharves and piers fronting on and adjacent to the slip lying between the foot of Cortlandt street and the foot of Liberty street, on the North river, Steamboats.

are hereby designated and appropriated for the exclusive use of steamboats.

Removal of Vessels.

§ 10. If the master, owner, or person having charge of any vessel or small craft, which shall lay in any of the aforesaid public slips, shall not remove the same out of such slip, or from one part of such slip to another part thereof, as may be directed, by the expiration of the time within which he, or any seaman, mariner or person employed on board, may be so ordered to remove such vessel or small craft, either by the Mayor or Superintendent of Wharves, every such owner or master of such vessel or small craft shall respectively forfeit and pay for every such offense the sum of twenty-five dollars.

Orders as to laying, &c. of vessels.

§ 11. Either of the persons mentioned in the preceding sections of this chapter, may give such order and directions, from time to time, to the owner, master or person having charge of any sloop, boat or other vessel whatsoever, laying at or within any of the said public wharves, docks, piers or slips, or to any seaman, mariner or person employed on board, as they shall respectively think just and proper, touching the laying, fastening and berth of any such sloop, boat or other vessel whatsoever.

Penalty.

§ 12. For every neglect or refusal to comply with any such order and direction, mentioned in the last preceding section of this chapter, the owner, master or person having charge of any such sloop, boat or other vessel, shall forfeit and pay the sum of twenty-five dollars.

Ferry slips, and obstructing Ferry boats.

§ 13. If any boat or vessel of any description whatsoever, excepting ferry boats, shall come into and lay in any slip used and appropriated for a ferry, without permission of the Mayor, or Superintendent of Wharves, or shall lay at any dock or wharf, so as to incommode the going into or coming out, or the turning of any ferry boat; or if any vessel, in hauling up or dropping down before either of the slips in which any ferry is kept, shall not drop its fast or anchor on the approach of any ferry boat, so as not to incommode or obstruct the same, the master, owner or person having charge of such boat or other vessel, shall forfeit and pay, for every such offense, the sum of ten dollars.

§ 14. No ship or other vessel shall lay at anchor in the East river, within a distance of sixty yards from a direct line between the landing places of either of the public ferries across the said river, under the penalty of twenty-five dollars for each offense, to be paid by the master, owner, or other person having charge of such ship or vessel. Obstruction of Ferries in East river.

§ 15. No person shall bring any vessel or vessels whatsoever, excepting market boats, and other small boats, within the slip belonging to the Corporation, at the foot of Spring street, under the penalty of five dollars for every such offense, to be paid by the owner or owners, master or persons having charge thereof. Spring street Slip.

§ 16. If any vessel, excepting such as shall belong solely to persons residing in the States of New Jersey, Connecticut and New York, or either of those States, and trading to and from either of the said States and this city, shall be brought into or shall lay at or within Peck slip, the owner, master or person having charge of any such vessel shall forfeit and pay for every such offense, the sum of ten dollars. Peck slip.

§ 17. If any vessel or small craft shall be brought into or shall lay at or within Coenties slip, the owner, master or person having charge of any such vessel or small craft, Coenties slip.

shall forfeit and pay for every such offense the sum of twenty-five dollars, and the further sum of ten dollars for every twenty-four hours the same shall lay at or within the said slip.

Coenties slip. § 18. The last preceding section of this chapter shall not be construed to apply to vessels or small craft belonging solely to persons residing either in the State of New York, New Jersey or Connecticut, and which trade to and from either of the said States and this city.

Fulton market slip. § 19. No person shall bring any vessel or vessels whatever, excepting market boats, periaugers, canoes or small craft, within the bulkhead and piers of the Corporation slips in front of Fulton market, under the penalty of ten dollars for each offense, to be recovered from the owner or owners, or person or persons having charge thereof, severally and respectively.

bid § 20. All market boats, periaugers and canoes, or other small craft, of not more than the burden of five tons, coming to the bulkhead and piers mentioned in the last preceding section, shall have the owner's name painted at full length, in legible letters, in a conspicuous place on the inside of the stern, under the penalty of ten dollars, to be paid by the owner, master, or person having charge of the same, severally and respectively.

Market boats Periaugers & Canoes. § 21. All market boats, periaugers and canoes, of not more than the burden of five tons, coming to any of the said public docks, wharves, piers or slips, shall have the owner or owners' name or names painted at full length, in legible letters, on the inside of the stern, under the penalty of ten dollars for each offense, to be paid by the owner, master or person having charge of the same.

Slip between Amos and Charles sts. § 22. The basin or slip fronting to West street, on the Hudson river, and laying between Amos street and Charles street, is hereby appropriated and set apart exclusively for the use of boats bringing hay to the city.

ARTICLE III.

OF THE RATES OF WHARFAGE.

§ 23. The master, owner, or person having charge of any ship or vessel, or small craft whatever, using or coming to lay with such ships or vessels, at or within any of the docks, wharves, piers or slips within the city of New York, belonging to the said Corporation, if such vessel be of not more than five tons burthen, shall pay to the lessee for the time being, of the small boat district, the like rate of fees of wharfage for so laying or using, as now are or hereafter may be, established and allowed by the Legislature of the people of the State of New York, to be taken and removed by the proprietors of private wharves in said city. Rates of Wharfage.

§ 24. If any such vessel, as mentioned in the preceding section of this chapter, be of more than five tons burthen, such owner or person having charge thereof, shall pay to the lessee or lessees for the time being, of the dock, wharf, pier or slip, at or within which such slip or vessel shall lay, the like rate or fees of wharfage, as now are or hereafter may be established and allowed by the Legislature of the people of the State of New York, to be taken and received by the proprietors of private wharves in the said city. Ibid.

§ 25. The preceding sections of this article shall be so construed, that for all vessels of not more than five tons burthen, there may be paid as aforesaid, in case the owner or master shall elect so to do, on their coming to lay at any of the said docks, wharves, piers or slips, after the Ibid.

first day of May inclusive in every year, the sum of two dollars and fifty cents, for the use of all the Corporation docks, wharves, piers and slips, within the said city which by law they may use, for the year ending on the last day of April ensuing; which sum shall be paid to the lessee of the small boat district, and shall exonerate such vessel from all other fees of wharfage for the year then current.

Rates of Wharfage.

§ 26. The preceding sections of this article shall also be so construed, that for all vessels of more than five tons burthen, and under twenty tons burthen, there shall be paid only thirty cents per day, subject to abatement or half wharfage, according to the provisions of the laws of this State, when not having dock berths.

Ibid.

§ 27. If the master, owner, or person having charge of any such ship or vessel, coming to lay with such ship or vessel, at or within any of the said docks, wharves, piers or slips, on or after the said first day of May, as mentioned in the 25th section of this chapter, shall elect to pay to the lessee for the time being, of the district in which such dock, wharf, pier or slip is situate, at and after the rate, and in the manner mentioned in the next succeeding section of this article, such ship or vessel shall be exonerated from any other or further payment in said district, for the residue of such year.

Ibid.

§ 28. The following are the rates of wharfage mentioned in the last preceding section of this article, to wit:

1. Between the first day of May and the last day of July inclusive, sixty cents per ton.
2. Between the first day of August and the last day of October, inclusive, forty-five cents per ton.
3. Between the first day of November and the last day of January, inclusive, thirty cents per ton.

4. Between the first day of February and the last day of April, inclusive, fifteen cents per ton.

§ 29. The two last preceding sections of this article shall be so construed, that in case any ship or vessel shall remain in any of the public slips more than fifteen successive days, such ship or vessel shall be subject to daily wharfage thereafter, until such ship or vessel shall depart from such slip, notwithstanding such ship or vessel shall have elected to pay wharfage by the year. Rates of Wharfage.

§ 30. Notwithstanding anything herein contained, any vessel paying daily wharfage, entitled to lay within or at any of the said docks, wharves, piers or slips, and which shall be laid up and out of employ, with their cargoes landed and sails unbent, between the tenth day of December and the tenth day of March inclusive, in any year, shall be subject for the time during which said vessel shall be so laid up, to the payment of a sum or sums not exceeding one half of the wharfage which they are subject to pay when in active employment; but such vessels shall be liable to be ordered to be removed; agreeably to the provisions of the second article of this chapter. Ibid.

§ 31. The owner, master, or person having charge of any ship or vessel, coming to lay with any such ship or vessel, at or within any of the docks, wharves, piers or slips, within this city, belonging to the Corporation, on or after the first day of May, in any year, shall not be exonerated from the payment of the daily rates or fees of wharfage allowed by the laws of this State, unless the said persons, or some one of them shall, upon such vessel first coming in, and such person or persons being called on by the lessee or his agent for that purpose, forthwith elect to pay to the lessee of the district in which such dock, wharf, pier or slip is situated, the yearly or periodical Ibid.

rates or fees of wharfage allowed by the 27th and 28th sections of this chapter.

ARTICLE IV.

OF INCUMBERING THE SLIPS.

Laying up of vessels.

§ 32. It shall not be lawful for the owner or master, or person having charge of any vessel that shall be out of employ, to lay up the same at any of the public docks, wharves, piers or slips, between Stanton street and Whitehall slip, except with the written consent of the Superintendent of Wharves.

Careening of vessels.

§ 33. No person shall careen or cause to be careened, any vessel at or within any of the public docks, wharves, piers, quays or slips, under the penalty of ten dollars, for every day for which such vessel shall continue to be careened, to be paid by the owner or owners, master or person having charge of such vessel, severally and respectively.

Wrecks not to encumber the slips.

§ 34. No person shall bring into any of the said public docks or slips, nor make nor leave there, the wreck of any ship or vessel, whereby such dock or slip may be incommoded, or the entrance or departure of any vessel or small craft in anywise obstructed, under the penalty of twenty-five dollars for every such offense; and the further penalty of ten dollars for every day, or part of a day the wreck of such ship or vessel shall so continue or remain in any such dock or slip.

Casting anchors &c., in the docks, &c

§ 35. No person shall cast any anchor, grappling or killock into or near any of the docks, wharves, piers, quays or slips of the said city; or shall place any cable, rope, chain, or line across the entrance of any slip; or shall permit or cause any vessel to lay at the end of or within any pier, with the jib-boom rigged out; or shall take away any stones, earth, timber, or ballast, belonging to any dock, wharf, pier or slip, from any of the same, under the penalty of ten dollars for every such offense.

§ 36. No person shall throw any stones, earth, timber, ballast, shells, ashes, or other dirt or rubbish whatsoever, into, or bring any masts, yards, spars or other kinds of timber, or stages or platforms for working on, within any of the docks, wharves, piers, quays or slips in the said city, under the penalty of ten dollars for every such offense; and the additional penalty of five dollars for every day or part of a day, such masts, yards and spars, or other kind of timber, or stages or platforms for working on, shall remain in any of the said docks, wharves, piers, quays or slips. Incumbrances.

§ 37. If any shells, ashes, stones, or dirt whatsoever, shall be thrown from any vessel into any of the slips or docks aforesaid, the person throwing the same, and the master, or owner or possessor of such vessel, shall forfeit and pay for every such offense, the sum of five dollars. Throwing dirt, &c., in the slips.

§ 38. No steamboat, small boat, or other craft, shall at any time lay alongside of the Battery wall, for the purpose of landing or receiving passengers or freight, and the proprietor or proprietors, or persons having charge of any such steamboat, small boat, or other craft, which shall land or receive any passengers or freight at the said Battery wall, shall be fined fifty dollars for each offense. Battery wall.

§ 39. The Street Commissioner shall hereafter insert a clause in all contracts for building piers and bulkheads or repairing the same, that no more timber or other materials shall be deposited in the slips or basins than is necessary for the completion of the work specified in the contract. Clause in contracts.

ARTICLE V.

OF THE RINGING OF BOAT-BELLS.

Ringing of Boat-bells.

§ 40. No bell, on board of or near any boat or vessel, or ferry-boat, at any of the wharves, piers or slips in the city of New York, shall be rung before sunrise in the morning, on any pretence whatever, nor shall such bell be rung or tolled at any other time, or for any greater length of time than is herein expressed, under the penalty of twenty-five dollars, to be paid by the master, owner, agent or person or persons having charge of such bell or vessel, and the person ringing or tolling the same, severally and respectively.

1. All such bells may be rung or tolled at the time of starting, one minute, and no longer.
2. They may also ring at or within a quarter of an hour before starting, on each trip, for the space of two minutes.

Blowing horns, &c.

§ 41. No horn, trumpet or other instrument, shall be blown or used in any of the streets, wharves, slips or piers in the city of New York, under the penalty of ten dollars for each offense.

Exception.

§ 42. The last preceding section of this chapter shall not be construed, to prevent the playing of any band of music, or any single instrument, on board of any vessel at or near any wharf or pier.

Soliciting Passengers.

§ 43. No person shall solicit or request any person or persons, in the public streets, or on any wharf or pier in the city of New York, to go on board of, or take passage in, any steamboat or vessel, under the penalty of five dollars for each offense.

ARTICLE VI.

OF THE LUMBER DOCK.

§ 44. There shall be appointed a suitable person, to be called "The Superintendent of the Public Lumber Dock," whose duty it shall be to to take the charge and superintendence of the Lumber Dock; to direct the mode of occupying the same; and collect the fees or charges therefor, as hereinafter established, and pay over the same to the Chamberlain of the city. Superintendent of Lumber Docks.

§ 45. Such superintendent shall take an oath, faithfully to perform the duties of his office; and before entering upon the duties of his office, shall execute a bond with two or more sureties, in the penal sum of five thousand dollars conditioned for the faithful discharge of such duties. Ibid.

§ 46. He shall receive an annual salary of seven hundred and fifty dollars, payable quarterly, for his services; and shall hold his office during the pleasure of the Common Council. Ibid.

§ 47. He shall, on the first Monday of every month, render to the Comptroller, a full and particular statement of all moneys received by him as such officer, verified by oath, stating the names of the persons from whom such moneys were received; the date, the amount and the quantity of timber or logs on which the same was charged; and shall, once in each year, on the first Monday of January, and oftener, if required, furnish a statement to the Common Council, of the whole quantity of timber, logs, spars and other articles which shall have been brought into the said lumber dock during the preceding year; and also the amount remaining therein at the time of making such report. Ibid.

Superintendent of Lumber Docks.

§ 48. He shall also keep a book, in which shall be entered the names of all persons bringing timber to the said lumber dock, specifying therein, the dates, qualities and prices charged therefor, and when the same shall be taken away.

Deposit of Mahogany, Marble, &c.

§ 49. No mahogany or other imported wood, or any blocks of granite or marble, shall be allowed to be deposited in any slip below Pike street, on the east, or Canal street on the west side, and not without the written permission of the Superintendent of Wharves.

Superintendent of Lumber Dock.

§ 50. The said superintendent shall not, in any manner or way whatever, either directly or indirectly, be concerned in the purchase or sale of any timber or lumber whatever, either in the said dock, or to be brought therein, and in case of any breach of the provisions of this section, he shall forfeit his office, and shall not afterward be eligible thereto.

Rates for Lumber Dock.

§ 51. The following rates shall be fixed and collected by the superintendent, on all the articles hereafter mentioned, for admission and storage within the Lumber Dock, viz:

On all squared oak timber, three-eighths of one cent for admission, and one and a half cent per year, for every cubic foot.

On all squared pine or other timber, except oak, one quarter of one cent for admission, and one cent per year, for every cubic foot.

On all dock or pump logs, four cents admission, and sixteen cents per year for each piece.

On all spars or masts, not over fifty feet in length, twenty-five cents for each admission, and one dollar per year, for each piece.

On all spars or masts over fifty feet in length, and not exceeding eighty feet, fifty cents for each admission, and two dollars a year, for each piece.

On all spars or masts eighty feet or upward in length, seventy-five cents each for admission, and three dollars per year, for each piece.

On all plank and other sawed lumber, four cents admission, and sixteen cents per year, for every thousand feet.

Such charges for admission shall be paid, whenever the articles shall be placed within the dock, and be deducted from the payment for rent, when the lumber is taken out of the dock; the rent shall be paid quarterly; and whenever any timber or other articles shall not be kept within the dock for the period of three months from the time of admission therein, the charge thereon shall be the same as if such timber or other articles had remained therein for the period of three months, and so for every three months thereafter. Any expenses which may be incurred, by reason of the removal of any timber or spars, within the basin, by the direction of the superintendent, shall be chargeable to the owner or owners of such timber, and paid by him or them, in the same manner as the other charges under this law.

§ 52. The Comptroller shall lease at public auction, such portion of the wharves and piers around the Lumber Dock, as may not be required for the use of the dock; and may grant the privilege of piling lumber thereon, until the first day of May next; and shall lease the same annually thereafter, at the same time and in the same manner as the other wharves are leased by him. Wharves,&c. at Lumber Dock.

Superintendent of Lumber Dock.

§ 53. It shall be the duty of the superintendent not to permit any timber or other articles within said Lumber Dock, to be removed therefrom, until all charges thereon are first paid.

Ibid.

§ 54. The Comptroller shall furnish the superintendent with a suitable book, for the purpose of keeping all accounts therein, which shall be handed over to his successor in office, from time to time.

CHAPTER XXVII.

OF SALES IN THE PUBLIC STREETS.

ARTICLE I.—OF PLACES AT WHICH FURNITURE MAY BE SOLD AT AUCTION IN THE STREETS.
II.—OF THE REGULATION OF SALES IN THE PUBLIC STREETS.

ARTICLE I.

OF THE PLACES AT WHICH FURNITURE MAY BE SOLD AT AUCTION IN THE STREETS.

§ 1. The following places are hereby designated as the places at which articles of furniture may be exposed for sale and sold, that is to say: Places for sale of Furniture.

1. At Peck slip, between Pearl street and Front street.
2. At Burling slip, between Pearl street and Front street.
3. At Old slip, between Water street and Front street.
4. In Broad street, between Front street and South street.
5. In Vesey street, between Church street and Washington street.
6. In the square in front of Greenwich market, on a line with Christopher street, west of Greenwich street.

§ 2. No goods, wares, merchandise, or other thing whatever, shall be sold at auction, or exposed for sale in any street, road, lane, highway or public place in the city of Time of sales in streets.

New York, except between the hours of nine o'clock in the morning and two o'clock in the afternoon of each day, under the penalty of ten dollars for every such offense, to be sued for and recovered from the seller, auctioneer, or his agent, severally and respectively.

ARTICLE II.

OF THE REGULATION OF SALES IN THE PUBLIC STREETS.

Permission to be gotten of owners of premises.

§ 3. No auctioneer, or his agent or servant, or any other person, shall sell at auction, or expose for sale, or lay or place any goods, wares, merchandise or other thing, in any street, road, lane, highway, or public place in the city of New York, unless such person shall first obtain the consent or permission, in writing, of the occupant of the lot or building before which such articles, or any part thereof, shall be placed or exposed for sale, under the penalty of ten dollars for every such offense, to be sued for and recovered from the seller, auctioneer or his agent, severally and respectively.

Extent to which streets may be occupied.

§ 4. Such articles, after permission granted as required in the third section of this chapter, when placed or exposed for sale, shall not occupy more than one third part in width of the carriage-way of any street, under the penalty of ten dollars for every such offense, to be sued for and recovered from the seller, auctioneer or his agent, severally and respectively.

Regulations as to certain articles.

§ 5. No person shall sell, or expose for sale, or lay or place in any street, lane, road, highway or public place, at any time between the first day of June and the first day of November in each year, any salted beef or pork, dried or pickled fish, blubber, hides, cotton or wool, under the penalty of ten dollars for each offense, to be sued for and recovered from the seller, auctioneer or his agent, severally and respectively.

As to sale of carriages and animals in the streets.

§ 6. No person shall sell, or expose for sale at auction any carriage or carriages, or any animal or animals, of any description, in any public street or place in the city of New York, except in the Fourth avenue, at the corner of Eighty-sixth street, under the penalty of ten dollars for each offense, to be sued for and recovered from the seller, owner or purchaser thereof, severally and respectively.

Things sold in streets to be immediately removed.

§ 7. Every article exposed to sale at auction, or sold in any public place, street, lane, road or highway in the city of New York, shall be removed from the same by the setting of the sun of the day of selling or exposing to sale, under the penalty of ten dollars for each offense, to be sued for and recovered from the auctioneer, his agent, or the purchaser thereof, severally and respectively.

Advertising Sales.

§ 8. No bellman or crier, nor any drum or fife, or other instrument of music, nor any show signal, or means of attracting the attention of passengers other than a sign or flag, shall be employed, or suffered or permitted to be used, at or near any place of sale, or at or near any auction-room, or at or near the residence of any auctioneer, or at or near any auction whatsoever, under a penalty of ten dollars for each offense, to be sued for and recovered from the person using the same, and the auctioneer or his agent, suffering or permitting the same, severally and respectively.

Sales of certain articles in streets prohibited.

§ 9. No auctioneer, or other person, shall sell or expose for sale at public auction or vendue, any dry goods, hardware, wooden ware or tin ware, by retail or in small parcels or pieces, in any public street, lane, highway or public place in the city of New York, (articles of household furniture at the places, and as is hereinbefore provided, alone excepted,) under the penalty of ten dollars for each offense, to be sued for and recovered from the seller, auctioneer or his agent, severally and respectively.

Sales at auction.

§ 10. No auctioneer, or his agent, or servant shall sell or expose for sale at public auction, any goods, wares, merchandise, or other thing whatsoever, to any person or persons who, at the time of bidding for the same, or whilst examining the same, shall be on the sidewalk or carriage-way of any of the streets of the city, under the penalty of ten dollars for every such offense.

Construction.

§ 11. This chapter shall not be construed to prevent the sale of goods to persons who may be standing on the carriage-way of such streets or parts of streets or places, as are hereinbefore mentioned and designated.

Sale of meat, fish or food.

§ 12. No person shall sell, or expose for sale, any meat, fish, or food of any description, in any of the streets or public squares in this city, other than in the markets of said city, under the penalty of ten dollars for each offense, except as follows:—Permission is hereby given to farmers and market gardeners to occupy daily, until 12 o'clock, M., free of charge, the vacant space of the northern and southern extremities of the intersection of Broadway and Sixth avenue, between Thirty-second and Thirty-fifth streets, without infringing upon the streets which the said space intersects, for the purpose only of selling vegetables and market produce of their own farms or gardens, under the supervision and control of the City Inspector.

Penalty.

§ 13. All persons offending against the last preceding section, shall be deemed guilty of a misdemeanor, and be punished, on conviction before the Mayor, Recorder, or one of the Police Justices of said city, by a fine not exceeding ten dollars, or in default of the payment of such fine, by imprisonment, provided such imprisonment does not exceed ten days.

§ 14. No auctioneer, or his agent, or servant, or any other person, shall lay, or place, or sell or expose for sale, any article of household furniture in any street, or public place in the city of New York, other than such as is hereinbefore designated or mentioned, under the penalty of twenty dollars for every such offense, to be sued for and recovered from the seller, auctioneer, or his agent or servant, severally and respectively. Sale of Furniture.

§ 15. No furniture, goods, wares, merchandise, or other article or thing whatever, shall be sold at auction, or exposed for sale by any auctioneer, his agent or servant, or by any other person or persons, upon the sidewalk of Chatham square, between James street and Catharine street, in the city of New York, under the penalty of twenty dollars for every such offense, to be sued for and recovered from the seller, auctioneer, or his agent or servant, or any other person or persons offending, severally and respectively. Sales in Chatham square.

§ 16. Such articles, when exposed for sale, shall not occupy more than twenty feet in width, and not more than twenty-five feet in length, of the carriage-way of Chatham square, between James street and Catharine street, in the said city, and shall not be placed within ten feet of each corner of the streets intersecting Chatham square, nor shall any such articles be placed upon, sold or exposed for sale upon any of the cross-walks or intersections of or in said Chatham square, under the penalty of twenty dollars for every such offense, to be sued for and recovered from the seller, auctioneer, or his agent or servant, severally and respectively. Ibid.

§ 17. All furniture, goods, wares, merchandise or other article or thing whatsoever, sold or exposed for sale in Ibid.

Chatham square, between James street and Catharine street, and authorized to be sold there under and by virtue of this chapter, and all auctioneer stands and conveniences used by or for the auctioneer, or person selling or exposing the same for sale, shall be removed from the said place before two o'clock of the afternoon of the day on which the sale, or offering for sale is by this chapter directed to be made, under the penalty of twenty dollars for every such offense, to be sued for and recovered from the seller, auctioneer, or his agent or servant, severally and respectively.

Sale in Chatham square.

§ 18. No auctioneer or other person shall sell, or expose for sale, at public auction or vendue, any dry goods, hardware, wooden ware, tin ware, earthen ware, china ware, glass ware, goods, wares or merchandise of any description, or any other article whatever, by retail, or in small parcels or pieces, in Chatham square, between James street and Catharine street aforesaid, under the penalty of ten dollars for each offense, to be sued for and recovered from the seller, auctioneer, or his agent or servant, severally and respectively.

Sales of certain things prohibited in streets.

§ 19. No person shall sell, or expose for sale, in any of the streets or slips in the city of New York, any tin plate ware, earthenware, china ware, glass ware, goods, wares and merchandise of any description, or any other article, under the penalty of ten dollars for each offense.

Firewood.

§ 20. No person shall sell, or expose for sale, in any of the streets of said city, any fire-wood of any description, under a penalty of ten dollars for each offense; but nothing herein contained shall prevent the sale, by any licensed cartman of said city, of any fire-wood on any of the wharves of said city.

CHAPTER XXVIII.

OF PUBLIC WORSHIP IN THE STREETS AND PUBLIC PLACES.

§ 1. No person shall be concerned or instrumental in collecting or promoting any assemblage of persons, under pretence of, or for public worship or exhortation, in the Park or Battery, or in any of the markets or streets, or any public place in the city of New York, laid out and appropriated for the common use of the citizens, under the penalty of twenty-five dollars for each offense. Prohibition.

§ 2. It shall be the duty of all magistrates, constables and police officers of the said city, to prevent all such assemblies, and to prosecute, apprehend and report to the attorney of the Board, all persons concerned or instrumental in promoting the same. Apprehension of offenders.

§ 3. Every constable or police officer who shall neglect or refuse to perform his duty in the premises, shall, for every neglect, forfeit and pay the sum of five dollars. Ibid.

§ 4. Nothing contained in the preceding sections of this chapter shall be construed to prevent any clergyman or minister of any denomination from preaching in any place in this city, who shall have obtained the written permission of either the Mayor, or one of the Aldermen or Councilmen of this city therefor. Permission to preach in the streets.

§ 5. The first section of this chapter shall not be construed to prevent any ministers or people of any church, usually called Baptists, from assembling in proper places in the city of New York, for the purpose of performing Baptists.

the rites of baptism according to the ceremonies of such church.

Disorders provided against.

§ 6. No person shall disturb, molest or interrupt any clergyman or minister who shall have obtained permission according to section four of this chapter, or who shall be performing the rites of baptism, as permitted by section five of this chapter, or shall commit any riot or disorder in any such assembly, under the penalty of twenty-five dollars for each offense.

CHAPTER XXIX.

OF DRIVING HORSES IN THE CITY.

§ 1. No person shall ride or drive any horse or horses in the city of New York, with greater speed than at the rate of five miles an hour, under the penalty of ten dollars for each offense, to be recovered from the owner or driver thereof, severally and respectively. Speed

§ 2. No person, upon turning the corner of any street in the city of New York, shall ride or drive any horse or horses, otherwise than on a walk, under the penalty of five dollars for each offense, to be paid by the owner or driver thereof, severally and respectively. Turning corners.

§ 3. No horse shall be suffered or permitted to go loose or at large, in any of the streets in the city of New York, under the penalty of ten dollars for every such offense, to be paid by the owner or person having the care, charge or keeping thereof, severally and respectively. Horses running at large.

§ 4. No person shall suffer or permit to go, or lead, or ride, or drive any horse upon any sidewalk in the city of New York, under the penalty of five dollars for each offense, to be paid by the owner or person having the care, charge or keeping thereof, severally and respectively. Horses on side-walks.

§ 5. No person shall run, or race any horse in any public street, road or avenue, in the city of New York, nor shall consent to or suffer such racing, under the penalty of fifty dollars, to be recovered from the person or persons who shall so race, or suffer, or permit such racing, and the owner, rider, and the person having charge of any animal which shall so race and run, severally and respectively. Racing.

Racing.

§ 6. The last preceding section of this chapter shall be construed to prevent and punish the running, racing or trotting of any horse or horses, for any trial of speed, or for the purpose of passing any other horse or horses, whether the same be founded upon any stake, bet or otherwise.

Tandem.

§ 7. No person shall drive one horse before another, in the manner commonly called tandem, otherwise than on a walk, in any street in the city of New York, under the penalty of five dollars for each offense, to be paid by the owner or driver thereof, severally and respectively.

Sale of horses at auction.

§ 8. No person shall show or expose for sale at auction, any horse or other animal, in any street, lane or avenue in the city of New York, under the penalty of five dollars for every such offense.

Bells to sleigh horses.

§ 9. No person shall drive any horse before a sleigh or sled, through any of the public streets or avenues of this city, unless there shall be a sufficient number of bells attached to the harness of such horse and sleigh or sled, to warn persons of his approach, under the penalty of ten dollars for each offense, to be paid by the driver, owner or person having the care, charge or keeping thereof, severally and respectively.

CHAPTER XXX.

OF SINKS, PRIVIES AND CESSPOOLS.

§ 1. No sink, privy or cesspool shall hereafter be constructed, or made in any part of the city of New York, south of Fourteenth street, unless the same shall be constructed of brick or stone, and be, at least, ten feet in depth from the surface of the ground, when such depth is practicable, under the penalty of fifty dollars, to be recovered from the owner and builder of the same, severally and respectively. Regulation of construction.

§ 2. No person shall inclose or cover any sink, privy or cesspool, or arch over or place upon the same, any house, shed or covering, until such sink, privy or cesspool shall have been examined, and measured by the City Inspector or the Health Warden, of the ward in which the same may be, under the penalty of twenty-five dollars for every such offense, to be recovered from the owner and builder of the same, severally and respectively. To be examined and measured before being covered.

§ 3. No privy, sink or cesspool, shall hereafter be made or constructed, within thirty feet of any public well or pump, under the penalty of one hundred dollars, to be paid by the owner and builder thereof, severally and respectively. Regulations of construction.

§ 4. No person shall dig any sink or cesspool, or build or erect any privy, without leaving, at least, two feet of solid earth, or solid mason work laid in mortar or cement, to be measured from the interior line of said sink, between such sink, cesspool or privy and the adjoining lot, under the penalty of twenty-five dollars, to be paid by the owner and builder thereof, severally and respectively. Ibid.

Covering privies and removing contents.

§ 5. No person shall cover over any sink or privy that may be full, or partly full, nor draw off the contents thereof into any hole or place dug or made to receive the same, under the penalty of twenty-five dollars, to be recovered from the owner of such premises or the person doing the same.

Contents to be kept two feet below the surface.

§ 6. The owner or occupant of any house, store, building or premises, to which any sink, privy or cesspool shall belong or appertain, shall not permit the contents thereof to rise within two feet of the surface of the earth, under the penalty of twenty-five dollars, to be recovered from the owner or occupant thereof, severally and respectively.

Emptying Sinks, &c.

§ 7. The owner or occupant of any house, lot or premises in the city of New York, shall not empty or remove, or cause, or suffer, or permit to be emptied or removed, the contents of any sink, privy or cesspool, between the last day of May and the last day of September in each year, without the express permission of the City Inspector, obtained for that purpose, under the penalty of twenty dollars for each offense.

Removal of tubs kept in privies.

§ 8. The owner or occupant of any house, lot or premises shall not cause, or suffer or permit any tub used in any necessary house, sink or privy to be removed, except between the hours of eleven o'clock in the evening and three o'clock in the morning, from the first day of May to the last day of September, in any year; and between the hours of ten o'clock in the evening and six o'clock in the morning, during the remainder of the year, under the penalty of ten dollars for each offense.

Contents not to run in streets, &c.

§ 9. No person shall cast, lay, or suffer to run in or upon any street, wharf or pier, or in any slip or dock, or upon or within the distance of three feet of any wharf, or in any lane, alley, lot or vacant place to the southward of

Fourteenth street, the contents of any sink, tub, privy or cesspool, under the penalty of ten dollars for each offense.

§ 10. No person shall throw or deposit, or cause or suffer to be thrown or deposited in any sink, privy or cesspool, any vegetable substance or garbage, or offal of fish or poultry, or any dead animal, under the penalty of twenty-five dollars for every such offense. Garbage, &c. not to be thrown in sinks.

§ 11. The owner or occupant of any house, lot or premises in the city of New York, shall not cause or suffer or permit any tub to be used in any necessary house, sink or privy, appertaining or belonging to such premises, unless such tub shall be made perfectly tight, and well secured with copper, brass or iron hoops and handles, under the penalty of ten dollars, to be recovered from the owner or occupant, severally and respectively. Regulations of tubs in privies.

§ 12. The owner or occupant of any house, store, building or premises to which a sink, privy or necessary house shall belong or appertain, in which tubs shall be used, shall not suffer or permit the contents thereof to rise within three inches of the top of said tub, under the penalty of ten dollars for each offense, to be recovered from the owner or occupant, severally and respectively. Ibid.

§ 13. No person shall empty or remove the contents of any tub, sink or privy, in the city of New York, otherwise than in tubs, boxes, or casks made tight and closely covered; each tub, box, cask and cover to be approved by the City Inspector; and any person who shall use for such purposes, any tub, box, cask or cover, other than those approved as aforesaid, shall forfeit and pay the sum of fifty dollars for each offense. Removal of contents of privies.

§ 14. It shall not be lawful for any person or persons to throw the contents of any tub, box, cask, sink or privy into As to throwing contents in rivers.

the North or East rivers, south of Forty-second street, save and except under the circumstances hereinafter mentioned, under the penalty of fifty dollars for each offense.

Regulations of vessels receiving contents of privies, &c.

§ 15. The several wharves or piers on the North and East rivers, where the contractors for cleaning the streets are permitted to heap up manure, excepting pier number one, East river, are hereby designated and set apart for vessels to come and be fastened to, subject to the directions and regulations of the City Inspector. A pier in the First Ward, to be selected by the Alderman of that District, for the same purpose, from which piers and in which vessels the night-scavengers shall deposit the contents of tubs, boxes, casks, sinks and privies, provided the same shall not be what is called "water;" and it shall be lawful for the night-scavengers to ask, demand, and receive therefor, from the owner of such vessel or vessels, the sum of twenty-five cents for each and every full load of twenty-four cubical feet; but in case there shall not be at the time, a vessel or vessels at said wharves or piers, capable of containing or receiving the contents so removed, or in case the contents shall at any time be what is called "water," then, and in each of the cases above-mentioned, the night-scavengers may deposit the contents of the tubs, boxes, casks, sinks or privies, from the ends of the said piers, or if vessels shall be lying at the ends of said piers, from a point as near as practicable to the outer ends of the said piers, into the river; and in case any night-scavenger or other person shall deposit the contents of any tub, box, cask, sink or privy at any other wharf, or from any other pier, than those before-mentioned, then such night-scavenger or other person shall forfeit and pay the sum of fifty dollars, for each and every offense; and, if a night-scavenger, he shall be subject, in case of any subsequent offense to forfeit his license, at the option of the City Inspector.

§ 16. No person shall remove, or cause to be removed, the contents, or any part thereof, of any tub, box, cask, sink or privy, south of Forty-second street, without a written or printed permission from the City Inspector, which permission shall specify the time within which the said contents may be removed, and the piers to which the same may be taken and deposited as mentioned in these ordinances, either of which piers the scavenger may elect; and if any person shall remove, or cause, or allow, or assist in removing the contents, or any part thereof, of any tub, box, cask, sink or privy, without such permission, or at any other time than that specified therein, or shall convey to and deposit, or assist in conveying and depositing, any of the contents aforesaid, from any other pier than one of those described in this chapter, he shall forfeit and pay for each and every offense, the sum of fifty dollars. Permission to remove contents of privies.

§ 17. It shall be the duty of the City Inspector or Health Warden, to examine each sink or privy in each Ward or District, once in each year, and a report shall be made to the City Inspector, on or before the first day of April in each year, of the situation of each sink or privy in each ward or district, and when any sink or privy requires emptying before the tenth of September next thereafter, notice shall be given to the owner of such sink or privy, or his agent, or, if they cannot be found, the tenants thereof, requiring the removal of the contents of such sink or privy to be performed forthwith; but the omission of such notice shall not excuse the person, whose duty it is to cause such sink to be emptied, from the payment of the sum of ten dollars, as hereinbefore specified. Examination of Privies.

§ 18. The City Inspector is directed to advertise, and sell to the highest bidder, in conformity with law, the right for five years, to all the night-soil taken from the sinks in Sale of Night soil.

the city; and the same shall be deposited by the scavengers in boats to be furnished by the person receiving the right; the boats to be used to be tight deck boats of no less than fifty tons, custom house measurement; the person who shall receive the right, shall be bound to enter into a contract with the City Inspector for the faithful performance of his contract for five years, and give security to the amount of one thousand dollars. The person or persons who shall have the contract awarded to him or them, shall have the right of the exclusive use of two berths at each of the following named piers, to wit: The pier foot of Clarkson street; the south side of pier foot of Twenty-sixth street, North river; the south side of pier foot of Thirty-eighth street, East river; also the north side of pier foot of Rivington street, and that the scavengers be compelled, under a penalty of twenty-five dollars, to proceed directly from the place where such soil shall be gathered, to the river, or to a street leading directly to the nearest dumping place, and dump all the night-soil taken from the privies or sinks into the boats of such person or persons who shall receive the contract from the city; and return the contract to the Common Council for confirmation.

Removal of dead animals

§ 19. The City Inspector hereby is authorized and directed immediately to advertise, for thirty days, proposals for the sale of, and then, in conformity to the provisions of the laws of the State, to sell to the highest bidder, who shall furnish adequate security, the right and privilege of collecting and removing dead horses, and other dead animals, blood, offal and other refuse matter and nuisances, in accordance with the following specifications, for the term of five years next thereafter; the contract to be prepared by the Counsel to the Corporation.*

* NOTE.—This section was passed on 14th December, 1855. Though temporary in its character, its operation may extend over five years, and it may be the basis of a permanent system.

SPECIFICATIONS.

First. The contractor shall collect, and remove from all parts of the city to the dock and slip, at the foot of Forty-fifth street, East river, or to such other docks or slips as the Common Council may, at any time or times hereafter designate and provide, all dead horses and other dead animals; and shall, at all times, provide and keep, at his own cost and expense, such a number of suitable carts as shall be necessary, for a prompt and faithful performance of such work; said carts shall be approved and licensed by by the City Inspector. Removal of dead animals.

Second. The contractor shall, at all times, provide and keep, at such dock or slip as aforesaid, a suitable number of suitable boats, scows, barges or vessels for receiving, and shall receive therein all dead horses, and other dead animals, and all blood, offal and other refuse matter from butchers' slaughter-houses, and all bones, fish, fish offal, diseased or tainted meats, and all other nuisances of a similar kind, which may or shall be offered by any person or persons at such dock or slip.

Third. The contractor shall furnish, at his own cost and expense, suitable boxes for the reception of all orders or complaints; the same to be placed, one at each police station-house in the city, and one at the office of the City Inspector, and to cause all orders and complaints to be collected from each and every station-house, and from the office of the City Inspector, at least twice every day; and shall cause all dead animals to be removed, in accordance with the contract, as soon as possible after the reception of any such order or complaint, or other notice.

Fourth. The contractor shall, at least once in every day, remove all such dead horses, animals, blood, offal, and other matters and nuisances as aforesaid, to some suitable

Removal of dead animals

and proper place or places beyond the limits of the city; and whenever the City Inspector shall so direct, such removal shall be made twice in each day, during the months of June, July, August and September.

Fifth. Approved sureties, to the amount of thirty thousand dollars, will be required for the faithful performance and execution of the contract, to the end of the term, which security shall be renewed within three weeks of the close of the year. In every respect, the work to be performed as required, and any neglect or refusal, on the part of the contractor to perform the whole or any part of the stipulations of the contract, or of the requirements of these specifications, shall be sufficient to empower and authorize the City Inspector to proceed to perform so much thereof as shall be neglected or refused, at the expense of, and chargeable by the Corporation to the contractor and his sureties, and such refusal or neglect, shall authorize and empower the Common Council at any time to revoke and annul such contracts.

Sixth. The bid shall state the amount which the bidder will pay per annum for such right and privilege, which amount shall be paid by the contractor to the Comptroller, in equal quarterly sums, at the end of each quarter.

Seventh. A strict compliance with the provisions of the chapters relating to "Contracts for supplies, and work done for the Corporation," and amendments thereto, will be observed and required.

Eighth. Should the person or persons to whom the contract shall be awarded, fail to attend with his or their sureties, and to execute the same in writing, within three days after being notified that such contract is ready, he or they shall be considered as having abandoned it, and shall forfeit all right to such award.

CHAPTER XXXI.

OF PARTITION FENCES AND WALLS.

§ 1. All partition fences in the city of New York shall be made and maintained by the owners of the land on each side; and each party shall make and keep in repair one half part thereof, when it can be conveniently divided. How made & kept in repair.

§ 2. In case of any dispute between the parties, concerning the division of any such fence, or as to what part or portion of it shall be made or repaired by each party respectively; and in all cases of dispute concerning the sufficiency of any fence in the city of New York, the matter shall be determined by the Alderman and Councilmen for the time being, of the district of the ward in which such partition or other fence may be situated. Disputes, how settled.

§ 3. When any partition fence cannot be conveniently divided, the same shall be made and kept in repair at the joint and equal expense of the owners of the land on each side. How made & kept in repair.

§ 4. When the regulation of a lot, in conformity with the street on which it is situated, shall require the ground of such lot to be raised and kept up higher than the ground of the adjoining lot or lots, and a partition wall for supporting the same shall be necessary, such partition wall shall be made and maintained by the owners respectively of the land on each side; and when the same can be equally divided, each party shall make and keep in repair one-half part thereof. Ibid.

§ 5. If any dispute shall arise concerning the division of such partition wall between the parties, or as to what Disputes, how settled, part or portion of it should be made or repaired by each respectively, or concerning the sufficiency of any such partition wall, the same shall be determined by the Alderman and Councilmen as aforesaid.

How made & kept in repair.

§ 6. Where any partition wall cannot be conveniently divided, the same shall be made and kept in repair at the joint and equal expense of the owners of the land on each side.

Regulation of Lots.

§ 7. The regulation of lots in conformity with the street shall be calculated not to exceed a descent of two inches on every ten feet.

How made & kept in repair.

§ 8. Where any owner or owners shall insist on maintaining his, her, or their ground higher than such regulation, the surplus partition wall which may be necessary to support such height, shall be made and maintained at the individual expense of such owner or owners.

Ibid.

§ 9. Where any such owner or owners shall insist on regulating his, her or their ground with a descent less than two inches on every ten feet, the surplus partition wall necessary to support the ground in the adjoining lot, regulated in conformity with the preceding 6th section, shall, in like manner, be made and maintained at the individual expense of such owner or owners.

Ibid.

§ 10. If any person whose duty it may be to make or repair any partition fence or partition wall, or any part thereof, in pursuance of the provisions of this law, shall neglect so to do, for six days after being requested, in writing, by the owner or occupant of the adjoining ground, it shall be lawful for such owner or occupant, to make, or repair such partition fence or wall, or cause the same to be done, and to recover from such person the expense of making or repairing so much thereof as ought to have been made or repaired by him or her, together with costs of suit in any court having cognizance thereof.

§ 11. All outside and boundary fences, and all fences erected on the line of any public road, street, lane or avenue in the city of New York, shall be at least five feet high, and shall be built of good and substantial materials, and sufficient in all respects to keep out and prevent the encroachment of cattle, sheep, hogs and other animals, and shall be kept in good repair, and of the height above-mentioned. Height and construction of fences.

§ 12. The owner or owners, lessee or lessees, tenant or tenants of any lot, piece of ground or premises upon which any fence not of the height, and that shall not be erected in the manner, and maintained at the height mentioned in the preceding section, or who having so erected the same shall not keep the same in good repair, shall not recover for any damage he, they or she may sustain from any cattle, sheep, hog or other animal, doing damage upon his, their or her premises; nor shall any cattle, sheep, hog or other animal be placed in pound for doing damage, unless such fence be erected and kept of the height, and in the manner mentioned in the 11th section. Neglect of repairs, &c.

§ 13. In case of any dispute between the parties, concerning any fence embraced within this chapter, or the sufficiency thereof, the matter shall be determined by the Alderman and Councilmen, for the time being, of the district of the ward in which such fence may be situate. Disputes, how settled.

CHAPTER XXXII.

OF THE BLASTING OF ROCKS.

Regulations for Blasting.

§ 1. In all cases of blasting rocks or stones within the city of New York, south of a line drawn across the island, one hundred feet northerly of Eighty-sixth street, each blast, before firing it, shall be securely covered with six timbers, of not less than four inches thick, ten inches wide and ten feet long each, to be placed over and around each charge, and to be held in place by at least three hundred pounds of large stones piled on top of them.

Ibid.

§ 2. Three minutes' notice, before firing the blasts, shall be given, by displaying a red flag on a staff, not less than ten feet high, set in a conspicuous place, within twenty-five feet of the point where the charge is placed, and also by calling out the words "a blast," several times repeated, and loud enough to be distinctly heard at a distance of two hundred feet from the point of discharge.

Penalties.

§ 3. For every violation of either of the preceding sections of this chapter, the offending party, or, if the work be done under a contract, the contractor, upon complaint and conviction thereof, before a police justice, shall be liable to a fine of twenty-five dollars, and stand committed until the same is paid.

CHAPTER XXXIII.

OF HOISTWAYS.

§ 1. The owner or occupant of each and every store or other building in the city of New York, in which there is a hoistway, shall cause the said hoistway on each story of said store or other building, to be forthwith inclosed by a good and sufficient railing around the opening thereof, and provide for the inclosing of such opening by a trap door; and each owner or occupant of any such building or store, shall cause said railing to be securely fastened up, and said trap-door to be closed, on the completion of the business of each day in such store or building; and for every violation of the provisions of this section, or of any of them, the owner or owners, occupant or occupants of any such store or building, shall be liable to a penalty of fifty dollars for each and every offense. Regulations for hoistways and penalties

§ 2. The penalties imposed by this chapter, shall, when recovered, be paid by the Attorney to the Corporation, to the Treasurer of the Fire Department of the city of New York, for the use and benefit of said Fire Department. Recovery of Penalties.

§ 3. It shall be the duty of the Fire Wardens of the city of New York to examine into all violations of this chapter, and to give, or cause to be given, a notice in writing, signed by at least one of them, to the owner or owners, occupant or occupants, or by leaving such notice with any person of suitable age on the premises, requiring such cause of violation to be removed within ten days after service of such notice; if said violation is not removed, to report the same in writing to the Corporation Attorney. Duty of Fire Wardens.

CHAPTER XXXIV.

OF WEIGHTS AND MEASURES.

ARTICLE I.

OF THE DISTRICTS FOR SEALING AND INSPECTING WEIGHTS AND MEASURES,

First district defined.

§ 1. All that part of the city of New York, lying southerly and westerly of a line running from the East river through the centre of Fulton street to Broadway; thence through the centre of Broadway to Bloomingdale road at Tenth street; thence through the centre of the Bloomingdale road to Union place at Fourteenth street; thence through the centre of Fourteenth street to the Bowery; thence along the easterly side of Union place to the Fourth avenue; and thence through the centre of the Fourth avenue to Harlem river, shall be known as the First District for the sealing and inspection of weights and measures; and the Sealer and Inspector of Weights and Measures who may be appointed for the said First District, shall be confined thereto in the performance of their respective duties.

§ 2. All the remaining part of the said city, not embraced within the limits of the said First District, shall be known as the Second District, for the sealing and inspection of weights and measures; and the Sealer and Inspector of Weights and Measures who may be appointed for the said Second District, shall be confined thereto in the performance of their respective duties. Second District.

ARTICLE II.

OF THE SEALING AND INSPECTION OF WEIGHTS AND MEASURES.

§ 3. All persons using weights, measures, scale-beams, patent balances, steelyards or any other instrument, in weighing or measuring any article intended to be purchased or sold in the city of New York, shall cause the same to be sealed and marked by a City Sealer of Weights and Measures in the said city. All weights, &c., to be sealed and marked.

§ 4. Any person who shall, in weighing or measuring any article for purchase or sale within the city of New York, use any weight, measure, scalebeam, patent balance, steelyard or other instrument, not sealed and marked as is required by the third section of this chapter, shall forfeit and pay the sum of fifty dollars for each and every offense. Penalty.

§ 5. All weights, measures, scalebeams, patent balances, steelyards and other instruments for weighing, to be sealed and adjusted by a City Sealer of Weights and Measures in the city of New York, shall be made conformable to the standard of the State; and shall be marked by him with the initials of his name, and the year in which the same shall be sealed and marked. Standard.

§ 6. If any person shall use in the city of New York, in weighing or measuring, as aforesaid, any weight, mea- Penalty.

sure, scalebeam, patent balance, steelyard or other instrument, which shall not be conformable to such standard, or shall use, in weighing as aforesaid, any scalebeam, patent balance, steelyard or other instrument, which shall be out of order or incorrect, or which shall not balance, he, she, or they shall forfeit and pay, for every such offense, the sum of twenty-five dollars.

Time of Inspection.

§ 7. It shall be the duty of the Inspectors of Weights and Measures, and each is hereby authorized to inspect and examine, at least once in each and every year, and as much oftener as he may think proper, all weights, measures, scalebeams, patent balances, steelyards and other instruments used in his district in weighing and measuring as aforesaid.

Rules of Inspection.

§ 8. No person shall refuse to exhibit any weights, measures, scalebeams, patent balances, steelyards, or other instruments, to either of said inspectors, for the purpose of being so inspected and examined, under the penalty of twenty-five dollars for every such offense.

Ibid.

§ 9. No person shall, in any way or manner, obstruct, hinder, or molest any Inspector of Weights and Measures in the performanee of his duties as hereby imposed upon him, under a penalty upon every such person, of twenty-five dollars for every such offense.

ARTICLE III.

OF THE FEES OF THE INSPECTORS OF WEIGHTS AND MEASURES.

Fees of Inspectors.

§ 10. The said inspectors shall be entitled to demand and receive the following fees for inspecting and examining weights, measures, scalebeams, patent balances, steelyards, and other instruments for weighing, used in the city of New York, namely :

1. For every weight of fourteen pounds, or upward, three cents.
2. For every weight of a smaller denomination, one cent and a half.
3. For every liquid measure, two cents.
4. For every yard and dry measure, three cents.
5. For every scalebeam, patent balance, steelyard or other instrument used for weighing, three cents.

§ 11. All weights, measures, scalebeams, patent balances, steelyards, and other instruments used for weighing, shall be inspected at the stores and places where the same may be used; but in case they, or any of them, shall be found not conformable to the standard of this State they shall be sent by the owner thereof, at his expense, to the office of the City Sealer, for the purpose of being adjusted and sealed, within three days after the owner thereof shall be required so to do, in writing, by the said inspector, under the penalty of ten dollars for every such neglect. Rules of Inspection.

§ 12. It shall not be lawful for the said inspectors to made the aforesaid charges for inspecting and examining weights, measures, scalebeams, patent balances, steelyards or other instruments used for weighing, more than once in each year, unless they shall be found to be not conformable to the said standard. Fees of Inspection to be charged but once a year.

§ 13. It shall be the duty of each of the said inspectors to make a register of all the weights, measures, scalebeams, patent balances, steelyards and other instruments used for weighing, inspected by him, in which he shall state the names of the owners of the same, and whether they are conformable to the standard of the State. Record of Inspection.

§ 14. It shall also be the duty of the said inspectors to report, forthwith, to the Sealer of Weights and Measures, Report of Incorrect weights, &c.

the names of all persons whose weights, measures, scalebeams, patent balances, steelyards or other instruments used for weighing, shall be found to be incorrect.

Copy of Register to be delivered to Clerk of C.C.

§ 15. It shall also be the duty of the said Inspectors of Weights and Measures, once in every three months, to deliver a copy of the register made or kept by them, as mentioned in 13th section of this chapter, during the preceding quarter of the year, to the Clerk of the Common Council.

Report to Corporation Attorney.

§ 16. It shall be the duty of the Inspectors of Weights and Measures and Sealer of Weights and Measures, to report, forthwith, to the Attorney of the Corporation, the names and places of business of all persons violating this chapter, and of all persons making use of any fraudulent or unsealed weights and measures, guage or balances.

Sealers and Inspectors not to sell weights, &c.

§ 17. It shall not be lawful for the said inspectors or sealers to vend any weights, measures, scalebeams, patent balances, steelyards or other instruments to be used for weighing, or to offer or expose the same for sale in the city of New York, under the penalty of fifty dollars for every such offense.

ARTICLE IV.

OF THE FEES OF THE CITY SEALERS OF WEIGHTS AND MEASURES.

Fees of Sealers.

§ 18. The said Sealers of Weights and Measures shall be entitled to demand and receive the following fees for their services:

For sealing and marking every scalebeam, patent balance, steelyard or other instrument used for weighing in the city of New York, twelve and a half cents.

For sealing and marking measures of extension, at the rate of twelve and a half cents per yard, not to exceed fifty cents for any one measure.

For sealing and marking every weight, three cents.

For sealing and marking liquid and dry measures: for every measure under one gallon, three cents; for one gallon and over, twelve and a half cents each.

For sealing and marking every measure of half a bushel, twelve and a half cents; for every measure of two bushels, seventy-five cents; and for every measure of three bushels and over, one dollar.

The said sealer shall also be entitled to a reasonable compensation for making such weights and measures conform to the standard established by law.

Standard Weights and Measures, custody of.

§ 19. Whenever any Sealer of Weights and Measures shall resign, be removed from office, or remove from the city, it shall be the duty of the person so resigning, removing or removed, to deliver, at the City Inspector's office, all the standard beams, weights and measures in his possession.

CHAPTER XXXV.

OF THE PUBLIC MARKETS.

ARTICLE I.

OF MARKET AND MARKET DAYS.

Public Markets designated. § 1. The following places are hereby severally designated and declared to be the public markets of the city of New York, to wit: Catharine market, Centre market, Clinton market, Essex market, Franklin market, Fulton market, Gouverneur market, Monroe market, Greenwich market, Jefferson market, Tompkins market, Washington market and Union market.

Hay market. § 2. The ground formerly occupied for a market at the foot of Grand street, East river, is hereby declared to be a hay market. Provided always, that the carts or wagons shall stand in one line only.

Market days. § 3. Every day in the week, excepting Sunday, shall be a public market day within the city.

Lease of Stalls and Stands. § 4. The Comptroller, under the direction of the Common Council, shall, from time to time, lease at auction, pursuant to law, for one or more years, all the butchers' stalls, and so many of the stands for fishermen, country people, and sellers of vegetables and fruit, as they may think proper.

Rent of stalls, &c. § 5. The rent of all stalls and stands in the public markets shall be payable daily, under condition of forfeiture;

and it shall be the duty of the clerks of the respective markets to collect the same, each day, and pay over the amount thereof, together with all other fees, to the City Chamberlain, on Thursday in every week.

ARTICLE II.

OF CLERKS OF THE MARKETS.

§ 6. It shall be the duty of the clerks of each market, provided with a market bell, to cause the same to be rung for five minutes previously to the closing of such market on every market day, and every butcher or other person attending such market, with articles for sale, who shall remain within the limits of the same for fifteen minutes after the bell shall have been rung as aforesaid, for the purpose of selling or exposing for sale any article or thing, shall forfeit and pay five dollars for every such offense. **Opening and closing of Markets.**

§ 7. It shall be the duty of the said clerks to examine all articles, in each of their markets respectively, which they may suspect to be unwholesome or stale, or blown, plaited, raised or stuffed meat, or measly pork, or flesh of animals dead by accident or disease, or known or suspected to be diseased at the killing of the same. And no person shall hinder, obstruct or molest any clerk in the performance of the duty herein enjoined, under the penalty of fifty dollars for each offense. **Unwholesome food, examination of.**

§ 8. It shall be the duty of the said clerks to assign and set apart certain portions of the street at or near the said public markets, for the purpose of exposing for sale and selling garden produce; and no person shall expose for sale or sell any garden produce or other thing whatsoever, in any street at or near the said public markets, other **Garden produce.**

than in the place or places so assigned and set apart by the said clerks, under the penalty of ten dollars for every such offense.

General Arrangements. § 9. It shall be the duty of the said clerks, to give directions respecting the arrangement or removal of any article, vehicle, cart, wagon, box, basket or other thing, in the market, or streets adjoining thereto. And any person who shall neglect or refuse to obey such direction, shall forfeit and pay, for every such offense, the sum of twenty-five dollars.

Ibid. § 10. In case of the refusal or neglect to obey the directions of the said clerks or either of them, it shall be lawful for, and shall be the duty of the said clerk of any such market, forthwith to remove, or cause such article, cart, vehicle, wagon, box, basket, or other thing, to be removed to such place as he shall have previously directed, or to such other place as he shall think proper in such market or street adjoining thereto.

Ibid. § 11. If such article, cart, vehicle, wagon, box, basket, or other thing shall be replaced, after having been removed, as provided in the last preceding section of this chapter, or shall remain in, or incumber or obstruct, such market or street adjoining thereto, it shall be lawful for, and shall be the duty of the clerk of such market, to order and cause the same to be removed into the yard of the Superintendent of Repairs to Public Buildings of the city of New York, or other suitable place within the said city.

Suspension of persons having stalls or stands. § 12. The said clerks shall have power to suspend any person having a stated stall or stand in any public market, or occupying any part of said market, or the streets adjoining the same, from occupying or using any part of such market, or the streets adjacent thereto, whether such person be a licensed butcher or not; and the said clerk shall, immediately after such suspension, report to the Superintendent of Markets the reasons of such suspension, and the decision of said Superintendent, in all cases, shall be final.

§ 13. In case of such suspension, the said clerk making such suspension shall, with all convenient dispatch, make a report of the same in writing, with the reasons therefor, to the Superintendent of Markets. Suspension of persons having stalls or stands.

§ 14. No person, suspended as aforesaid, after being served with a written notice of such suspension, shall occupy any part of such market, or the streets adjoining the same, with any thing whatsoever, until the said Superintendent shall have acted in the matter, and either restored such person, or confirmed the said suspension and removed such person from the market, under the penalty of ten dollars for each offense. Ibid.

§ 15. The said clerks shall keep a list of the names of all persons holding permits from the Superintendent of Markets, and shall interchange such lists with each other, from time to time, at least once in every three months. List to be kept by clerk

§ 16. In case of suspicion respecting the weight of any article sold, or offered for sale by weight, or of the quantity of any article sold or offered for sale by measure, in any of the public markets, market places or streets contiguous thereto, it shall be the duty of the said clerk of such market, to weigh or measure the same; and if any such article shall be found deficient in weight, or measure, the person selling or offering the same for sale, shall forfeit and pay ten dollars for each offense. Suspicion of short weight, &c., how determined.

§ 17. It shall be the duty of the said clerks, once in every month, or oftener if they shall think fit, to inspect and examine all the weights, measures and beams used in Inspection of weights and measures by clerks.

weighing or measuring in their respective markets, or in the streets at or near the said markets. And if any person shall neglect or refuse to exhibit his or their weights, measures or beams, or any of them, for the purpose of examination or inspection as aforesaid, or shall obstruct, hinder or molest either of the said clerks, in the performance of the duties enjoined by this section, he, she or they shall forfeit, for every such offense, the sum of twenty-five dollars.

Attendance of Clerks.

§ 18. It shall be the duty of the said clerks to attend constantly in their respective markets, from sunrise to the close of the market, for the purpose of carrying the provisions of this chapter into effect.

Report to Corporation Attorney.

§ 19. It shall be the duty of the said clerks to keep a list of all persons holding stalls or stands in their respective markets; and the said clerks are hereby enjoined and required forthwith to report all violations of any of the provisions of this chapter to the Attorney of the Corporation, for prosecution.

Chains at Fulton market.

§ 20. It shall be the duty of the Clerk of Fulton Market to cause chains to be placed across the entrance of the inner court or square of said market, immediately after the ringing of the first bell of said market, leaving a space sufficiently large for the admission of foot passengers within the said court.

Clerk at Fulton market.

§ 21. The Clerk of Fulton Market shall attend daily at the said market, from the closing of the same until ten o'clock at night, and also on Sundays, for the purpose of preventing disorderly assemblages of persons, and of arresting all vagrants and persons who shall be found at the said market disturbing the peace.

Exclusion of Forestallers, &c.

§ 22. It shall be the duty of the said clerks to exclude from their respective markets all persons who shall be engaged in combinations to raise the price of provisions, or who shall have been guilty of forestalling therein; and the said clerks shall also report forthwith to the said Superintendent, the names of all persons engaged in any of the said practices.

§ 23. The clerk of each market now in the city of New York, or which may be hereafter erected therein, shall assign some proper and convenient place in his market, for persons wanting employment, to stand, and to which those having occasion to hire, may also resort for their mutual accommodation. Persons wanting employment.

§ 24. The clerks of the respective markets shall report, at least once in three months, to the City Inspector, the amount of fees and rents received by them from persons occupying stalls and stands in the public markets, and who are permanent occupants, stating particularly the names of the different occupants, and the amount each of them pay, and how often they pay. Report of Fees and Rents.

ARTICLE III.

OF BUTCHERS.

§ 25. The Mayor of the city of New York shall, from time to time, issue licenses, under his hand and seal, to exercise and carry on the trade and business of butchers, in such public market as may be designated in such licenses. Licenses to Butchers fo markets.

§ 26. All licenses so issued, or which have been issued heretofore, shall expire and cease on the first Monday of December, after the granting thereof, and shall be renewed by the said Mayor. Duration of Licenses.

§ 27. For every license issued as aforesaid, shall be paid the sum of one dollar to the Mayor, on granting the same; License fee.

and for every renewal of such license, the sum of twenty-five cents.

Butchers in markets to be licensed.

§ 28. No person shall exercise or carry on the trade or business of a butcher, or any branch or part thereof, in the public markets, without being licensed or permitted for that purpose, by or under the authority of the Common Council, under the penalty of fifty dollars for each offense.

Persons not to sell meat without License.

§ 29. No person, other than those licensed so to do, shall cut up, in any of the markets of the city of New York, any beef, pork, veal, mutton or lamb, and sell or expose the same for sale, by the joint or in pieces, under the penalty of fifty dollars for each offense.

Sales to be at their own stalls.

§ 30. No licensed butcher, or his agent or servant, shall cut up, or expose for sale, or sell any beef, pork, veal, mutton or lamb, in any part of any of the public markets, other than at his own licensed stall, under the penalty of ten dollars for each offense.

Weights, Scalebeams, &c., regulation, &c.

§ 31. Every butcher shall have and use his own scale-beams and weights, which shall be suspended in some conspicuous place in front of, or at the side of his stall, on a line parallel with the front of his stall, under the penalty of five dollars for every day's omission or neglect.

Ibid.

§ 32. The last preceding section shall not be construed to prevent any two butchers, whose stalls are adjoining each other, from using one set of scales and weights in common, provided the same be suspended in a conspicuous place on a line with, and between the said stalls.

Weights, &c. to be sealed.

§ 33. No butcher or other person shall use, within the limits of any public market, any weight, measure or beam which is not sealed by the Sealer of Weights, Measures and Beams, under the penalty of ten dollars for each offense.

ARTICLE IV.

OF MARKET FEES.

§ 34. The following shall be the rent or daily payment to be demanded and received by the clerks of the several markets, for the occupation of unrented stalls or stands, to be collected by the said clerks, immediately on such stall or stand being occupied, to wit: Rents of Stalls and Stands.

1. For a stand for the sale of vegetables and fruits out of the country market, one shilling per day.
2. For every stand for a fisherman, six cents and one quarter per day.
3. For every stand occupied by a countryman bringing the produce of his own farm to market, six cents and one quarter a day.
4. Whenever another person shall be employed, he shall be considered an agent, and if he be agent for one farmer only, he shall pay fifty cents for a stand per day.
5. Whenever a person is agent for more than one person, he shall pay fifty cents for each agency, not exceeding two dollars per day.
6. If the captain of a vessel, or one of his hands, comes to the market with the produce brought in the vessel, he shall pay fifty cents for a stand per day.
7. If the captain of a vessel employs any other agent than one of his own hands, such agent shall pay two dollars per day.
8. All women hucksters, twenty-five cents per day.
9. All men hucksters, fifty cents per day.

§ 35. No person or persons shall occupy any part of any public market, or the streets contiguous thereto, within the Stands near the markets prohibited.

distance of three hundred yards from any part of such market, for the purpose of exposing and offering for sale and selling any article or thing whatsoever, without having first paid the rent or market fees, according to the rates specified in the 34th section of this chapter, when demanded by the clerk of the said market, under the penalty of twenty-five dollars for every such offense.

ARTICLE V.

GENERAL RULES AND REGULATIONS.

Sales of meat to be at stalls

§ 36. No person shall sell or expose for sale any meat, beef, mutton, veal or lamb, in any of the said public markets, other than at a butcher's stall, under the penalty of ten dollars for each offense.

Countrymen.

§ 37. The last preceding section shall not be construed to prevent countrymen from bringing to market and selling the meats raised and slaughtered on their own farms.

Articles of provision to be sold at stalls.

§ 38. No person shall sell or expose for sale any article of provision, or other thing whatsoever, in any market or the limits thereof, or in any street within the distance of three hundred yards from any part of such market, except at a stall or stand, to be hired by such person of the clerk of the said market, under the penalty of ten dollars for each offense.

Unwholesome provisions.

§ 39. No butcher or other person shall sell, or offer, or expose for sale in any of the public markets, or in any part of the city of New York, any unwholesome or stale articles of provisions, or any flesh of any animal dead by accident or disease, or known or suspected to be diseased at the killing of the same, under the penalty of twenty-five dollars for each offense.

Ibid.

§ 40. No person shall bring into any market or the limits thereof, or offer, or expose for sale, any blown, plaited, raised or stuffed meat, within the city of New York, under the penalty of ten dollars for each offense.

§ 41. No butcher or other person shall, between the first day of May and the first day of November in any year, bring into, or place, or suffer, or permit to be brought into, or placed in any market, any untried fat, commonly called gut fat; nor at any time or season, the head of any sheep or lamb, unless the same shall be skinned and properly cleaned; nor any sheep or lamb in carcass or quarter, with any foot or trotters thereto; nor any hides or skins, excepting calves' skins, under the penalty of ten dollars for each offense. Gut fat, heads of sheep, &c.

§ 42. No person shall, at any time, bring into any market, or sell, or offer or expose for sale, in any public market or other place in the city of New York, any meagre or back shad, under the penalty of ten dollars for every such offense. Back shad.

§ 43. No person or persons, shall sell, or expose for sale, any fresh fish in any of the said markets, or the streets contiguous thereto, excepting fishermen, or persons who shall have purchased the fish at the fishing places, from the fishermen, under the penalty of ten dollars for each offense. Sales of Fresh Fish.

§ 44. No person shall sell, or expose for sale, any poultry, eggs, or butter, in any of the said markets, or streets contiguous thereto, except the same shall have been raised on the farm of such person, or unless such person shall have been himself or herself into the country, and there purchased the same from the farmer who raised the same, under the penalty of ten dollars for each offense. Poultry, eggs and butter.

§ 45. Any person having market produce in any of the Agents.

said markets, of which he is not the owner, shall, when required by the clerk of said market, procure a written authority from the owner of such produce, describing the quantity thereof, and authorizing such person to sell the same; and any person who shall neglect or refuse to produce such authorization, or who shall produce a fictitious or false one, shall be considered a forestaller in the said market, and shall forfeit and pay for every such offense, the sum of twenty-five dollars.

Butter. § 46. No person shall sell, or offer, or expose for sale in any of the public markets or the limits thereof, any butter, except by weight, under the penalty of five dollars for every such offense.

Ibid. § 47. No person shall sell, or offer, or expose for sale in any of the public markets or the limits thereof, any butter in less quantities than in rolls, one pound weight each, without any fraction of a pound, or if the butter be contained in tubs, pails or firkins, the same shall be sold by the tub, pail or firkin, and by no less quantity, under the penalty of five dollars for each offense.

Ibid. § 48. No person shall sell, or offer, or expose for sale, in any of the markets, or the limits thereof, any butter, in any vessel, other than such as hath the weight of such vessel marked thereon, before the same is brought into the market, under the penalty of five dollars for each offense.

Hucksters to have a permit. § 49. No person, commonly called a huckster, shall sell or expose for sale, in any of the public markets, or in any street within the city of New York, any provisions or articles of any kind, excepting vegetables or fruit, without having received a permit for the sale of the same, under the penalty of ten dollars for each offense.

§ 50. No person shall occupy any part of the said markets or market places, for the purpose of selling or exposing for sale, any article or thing whatsoever, without having first obtained a permit in writing for that purpose, and having the same registered with the deputy clerk of said market, under the penalty of twenty-five dollars for each offense. Permits generally.

§ 51. No provisions, country produce or other article, which shall have been sold or bargained for in any manner after its arrival in the city of New York, shall be exposed for sale, or sold in any of the public markets of the said city, under the penalty of ten dollars for each offense. Forestalling.

§ 52. No person shall purchase, in any public market until after the hour of twelve o'clock at noon, any provisions or articles of any kind, with intent to sell the same again at any place in the city of New York, under the penalty of ten dollars for each offense. Purchase with intent to sell again.

§ 53. No licensed butcher, or any other persons, shall sell or expose for sale, any kind of meat, or other article, in any of the said public markets, or the limits thereof after the hour of one o'clock in the afternoon of each day, between the first day of May and the last day of October, in every year; nor after the hour of two o'clock in the afternoon of each day between the first day of November and the last day of April in every year, except on Saturday, nor on that day after the hour of eleven o'clock in the evening, under the penalty of five dollars for each offense. Market hours

§ 54. Every cart, wagon or other vehicle, in which articles shall be brought to market, or which shall come within the limits of any market, shall be removed there- Removal of carts, &c.

from, at or before seven o'clock in the morning of each day, between the first day of May and the first day of October, and at or before eight o'clock in the morning of each day during the remainder of the year, under the penalty of five dollars for each offense, to be paid by the owner or person having charge thereof.

Removal of Carts, &c.

§ 55. Every cart, wagon, or other vehicle, in which any garden produce or other thing shall be brought to market, shall be unloaded immediately, on its arrival at the said market, and forthwith removed from the said market or the limits thereof, under the penalty of ten dollars for every refusal or neglect to remove the same, to be recovered from the owner or owners, or person or persons, having charge thereof, severally and respectively.

Removal of Carts, Produce, &c.

§ 56. All carts, wagons, or other vehicles, and all boxes, baskets or other things, and all market produce or other articles whatsoever, which shall not be removed, as directed by the clerks of their respective markets, as hereinbefore in this chapter provided, shall be removed by the said clerks to the Corporation yard; and such part thereof as will pay the penalty imposed by this chapter, shall be forthwith sold, and the said penalty, when thus received, shall be paid over by the said deputy clerks to the Chamberlain of the city.

Ibid.

§ 57. The said clerks shall also sell so much of the said article or thing as will pay the expense of removal, and the remainder thereof shall continue in the place to which it was removed, until the owner thereof shall pay to the said clerk, for the use of the city of New York, the sum of six cents for every cart or wagon load thereof, for every day the same shall have remained in the said place of removal.

§ 58. The owner of every cart or other vehicle used for the purpose of bringing meat, garden produce or other thing, to any of the public markets to be sold, shall cause his or her name to be painted, in a plain manner, and on a conspicuous part of such cart or other vehicle, under the penalty of five dollars for every time the same shall be used or driven in the city of New York, without such name, to be recovered from the owner or driver thereof, severally and respectively. Name to be painted on vehicles.

§ 59. The last preceding section shall not be construed to apply to the carts used by licensed cartmen of this city, nor to wagons, carts or other vehicles, owned by countrymen and bringing such countrymen's produce to market. Ibid.

§ 60. No butcher or other person shall erect, under his shambles or stall, in any market, any box, drawer or closet, which shall approach within twelve inches of the floor of the market, under the penalty of five dollars for each offense. Boxes, Drawers and closets in stands, &c.

§ 61. No person shall bring into any market any articles intended for sale, which shall be conveyed in any covered chest or other thing, where it is hidden from the sight or view, under the penalty of five dollars for each offense. Goods to be exposed.

§ 62. No butcher or any other person shall have or keep, in any of the public markets, any refrigerator, ice-box, or cask containing ice or pickle, unless the same be placed within the limits of, and in the rear of his stall or stand, and be lined with lead or some other metallic substance, so as to be water-tight, and provided with a pipe of lead, zinc or copper, leading therefrom to the nearest gutter, under the penalty of twenty-five dollars for the violation of each and every provision of this section. Refrigerators pickle casks, &c.

Trout. § 63. No person shall expose for sale, or have in his or her possession, in the city of New York, any trout, between the fifteenth day of October and the fifteenth day of March, in any year, under the penalty of five dollars for each trout so exposed for sale, or had in possession.

Heath hens. § 64. No person shall expose for sale, or have in his or her possession, in the city of New York, any heath-hens, between the first day of January and the first day of October, in any year, under the penalty of ten dollars for each heath-hen so exposed for sale, or so had in possession.

Quail. § 65. No person shall expose for sale, or have in his or her possession, in the city of New York, any quail, between the *fifth* day of January and the *twenty-fifth* day of October, in any year, under the penalty of five dollars for each quail so exposed for sale or had in possession.

Partridges. § 66. No person shall expose for sale, or have in his or her possession, in the city of New York, any partridge, between the *fifth* day of January and the *twenty-fifth* day of October, in any year, under the penalty of ten dollars for each partridge so exposed for sale, or had in his or her possession.

Woodcock. § 67. No person shall expose for sale, or have in his or her possession, in the city of New York, any woodcock, between the first day of February and the first day of July, in any year, under the penalty of five dollars for each woodcock so exposed for sale, or so had in his or her possession.

Penalties, how recovered. § 68. The above penalties may be sued for and recovered in any justice's court, by any person or persons who will prosecute for the same; in which case one half of the said penalty shall go to the person or persons who shall prosecute to conviction, and the other half to the Commissioners of the Alms-house, for the benefit of the poor.

CHAPTER XXXVI.

OF THE SALE, &c., OF FIREWOOD, HAY, STRAW, LIME AND COAL.

ARTICLE I.

OF FIREWOOD.

§ 1. No firewood, brought to this city for sale, shall be landed on any of the docks, wharves, or piers of this city, until the same shall have been sold; and all firewood so sold and landed shall be immediately carried away, under the penalty of one dollar for every load which may be so landed before sale, or not taken away when sold. Firewood, landing and carting.

§ 2. No firewood shall be sold otherwise than according to the following regulations, that is to say: the stanchions of each cart or sled which shall be employed in the carrying of such wood, shall be five feet four inches high from the floor of the cart or sled, and no higher; and the breadth of such cart or sled, between the two foremost stanchions, shall be two feet five inches, and between the two hindmost stanchions, two feet nine inches and no more; in which space between the said stanchions, every cartman who shall cart any wood, shall stow as much and as close together as can conveniently be put, or as much of it as will amount to thirty-seven feet ten inches and two-thirds of an inch, cubic measure, which shall consti- Regulations of sales of Firewood.

tute, and be deemed a load, and shall and may be bought and sold accordingly.

Penalties.

§ 3. No person or persons shall buy or sell any firewood, contrary to the above regulations; and no cartman shall cart any firewood brought to this city for sale, except in carts and sleds made and constructed as by law directed, and loaded as above-mentioned, under the penalty of five dollars for each offense.

Crooked firewood.

§ 4. No crooked wood shall be stowed in any cart or sled constructed in manner aforesaid, with other wood, but the same may be sold or disposed of as refuse wood, not subject to the above regulations; and if any cartman who shall cart firewood, shall put or suffer to be put into his cart any such crooked wood as will prevent his cart from containing a full load between the stanchions thereof, he shall, for every load so carted, forfeit the sum of one dollar.

Sale of wood by cartmen and wood-sawyers.

§ 5. No cartman or wood-sawyer, or other person for, or on account of such cartman or wood-sawyer, shall purchase any firewood which shall be brought to this city for sale, except it be for the only use of such cartman, wood-sawyer, or his family, under the penalty of twenty-five dollars for each offense, except such cartman or wood-sawyer shall have received an order, which it shall be incumbent upon him to prove, to purchase wood. And further, that no cartman or wood-sawyer shall sell or expose to sale, any firewood which shall be brought to this city for sale, on his own account, or as agent for or on account of any person or persons, under a penalty of fifteen dollars for each offense.

ARTICLE II

OF HAY AND STRAW.

§ 6. No cartman shall cart or carry for hire or wages, any hay brought to this city for sale, unless he shall be duly licensed for that purpose by the Mayor, under the penalty of five dollars for every load or part of a load which he shall so cart or carry. Hay cartmen

§ 7. Every cartman to be so licensed shall first take and subscribe an oath or affirmation, before the said Mayor, well and carefully to examine and inspect all the hay to be carted or carried by him, for the purpose of ascertaining whether it be well and sufficiently cured and dry; and no such cartman shall cart or carry any hay and pass the same as good and merchantable, unless the same be well and sufficiently cured and dry, under the penalty of five dollars for every load or part of a load which he shall so cart or carry. Ibid.

§ 8. Nothing in the last section contained shall be taken or construed to prohibit the importation within this city, or the cartage or sale of any injured or damaged hay, as being so injured or damaged. Damaged Hay.

§ 9. Every cartman to be so licensed shall cause the number of his license to be fairly painted on a tin plate, with red paint upon a white ground, easily to be seen, and shall fix and keep such tin plate so fairly painted and easily to be seen, on the square of the after part of the shaft of his cart, under penalty of twenty dollars for every neglect or default. Hay carts.

§ 10. The street or place known as Hall street, between Sixth and Seventh streets, in the Seventeenth Ward of this city, is hereby designated as the place for the sale of hay coming from the country, by the wagon, cart, or sled load. Hay stand.

Straw. § 11. All the foregoing provisions of this law, shall apply to the sale of straw in this city, except straw made up into bundles, and sold by the bundle.

Slips for boats with hay & straw. § 12. The boats employed in bringing loose hay or straw to this city for sale, shall have the privilege, in preference to all other vessels, of occupying the whole of Gouverneur slip on the East river; and the basin at the foot of Amos street, on the North river; and no person having the charge of any other boat or vessel as master owner or otherwise, shall interfere with boats employed in bringing hay to the said places, or prevent their approach thereto, under the penalty of ten dollars for every such offense.

Ibid. § 13. The pier at the foot of Charles street, with one half of the bulkhead south of said pier, is hereby appropriated for vessels laden with loose hay for sale, to the exclusion of all other vessels.

ARTICLE III.

OF LIME.

Vessels with Lime. No sloop or other vessel which shall bring any slaked or unslaked lime to this city for sale, shall be permitted to lay in any of the public slips or at any of the public wharves in this city, while she has lime on board, except as hereinafter provided, under the penalty of fifty dollars for each offense.

Ibid. § 15. The last preceding section of this chapter shall not be construed to prevent the laying of vessels having lime on board, at the public wharves and in the slips, while discharging cargo, or during the period the lime is bona fide for sale, and the person having charge of said vessel and lime, is ready and willing to sell and deliver the same.

§ 16. Any cartman who shall cart any slaked lime, whether merchantable or not, shall provide his cart with a tight box, sufficient to contain sixteen bushels, struck measure; which box shall, whenever any lime is contained therein, be covered with cloth or other sufficient covering to keep the contents from wasting. Regulation of carts carrying lime.

§ 17. Every cartman who shall cart any slaked lime, excepting in the box, and furnished in the manner provided for in the last preceding section, with the covering therein mentioned, shall forfeit and pay the penalty of five dollars for every such offense. Ibid.

§ 18. No person shall keep a lime-house in any of the public streets, lanes, or alleys, of the city of New York, between the first day of December and the first day of April, in any year, under the penalty of fifty dollars for every twenty-four hours the same shall be kept therein. Lime houses.

§ 19. It shall not be lawful for any person to keep a lime-house in any of the public streets, lanes or alleys of the city of New York, for a longer period than three months, under the penalty of ten dollars for every twenty-four hours the same shall be kept therein. Ibid.

ARTICLE IV.

OF COAL.

§ 20. All coal which shall be sold from any coal yard, or any other place in this city, shall be sold by the bushel, except anthracite coal, which may be sold by weight. Coal, how to be sold.

§ 21. No person shall unload, vend, or expose for sale, any charcoal at either of the slips in front of any of the public markets of this city, under the penalty of ten dollars for every such offense. Charcoal.

§ 22. In the sale of anthracite coal the hundred weight shall consist of one hundred pounds avoirdupois, and twenty such hundred weight shall constitute a ton. Anthracite coal.

CHAPTER XXXVII.

OF CARTS AND CARTMEN, DIRT CARTS, PUBLIC PORTERS AND GARBAGE CARTS.

ARTICLE I.—OF CARTS AND CARTMEN.
II.—OF DIRT CARTS.
III.—OF PUBLIC PORTERS.
IV.—OF GARBAGE AND OTHER CARTS.

ARTICLE I.

OF CARTS AND CARTMEN.

Public carts defined.

§ 1. Every cart, truck, wagon, dray, or other vehicle, drawn by one or more horses or other animals, which shall be kept, used, driven or employed for the transportation or conveyance of any thing whatsoever, from place to place within the city of New York, for hire, wages or pay for such transportation, shall be deemed a "public cart" within the meaning of this chapter; and every person who shall set up, or so keep, use, drive or employ any such public cart, without first obtaining license therefor, from the Mayor of said city, as is hereinafter provided, shall be deemed guilty of a violation of this chapter.

Cartmen to be licensed

§ 2. The Mayor shall, from time to time, license and appoint so many and such persons as he may think proper to set up and keep public carts in said city, provided that no one person shall be so licensed to keep more than three such public carts. And he shall also license so many, and such persons as he may think proper, to be public cartmen of said city, and he may revoke or suspend any or all of such licenses at his pleasure; all persons licensed, as aforesaid, to keep public carts, shall be deemed to be public cartmen within the meaning of this chapter; but it shall not be lawful for any person to receive or hold a license to keep public carts, or to be a public cartman, unless he be a citizen of the United States, and resident within the State of New York, and is the actual owner of the cart or carts, with good horses therefor, so licensed to be kept as public carts ; and the Mayor may examine, under oath, all persons applying for, or holding any such license, or the renewal thereof, touching their qualifications as aforesaid; and all licenses, other than to persons so qualified, shall be void.

§ 3. The Mayor shall require and receive for the use of the city, from every person to whom he may grant license to keep public carts as aforesaid, two dollars and fifty cents for every cart so licensed; and from every person licensed as aforesaid to be a public cartman, one dollar; and fifty cents for the license for each cart and public cartman renewed, as hereinafter provided. License Fee of cartmen.

§ 4. All licenses to persons to keep public carts and to be public cartmen, shall expire on the last day of October next after the date thereof ; and it shall be lawful for the Mayor to renew and continue any or all of such licenses for a year succeeding such last day of October, provided that the applicant therefor continues in all things qualified, as hereinbefore provided, to hold such license, and the application be made therefor prior to the expiration thereof, at such time as may be appointed by the Mayor. Term of License and renewal.

§ 5. No public cart shall be driven or used within said city, except by a duly licensed public cartman ; and the person to whom license is granted to keep and use a public cart, shall, for all the pnrposes of this chapter, be considered the owner thereof, and responsible for all articles intrusted to, and for the conduct of the driver thereof, and liable to all forfeitures, penalties and punishments herein contained or provided. Carts to be Licensed. Responsibility of cartmen

Numbers to be painted on carts.

§ 6. Every public cart shall have fairly painted on the outside of the square of the after part of the shaft, or on some other conspicuous place, on each side, with black paint on a white ground, so as to be easily seen, the number of the license therefor, in plain figures of at least two and a half inches in length, and the driving or using of a public cart, without its being so numbered, shall be deemed a violation of this chapter.

Numbers to be defaced on expiration of license.

§ 7. Every person licensed as aforesaid to keep a public cart, upon failing to renew the license for, or disposing of, or parting with the same, shall deface, remove and obliterate the license number therefrom, and failing or neglecting to do so, shall be deemed to be a violation of this chapter.

Cartmen to report their residence.

§ 8. Every person, upon receiving a license to keep a public cart, or to be a public cartman, shall report his residence to the Mayor; and upon changing his residence, shall in like manner report his new residence, and the failing or neglecting to do so, shall be deemed to be a violation of this chapter.

Regulation as to numbers.

§ 9. It shall not be lawful for any person other than a public cartman, to keep, use, drive or employ any cart or other vehicle with numbers or figures thereon similar to or resembling the numbers on public carts, or for any person licensed to keep public carts, to place or have any number for which he may have received license, on more than one cart, or to use more carts as public carts than he may have license for.

Stands for Cartmen.

§ 10. The Mayor may assign to the owner of each duly licensed public cart, a stand, where such cart may remain, waiting to be employed, and also a stand where it may remain at other times, provided that no such stand shall be assigned for a cart to remain at such other times in front of the premises of any person other than the owner of such cart, against the wishes of the occupant thereof, and provided further, that carts shall not be permitted to so stand two abreast in any of the streets; and every public cartman who shall permit his cart to stand loaded, or waiting for employment, or to remain at other times at any place other than the one so assigned for such carts, shall be deemed guilty of a violation of this chapter.

§ 11. The Mayor, and the several officers and members of the police department and magistrates, shall have power and authority to order the driver or other person having charge of any public cart or any other vehicle, to remove such cart or other vehicle away from any place in any of the streets, or on any of the wharves or docks of said city which, in his or their opinion, may be improperly incumbering such street or wharf, or obstructing or impeding the public travel; and any and every person neglecting or refusing to comply with or obey any such order, shall be deemed guilty of a violation of this chapter.

Carts encumbering the streets.

§ 12. It shall be the duty of every person driving or having charge of a public cart, to give to any person requesting it, his name and place of residence, his number, and the number of the cart he is driving or in charge of, and the name and place of residence ot the owner thereof; and the refusal to do so shall be deemed a violation of this chapter.

Names to be given when demanded.

§ 13. If any accident or injury shall happen to any person, or any carriage, vehicle or other thing, by reason of coming in contact with any public cart, or other cart, or vehicle, or the horse or horses attached thereto, or any thing loaded thereon, while the same is moving, it shall be the duty of the person driving or having charge of the same, to immediately stop, and if necessary, render his

Provision respecting accidents.

assistance, and to give his name and residence, and to give the number of the cart or other vehicle he was driving, and the name and residence of the owner thereof, under the penalty of fifty dollars, to be recovered from the driver or owner of any such cart or other vehicle.

Driving carts on sidewalks, wharves, &c.

§ 14. It shall not be lawful for any public cartman, or for any person driving or having charge of any public cart or any other cart, wagon or other vehicle, to drive or back any such public cart, or any other vehicle, on to the sidewalk of any of the streets of said city, or to stop any such cart, or any other vehicle, on any of the crosswalks or intersection of streets, so as to obstruct or hinder the travel along such crosswalks or intersections of streets, or to place any such carts or other vehicles cross-wise of any street or wharf of said city, except to load thereon, or unload therefrom, articles of greater weight each than two hundred pounds; but in no case shall it be lawful for any person to permit such cart or other vehicle to remain so crosswise of any street for a longer period than may be actually necessary for such purpose, and not to exceed five minutes.

Speed of carts.

prevention of accidents, &c.

§ 15. It shall not be lawful for any cart, wagon, coach, public cart or any other vehicle, to be driven through any of the streets of the city of New York at a greater speed than six miles an hour; nor shall it be lawful for any such vehicle to be driven around the corner of any of the streets of said city, with the horse or horses thereto traveling at a faster gait than a walk; and all and every such public carts, and all other vehicles, when passing through or along any of the streets of said city, shall, when meeting any other vehicle, be driven to the right-hand side of the way, so that such vehicles shall pass clear of each other; and it shall be unlawful for any such public cart, carriage or any other vehicle, or the horse or horses attached thereto, to be driven foul of, or against any person, vehicle, or any other thing whatever, in any of the streets, or on any of the docks and wharves of said city.

§ 16. No cart, dray, truck or wagon shall be driven over any of the wharves or piers of the city of New York, at a greater rate of speed than a walk, under a penalty of five dollars, to be sued for and recovered from the owner or owners, or driver thereof, severally and respectively. Speed on Wharves, &c.

§ 17. Each sled, cart or dray employed in the transportation of any goods, wares, merchandise or other things excepting firewood, shall be two feet five inches wide between the foremost rungs, and two feet nine inches wide between the hindmost rungs, and no more; and all the rungs shall be three feet eight inches high above the floor of the sled or cart, and no more, under the penalty of five dollars for every such offense. Size of carts.

§ 18. Licensed cartmen of the city of New York shall and may be permitted to use iron-shod wheels, under the regulations following: Iron shod wheels.

1. The iron or tire round the wheels shall be in breadth not less than three inches, and the nails with which the tire shall be nailed or fastened to the wheels, shall be sunk into the iron or tire, so that the heads of such nails shall not project beyond the surface thereof.
2. The rims of the wheels of all carts not shod with iron in the manner aforesaid, shall not be less than four inches and a half broad, and eight inches deep, when new.
3. If any cartman shall use any cart in violation of either or any of the provisions of this section, he shall forfeit and pay the sum of five dollars for every such offense.

Furniture carts.

§ 19. Furniture or spring carts hereafter licensed, shall be ten feet in length, and no more, and four feet four inches wide, and no more; and the tires thereof shall be not less than two inches in width ; and all other provisions of this chapter, not inconsistent herewith, shall be applicable to all furniture or spring carts now in use, or hereafter to be made or licensed.

Rates of charges.

§ 20. The prices or rates to be taken or charged for the loading, transportation and unloading of goods, wares or other articles, shall be as follows, to wit:

	Cents.
Oils, molasses, and all wet casks containing less than twenty-five gallons, for every load ... $	38
Of twenty-five and under fifty gallons, for every four	40
Of fifty and under one hundred gallons, for every two	45
Of one hundred gallons and upward, for every one hundred gallons....................	50
Sugar, tobacco, copperas, and all dry casks of under one thousand pounds' weight, for every load	38
Of one thousand pounds, and under one thousand five hundred pounds, each............	45
Of one thousand five hundred, and under two thousand pounds, each..................	50
Of two thousand pounds and upward, for every hundred pounds and other ponderous articles of one thousand pounds' weight and upward, at the same rate....................	5
Hay, loose, per load...	1 00
Bricks, when handled and piled, per load.....	40
Hoop poles, loose, per load.................	50
Timber and lumber, per load................	35
Hemp, loose, for every one thousand two hundred pounds...........................	50

	Cents.	
Beef and pork, for every five barrels.........	38	Rates of Charges.
Calves, sheep and lambs, per load............	35	
Coal, per ton..............................	50	
Coal, per half chaldron....................	40	
Cotton, for every three bales................	38	
Earthenware, loose, per load................	40	
Oil floor cloths, in boxes or rolls of less than ten feet in length, per load................	33	
Of ten feet, and less than fifteen feet in length, each	33	
Of fifteen feet, and less than twenty feet in length, each..........................	50	
Of twenty feet, and less than twenty-four feet in length, each..........................	65	
Of twenty-four feet and upward, as may be agreed on.		
Plaster of Paris, loose, per ton...............	65	
Salt, for every twenty bushels..............	33	
Cut stone, per load........................	35	
Slates or tiles, per load	35	
Household furniture, loose, per load.........	50	
For loading, unloading and housing furniture in the removal of families, extra per load...	50	
Bedding, tied up, chests, trunks and boxes, per load	33	
Cassia, in mats, per one hundred mats........	25	
Anchors, of under three hundred pounds' weight, per load...............................	38	
Of three hundred pounds' weight and upward, per one hundred pounds...........	10	
Chain cables of under one thousand pounds' weight, per load........................	40	
Of one thousand pounds' weight and upward, per one hundred pounds..................	5	

	Cents.
Iron hollow ware, per load................	40
Iron and steel, per load..................	45
Fish, dry, per load.......................	50
And for every load of goods, wares and merchandise, or other things not enumerated....	38

Provided, That when the distance exceeds half a mile, and is within a mile, one third more shall be added to the above rates and prices, and in the same proportion for any greater distance. And if any public cartman shall ask, demand, receive, take, exact or extort any greater rate, price, pay or compensation, for carting or transporting any article or thing whatsoever, than is mentioned, allowed, expressed and limited as aforesaid, it shall not be lawful for him to receive any compensation for the said carting or transportation, and the said asking or receiving shall be deemed a violation of this chapter.

Regulation as to loads.

§ 21. It shall not be lawful for any public cartman to neglect or refuse to carry and transport a good and sufficient load, as much as can be conveniently and safely stowed on his cart, or is reasonable for one horse to draw, nor any article of less than two thousand pounds' weight, when required so to do, unless he be then actually otherwise employed; and every public cartman and public porter shall be entitled to be paid the legal rate or compensation allowed and provided in this chapter, immediately upon the carting or transportation of any article or thing; and it may be lawful for any such public cartman or public porter, to retain any article or thing so carted or transported by him, for which he is not so paid his cartage, and to convey the same without delay to the office of the Superintendent of Police, and he shall be entitled to the lawful rate of pay or compensation for the so conveying. All disputes or disagreements as to distance or rates of compensation, between public cartmen or public porters, and persons employing them or owing for cartage or transportation, shall be determined by the Mayor. Disputes with cartmen.

§ 22. It shall not be lawful for any public cartman, or any other person, to cart or transport through any of the streets of said city, any planks, poles, spars, timber or other thing exceeding thirty feet in length, except on a suitable truck or other vehicle, and such plank or other thing shall be placed lengthwise thereon, so as not to project at either end beyond the line of the side, or width of such truck or other vehicle; and all persons so carting or transporting any such poles, plank, timber, spars, or other things, in any other manner, shall be deemed guilty of a violation of this chapter. Carting articles over 30 feet in length

§ 23. It shall not be lawful for the driver or other person having charge of any public cart, dirt cart or any other vehicle, to be off, or away from any such cart, or any other vehicle, while the same is moving or passing along any of the streets or avenues of said city; nor shall it be lawful for any public cartman, while waiting for employment at any place assigned for his cart, to stand waiting for employment, at any other place, or to snap or flourish his whip, or to be away from his cart, unless from necessity or on business, or to sit or stand about the door-steps or platforms, or in front of any house, store or other building, to the annoyance of the occupants thereof. Cartmen to attend their carts.

§ 24. It shall not be lawful for any person, who has been licensed to keep public carts, or to be a public cartman, and whose license has been suspended or revoked by the Mayor, to keep, drive or use any public cart in the city of New York, under the penalty of twenty-five dollars for every such offense. Cartmen suspended, &c.

Stanchions of carts for Firewood.

§ 25. The stanchions of every public cart employed in the transportation of any fire-wood, shall be shouldered with a band of iron around the part which enters the mortice, and the mortice cased with iron, so as to prevent the wearing of the stanchion or mortice ; and, at least three feet distant from the floor of the cart, there shall be fixed across from one stanchion to the other an iron chain, so as to prevent the stanchions from spreading, and no public cartman shall cart any fire-wood in violation of any of these provisions.

Privatecarts

§ 26. It shall not be lawful for any person to keep, drive, use or employ any cart, wagon, truck, dray or other vehicle, other than such as are licensed as herein provided, for the transportation or conveyance of any article or thing, from place to place in the city of New York, unless the name and residence or place of business, where such owner can be found, (of the owner thereof,) be fairly and distinctly painted, with red paint, on a white ground, in plain letters and figures, at least two and a half inches long, in a conspicuous place, on both sides of such cart or other vehicle, or so as at all times to be easily seen thereon.

Standing of carts in front of cartman's premises.

§ 27. Every cartman who shall be duly licensed in the city of New York, shall be permitted to place and leave his cart, when unemployed, in front of the house or premises where he shall at the time reside, or in front of the stable where he shall at the time stable his horse; provided that such cart shall be placed on the street upon the carriage-way thereof, in close proximity to the curb stone next to his said residence or stable, and shall not extend beyond said curb stone any greater distance than the width of such cart, nor beyond the line of the lot on which his said residence or stable is situated, and provided that such place of residence or stable shall be specified upon the license for such cart.

§ 28. Nothing in the last section contained shall be construed to apply to any vehicle other than public carts in the city of New York. Ibid.

§ 29. It shall be the duty of the person or officer exercising the duties of Superintendent of Carts to visit daily, the several stands and places in the city, where cartmen are in the habit of waiting for employment, and to see that all the ordinances regulating carts and cartmen, including dirt carts, are in every respect complied with. Duty of Superintendent

§ 30. It shall be the special duty of the said person or officer to ascertain whether any carts are driven for hire by persons who have not received licenses therefor, and to report such and all other offenses or violations of the law to the attorney of the Corporation. Ibid.

ARTICLE II.

DIRT CARTS.

§ 31. The Mayor of the city of New York may grant license to such and as many persons as he may deem proper, to keep and use such number of dirt carts as he shall think expedient, to be employed exclusively in the carting and transportation of dirt, sand, gravel, clay, paving stones, ashes, garbage and building rubbish, and revoke or suspend any or all such licenses at his pleasure; and it shall not be lawful for any person to drive or use any cart, wagon or other vehicle, for the transportation of any such dirt, sand, gravel, clay, paving stones, ashes, garbage, or building rubbish within the city of New York, for hire, wages or pay, for such transportation, unless the said cart or other vehicle be licensed as aforesaid. Provided, that License of Dirt carts.

nothing herein shall prevent any person licensed as a public cartman, or to keep public carts from driving or using any such public cart in the carting and transporting of any such sand, gravel, clay, paving stones, ashes, garbage or building rubbish, the same as if they were licensed as dirt carts. This section shall not be construed to permit any dirt cart to be used in the transportation for hire, wages or pay, of any article or thing whatsoever, other than is herein specified.

Duration of License.

§ 32. Every license granted as aforesaid, shall continue in force for one year, from the date thereof, and may be renewed by the Mayor at any time before the expiration thereof, for a succeeding year.

License Fee.

§ 33. Every person, upon receiving a license to keep and use one or more dirt carts, as hereinbefore provided, shall pay to the Mayor, for the use of the city, one dollar for every cart so licensed; and the further sum of twenty-five cents upon the renewal of the license for every such cart.

Construction of Dirt carts.

§ 34. Every dirt cart, and every public cart, when used as a dirt cart, shall be furnished with a good and tight box, the sides and forepart of which shall be two feet, and the tail-board eighteen inches high, and of capacity to contain twelve cubic feet; and on all dirt carts the letters D. C., and the number of the license therefor, shall be fairly and distinctly painted, with black paint, on a white ground, on the square of the after part of the shaft, on both sides, in plain legible letters and figures at least two and a half inches long, so as to be easily and distinctly seen, and so continued; and every person driving or using a dirt cart, without being so furnished and numbered, shall be deemed guilty of a violation of this chapter.

§ 35. It shall not be lawful for the owner or driver of any dirt cart or any other vehicle, or for any other person, to use or employ, or permit to be used or employed, any such dirt cart or any other vehicle, for the conveyance or removal of any dirt, sand, gravel, stones or other thing, from any of the streets, or avenues, or highways, or from any lot of land or other place, or to dump, deposit, or leave any dirt, sand, gravel, rubbish, or other thing, in any of the streets or highways, or on any dock or wharf, or on any lot or lots of land within said city, without being duly authorized or permitted so to do by the public officer or other person competent to give such authority or permission.

Permission to remove dirt to be obtained.

§ 36. All persons offending against the provisions of the last section, shall forfeit and pay twenty-five dollars for each offense.

Penalty.

ARTICLE III.

OF PUBLIC PORTERS.

§ 37. The Mayor shall license and appoint as many and such persons as he may think expedient, to be public porters of the city of New York, and revoke or suspend any or all of such licenses at his pleasure; and it shall not be lawful for any person to use any wheelbarrow or hand-cart to carry, transport or convey baggage, goods or other things, from place to place within said city, for hire, wages or pay for such conveyance, or to be at any hotel, boarding-house, ferry, steamboat landing, railroad station or depot, and solicit of strangers, travelers, citizens or other persons, or accept the conveyance of baggage or other articles, without being licensed as aforesaid by the Mayor.

Porters to be licensed.

This section shall not be construed to prevent any person keeping, or employed in, any hotel or boarding-house,

Keepers of public houses excepted.

from conveying any baggage or other articles to or from such hotel or boarding-house, and using a hand-cart or wheelbarrow therefor; provided the name of the hotel or boarding-house, and the keeper thereof, be painted distinctly on both sides of such wheelbarrow or hand-cart, and on a badge worn on the front of his hat or cap, so as to be easily and distinctly seen.

Duration of Licenses.

§ 38. All licenses to public porters, granted as aforesaid, shall run one year from the date thereof, and may be renewed by the Mayor at any time within the said year for a succeeding year.

License Fee.

§ 39. Every person receiving a license to be a public porter, as aforesaid, shall pay to the Mayor for the use of the city, one dollar; and a further sum of twenty-five cents upon the renewal of every such license.

Badges of Porters.

§ 40. Every public porter shall wear, in a conspicuous place about his person, so as to be easily seen, a brass plate or badge, on which shall be engraved his name, the words "public porter," and the number of his license; and it shall be unlawful for any other person to wear or exhibit any badge purporting to be, resembling, or similar to, the badge of a public porter; and no public porter shall permit any other person to wear his badge or use his name in any way whatever, in the transportation or conveyance of any thing.

Porter's fees.

§ 41. Public porters shall be entitled to charge and receive for the carrying or conveyance of any article, any distance within half a mile, twelve cents, if carried by hand; and twenty-five cents if carried on a wheelbarrow or hand-cart; if the distance exceeds half a mile, and is within a mile, one half of the above rates in addition thereto, and in the same proportion for any greater distance.

§ 42. No public porter or hand-cartman shall be entitled to recover or receive any pay or fare, from any person for the transportation of any article or articles, unless his name and number of his license, and the rates shall be fixed, and the badge worn, agreeably to this chapter. Porter's fees.

§ 43. Upon the trial of any cause commenced for the recovery of any of the aforesaid prices or rates, it shall be incumbent on the plaintiff in such action, to prove that the badge was worn and the prices fixed, agreeably to the last preceding section, at the time the services were rendered for which the suit was brought. Ibid.

§ 44. No public porter or hand-cartman shall neglect or refuse to transport any article or articles, when required so to do, unless he shall then be actually and otherwise employed, or unless the distance he shall be required to go shall be more than two miles, under the penalty of five dollars for each offense. Refusing employment.

§ 45. No public porter or hand-cartman shall suffer or permit any other person than himself to carry any article or articles, in his wheel or hand-barrow, or hand-cart, or to wear his badge, under the penalty of five dollars for every such offense. Substitution of others.

§ 46. If any public porter shall ask or demand any grater rate of pay or compensation for the carrying or conveyance of any articles than is herein provided, he shall not be entitled to any pay for the said service; and to so ask, demand or receive any such greater pay or compensation, shall be deemed a violation of this chapter. Porter's fees.

§ 47. It shall not be lawful for any person to represent himself as, or to wear or exhibit any badge, inscription, card or device purporting or implying that he is employed or authorized by the keeper, proprietors, agent or officer False representation.

of any hotel, boarding house, vessel, steamboat or railroad company, to solicit, receive or convey persons, baggage or other things to or from any such hotel, boarding-house, vessel, steamboat or railroad company's station or depot, without being actually and duly authorized by such keeper, proprietor, officer, or agent, so to do, under the penalty of twenty-five dollars for every offense.

General Provision.

Penalties. § 48. All persons who shall violate or fail to comply with any of the provisions of this chapter, shall be deemed guilty of a misdemeanor, and on conviction thereof shall be punished, pursuant to the provisions of sections 20 and 21 of an act relative to the powers of the Common Council of the city of New York, and the criminal courts of said city, passed by the Legislature of the State of New York, January 23d, 1833 : — or in lieu thereof, shall forfeit and pay, for the use of said city, ten dollars for each and every offense, except where a penalty is prescribed in said chapter.

ARTICLE IV.

OF GARBAGE AND OTHER CARTS.

Regulations. § 49. Every cart or other vehicle used to convey or transport dirt, manure, sand, gravel, mud, ashes, lime, garbage, swill, offal, or other loose materials, in any of the streets of said city, shall be fitted with a good and substantial tight box thereon, the sides of which shall be twenty-four inches, and the tail-board eighteen inches high, so that no portion of such dirt, sand or other loose material be scattered or thrown into any of said streets ; and all carts or other vehicles, when used in carting slaked lime, garbage, offal, swill, or other offensive matter, or ashes, shall have the box thereof closely covered with a sufficient covering of cloth, or boards closely fitted, so as to prevent the escape or flying about of any of the contents, or effluvia therefrom; and every person using any cart or other vehicle for any such purpose, without its being so fitted shall be deemed guilty of a violation of this chapter. Regulations.

CHAPTER XXXVIII.

OF EXPRESS WAGONS.

Provisions applicable.

§ 1. All the provisions of the preceding chapter of these ordinances, as far as relates to carts and cartmen, and not inconsistent herewith, excepting sections 2, 3, 6, 10, 20 and 21 of said chapter, are extended to, and shall include and be applicable to all wagons and other vehicles, commonly known as express wagons, which shall be kept, used, driven or employed for the transportation of any thing whatsoever, to or from any place within the city of New York, from or to any place wheresoever, for hire, wages or pay; provided always, that the owner or owners of such wagons or vehicles shall have a place in the city of New York, for the transaction of such business.

Owners to be licensed.

§ 2. The Mayor shall, from time to time, license and appoint so many and such persons as he may think proper to set up and keep one or more express wagons in said city; and he may revoke or suspend any or all such licenses at his pleasure; but it shall not be lawful for any person to receive or hold a license to keep such express wagons, unless he is the actual owner of the wagon or wagons, and of a good horse or horses therefor, nor unless he be a citizen of the United States, and has a family, and resides with his family in said city; or if not having a family, shall have resided himself therein during the six months preceding, and the Mayor may examine, under oath, all persons applying for or holding any such license or the renewal thereof, touching their qualifications, as aforesaid; and all licenses, other than to persons so qualified, shall be void.

§ 3. The Mayor shall require and receive, for the use of the city, from every person to whom he may grant license to keep such express wagons, five dollars for every wagon so licensed, and two dollars and fifty cents for the licenses of each wagon renewed. License Fee.

§ 4. Every such express wagon shall have fairly painted on the outside thereof, in a conspicuous place, on each side, so as to be easily seen, in plain letters and figures of at least two and a half inches in length, the name of the owner or owners, the place of business in said city, and the number of the license for such wagon, and such owner or owners shall be responsible for all articles intrusted to such wagon or to the driver thereof, and for the conduct of such driver, whilst in charge of or with such wagon. Names of owners to be painted on wagons.

§ 5. No person shall drive such express wagon unless he be twenty-one years of age, and have obtained license from the Mayor for such purpose, under the penalty of ten dollars for every such offense, to be recovered from the owner or owners of such express wagon, and from such driver, both or either. Drivers to be licensed.

§ 6. The Mayor is hereby authorized to grant licenses, from time to time, to drivers of such express wagons, as are herein mentioned, as often as may be necessary, and to suspend and revoke the same whenever he may deem it expedient. Ibid.

§ 7. Any driver of an express wagon who shall be thrice convicted of a breach of any of the sections of this chapter of these ordinances, shall be deprived of his license and forever debarred of a license under this chapter. Revocation of License.

CHAPTER XXXIX.

OF STAGES, OR ACCOMMODATION COACHES.

ARTICLE I.

OF LICENSING STAGES OR ACCOMMODATION COACHES AND DRIVERS.

License of Owners.

§ 1. The Mayor of the city of New York, for the time being, is hereby authorized and required, from time to time, to issue licenses, under his hand and seal, in accordance with the provisions of the laws of the State of New York, to persons to keep and use accommodation coaches or stage coaches. Such licenses shall specify, in each case, and for each coach or stage, the name of the owner; the number of the coach or stage; the route to be taken in going to, and returning from, such parts of the city for which it shall be licensed.

Term of License.

§ 2. All licenses granted by virtue of this chapter, shall expire on the first Monday in July next after the date thereof, and shall be renewed by the Mayor, on application,

§ 3. A separate license shall be taken out for every accommodation stage or coach. Each stage to be licensed

§ 4. Every person licensed, by virtue of the provisions of this chapter, shall pay to the Mayor of the city of New York, for the use of the city, for every accommodation coach or stage, or stage coach which such person shall keep, the sum of thirty dollars, when drawn by four horses, and twenty dollars, when drawn by two horses; and half those prices respectively, when the tire of any accommodation coach or carriage licensed by this act shall be of the width of four inches or upwards. License fee of owners.

§ 5. No accommodation coach or stage drawn by more than two horses, except such as were licensed before the seventh day of April, one thousand eight hundred and thirty-five, shall be licensed, or permitted to run in the streets of this city. Horses.

§ 6. The owner of any coach or stage, driven without license, or taking any other route than that designated by license, or using any other street or place than that assigned by license to it, shall, in each, or any, or every case of such violation of this chapter, be subject and held to pay the penalty of twenty-five dollars. Penalty.

§ 7. No person shall keep or drive for hire or wages in the city of New York, any accommodation coach or stage, or stage coach, by whatever name or title the same may be known or designated, without being licensed as aforesaid, under the penalty of fifty dollars for every such offense, to be recovered from the owner or owners, or driver thereof, severally and respectively. No stage to be used without license.

§ 8. No person shall drive any such coach or stage, unless he be twenty-one years of age, and have obtained license from the Mayor for such purpose, under the pen- License of Drivers.

alty of ten dollars for every such offense, to be recovered from the owner of such coach or stage, and from such driver, both or either.

License fee of Drivers.

§ 9. The Mayor is hereby authorized to grant licenses, from time to time, to drivers of such coaches as are herein mentioned, as often as may be necessary, and to suspend and revoke the same whenever he may deem it expedient; and every driver of a stage or accommodation coach shall, on receiving his license, pay to the Mayor of the city of New York, for the use of the city, the sum of twenty-five cents.

Revocation of Driver's license.

§ 10. Any driver of any stage, coach or carriage, who shall be thrice convicted of a breach of any of the sections of this article of thschapter, shall be deprived of his license, and forever debarred of a license under this ordinance.

Penalties.

§ 11. The provisions and penalties of the several sections of the ordinances regulating hackney coaches, shall apply, in every respect, to all accommodation stages or coaches, or stage-coaches, which shall or may be licensed, by virtue of the provisions of this chapter.

ARTICLE II.

OF THE PLACES AT WHICH STAGES MAY STAND WAITING FOR HIRE.

Stands for Stages.

§ 12. Accommodation stages or coaches, or stage-coaches may stand, waiting for hire or employment, at all times, Sundays excepted, at the stands herein named, to wit:

Ibid.

All those stages or coaches which run or ply between Wall street and Greenwich Village, may stand, for the purpose of receiving passengers, on the westerly side of Nassau street, between Wall street and Pine street, and on the westerly side of Broad street, at its junction with Wall street, and at such other places as may be designated by the Mayor.

§ 13. The stage-coaches or carriages named in the last preceding section of this chapter may, from time to time, in their passage northward from the said stand, call at the southwesterly corner of Nassau street and Pine street, to take up and receive passengers, provided, that no such stage-coach or carriage shall remain or stand at the said corner longer than five minutes at any one time. Stopping place for stages.

§ 14. It shall be the duty of the Alderman and Councilmen of the respective districts, where it may be necessary to fix a stand for the accommodation of stage-coaches, together with the Mayor, to designate a place for the accommodation of said coaches; and the place so fixed upon by a majority of them, shall be the stand or place until a change shall be made by the same authority. Stands.

§ 15. The Aldermen and Councilmen of the districts embracing the Fourth, Sixth, Seventh and Tenth Wards are hereby authorized to designate a place or stand, on Chatham square, for the accommodation of stages from Harlem, Yorkville, or any intermediate places, and which receive or discharge their passengers in the Bowery, and also to fix the period of time which they shall be permitted to remain there; and the stand so designated shall be appropriated for said stages. Stands.

§ 16. If any stage or accommodation coach or carriage shall be allowed to stand, for hire or employment, in any other street or place, or for any longer time than is prescribed by or under this chapter, the owner or driver thereof shall forfeit and pay, for every such offense, the sum of five dollars, to be sued for and recovered from the owner and driver thereof, severally and respectively. Ibid.

ARTICLE III.

OF STAGES WHILE ON THE STAND, OR MOVING FROM ONE PART OF A STAND TO ANOTHER.

Regulations of Stands. § 17. Every stage-coach or carriage named or referred to in the second article of this chapter shall, on returning to the stands designated for them, take its station in the rear of the stage-coaches or carriages then occupying the stands; and each stage-coach or carriage, when leaving the said stand, shall wait for its turn in the order in which it arrives on said stand, under a penalty for a violation of either of the provisions of this section, of ten dollars, to be sued for and recovered from the owner or driver thereof, severally and respectively.

Ibid. § 18. No stage-coach or carriage, occupying either of the stands designated for them, shall, for the purpose of taking and conveying passengers, leave the stand or place which it occupies, until its turn, under the penalty of five dollars for every offense, to be sued for and recovered from the owner or driver thereof, severally and respectively.

Ibid § 19. No stage-coach or carriage, while upon, at, or near either of the said stands, shall stand abreast, or alongside of any other stage-coach, or carriage, under the penalty of five dollars for every such offense, to be sued for and recovered from the owner or driver thereof, severally and respectively.

Ibid. § 20. No stage-coach or carriage shall leave the stands designated for them, until five minutes shall have elapsed after the departure of the stage-coach or carriage immediately preceding, under the penalty of five dollars, to be sued for and recovered from the owner or driver thereof, severally and respectively.

§ 21. The Mayor of the city of New York, by and with the consent of the Aldermen and Councilmen, representing the respective districts, shall have full power and authority to make such rules and regulations, and give such orders respecting the standing of accommodation stages or coaches or stage-coaches, at and upon the stands designated and specified for such coaches or stages, as may be necessary to preserve order and decorum. Regulations at Stands.

§ 22. Every owner or driver of any such stage-coach or carriage, who shall neglect to obey any of the said rules, regulations or orders, shall forfeit and pay, for every such offense the sum of five dollars, to be recovered from the owner or driver of any such coach or carriage, severally and respectively. Penalties.

§ 23. No person, whether driver or owner of any hackney coach or accommodation stage coach, while waiting for employment, at either of the said stands, shall snap or flourish his whip, or shall leave such coach or carriage under the penalty of five dollars for every such offense, to be recovered from the owner or driver thereof, severally and respectively. Regulation at Stands.

ARTICLE IV.

OF THE STAGES WHILE GOING OR DRIVING.

§ 24. The owner or driver, or person having charge of any stage or accommodation coach, shall not drive, or permit the same to be driven in the city of New York, at greater speed than at the rate of six miles an hour, nor at a less rate than four miles an hour, unless obstructed in the streets, under the penalty of ten dollars for every such offense. Speed.

§ 25. The owner or driver, or person having charge of any stage or accommodation coach, shall not, on any Passing other vehicles.

street, road, avenue or highway in the city of New York, pass or attempt to pass with the same any other stage or accommodation coach, which shall be driving or going the same route or direction on the same street, road or way, at the rate or speed of four miles and upwards an hour, under the penalty of ten dollars for every such offense.

Stopping on route.

§ 26. No coach or stage, after the commencement of its route in going or returning, shall stop until its arrival at the termination of such route, unless an actual necessity shall exist therefor, (or to set down a passenger or passengers, or to take up and into such stage a passenger or passengers claiming to be admitted); and no such coach or stage shall be stopped or driven abreast of another, or stopped so as to obstruct the free passage of any cross-walk or cross street, or the passage-way at the intersection, head or termination of any street, under the penalty of ten dollars for each and every offense.

Taking up & setting down passengers.

§ 27. No driver shall take up or set down any passenger or passengers, except upon the right hand side of the way, in going and returning on his route, between Tenth street, in Broadway, Chatham square, head of Chatham street, and the southerly or easterly termination of his route, under the penalty of ten dollars for each offense.

Numbers of Stages.

§ 28. Every stage or coach shall be numbered, on each side near the centre thereof, and on the door behind, both on the inside and the outside panel, with the license number thereof, in plain, distinct figures, four inches in length, painted on a ground of a distinct contrast color, and so placed as to be readily seen and known at all times, under the penalty of twenty-five dollars for each and every day's use of such stage or coach not so numbered.

Lamps with numbers.

§ 29. Every stage or coach when driven or used in the

night, shall have fixed upon the inside of the front of the stage, a sufficient lighted lamp or candle, and shall have the number of its license, in plain legible figures of at least four inches in length, and no other figure or device, painted on each front side sash-light of such stage or accommodation coach, in such a manner that the same may be distinctly seen and known by persons either inside or outside, (whether the said stage or accommodation coach may be standing or driving); said sashes to be made and kept stationary, under a penalty of ten dollars for every violation.

Numbers.

§ 30. No stage or coach shall have exhibited, on any part thereof, any other number than the number of its license, under the penalty of fifty dollars.

Stopping of Stages.

§ 31. All stages shall be prohibited from stopping by the sidewalk, in front of any hotel or private residence, without express permission of the occupants thereof, except for the purpose of taking up such passengers as may hail them, or of setting down those who may desire to quit them.

Watering horses.

§ 32. No stage shall be allowed to stop, for the purpose of watering the horses attached thereto, excepting at such points as may be selected and designated by the City Marshal.

Penalties.

§ 33. The owner or owners, driver, and any person having the charge of any stage or accommodation coach, shall be liable, severally and respectively, for the penalty or penalties prescribed for any and every infringement of the provisions of this chapter.

Report of offences.

§ 34. It shall be the duty, especially of all day and other police officers and Mayor's marshals, to daily report all violations of the laws and regulations appertaining to stages or accommodation coaches, to the Attorney of the Corporation.

ARTICLE V.

OF THE SUPERINTENDENCE OF STAGES.

Duties.

§ 35. It shall be the duty of the person or officer exercising the duties of Superintendent of Stages, to visit the stands designated in this chapter, and such other places as may, by law, be designated as stands for stages. He shall have full power and authority to order away from the stands, any coach or stage not provided with proper and sufficient horses or harness: or if the horses attached thereto are unruly; or if the driver or person having charge thereof is intoxicated, or in any manner misbehaves himself.

Orders by Superintendent.

§ 36. If any person or persons having charge of any such stage or coach, shall refuse or neglect to obey such order of the said person or officer, he or they shall forfeit and pay, for every such offense, the sum of five dollars, to be recovered from the owner or driver thereof, severally and respectively.

Duties of Superintendent

§ 37. It shall be the duty of the said person or officer, to see that all the laws regulating accommodation stages and coaches, are in every respect complied with; and it is particularly enjoined upon the said person or officer, that he report all offenders thereof to the Attorney of the Corporation.

Ibid.

§ 38. The said person or officer, under the direction of the Mayor of the city of New York, shall determine the number of coaches or stages for any particular stand; and he shall also designate the proper boundaries and limits of every stand.

ARTICLE VI.

GENERAL PROVISIONS.

§ 39. All the provisions and penalties of this chapter, except those requiring lamps, shall apply to sleighs which shall come upon and use the stands designated for them, and to the owner or owners, or drivers thereof; and shall also apply, in all respects, to sleighs which shall be driven and used for the conveyance of passengers, in the city of New York, for hire or wages. Sleighs.

§ 40. Every owner, driver or person having charge of any accommodation coach or stage, shall, upon being requested so to do, give to any person or persons the number of his coach or stage, the name of the owner thereof, and his place of abode; and in default thereof, shall forfeit and pay the sum of ten dollars to be sued for and recovered from the owner or driver of any such coach or stage severally and respectively. Number and name to be given when demanded.

CHAPTER XL.

OF HACKNEY COACHES AND CABS.

ARTICLE I.

OF LICENSING OWNERS OF HACKNEY COACHES.

License of owners.

§ 1. The Mayor of the city of New York, for the time being, shall, from time to time, issue licenses under his hand and seal, to so many and such persons as he shall think proper, to keep hackney coaches and carriages for hire in the said city, and to revoke all or any of the said licenses.

Ibid.

§ 2. No person who is not a citizen of the United States, a resident of this city for the last six months, of the age of twenty-one years and upward, and the owner of two good horses, and a sufficient hackney coach or carriage, shall be licensed as aforesaid.

Oath.

§ 3. The Mayor of the said city may administer to any person applying for a license, an oath or affirmation, and shall examine such person orally, touching his said application and qualifications to receive said license.

§ 4. All licenses to the owners of hackney coaches and carriages, shall expire on the first Monday of June, next after the date thereof. Term of License.

§ 5. If the owner of any hackney coach, who may have received a license, shall sell or dispose of such coach before the expiration of such license, such licensed owner shall, within ten days after such sale, report the same to the person exercising the duties of Superintendent of Hackney Coaches, who shall be authorized with the consent of the Mayor, to transfer such license to the purchaser of such hackney coach. on the payment of one dollar; and every owner of a hackney coach who shall neglect to report any such sale to the said person, shall forfeit and pay the sum of five dollars. Transfer of License.

§ 6. No licensed person shall be entitled to have his license renewed, unless he shall make it satisfactorily appear on oath, as aforesaid, that he still owns two good horses, and a sufficient and proper hackney coach, as aforesaid. Renewal of License.

§ 7. Every license shall state the number of the carriage for which the same is granted. Number.

§ 8. Every person who may be licensed as aforesaid shall pay the Mayor, for the use of the city, for each hackney coach or carriage, which such person shall keep for hire, the sum of five dollars. License Fee of owners.

§ 9. Every person who shall keep or drive any hackney coach or carriage, for hire, in the city of New York, without being first licensed as aforesaid, shall be liable to the penalty of twenty-five dollars for every such offense. Penalty.

ARTICLE II.

OF LICENSING DRIVERS OF HACKNEY COACHES.

Driver's License. § 10. The Mayor of the city of New York shall have full power and authority, from time to time, to issue licenses, under his hand and seal, to so many and such persons as he may think proper, to drive hackney coaches and carriages, and at pleasure, to revoke all or any of the said licenses.

Ibid. § 11. All licenses to drivers of hackney coaches or carriages, shall expire on the first Monday in June next after the date thereof.

License Fee of Drivers. § 12. Every driver of a hackney coach or carriage shall, on receiving his license, pay to the Mayor of the city of New York, for the use of the said city, the sum of one dollar.

Penalty. No person shall drive any hackney coach or carriage, without being at the time licensed as aforesaid, under the penalty of five dollars for each offense.

None to drive without License. § 13. No owner of any hackney coach, carriage or cab, shall suffer or permit any person to drive such hackney coach, carriage or cab, who is not licensed as aforesaid; nor shall the owner permit any driver who has received any license as aforesaid, to drive any coach, carriage or cab, other than the number for which he is licensed, under the penalty of ten dollars for every such offense.

Annulling License. § 14. Any driver who shall be thrice convicted of a breach of any of the sections of this chapter, shall be deprived of his license, and forever debarred of a license under this chapter.

Badge of persons driving. § 15. Every licensed owner or driver of any hackney coach, carriage or cab in the city of New York, whenever he shall drive any such coach, carriage or cab, or shall be with his coach, carriage or cab on any public stand, or at any of the steamboat or other landings, or railroad depots, or while waiting for employment at any place in said city, shall wear conspicuously on his hat a badge, with the number of his license fixed thereon—the figures composing which number shall be of brass, or some other metal, and at least one inch in length. The form and material of the said badge shall be determined by the Mayor of said city.

§ 16. No owner of any such coach, carriage or cab in said city shall suffer or permit any licensed driver to drive any such coach, carriage or cab, unless such driver shall have fastened on his hat, conspicuously displayed, a badge, with the number of his license thereon, as aforesaid. Badge of persons driving.

§ 17. No person, except a licensed owner or driver of any such coach, carriage or cab in the said city, shall wear the badge of any such licensed owner or driver, or any badge purporting to be the badge of any such licensed owner or driver; nor shall any person other than a licensed driver or owner solicit passengers for any such coach, carriage or cab; nor shall any such licensed owner or driver wear any other than his own badge, or suffer or permit any other person to wear the same. Ibid.

§ 18. Every driver of any such coach, carriage or cab, shall present to every passenger employing him, a card, on which shall be legibly printed, the number of his license, and also the name and stable of the owner, and the number of the coach, carriage or cab driven by him, together with the place of the Mayor's office; and every such owner may, with the consent of the captain, agent, or superinten dent of any steamboat or ship, or railroad company land Cards.

ing at, or terminating in said city, enter on board such steamboat or ship, or into the depot of such company, for the purpose of soliciting passengers, providing he shall comply, in every respect, with the provisions of this chapter.

Penalty.

§ 19. Any licensed owner or driver of any hackney coach, carriage or cab, or any other person who shall neglect to comply with, or violate either of the provisions of the 15, 16, 17 or 18th sections of this chapter, shall be liable to a penalty of ten dollars for every such neglect or violation.

Special License excepted.

§ 20. The last five sections shall not apply to any licensed owner or driver of any coach, carriage or cab having a special license.

ARTICLE III.

OF THE RATES AND PRICES OF FARES.

Rates of Fare.

§ 21. The prices or rates of fare to be taken by or paid to the owners or drivers of hackney coaches or carriages, shall be as follows, to wit:

1. For conveying a passenger any distance not exceeding one mile, fifty cents; for conveying two passengers the same distance, seventy-five cents, or thirty-seven and a half cents each; and for every additional passenger, thirty-seven and a half cents.
2. For conveying a passenger any distance exceeding a mile, and within two miles, seventy-five cents; and for every additional passenger, thirty-seven and a half cents.
3. For conveying a passenger to the new Alms-house and returning, one dollar; and for every additional passenger, and returning, fifty cents.

4. For conveying one passenger to Fortieth street and remaining half an hour, and returning, one dollar and a half; and for every additional passenger, fifty cents. Rates of Fare,

5. For conveying one passenger to Sixty-first street, and remaining three-quarters of an hour, and returning, two dollars; and for every additional passenger, fifty cents.

For conveying one passenger to Eighty-sixth street, and remaining one hour, and returning, two dollars and a half; and for every additional passenger seventy-five cents.

7. For conveying one or more passengers to Harlem, and returning, with the privilege of remaining three hours, five dollars, or to the High Bridge, five dollars, with the same privilege.

8. For conveying one or more passengers to Kingsbridge and returning, with the privilege of keeping the carriage all day, five dollars.

9. For the use of a hackney coach or carriage by the day, with one or more passengers, five dollars.

10. For the use of a hackney coach or carriage by the hour, with one or more passengers, with the privilege of going from place to place, and stopping as often as may be required, one dollar an hour.

11. In all cases where the hiring of a hackney coach or carriage is not, at the time thereof, specified to be by the day or hour, it shall be deemed to be by the mile.

12. For children between two and fourteen years of age, half price is only to be charged; and for children under two years of age, no charge is to be made.

13. Whenever a hackney coach or carriage shall be detained, excepting as aforesaid, the owner or driver shall be allowed after the rate of seventy-five cents an hour.

14. For attending a funeral within the lamp and watch district, two dollars; and to the Potter's Field, three dollars; which charges shall include for the necessary detention and returning with passengers.

15. Every driver or owner of a hackney coach, carriage or cab, shall carry, transport and convey, in and upon his coach, carriage or cab, in addition to the person or persons therein, one trunk, valise, saddle-bag, carpet-bag, portmanteau or box, if he be requested so to do, for each passenger, without charge or compensation therefor; but for every trunk or such articles as above-named, more than one for each passenger, he shall be entitled to demand and receive the sum of six cents.

Disputes.

§ 22. In case of disagreement as to distance or price, the same shall be determined by the Mayor.

Collecting Fare.

§ 23 The owner of any hackney coach or carriage shall not demand or receive any pay for the conveyance of any passenger, unless the number of the carriage, and the rates and prices of fare shall be fixed and placed in the manner hereinafter directed by section 30 of this chapter, at the time such passenger may be conveyed in such carriage.

Ibid.

§ 24. The owner or driver of any hackney coach or carriage shall not be entitled to recover or receive any pay from any person from whom he shall have demanded any greater price or rates than he may be authorized to receive as aforesaid.

§ 25. Upon the trial of any cause commenced for the recovery of any of the aforesaid prices or rates, it shall be incumbent upon the plaintiff or plaintiffs in such action to prove that the number and prices or rates were placed and fixed in pursuance of the provisions of this chapter, at the time the services were rendered, for which the suit may be brought. Proof in actions.

§ 26. No owner or driver of any hackney coach or carriage in the city of New York, shall ask, demand or receive any larger sum than he or they may be entitled to receive as aforesaid, under the penalty of ten dollars for every such offense, to be sued for and recovered from the owner or owners, or driver of any such hackney coach or carriage, severally and respectively. Demand of excessive fare.

ARTICLE IV.

OF THE REGULATING AND NUMBERING OF HACKS.

§ 27. Every hackney coach or carriage which shall resort to or come upon any of the stands hereinafter designated, or which shall be found waiting for hire at a place other than the house or stable of the owner thereof, shall be marked and numbered in the manner following, that is to say: The number of the license of the owner thereof shall be fixed in plain legible brass figures of at least two inches in length and a quarter of an inch thick on each side of the rocker, immediately under the doors of the carriage, on the outside thereof, and such conspicuous place on the inside of the carriage as shall be designated and approved by the Mayor. Numbering of Hacks.

§ 28. Every hackney coach or carriage, when driven or used in the night, shall have fixed upon some conspicuous part of the outside thereof, two lighted lamps with plain Lamps with numbers.

glass fronts and sides, and having the number of the license of the owner of such hackney coach or carriage in plain legible figures, at least two inches in length, and no other figure or device, painted with black paint upon each of the said lamps, in such a manner that the same may be distinctly seen and known, when the said hackney coach or carriage may be standing or driving.

Penalty. § 29. Any person or persons who shall keep or drive such hackney coach or carriage, in violation of any or either of the preceding provisions of this chapter, shall forfeit and pay for every such offense, the sum of ten dollars, to be sued for and recovered from the owner or driver thereof, severally and respectively.

Card to be fixed in the Coach. § 30. There shall be fixed in every hackney coach or carriage, in such a manner as can be conveniently read by any person in the same, a card containing the name of the owner of said carriage, the number of his license, and the whole of the third article of this chapter printed in plain legible characters.

Exhibition of card. § 31. Every driver or owner of such hackney coach or carriage shall, when required so to do by any passenger in such hackney coach or carriage, exhibit to such passenger a card in every respect similar to the one above-mentioned and described in the preceding section.

Penalty. § 32. Any person who shall violate any or either of the provisions of this chapter, shall forfeit and pay for every such offense the sum of ten dollars, to be sued for and recovered from the owner or driver of such hackney coach or carriage, severally and respectively.

Refusal of employment. § 33. No owner or driver of any hackney coach, carriage, or cab, whilst on any of the stands, or any stand which may hereafter be made, or at any steamboat landing, or other landing, or whilst waiting for employment at any place other than at the stable or residence of the owner thereof, shall refuse or neglect to convey any person or persons to any place or places on the island of New York on his being applied to for that purpose; and on the person or persons being placed in such coach, carriage or cab, shall immediately carry him, her, or them, (as the case may be,) to such place as he, she or they may request; nor shall the owner or driver place any other person or persons in such coach, carriage or cab, without the consent of the person or persons therein, or who first engaged or called upon him, under the penalty of ten dollars for each and every refusal, neglect, or offense, to be sued for and recovered from the owner or driver of any such hackney coach, carriage or cab, severally and respectively.

Drivers not to leave the coach, &c

§ 34. No person, whether owner or driver of any hackney coach, carriage or cab, or accommodation stage coach, while waiting for employment at either of the public stands, or at any stand that may hereafter be made, or at any steamboat landing, or other landing, shall snap or flourish his whip, or leave such coach, carriage or cab, or accommodation stage coach, and go on board of any steamboat or other vessel, or on any pier or wharf, for the purpose of looking for employment for such coach, carriage or cab, or accommodation stage coach, under the penalty of ten dollars for each and every offense, to be sued for and recovered from the owner or driver thereof, severally and respectively.

Sleighs.

§ 35. All the provisions and penalties of this chapter, except those requiring lamps, shall apply to the sleighs, which shall come upon and use the stands hereinbefore designated, and to the owner or owners, or drivers thereof; and shall also apply, in all respects, to sleighs which shall be driven and used for the conveyance of passengers in the city of New York, for hire or wages.

Name and number to be given when required.

§ 36. Every owner, driver or person having charge of any hackney coach or carriage, shall, upon being requested to do so, give to any person or persons the number of his coach, the name of the owner thereof, and his place of abode; the name of the driver thereof, and his place of abode; and in default thereof, shall forfeit and pay the sum of ten dollars, to be sued for and recovered from the owner or driver of such coach, severally and respectively.

Soliciting passengers

§ 37. No person shall solicit or request, nor shall the licensed owner or driver of any hackney coach, carriage or cab, or accommodation stage coach, solicit or request, hire, employ, suffer or permit any person to solicit or request in any way, directly or indirectly, any person or persons in the public streets, or at any place of public amusement, or on board of any steamboat or other vessel, or at any steamboat landing or other landing, or upon any wharf or pier in the city of New York, to ride in, or hire, or engage, or employ any hackney coach, carriage or cab, or stage coach, under the penalty of ten dollars for each and every offense, to be sued for and recovered from such person, owner or driver, any or either of them, severally and respectively.

ARTICLE V.

OF PLACES AT WHICH HACKS MAY STAND FOR HIRE.

Stands for Hacks.

§ 38. Hackney coaches and carriages may stand waiting for employment, at all times, Sundays excepted, at the stands herein named, that is to say:

1. On the northerly side of Chatham street, along the Park.
2. In Broadway, around the Bowling Green.

3. In Barclay street, west of Washington street,
4. In Pearl street, at Hanover square.
5. In Maiden lane, southeast of Water street.
6. In Murray street, between Washington street and West street.
7. In Hudson street, along St. John's Park.
8. In Beekman street, southeast of Water street.
9. In Hudson street, near the Little Park.
10. In Reade street, west of Washington street.
11. In Canal street, west of Washington street.
12. In Chatham square.
13. In Grand street, southeast of Mangin street.
14. In Catharine street, southeast of Cherry street, after market hours.
15. On the northerly side of Canal street, east of Broadway.

§ 39. The Mayor of the city of New York, with the advice and consent of the Alderman and Councilmen of each district, may, from time to time, designate such other place or places in each ward, as they shall deem proper, at which hackney coaches and carriages may stand waiting for employment. Stands for Hacks.

§ 40. The owner or driver of any hackney coach or carriage, which shall stand waiting for employment at any other time or place than herein are designated or may be designated as aforesaid, shall forfeit and pay for every such offense, the sum of ten dollars, to be recovered from the owner or driver thereof, severally and respectively. Ibid.

§ 41. The Mayor of the city of New York, by and with the consent of the Aldermen and Councilmen of the several Regulation of Hacks.

districts, shall have full power and authority to make such rules and regulations, and give such orders respecting the standing of hackney coaches and carriages at and near the theatres and other places of amusement, at night, and at and near steamboats and other vessels at all times, and at and upon the stands designated and specified for such coaches, as may be necessary to preserve order and decorum.

Obeying regulations.

§ 42. Every owner or driver of any such hackney coach or carriage, who shall neglect to obey any of the said rules, regulations or orders, shall forfeit and pay for every such offense, the sum of five dollars, to be recovered from the owner or driver of any such coach or carriage, severally and respectively.

Seeking employment on Sunday.

§ 43. No owner or driver of any hackney coach, carriage, cab or stage coach, shall drive, or lead his hackney coach, carriage, cab or stage coach, up or down any street, avenue, dock, wharf or pier, on the Lord's Day, commonly called Sunday, for the purpose of looking for employment, under the penalty of ten dollars, for each and every offense, to be sued for and recovered from the owner or driver of such coach, carriage, cab or stage coach, each severally and respectively.

Penalties, to whom paid.

§ 44. Any penalty recovered under the provisions of this chapter, shall be paid to the Comptroller of the city for the use thereof.

ARTICLE VI.

OF SPECIAL HACKNEY COACHES OR CARRIAGES.

Special Licenses.

§ 45. The proprietor of any hackney coach or carriage, who does not intend to come upon and use the public stands with such hackney coach or carriage, shall, at the time of applying for a license for the same, state, in writing, to the Mayor, such intention; and, thereupon, a special license may be granted, in the discretion of the Mayor, to such proprietor.

§ 46. For every such special license granted by virtue of the provisions of this chapter, shall be paid the sum of five dollars. Fee for Special License.

§ 47. Every such license shall expire on the first Monday of June next after the date thereof, and may be renewed on application for such purpose. Term of Special License.

§ 48. No hackney coach or carriage, which shall be specially licensed, by virtue of the provisions of this chapter, shall make use of, or come upon, or stand, or wait for employment at any of the public stands, or at any other place in the city of New York, except upon the premises of the owner thereof, under a penalty of ten dollars for every such offense, to be recovered from the owner or driver thereof, severally and respectively. Regulation under Special License.

§ 49. The person or officer exercising the duties of the office of Superintendent of Hacks, shall, at all reasonable times, have free access to such hackney coaches and carriages, within the premises of their several proprietors, as shall be necessary to the performance of his duties, under a penalty of ten dollars upon each and every person who shall obstruct, disturb, or molest the said person or officer, whilst in the discharge of his duties as aforesaid. Ibid.

§ 50. The several provisions and penalties of article one, and of sections 12, 13 and 14, in article two of this chapter, shall, in all and every respect, apply to hackney coaches and carriages, which may be licensed, by virtue of the provisions of this article, and the owners and drivers thereof, severally and respectively. Other provisions applicable.

ARTICLE VII.

OF THE SUPERINTENDENCE OF HACKNEY COACHES AND CARRIAGES.

Duties of Superintendent

§ 51. It shall be the duty of the person or officer exercising the duties appertaining to the office of Superintendent of Hacks, to visit the public stands, and all places where hackney coaches and carriages are permitted to stand; he shall have power and authority to order away from the stands, and from all other places, any hackney coach or carriage not provided with a number, or with lamps fixed up, lighted and numbered as hereinbefore required; or not furnished with proper and suitable harness and horses; or, if the same, in his opinion, shall be improperly obstructing the way or street; or if the horses attached thereto are unruly; or if the driver or person having charge of any such hackney coach or carriage is intoxicated, or in any manner misbehaves himself.

Orders of Superintendent

§ 52. If any person having charge of any such hackney coach or carriage, shall refuse or neglect to obey any such order of the said person or officer, he or they shall forfeit and pay for every such offense the sum of ten dollars, to be recovered from the owners or driver of every such hackney coach or carriage, severally and respectively.

Duties of Superintendent

§ 53. It shall be the duty of the said person or officer, to see that all the laws regulating hackney coaches and carriages, are, in every respect, complied with; and it is particularly enjoined upon the said person or officer, that he report all offenders thereof to the Attorney of the Corporation.

Ibid.

§ 54. The said person or officer, under the direction of the Mayor, shall determine the number of coaches or carriages for any particular stand; and he shall also designate the coaches or carriages which shall wait for employment at any particular stand; and also, the proper boundaries and limits of every stand.

ARTICLE VIII.

OF CABS.

§ 55. The several ordinances heretofore passed regulating cabs as distinct and separate from hackney coaches, shall be, and the same are, by effect hereof, at that time repealed. And all cabs shall hereafter be regulated, numbered, licensed, and, in all respects, governed by the chapter relative to hackney coaches, provided, however, that the fee for license of a cab drawn by one horse only shall be no more than three dollars. Cabs.

CHAPTER XLI.

OF THE LICENSING OF CITY RAILROAD PASSENGER CARS.

License Fee. § 1. Each and every passenger railroad car running in the city of New York below One hundred and twenty-fifth street, shall pay into the city treasury the sum of fifty dollars annually for a license, a certificate of such payment to be procured from the Mayor, except the small one horse passenger cars, which shall each pay the sum of twenty-five dollars annually for said license as aforesaid.

§ 2. Each certificate of payment of license shall be affixed to some conspicuous place in the car that it may be inspected by the proper officers.

Penalty. § 3. For every passenger car run upon any of the city railroads below One hundred and twenty-fifth street, without the proper certificate of license, the proprietor or proprietors thereof shall be subject to a penalty of fifty dollars, to be recovered by the Corporation Attorney, as in the case of other penalties, and for the benefit of the city treasury.

CHAPTER XLII.

OF PAWNBROKERS, DEALERS IN SECOND-HAND ARTICLES AND KEEPERS OF JUNK SHOPS.

ARTICLE I.

OF PAWNBROKERS.

§ 1. The Mayor may, from time to time, grant licenses under his hand and seal, to such persons as shall produce to him satisfactory evidence of their good character, to exercise or carry on the business of a pawnbroker. License to Pawnbrokers.

§ 2. Every person receiving such license, shall pay therefor the sum of fifty dollars, for the use of the city. License Fee.

§ 3. Every person so licensed, shall, at the time of receiving such license, enter, with two sufficient sureties, into a joint and several recognizance to the Mayor, Aldermen and Commonalty of the city of New York, in the penalty of five hundred dollars, conditioned for the due observance of all such ordinances of the Common Council, as may be passed or in force respecting pawnbrokers, at any time during the continuance of such license. Sureties.

§ 4. Every pawnbroker shall keep a book, in which shall be fairly written, at the time of each loan, an accurate account and description of the goods, article or thing pawned, the amount of money loaned thereon, the time of pledging the same, the rate of interest to be paid on such Record of things pawned.

loan, and the name and residence of the person pawning or pledging the said goods, article or thing.

Pawn ticket.

§ 5. Every pawnbroker shall, at the time of each loan, deliver to the person pawning or pledging any goods, article or thing, a memorandum or note, signed by him or her, containing the substance of the entry required to be made in his or her book, by the last preceding section; and no charge shall be made or received by any pawnbroker, for any such entry, memorandum or note.

Record of articles pawned

§ 6. The said book shall, at all reasonable times, be opened to the inspection of the Mayor, Recorder, Aldermen, Councilmen, and special justices for preserving the peace of the city of New York, or any or either of them; or of any person who shall be duly authorized in writing, for that purpose, by any or either of them, and who shall exhibit such written authority to such pawnbroker.

Penalty.

§ 7. Every pawnbroker who shall violate or neglect, or refuse to comply with any or either of the provisions of the 4th, 5th or 6th sections of this chapter, shall, for every such offense, forfeit and pay the sum of twenty-five dollars.

Rate of Interest.

§ 8. No pawnbroker shall ask, demand, or receive any greater rate of interest than twenty-five per cent. per annum, upon any loan not exceeding the sum of twenty-five dollars; or than seven per cent. per annum upon any loan exceeding the sum of twenty-five dollars, under the penalty of one hundred dollars for every such offense.

Pledge to be kept 1 year.

§ 9. No pawnbroker shall sell any pawn or pledge, until the same shall have remained one year in his or her possession; and all such sales shall be at public auction, and not otherwise; and shall be made or conducted by such auctioneer as shall be approved of for that purpose, by the Mayor of the city of New York.

§ 10. Notice of every such sale shall be published for at least twelve days previous thereto, in one or more of the daily newspapers printed in the city of New York; and such notice shall specify the time and place at which such sale is to take place, the name of the auctioneer by whom the same is to be conducted, and a description of the goods or articles to be sold. Sale of things pledged.

§ 11. The surplus money, if any, arising from any such sale, after deducting the amount of the loan, the interest then due on the same, and the expenses of the advertisement and sale, shall be paid over by the pawnbroker to the person who would be entitled to redeem the pledge in case no such sale had taken place. Ibid.

§ 12. No pawnbroker shall make any loan on the separate or divided part or parts of any one article or thing, and which article or thing shall have been offered entire or collectively, to him or her, by way of pawn or pledge. Dividing Loans.

§ 13. No pawnbroker, shall, under any pretense whatever, purchase or buy any second hand furniture, metals or clothes, or any other article or thing whatever, offered to him or her as a pawn or pledge. Pawnbrokers not to purchase.

§ 14. Every pawnbroker who shall violate or neglect, or refuse to comply with any or either of the provisions of the 8th, 9th, 10th, 11th, 12th and 13th sections of this chapter, shall, for every such offense, forfeit and pay the sum of one hundred dollars. Penalty.

ARTICLE II.

OF DEALERS IN SECOND HAND ARTICLES.

§ 15. The Mayor may, from time to time, grant licenses under his hand and seal, to such persons as shall produce to him satisfactory evidence of good character to exercise Licenses to second-hand dealers.

or carry on the business of dealing in the purchase and sale of second hand furniture, metal, clothes, or other articles in the said city.

License Fee. § 16. Every person receiving such license, shall pay therefor the sum of twenty-five dollars, for the use of the city.

Sureties. § 17. Every person so licensed shall, at the time of receiving such license, enter, with two sufficient sureties, into a joint and several recognizance, to the Mayor, Aldermen and Commonalty of the city of New York, in the penalty of five hundred dollars, conditioned for the due observance of all such ordinances of the Common Council as may be in force or passed, respecting dealers in second-hand articles, at any time during the continuance of such license.

Record of articles purchased. § 18. Every such dealer shall keep a book, in which shall be fairly written, at the time of the purchase of any article or thing, in the way of his or her business, an accurate account and description of the article or thing so purchased, the price paid therefor, the precise time of making such purchase, and the name and residence of the person from whom such purchase was made.

Ibid. § 19. The said book shall, at all reasonable times, be open to the inspection of the Mayor, Recorder, Aldermen, Councilmen, Police Justices and Superintendent of Police, of the city of New York, or any or either of them, or of any person who shall be duly authorized, in writing, for that purpose, by any or either of them, and who shall exhibit such written authority to such dealer.

Penalty. § 20. Every such dealer who shall violate or neglect, or refuse to comply with, any or either of the provisions of the 18th and 19th sections of this chapter, shall, for every such offense, forfeit and pay the sum of twenty-five dollars.

§ 21. No article or thing, except wooden furniture, which shall have been purchased by any such dealer in the way of his or her business, shall be sold or disposed of by such dealer until the expiration of one month after such purchase. Things not to be sold within a month.

§ 22. No such dealer shall receive any article by way of pledge or pawn, or shall purchase or buy, at private sale, of any one person, in one day, any article or articles exceeding in value the sum of fifty dollars. Pledges and purchases.

§ 23. Every such dealer who shall violate or neglect, or refuse to comply with any or either of the provisions of the 21st and 22d sections of this chapter, shall, for every such offense, forfeit and pay the sum of one hundred dollars. Penalty.

ARTICLE III.

OF KEEPERS OF JUNK SHOPS.

§ 24. The Mayor may, from time to time, grant licenses to such persons as shall procure the recommendation for that purpose, of the Police Justices, or General Superintendent of Police of the city of New York, to keep what are commonly called junk shops, for the purchase and sale of junk, old rope, old iron, brass, copper, tin and lead, rags, slush and empty bottles. Licenses.

§ 25. Every person receiving such license, shall pay therefor the sum of twenty dollars, for the use of the poor of the city. License Fee.

§ 26. Every person so licensed, shall, at the time of receiving such license, enter with one sufficient surety, into a joint and several recognizance to the Mayor, Aldermen and Commonalty of the city of New York, in the penal sum of two hundred and fifty dollars, conditioned for the due observance of such ordinances of the Common Coun- Surety.

cil, as may be passed or in force, respecting the keeping of junk shops, at any time during the continuance of such license.

Purchasers and pledges.

§ 27. No keeper of a junk shop shall buy or sell any coin of any description, or any article of gold or silver, or any wearing apparel; or any article of household furniture, or any implement, tool or utensil, in a sound, unbroken or undamaged condition; nor shall such keeper receive, in the line of his business, any article or thing by way of pledge or pawn; nor shall he or she loan or advance any sum of money on the security of any such article or thing.

Record of purchases.

§ 28. Every keeper of a junk shop shall provide and keep a book, in which shall be fairly written, at the time of every purchase, a description of the article so purchased, the name and residence of the person from whom such purchase was made, and the day and hour of such purchase.

Ibid.

§ 29. Every such book shall, at all times, be open to the inspection of the Mayor, Aldermen, Councilmen and Police Justices, and Superintendent of Police of the city of New York, and each of them, or to any person who may be authorized for the purpose, in writing, by either of them, such person exhibiting to the said keeper his authority as aforesaid.

Penalty.

§ 30. Every such keeper of a junk shop, who shall violate or neglect, or refuse to comply with the foregoing provisions, or either of them, shall, for every such offense, forfeit and pay the sum of fifty dollars.

ARTICLE IV.

OF GENERAL PROVISIONS.

Place of Business.

§ 31. Every license to be granted to any dealer in second-hand articles, or keeper of a junk shop, shall designate the house or place in which the person receiving such license shall be authorized to carry on such business.

§ 32. Every such license shall continue in force until the second Monday in May, next following the granting thereof, unless sooner revoked by the Mayor, and no longer. **Duration of License.**

§ 33. On the renewal of every such license, the person receiving the same shall pay the same sum therefor, as is required to be paid on granting such license in the first instance. **Renewal of License.**

§ 34. No person shall use, exercise or carry on the trade or business of a dealer in second-hand articles, or of a keeper of a junk shop, without being specially licensed for such purpose as aforesaid, or shall carry on any such business at any other house or place than the one designated in such license, or shall continue to carry on such business after such license may have been revoked, under the penalty of fifty dollars for every such offense. **License.**

§ 35. No dealer in second-hand articles, or keeper of a junk shop, shall purchase any goods, article or thing whatsoever, from any minor, apprentice or servant, knowing, or having reason to believe him or her to be such, under the penalty of twenty-five dollars for every such offense. **Purchases from minors and others.**

§ 36. No dealer in second-hand articles, or keeper of a junk shop, shall receive or purchase, in the way of his or her business, any goods, articles or thing whatsoever, from any person or persons whomsoever, between the setting of the sun and the hour of seven o'clock in the morning, under the penalty of twenty-five dollars for every such offense. **Purchases after sun-down**

§ 37. No dealer in second-hand articles shall deface, mutilate, take apart, or, in any way, alter, or permit to be defaced, mutilated, taken apart, or in any way altered, any article or thing which shall come into his or her pos- **Defacing Goods.**

session, in the way of his or her business, but the same shall be sold, or offered for sale in the same form, state and condition in which it was when first received by him or her, under the penalty of one hundred dollars for every such offense.

Goods advertised. § 38. If any goods, article or thing shall be advertised in any daily newspaper printed in the city of New York, as having been lost or stolen, and if the said goods, article or thing, or any such answering to the description of the goods, article or thing so advertised, or any part or portion thereof, shall then be, or thereafter come into the possession of any dealer in second-hand articles or keeper of a junk shop, he or she shall, forthwith, give information thereof in writing, at the office of the General Superintendent of Police, and shall also state from whom the same were received under the penalty of two hundred and fifty dollars for every neglect or offense.

Lost or stolen goods. § 39. Every dealer in second-hand articles, or keeper of a junk shop, who shall receive or be in possession of any goods, articles or things, which may have been lost or stolen, or alleged or supposed to have been lost or stolen, shall, forthwith, on a demand to view the same, present the same to the Mayor or Recorder, or any Alderman or Councilman, or Police Justice, Superintendent of Police, or any policeman, who may be authorized by either of the above-mentioned officers or magistrates, to make such demand, under the penalty of two hundred and fifty dollars, for every neglect or refusal so to do.

Restricted to Special business. § 40. No dealer in second-hand articles shall, during his license as such, receive or hold a license to carry on the business of a pawnbroker or keeper of a junk shop; and, no keeper of a junk shop, shall, during his license as such, receive or hold a license to carry on the business of a pawnbroker, or of a dealer in second-hand articles.

§ 41. Every license granted, or to be granted, to any dealer in second-hand articles, or keeper of a junk shop, may be revoked by the Mayor, on satisfactory cause appearing to him for so doing. Revocation of License.

§ 42. No person shall keep what is commonly called a junk shop, for the purchase and sale of junk, rags, or old rope, old iron, brass, copper, tin, empty bottles, slush or lead; and no person shall draw or drive, or procure to be drawn or driven through the streets of this city, any hand-cart, wheel-barrow, or other carts or vehicles; and no person shall propel, or procure to be propelled through the waters of the city and county of New York, any boat, or other kind of vessel, for the purpose of collecting junk, rags, old rope, old iron, brass, copper, tin, empty bottles slush or lead, or deal in buying or selling either of such articles, without being first licensed by the Mayor for such purposes. License.

§ 43. Every licensed keeper of a junk shop, for the purchase and sale of rags, old rope, old iron, brass, copper, empty bottles, tin, slush or lead, shall be entitled to keep one or more carts, wagons, or other vehicles ; one or more boats or other vessels, for the purpose of collecting old junk, rags, old rope, old iron, brass, copper, empty bottles, tin, slush or lead, in the city of New York, provided he or she shall, before using such carts, wagons, boats or other vessels, or causing the same to be used, cause to be painted on the outer side of such hand-carts, wheel-barrows, or other carts or vehicles, boats or vessels, his name, at length, the street and number of his place of business—the number of his license in plain letters and figures, put on with paint, of not less than two and a half inches in length; and no person or persons except such as are regularly licensed for the purpose aforesaid, according to the provisions of this chapter, or persons in the employ of such licensed dealer, Vehicles and Boats.

shall draw or drive, or procure to be drawn or driven, or propelled, any such hand-carts, wheel-barrows, carts, wagons, or other vehicles, boats, or other vessels.

License for Vehicles and Boats. § 44. A separate license shall be obtained, by the owner thereof, for each and every cart, wagon, or other vehicle, boat, or other vessel.

Ibid. § 45. Every owner of a cart, wagon, or other vehicle, boat or other vessel, on receiving his or her license, shall pay for each and every cart, wagon, or other vehicle, boat or other vessel, to the Mayor of the city of New York, for the use of said city, the sum of ten dollars.

Removal of place of business. § 46. In case any person so licensed as aforesaid, shall remove his or her store, or place of business, from the place designated in said license, he or she shall immediately thereupon give notice thereof to the Mayor, and have the same indorsed upon such license, and the number of his or her place of business shall thereupon be changed on the sides of the vehicle or vessel used by such licensed dealer, and made to correspond with such change of store or place of business.

Inspector. § 47. The Superintendent of Police, aided and assisted by such policemen as he may deem necessary, shall be the inspector of pawnbrokers, dealers in second-hand articles, junk shops and intelligence offices.

Penalties. § 48. Whoever shall violate any of the provisions of the 2d, 3d and 4th articles of this chapter, shall be subject to the penalties prescribed in and by said article, or, in lieu thereof, shall be deemed guilty of a misdemeanor, and shall be punished, on conviction, pursuant to the provisions of sections twenty and twenty-one of an act relative to the powers of the Common Council of the city of New York, and the police and criminal courts of said city, passed by the Legislature of the State of New York, January 23d, 1833.

CHAPTER XLIII.

OF INTELLIGENCE OFFICES.

§ 1. The Mayor of the city of New York, for the time being, shall, from time to time, issue licenses, under his hand and seal, to so many and such persons as he shall think proper, to keep intelligence offices in the said city, and shall have power to revoke all or any of the said licenses at pleasure. Licenses.

§ 2. Each license shall designate the house in which the person licensed shall keep his office, and the number of such license, and shall continue and be in force until the first Tuesday of May next ensuing the date thereof, and no longer, unless sooner revoked by the Mayor. Ibid.

§ 3. Every person who may be licensed under and by virtue of the provisions of this chapter, shall pay to the Mayor, for the use of the city, the sum of twenty-five dollars, and for the renewal of any such license, the sum of twelve dollars and fifty cents. License Fee.

§ 4. No person shall keep any intelligence office in the city of New York, without having such license as aforesaid, or after the same shall have been revoked, or shall have expired, or at any other house or place than is designated in such license, under the penalty of fifty dollars for every such offense. None to keep without License.

CHAPTER XLIV.

OF PROVISIONS CONCERNING DOGS.

Dogs running at large.

§ 1. No dog shall hereafter be permitted to go abroad in any of the streets, squares, lanes, alleys or public places of this city, without being properly muzzled, or being led by a chain or string, under the penalty of ten dollars for each offense, to be recovered against the owner, possessor or person who harbored such dog, within three days previous to the time of such dog being found so going abroad. And it shall be lawful for any person whosoever, to seize and kill any dog so running at large without being muzzled or led by a chain or string.

Killing dogs.

§ 2. The Mayor may, from time to time, and for such time as he shall think proper, appoint one or more suitable persons to kill and destroy all dogs found running loose or at large in the streets, roads, squares and public places of said city, unless they are properly muzzled.

Pay of dog killers.

§ 3. The persons so appointed shall receive the sum of two dollars per day, for each day they shall be so employed, and shall make weekly returns to the Mayor, of the number of dogs they may severally kill.

Dog killers not to be molested.

§ 4. No person shall hinder or molest any person or persons who may be engaged in seizing and killing any dog, or in removing the carcass thereof, under the penalty of one hundred dollars for each offense.

Killing Dogs.

§ 5. The Mayor is hereby authorized, from time to time, and for such time as he may think proper, and under such regulations as he may prescribe, to pay, or cause to be paid to persons who shall not be regularly appointed to kill or destroy dogs, a sum not exceeding fifty cents for each dog found running loose or at large in the city, below Forty-second street, without being properly muzzled, and which may be killed or destroyed by them.

§ 6. No part of this law shall apply to so much of the city as lies north of Forty-second street, to prevent dogs running at large between sunset and sunrise. Limit.

CHAPTER XLV.

OF NUISANCES AND NOXIOUS THINGS AND PRACTICES.

Made ground

§ 1. No made ground, or ground formerly covered with salt or stagnant water, within the city of New York, shall be turned up, or the surface thereof removed, at any time between the first day of June and the first day of October, in any year, unless by special permission of the Common Council, under the penalty of one hundred dollars for each offense.

Nuisances on premises.

§ 2. No person shall have, make, use, or keep, in his or her premises, at any place in the city of New York, any noisome, offensive or unwholesome substance, or any vat, pit or pool of standing water, whether for tanners, skinners, dyers or other use, under the penalty of fifty dollars for each offense.

Hides, blubber, &c.

§ 3. No tanner, skinner or other person shall bring to, or keep for the period of twenty-four hours, in any part of the city of New York, south of Fourteenth street, any undressed or uncurried hides, skins or leather, or any blubber or other materials whatever, for dressing the same, which may cause any noisome, offensive or unwholesome smell, under the penalty of fifty dollars for each offense.

Beekman's Swamp.

§ 4. The preceding sections, two and three, of this chapter, shall not be construed to affect any vat or vats, pit or pits, in the place commonly called Beekman's Swamp, in the city of New York, which were made and erected on or before the 29th day of March, in the year of our Lord one thousand eight hundred and six.

§ 5. Every butcher or other person occupying any slaughter-house or building, or who shall or may kill or slaughter in any slaughter-house or building in the city of New York, any animal, shall, on every day when any animal may be so slaughtered or killed therein, cause the slaughter house and yard thereof, to be washed out and thoroughly cleansed, under the penalty of ten dollars for each neglect or refusal to comply with this section. Slaughter houses.

§ 6. Every butcher or other person within this city, immediately after killing or slaughtering any animal, shall convey, or cause to be conveyed, in tight covered boxes or barrels, the blood, offal, garbage and other offensive or useless parts of said animal or animals so killed or slaughtered, to such place as the Common Council, or the City Inspector shall, or may, from time to time direct, under a penalty of ten dollars for each and every neglect or refusal to comply with this section. Ibid.

§ 7. It shall be the duty of the City Inspector to see that the two preceding sections are enforced. Ibid

§ 8. No person shall leave exposed, or cast into any street, yard, lot, lane or other place within the city of New York, the carcass of any horse, under the penalty of twenty-five dollars for each offense. Dead horses.

§ 9. No person shall cast or leave, or keep in or adjoining any street, lane, alley, avenue, square, public place, public road, or in any yard, lot, field or premises, in the city of New York, any bones, putrid, unsound, unwholesome, or refuse meat or beef of any animal, whether salted or otherwise, or any unsound pork, fish, hides or skins of any kind, or horns; or the whole or part of any dead animals, or any other unsound, putrid or unwholesome substances; or the offal, garbage or other offensive or useless Unwholesome things prohibited.

parts of any beeves, calves, sheep, hogs or other cattle, under the penalty of fifty dollars for every such offense.

Docks for offal, &c.

§ 10. There shall be designated and set apart, for the use of the City Inspector, two of the docks and slips of the city of New York; one on the East river, and the other on the North river; said docks and slips shall be under the sole control and direction of the City Inspector, and shall be used by him as a place of landing for such boats as may be required for the removal of the butchers' blood and offals, bones, dead animals and other refuse substances from the city.

As to boats for removing offal, &c.

§ 11. No ship, boat, or other vessel, shall come in or lay at or within any of said docks or slips, designated as aforesaid, unless by written permission of the City Inspector, under the penalty of twenty-five dollars for each offense, to be paid by the owner, master, or person having charge thereof, severally and respectively.

Ibid.

§ 12. The City Inspector may give such order or direction as he may deem proper, directing the laying, fastening or berth of any boat or vessel lying at or within said docks and slips, and may direct the same to be removed, from time to time, as he may deem just and proper, and for every neglect or refusal to comply with such order or direction, the owner, master, or person having charge of such boat or other vessel, shall forfeit and pay the sum of twenty-five dollars.

Carts for removing carcasses &c.

§ 13. The contractor or contractors for removing the aforesaid dead animals, bones and other refuse substances, shall furnish, from time to time, a suitable number of carts, to be licensed, under the hand and seal of the City Inspector, for the purpose of transporting and removing said dead animals, bones and other refuse substances in said city; and no person shall transport or remove any dead animals, bones or refuse substances in said city, unless licensed as aforesaid, under the penalty of twenty-five dollars for each offense, to be recovered from the person or persons so removing, or the owner or owners of the vehicle used for that purpose, severally and respectively.

§ 14. No dead animal shall be cast or thrown into East or North rivers, or any water within the limits of the said city, but shall be removed by the person licensed as aforesaid for that purpose, to the docks and slips of the City Inspector, under the penalty of twenty-five dollars for each offense. As to throwing carcasses in the river.

§ 15. No person or persons shall throw, cast or lay any ashes, offal, vegetables, garbage, dross, cinders, shells, straw, shavings, dirt, filth, or rubbish of any kind whatever, in any street, lane, alley, or public place in the city of New York. Throwing offal in the streets.

§ 16. The violation of any of the provisions of the preceding section shall be, and is hereby declared to be a misdemeanor, and shall be punishable by a fine of not less than one dollar, or more than ten dollars, or by imprisonment in the city prison, for a term not less than one or more than five days. Penalty.

§ 17. It shall be the duty of the Superintendent of Sanitary Inspection and Street Cleaning and the Health Wardens and Policemen of the said city to enforce the observance of this chapter, and the punishment of any party or parties who may violate the same. Enforcement of ordinance.

§ 18. It is hereby declared to be the duty of the proprietor or possessor of any foundries, forges, blacksmiths' shops, oyster stands, and other places for the sale of oysters or other shell fish, to employ carts, at their own ex- Oyster and fish dealers.

pense, for the purpose of removing the several articles enumerated in the 15th section of this chapter, which may accumulate in their respective premises.

Building rubbish. § 19. The owner or builder of any house or other building which may be erecting or repairing in the city of New York, shall cause all the rubbish, of every kind, occasioned thereby, which may accumulate in the street, or be cast into the street, and all the ground, stone, sand and clay which may be dug from the cellar or yard, or area or vault, and cast into the street, to be removed out of the said street, before sunset on each day, under the penalty of five dollars for each day's neglect, to be recovered from the owner or builder, severally and respectively.

Ibid. § 20. If any rubbish, ground, stone, sand, clay, shavings or other substance, shall be cast into the street, and shall not be removed, as required by the last section, it shall be lawful for the Superintendent of Sanitary Inspection and Street Cleaning and the Health Warden in whose round the same may be, to cause the same to be removed.

Ibid. § 21. In addition to the penalty imposed by the 19th section, the person who has so incurred the same shall also pay to the said Superintendent of Sanitary Inspection and Street Cleaning and the Health Warden, in whose round the said rubbish or other substance may have been, for removing the same, double the usual and ordinary sum for the removal thereof, to be recovered in the name of the Mayor, Aldermen and Commonalty of the city of New York, with costs of suit, by the Attorney of the Corporation, in any court having cognizance thereof.

Sifting ashes, &c., and carpet shaking. § 22. No person shall sift or screen any lime, ashes, dirt or sand, or shake any carpet, cloth or mat, in any street in the city of New York, or shall employ or suffer or permit any person so to do, under the penalty of five dollars for every such offense.

§ 23. No collector of ashes or other person shall unload from any cart, wagon or other vehicle in any of the streets of the city of New York, any ashes, by dumping or starting the same in the street or on the sidewalk, under the penalty of ten dollars for each offense. **Ash Carts.**

§ 24. No cinders or coal ashes, of any description shall be laid or cast into any street, lane or alley in this city; but shall be delivered to the ash carts provided for the purpose of receiving the same, under the penalty of three dollars for each offense; to be paid by the occupant or occupants of the house or premises from which the same shall be cast, or the persons casting the same, severally and respectively. **Cinders and coal ashes.**

§ 25. All ashes or cinders shall be kept for the purpose of delivering the same to the ash carts, in vessels of tin, iron or other metal, under the penalty of one dollar for each offense. **Ibid.**

§ 26. No person shall throw or deposit any water or other liquid, in any part of any street, alley, lane or public place, except in the side gutter thereof, under the penalty of two dollars for every such offense. **Throwing out liquids.**

§ 27. It shall be the duty of every person, from whose kitchen or lot any water may pass into any street, across the sidewalk, to cause the same to pass through a covered gutter under such sidewalk, and to keep such gutter at all times clear of ice and every other obstruction, so that the water shall pass freely through the same, without overflowing or running upon the surface of the sidewalk, under the penalty of ten dollars for every day that such duty may be neglected. **Gutters across sidewalks.**

Throwing out offensive Liquids.

§ 28. No person shall cast or throw, or suffer to run into any street, lane or alley in the city of New York, from his, her or their house, houses or premises, any stinking, noxious, impure, offensive or noisome water, or any substance or thing, in a liquid or flowing state, under the penalty of twenty-five dollars for each offense.

Water from manufactories, &c.

§ 29. No brewer, distiller, dyer, soapmaker, or other person, shall cast, or throw, or suffer the water to run from his manufactory, shop, house or establishment, into any street, except between the hours of eight in the morning, and five o'clock in the afternoon, from the first day of December, until the first day of April, in any year, under the penalty of twenty-five dollars for each offense.

Ibid.

§ 30. The last preceding section shall not be construed to prevent the casting of water from any steam engine, at any time during the year, in the city of New York.

Ibid.

§ 31. Whenever any water shall be cast or thrown, as provided in the twenty-ninth section of this chapter, the person or persons so casting, or suffering the same to run from their premises, shall clear a passage for the same along the gutter, to the river or public sewer, so that the same shall not overflow the curb-stone or sidewalk, under the penalty of twenty-five dollars for each neglect.

Swill and vegetable substances.

§ 32. No person shall convey or deposit, or cause or permit to be conveyed or deposited, into any street, sewer or drain in the city of New York, any swill or other vegetable fluid, liquid or substance, under the penalty of fifty dollars for each offense.

Shell fish.

§ 33. No person shall erect any booth, or establish or fix any stand in any of the streets or public grounds in the city of New York, for the purpose of opening and exposing for sale, or selling any oysters or other shell fish, under the penalty of five dollars for each offense.

§ 34. No person shall erect any booth, or establish any stand in the streets or public grounds in the city of New York, for the purpose of exposing for sale, or selling any kind of provisions, or any goods of any description whatever, under the penalty of five dollars for each offense. Booths and Stands in the streets.

§ 35. No cart, wagon or other vehicle, in or upon which there shall be any box, hogshead, barrel, cask or other vessel, used or intended to be used for the purpose of containing or conveying the article commonly called swill, shall, when not in actual use, incumber or stand in any of the streets, lanes or alleys in the city of New York, under any pretense whatever, under the penalty of five dollars for each offense, to be recovered from the owner or person having charge of any such cart, wagon or other vehicle, severally and respectively. Swill Carts.

§ 36. The last preceding section shall not be construed to prevent such vehicles, not exceeding four in number, from standing at or in front of the premises from which such swill is obtained, for the purpose of receiving such swill, but not elsewhere; provided the said vehicles do not stand abreast of each other. From the first day of May to the first day of November, in every year, all persons are forbid to use the Croton water for washing streets, sidewalks, steps or buildings, after 8 A. M., and from the first day of November to the first day of May following, after 9 A. M., under the penalty of five dollars for each offense. Ibid.

§ 37. All carts and other vehicles, used by any person or persons, to carry or transport any swill or garbage, shall have water-tight boxes or other vessels, so as to prevent the contents from leaking, spilling or scattering on the streets, under the penalty of one dollar for each and every offense, on conviction thereof, before any magistrate of the city. Ibid.

Bone boiling, skinning of animals, &c.

§ 38. It shall not be lawful for any person or persons, incorporated or unincorporated, to carry on, establish, prosecute or continue, within the city of New York, the occupation, or trade, or business of bone-boiling, bone-burning, bone-grinding, horse-skinning, cow-skinning, or skinning of dead animals, or the boiling of offal; and any such establishment or establishments, or place of such business, existing within the limits aforesaid, shall be forthwith removed out of said city, and such trade, occupation or business shall be forthwith abated and discontinued; provided, that nothing herein contained shall apply to the slaughtering or dressing of animals for sale in said city.

Ibid.

§ 39. Every person or corporation, violating, refusing, or failing to comply with the provisions of the thirty-eighth section of this chapter, shall, upon conviction thereof, before any court of competent jurisdiction, be liable for every such offense, to a penalty of five hundred dollars; and every person or persons engaged or employed in any such trade, or business or occupation, prohibited by the said section of this chapter, or violating the provisions thereof, or refusing or failing to comply with the same, shall, in addition to said penalty, be considered guilty of a misdemeanor, and on conviction shall be subject to fine or imprisonment, or both, at the discretion of the court. And it is made the especial duty of all magistrates and police officers to cause the arrest and detention of all persons guilty of violating the provisions of this chapter of the ordinances.

Ibid.

§ 40. It shall be the duty of the City Inspector to ascertain whether any such trade or business is carried on, or continued, or established within the limits aforesaid, and to cause notice, in writing, to be served upon the person, persons or corporation carrying on or continuing such trade or business, directing every such person, persons or corporation to discontinue the said trade or business, and to cause all offensive or unwholesome materials or things appertaining to said trade or business, to be removed without the limits aforesaid, within forty-eight hours after the service thereof.

§ 41. If the name of any such person shall be known to the said City Inspector, the same shall be inserted therein, but if any such name be unknown to said City Inspector, it shall be sufficient, after diligent inquiry for the same, to direct such notice in the following manner: "To the person, persons or incorporation concerned in the carrying on, or continuance of the business of, (specifying the same) at (specifying the place of such business) and every of them," without any other name or addition, and such notice may be served by leaving the same with any person of suitable age and discretion, upon the premises where such trade or business is so carried on, or if the same be closed, or no person be found upon the premises, upon whom the same can be served, then by posting such notice in a conspicuous place upon such premises, and in case the person or persons to whom such notice is directed be known to the City Inspector, the said notice may be served, by leaving the same at the place of residence of such person, with any person of suitable age and discretion.

Bone boiling, Skinning of animals, &c.

§ 42. If such trade or business, so carried on and continued, shall not be discontinued by the time specified in such notice, and all offensive or unwholesome material and things appertaining thereto, removed from within the limits aforesaid, within the time aforesaid, it shall be the duty of the said City Inspector to cause the same to be done, and he shall have authority to do all things necessary, in order to shut up and discontinue such trade or

Ibid.

28

business peaceably, and to remove beyond the limits aforesaid, all such offensive or unwholesome material or things.

Bone boiling, Skinning of animals, &c. § 43. It shall be the duty of the City Inspector to prepare a statement, showing the expenses incurred in the execution of the last preceding five sections, specifying the lot or lots whereon such trade or business has been so carried on or continued, and the name or names of the proprietor or proprietors, owner or owners of the same, so far as the same may be ascertained, and such statement shall be filed in the office of the Street Commissioner, and such proceedings shall thereupon be taken for the collection of the amount of the sum so expended in carrying the said section into execution, as are provided or allowed by law.

Removal of Nuisances. § 44. In all cases when the City Inspector shall deem it advisable for the public health of said city, forthwith to remove any nuisance in said city, it shall be the duty of said City Inspector to cause the said nuisance forthwith to be abated or removed, at the expense of the owner or owners of any lot or premises upon which the same may exist.

Ibid. § 45. It shall be the duty of such City Inspector forthwith, after the removal or abatement by him of any nuisance, to prepare a statement in writing, showing the expense thereof, and specifying therein the lot or lots, or premises upon which the same existed, and the name or names of the proprietor or proprietors, owner or owners of the same as far as the same may be ascertained, and particularly specifying the expense of the removal or abatement of such nuisance, from each separate lot; and such statement shall be filed in the office of the Street Commissioner; and such proceedings shall be thereupon taken for the collection of the amount of such expense, as are provided by law.

§ 46. No person shall bring into the city of New York, or have in his, her, or their possession, in the said city, any oysters between the first day of May and the first day of September, in any year, under the penalty of five dollars for any quantity not exceeding one hundred, and the further penalty of two dollars for every additional hundred. Oysters.

Provisions against certain Practices.

§ 47. No person shall expose, in any of the streets, lanes, avenues, or public places of the city of New York, any table or device of any kind whatever, upon or by which any game of chance or hazard can be played, or shall play at or upon any such table or device, under the penalty of twenty-five dollars for each offense. Games of Chance.

§ 48. No person shall, at any time, swim or bathe in the waters of the East and North rivers, adjacent to any ferry stairs, or to the Battery, in the city of New York, under the penalty of ten dollars for each offense. Bathing.

§ 49. No person shall swim or bathe in the waters of the East and North rivers, between the hours of six o'clock in the forenoon and eight in the afternoon, at any place in the city of New York, exposed to view, lying south of Thirtieth street, under the penalty of ten dollars for each offense. Ibid

§ 50. No person shall raise or fly any kite in any street, lane or avenue, or public place in the city of New York, to the southward of Fourteenth street, under the penalty of five dollars for each offense. Flying kites.

§ 51. No person shall place or post, or cause or permit to be placed or posted in any street in the city of New York, any handbill or advertisement, giving notice of any person having or professing to have skill in the treatment Posting notices of Quacks &c.

or curing of any disorder or disease, or giving notice of the sale, or exposure to sale, of any nostrum or medicine, under the penalty of twenty-five dollars for every such offense.

Washing in the streets.

§ 52. No dyer or scourer, or any other person, shall wash, rinse or cleanse, or cause or procure to be washed, rinsed or cleansed, any cloth, yarn or garment, in any street in the city of New York, under the penalty of ten dollars for each offense.

Drying clothes &c. in the streets.

§ 53. No dyer or scourer, or any other person shall place or suspend, or cause or procure to be placed or suspended, in or over any street in the city of New York, any cloth, yarn or garment, for the purpose of drying the same, under the penalty of ten dollars for each offense.

Flying horses &c.

§ 54. No grocer, inn-keeper, tavern-keeper, or any other person, shall have on his, her or their premises, or shall let, hire or use for public amusement, any flying horse or horses, or whirligig, or roundabout, or other similar machinery or device, by whatever name it may be called, under the penalty of fifty dollars for each offense.

Advertising shows.

§ 55. No person shall beat any drum or other instrument, or blow any horn or other instrument, for the purpose of attracting the attention of passengers, in any street in the city of New York, to any show of beasts or birds or other things in said city, under the penalty of ten dollars for each offense.

Garbage barrels, &c.

§ 56. The owner or owners of any buildings or tenements in the city, below Fortieth street, are hereby required to provide a barrel, or tub, or box, of sufficient size to contain all the rubbish, coal ashes and garbage, that may accumulate from day to day, on his or her premises, which said barrel, tub, or box, shall be placed on the sidewalk, in front of each house or tenement, or such convenient spot as shall be designated by the Street Inspectors of the several Wards; and it shall be the duty of the owners or occupants of all houses, tenements, &c., to put all their rubbish, coal ashes and garbage, into said barrels, tubs, or boxes, when so provided; and in case of negligence they shall be liable to a fine of one dollar for each offense.

Garbage barrels, &c.

CHAPTER XLVI.

OF CHARCOAL, FISH, VEGETABLE AND FRUIT WAGONS, AND VENDERS OF BROOMS, WOODEN WARE AND KINDLING WOOD.

General Regulations.

§ 1. No owner of, vender, or retailer of charcoal, fish, fruit, vegetables, brooms, wooden ware or kindling wood, shall affix to, or suffer, or permit to be affixed to the cart, wagon or any other vehicle, owned by, or employed or used by him for the purpose of transporting, conveying in, or selling thereout, in the streets of the city of New York, charcoal, or fish, or fruit, or vegetables, or brooms, or wooden ware, or kindling wood, any bell, iron, steel, or other metal bar, or any other instrument, nor shall blow upon or use, or suffer or permit to be blown upon, any horn or other instrument for the purpose of giving notice of the approach of any cart, wagon or other vehicle, in order to sell thereout charcoal, fish, fruit, vegetables, brooms, wooden ware, or kindling wood, under the penalty of five dollars for each offense, to be sued for and recovered of the owner of, employer of, driver of, or persons having charge of such cart, wagon or other vehicle, or of the owner of such coal, fish, fruit, vegetables, brooms, wooden ware, or kindling wood, severally and respectively.

Licenses

§ 2. The owner of, employer or driver of every cart, wagon or other vehicle, used for the purpose of selling thereout charcoal, fish, fruit, vegetables, brooms, wooden ware or kindling wood authorized or permitted to be sold by law, shall, before the same be used for such purpose, have the same licensed by the Mayor of the city of New York, which license shall contain the number of the cart, wagon or vehicle, and the name of the owner, employer and driver thereof; the owner, employer or driver of each cart, wagon or other vehicle used for the purpose of selling thereout charcoal, brooms, wooden ware or kindling wood, shall, at the time such license is granted, pay to the said Mayor the sum of two dollars and fifty cents for the use of the city; and the owner, employer, or driver of each cart, wagon or other vehicle, used or employed for the purpose of selling thereout fish, fruit or vegetables authorized or permitted to be sold by law, shall, at the time such license is granted, pay to the said Mayor the sum of five dollars for the use of the city; said license shall be in force for one year, and shall be renewed at the expiration of each year, and upon the renewal thereof, such owner, employer or driver shall pay, as aforesaid, the sum of fifty cents to the Mayor, for the use of the city, as upon the original granting of the license. Each cart, wagon, or other vehicle, shall have the number of its license painted upon it in a conspicuous place, and the figures composing said number shall not be less than two and a half inches in length, and shall at all times be kept legible.

§ 3. The owner of, employer or driver of any cart, **Penalty.** wagon or other vehicle, who shall employ or use the same, or suffer or permit the same to be employed or used, for any of the purposes above-mentioned, without having obtained a license therefor, as is above provided, shall forfeit and pay for each day such cart, wagon or other vehicle shall be so employed or used without license, the sum of fifty cents, and the like sum for neglecting or omitting to have the number painted upon his cart, wagon or vehicle, in the manner directed by this chapter, to be sued for and recovered of the owner of, employer of, driver of, or person having charge of such cart, wagon, or other vehicle, or of the owner of such coal, fish, fruit, vegetables, brooms, wooden ware or kindling wood, severally and respectively.

Exceptions as to Farmers, &c.

§ 4. Nothing herein contained shall be so construed as to prevent farmers and gardeners from bringing their produce to the city for the purpose of vending and disposing of the same from wagons or other vehicles.

Licenses.

§ 5. The Mayor is hereby authorized to grant licenses pursuant to the provisions above set forth.

CHAPTER XLVII.

OF THE SALE AND MANUFACTURE OF BREAD.

How made and sold.

§ 1. All bread baked and offered or exposed for sale in the city of New York, shall be made of good and wholesome flour and meal, and sold by avoirdupois weight.

Penalty.

§ 2. If any baker or other person shall make for sale, offer or procure to be sold, any bread of any other than wholesome flour or meal, or shall sell the same contrary to the preceding section of this chapter, such person shall forfeit and pay the sum of ten dollars for every such offense.

Forfeiture.

§ 3. All loaf-bread offered for sale in this city, not in conformity with the provisions of this chapter, shall be forfeited, and shall, and may be seized and disposed of for the use of the said city.

CHAPTER XLVIII.

OF SWINE AND NEAT CATTLE RUNNING AT LARGE, AND HEREIN OF PUBLIC POUNDS.

§ 1. No neat cattle shall go at large in any of the streets, lanes, alleys, piers, wharves, or public places in the city of New York, within the lamp and watch district, nor any swine in any part of the city of New York, under the penalty of five dollars for every such swine or animal which shall be found at large, to be paid by the owner or person having charge, care or keeping thereof, severally and respectively. Neat cattle & swine.

§ 2. There shall be appointed proper persons, as masters of the public pounds in the city of New York, who, before entering upon the duties of their office, shall take and subscribe an oath or affirmation, well and truly to execute the duties of their office. Pound masters.

§ 3. The said pound-masters shall enter into bonds with two good and sufficient sureties, to be approved by the Comptroller, in the penal sum of five hundred dollars, conditioned for the faithful performance of the duties of their office. Pound master's bonds.

§ 4. All swine or neat cattle found at large in the city of New York, in violation of this chapter, may be taken by any person or persons, and driven or carried to such place as may have been designated by the Common Council as a public pound; and it shall be the duty of the pound-master or person having charge of such public pound, to enter in a book, to be kept by him for that purpose, the names and places of abode of all persons who may bring Regulation of pounds.

any such swine or neat cattle to such pound, and the time of bringing the same, respectively, and the said pound-master shall pay to the person bringing any such swine or neat cattle, to such pound, one dollar for each beast or animal so brought.

Regulation of pounds.

§ 5. If the owner of any such swine or neat cattle, or any other person entitled to redeem the same, shall appear and claim the same, at any time before a sale thereof, it shall be the duty of the pound-master to deliver the same on receiving the amount of his fees for keeping and feeding the same, not exceeding fifty cents for each beast for every twenty-four hours, and at that rate for any less period of time, together with such sum as he may have paid to the person who brought the said beast to the pound.

Ibid.

§ 6. It shall be the duty of the pound-master, on making any delivery of swine or neat cattle, before sale, or on payment of surplus money after sale, to obtain from the person or persons claiming the same, his, her or their name or names and residence; and once in each month to report to the Attorney of the Corporation, the same, and the name or names of all persons claiming swine or neat cattle, and their places of residence, the date when the same were left, when the same were sold or redeemed, and the names of the persons leaving the same at the pound.

Ibid.

§ 7. If no person shall appear to claim such swine or neat cattle, within five days after the same may have been impounded, it shall be the duty of the pound-master to give three days' notice of the sale thereof.

Ibid.

§ 8. Such notice shall contain some general description of the beasts impounded, and shall be posted up in some conspicuous place at said public pound, and in the City Hall of the city of New York, and shall also be inserted in two or more of the public newspapers employed by the Common Council.

§ 9. In case of the sale of any impounded swine or neat cattle, the said pound-master shall retain out of the proceeds of such sale, sufficient to pay the amount of his fees, and all charges incurred by him on account of said swine or neat cattle. Regulation of Pounds.

§ 10. If, after any such sale, and whilst the proceeds thereof remain in the hands of the said pound-master, the former owner of any swine or neat cattle shall appear and claim the same, it shall be the duty of the said pound-master, to deduct from the proceeds of such sale, the fees and charges as provided in the last preceding section; to ascertain the name and residence of such owner, and to pay over the residue of the proceeds of such sale to the person so claiming to be the owner. Ibid.

§ 11. It shall be the duty of the said pound-master once in every month to account to the Comptroller of the city of New York, for all moneys received or expended by him, by virtue of this chapter, and to pay over to the said Comptroller, all such moneys remaining in his hands, after deducting his legal fees and charges. Pound Master's report.

§ 12. It shall be the duty of the persons exercising the duties of keepers of the Park, the Battery, and the Bowling Green, and the Washington Parade Ground, to drive to the said public pound, all swine or neat cattle found at large by them, respectively, and to report all violations of the first section of this chapter, to the Attorney of the Corporation. Running of cattle, &c., in Public grounds.

§ 13. No person or persons shall have or keep in the city of New York, in any pen or sty, more than three swine, at any one time, between the first day of May and Pig sties.

the last day of October in each year, under the penalty of five dollars for every swine above the aforesaid number.

Pig sties. § 14. All swine in the said city shall be kept in pens or sties, during the period mentioned in the 13th section of this chapter, which sties shall be properly and effectually cleaned at least once in every three days, under the penalty of five dollars for each and every violation of either of the provisions of this section.

Exception. § 15. So much of the foregoing provisions as relates to swine, shall apply to the whole city of New York.

Pound in New street. § 16. The premises known as Nos. 81 and 83 New street, in the First Ward of the city of New York, are hereby designated as and for a public pound, and a pound-keeper is assigned therefor, without any compensation or salary to be paid by the Corporation.

Pounds in Twelfth and Nineteenth Wards. § 17. There shall be established in the Twelfth Ward of the city of New York, two public pounds, and also one other public pound in the Nineteenth Ward of said city, wherein shall be impounded all stray swine and cattle that shall be found at large in any of the streets, lanes, alleys, piers, wharves, or public places, or trespassing upon private grounds; and all such swine or cattle as shall be impounded shall be subject to the provisions set forth and prescribed by this chapter.

Pound on King'sbridge road. § 18. One pound shall be located as near as possible to the intersection of Kingsbridge road and One hundred and sixtieth street; and also one near the intersection of Seventh avenue and One hundred and twenty-third street.

Pound in Nineteenth Ward. § 19. The public pound hereby authorized to be established in the Nineteenth Ward shall be located upon the grounds of the Corporation, at or near the corner of Fifth avenue and Eightieth street.

§ 20. The premises known as the north east corner of One hundred and fiftieth street and Tenth avenue is hereby designated as and for a public pound, and a pound-keeper shall be assigned therefor, without any compensation or salary to be paid by the Corporation.

Pound on One hundred and fiftieth street & 10th avenue.

§ 21. The premises known as the rear of lot on the north west corner of One hundred and twenty-seventh street and Third avenue, is hereby designated as and for a public pound, and a pound-keeper shall be assigned therefor, without any compensation or salary to be paid by the Corporation.

Pound in One hundred and twenty-seventh street & Third avenue

§ 22. The City Inspector of the city of New York is hereby empowered and directed to assume the control, direction and supervision of the public pounds, created by the two last preceding sections, and the said City Inspector is also hereby further authorized and directed to cause the enforcement of all laws of the State and ordinances of the Common Council in relation to the public pounds in the said city of New York.

Control of pounds

CHAPTER XLXIX.

OF THE INTERMENT OF THE DEAD.

Regulation for opening graves south of 86th street.

§ 1. No person shall dig or open any grave, or cause or procure any grave to be dug or opened in any burying-ground, cemetery, or church-yard, or in any other part or place in the city of New York, south of Eighty-sixth street, or shall inter or deposit, or cause or procure to be interred or deposited in any such grave, or in any vault or tomb, except in private vaults and private cemeteries now existing, any dead body, within the limits aforesaid, under the penalty of two hundred and fifty dollars.

New Cemeteries prohibited.

§ 2. No new cemetery or burying-ground shall hereafter be established in any part of the city and county of New York, and no person shall dig or open any grave, or cause or procure any grave to be dug or opened, in any such new cemetery or burying-ground, or shall inter or deposit, or cause to be interred or deposited, in any such grave, or in any vault or tomb, in any new cemetery or burying-ground, as aforesaid, any dead body, under the penalty of two hundred and fifty dollars for every such offense.

Regulation for opening graves north of 86th street

§ 3. No person shall inter any corpse in any vault or grave in the city of New York, north of the limits mentioned in the first section of this chapter, unless such vault or grave shall be at least six feet deep, and not less than six feet below the level of the adjacent streets, under the penalty of one hundred dollars for each offense.

Permission to remove bodies.

§ 4. No person shall remove, disturb or expose any dead body or coffin, that is now or may hereafter be interred in any grave-yard in the city of New York, unless permission be first obtained from the Common Council, or as provided in this chapter, under the penalty of two hundred and fifty dollars for each offense.

Sexton's report of burials.

§ 5. Every sexton or person having charge of any vault or burying-ground, in the city of New York, shall, between the hours of nine and two o'clock of Saturday in each week, make and deliver to the City Inspector, a return of the persons buried in such vault or burying-ground, during the week, according to the form following:

FORM.

An accurate list of Interments in the Burial-ground belonging to , from the day of , to

SEXTON.

	MALES.				FEMALES.				AGE.			PLACE OF RESIDENCE.				
Date of Decease.	Boys.	Married Men.	Widowers.	Batchelors.	Girls.	Married Women.	Widows.	Unmarried Women.	Years.	Months.	Days.	Number.	Street.	From what Country.	Disease.	Remarks.

Tolling of Church bells for funerals.

§ 6. No bell of any church shall be rung or tolled for any funeral, without the permission of the Common Council, under the penalty of twenty dollars, to be paid by the sexton or person having charge of the said church.

Penalty.

§ 7. Any person who shall violate the provisions of section five of this chapter, shall forfeit and pay for every such offense the sum of twenty-five dollars.

Sextons to be furnished with form of returns.

§ 8. It shall be the duty of the City Inspector to furnish the sextons and other persons having charge of any burying-ground or vault, with copies of the form set forth in section five of this chapter; and the said City Inspector shall report to the Attorney of the Corporation, all violations of any or either of the provisions of this chapter.

No burial without certificate.

§ 9. No sexton or other person having charge of any place of interment in the city of New York, shall, under a penalty of two hundred and fifty dollars, inter, or permit to be interred, any dead body therein, without having first received a certificate, stating the name, apparent age, birth-place, date, and place of death, and the disease of which he or she shall have died, signed by the attending physician, or in case no physician shall have attended such deceased person, then by some of the family of the deceased, or in case of an inquest having been held, by the Coroner, which certificate shall be deposited with the return, in the office of the City Inspector.

Permission to convey bodies from the city.

§ 10. No captain, agent or other person attached to any steamboat, ferry-boat, sailing or other vessel, or to any stage, railroad, or other conveyance, public or private, shall convey the body of any person who has died in the city of New York, beyond the limits of said city, without a permit from the City Inspector, under the penalty of two hundred dollars for each offense, to be collected from the person or persons so offending, severally and respectively.

Ibid.

§ 11. It shall be the duty of the City Inspector to grant a permit for the removal of the body of any deceased person from the city, which has not been buried, upon receiving a certificate of the death of said person, made in accordance with the provisions of section nine of this chapter.

Permission to convey bodies from th city.

§ 12. In ordinary cases, the Mayor and City Inspector are authorized to permit the removal of the remains of deceased persons from cemeteries or burial-places within the city; but if there are any extraordinary circumstances in the case, they shall refer all applications made to them on the subject, to the Common Council.

Ibid.

§ 13. It shall be the duty of the City Inspector to grant a general permit to the sexton of St. Patrick's Cathedral, for the removal of dead bodies, to be interred in the new Roman Catholic Cemetery, in Newtown, Queens' County, Long Island, provided that the said sexton comply with the ninth section of this chapter; and all captains, agents, or other persons attached to any steamboat, ferry-boat, sailing or other vessel, or to any stage, railroad or other conveyance, shall convey the said dead bodies so to be interred, upon the certificate of the said sexton.

CHAPTER L.

OF POLICE COURTS AND OTHER COURTS.

Division of Districts.

§ 1. The city is hereby divided into four Districts, for Police Courts, as follows:

The First District shall comprise the First, Second Third, Fourth, Fifth and Sixth Wards.

The Second District shall comprise the Eighth, Ninth, Fifteenth and Sixteenth Wards.

The Third District shall comprise the Seventh, Tenth, Eleventh, Thirteenth and Fourteenth Wards.

The Fourth District shall comprise the Twelfth, Seventeenth and Eighteenth Wards.

The Mayor's office, or a suitable portion thereof, shall be known and designated as part of the First District Police Court.

Location of Police Courts.

§ 2. In each of said districts there shall be a Police Court and office, and in the First District there shall be two Police Courts and offices.

The Police Courts of the First District shall be held at the Halls of Justice in Centre street, and in the basement of the City Hall.

The Police Court of the Second District shall be held at the Jefferson Market, Sixth avenue.

The Police Court of the Third District shall be held at the Essex Market in Grand street.

The Police Court of the Fourth District shall be held at the corner of Fourth avenue and Eighty-sixth street.

§ 3. The Mayor, Aldermen and Commonalty of the city of New York, shall, from time to time, designate the Justices and Clerks to be assigned to the various Police Courts. Designation of Justices.

§ 4. During the months from April to September, both inclusive, the said Police Offices shall be kept open every day ready for the transaction of business, from seven o'clock in the forenoon to seven o'clock in the afternoon. During the months from October to March, both inclusive, such offices shall be so kept open every day from eight o'clock in the forenoon to six o'clock in the afternoon. During such hours the magistrates and clerks shall attend in said offices for the discharge of their duties; and no extra compensation shall be allowed to them for attending on Sundays. Regulation of Police offices.

§ 5. No political or public meeting shall be held in any of the rooms assigned or occupied by the District or Police Courts or as police offices or stations. Political and public meetings.

§ 6. The magistrates of the several police offices in this city, are hereby directed to furnish to either party in any matter pending before them, or either of them, a bill of the costs and fees charged in such matter, such bill to state particularly all items charged and the fees therefor. Furnishing bill of fees.

§ 7. The several Justices of District Courts of this city, and the clerks of the respective District Courts are requested to place correct written or printed lists in some conspicuous part of their several court rooms, of all fees, costs, or other charges to which the said Justices and clerks, or police officers or constables, or other officers of said courts may be legally entitled, whether the same be chargeable to complainant or defendant, and such list to state particularly the service and the fee allowed therefor. Posting list of Fees.

Delivery of bill of costs.

§ 8. The Justices or clerks aforesaid, hereby are directed to deliver, when required, to either party to a suit in said courts, a bill of the costs charged to such party, specifying particularly the nature of the service performed, the officer by whom it may be performed, and the legal fees chargeable therefor.

Stationery.

§ 9. The Comptroller shall not be authorized to allow or audit any bills hereafter created, for any expenditure for any books, blanks or stationery for the use of the Superior Court, Supreme Court, Court of Common Pleas, Police Courts, Assistant Justices' Courts, or Marine Court, or the Justices or Clerks thereof, which shall be contracted for or purchased by said Justices and their clerks, but that all such books, blanks and stationery to be used by said courts and their clerks, shall be contracted for by the Comptroller, and the contractor therefor shall furnish the same to the said courts on a requisition from the justices thereof, except that until such contract is made, the Comptroller may furnish such books, blanks and stationery as may be necessary for the immediate use of said courts, from such sources as he may think proper.

City Prison & Bridewell.

§ 10. The various "District Head Quarters" in the several Wards, together with the office of the Superintendent of Police, are hereby respectively declared to be portions of the City Prison and Bridewell, for the purpose of detaining persons arrested until they can be duly examined according to law.

Collecting Costs.

§ 11. It shall be the duty of the clerks of the several District Courts, in the city of New York, to collect the costs of said court, to become due, to the Corporation from suitors in said courts, and they are authorized to proceed by prosecution in all cases when it may be found necessary.

§ 12. All moneys which shall be paid for fines imposed by the Police Courts or Justices, whether before or after commitment, shall hereafter be received by one of the clerks in the respective police offices, who shall, immediately upon the receipt of such moneys, enter an account of the same into a book to be denominated the "cash book," specifying the date when the fine was imposed, the name of the defendant, nature of the complaint, amount of fine and date of payment; and he shall, on the Tuesday succeeding the expiration of each week, pay into the Treasury all the moneys so received during the preceding week, and account for the same, under oath or affirmation, to the Comptroller. Fines.

§ 13. It shall be the duty of the Police Justice of each district, to designate one of the clerks in their respective offices, to receive the moneys and keep the accounts, as provided in the preceding section; and the clerks so designated shall perform such duties and be responsible for such moneys. Ibid.

§ 14. The Common Council of the city of New York, do hereby designate the seal last used by the Marine Court of the city of New York, (and which, by law, has been out of use for a few years last past) as the seal of the said court, to be used in future, in pursuance of the tenth section of an act in relation to the Marine Court of the city of New York, passed April 17, 1852—and that the said seal be hereby furnished to the Clerk of the Marine Court, as the seal of the said Court. Seal of Marine Court.

§ 15. The trustees of the Second District Police Court are authorized to appoint a suitable person as scrivener, at a salary of eight hundred dollars per annum. Scrivener of Second District Court.

§ 16. The office of scrivener is hereby created for the Third District Police Court, at a salary of one thousand dollars per annum. Scrivener of Third Dis-

CHAPTER LI.

OF CONSTABLES' BADGES.

Badges. § 1. All constables of the city of New York shall hereafter, when on duty, wear a badge, as hereinafter provided and designated.

Ibid. § 2. The badge mentioned in the preceding section shall be made of German silver (plain,) bearing the words "Constable," and the number of the Ward from which the constables respectively are elected, engraved thereon; as "Constable, First Ward," "Constable, Second Ward," &c.; the said badge to be round, and not to exceed two and a half inches in diameter.

Ibid. § 3. The said badges shall be deposited with the Mayor, to be distributed by him to the constables of the various wards of the city.

Ibid. § 4. The said badges shall be the exclusive property of the city of New York; and when any constable or constables shall resign, or be removed by death or otherwise, or his term of office expire, the said badge or badges shall be returned to the Mayor, for his or their successor or successors.

Penalties. § 5. Any person or persons, not constables, found wearing the said badge, shall be deemed guilty of a misdemeanor and shall be subject to imprisonment for a term not exceeding one year, or a fine of not less than two hundred and fifty dollars.

CHAPTER LII.

OF CHIMNEY SWEEPERS.

§ 1. It shall be lawful for the Mayor of the said city to grant licenses, under his hand and seal, to such persons as shall produce to him satisfactory evidence of their good character, to be sweepers of chimneys in the said city; and each person so licensed, shall pay therefor the sum of three dollars. Licenses.

§ 2. Any person so licensed, may keep and employ so many boys, apprentices or servants to assist him in his said business, as he may think proper; provided they are comfortably clad, and sufficiently provided with good and wholesome food, and not under eleven years of age. Apprentices and servants

§ 3. The said boys, apprentices or servants, shall not be required, by their master or employer, to work before six o'clock in the forenoon, nor after four o'clock in the afternoon, during the winter season; nor before five o'clock in the forenoon, nor after six o'clock in the afternoon, during the residue of the year. Ibid.

§ 4. No person so licensed as aforesaid, shall employ any boy under the age of eleven years, as a chimney sweeper, or shall omit or neglect to feed or clothe any of the boys, apprentices or servants in his employ, as above directed, or require or permit them, or any of them, to work at other hours than are above prescribed, under the penalty of five dollars, and the forfeiture of his license, for every such offense. Ibid.

§ 5. No person, without such license as aforesaid, or after the forfeiture thereof as aforesaid, shall carry on the Penalty.

business of a chimney sweeper, or shall suffer or permit any boy, apprentice or servant belonging to him or in his employ, to sweep any chimney in this city, under the penalty of five dollars.

Responsible for fires.

§ 6. Every person so licensed, shall be subject to all penalties that may be incurred by any chimney taking fire, within one month after having been swept by them respectively, or by any boy, apprentice or servant in their employ.

Regulation of License, &c.

§ 7. Each license granted as aforesaid, shall be numbered; and every person so licensed shall cause the boys, apprentices or servants in his employ, to wear a badge, upon which shall be inscribed the number of his license; and if any such boy, apprentice or servant shall at any time be found out of the house or premises of his master, or employer, and not wearing such badge, his said master or employer shall forfeit and pay the sum of two dollars.

Fees of Chimney Sweepers

§ 8. The licensed chimney sweepers of the said city shall be authorized to demand and receive the following sums for each and every chimney swept by them, or by their boys, apprentices or servants respectively, that is to say: for every chimney from the uppermost floor of any house, twelve and a half cents; for every chimney from the next floor below, fifteen cents; for every chimney from the next floor below, eighteen cents; for every chimney from the next floor below,. twenty-one cents; for every chimney from the next floor below, twenty-eight cents; for every chimney from the next floor below, thirty-seven and a half cents; and where a Franklin stove, coal grate or jack are used in any fire-place, twelve and a half cents may be demanded, and received in addition to the abovementioned sums.

§ 9. It shall be lawful for the Mayor of the said city from time to time, to appoint one of the licensed chimney sweepers, to be called "The Inspector of Chimney Sweepers," who shall hold his office for the term of one year, subject, however, to removal by the said Mayor, and whose duty it shall be to see that this law be duly observed by the said licensed chimney sweepers and all others, and to report the names of offenders to the Attorney of the Corporation. Inspectors of Chimney Sweepers.

§ 10. It shall be the duty of every sweeper of chimneys, licensed as aforesaid, to report to the Mayor the names of all persons employed by him for the purpose of sweeping chimneys, and also the names of all such as shall quit his employment. And if any person so licensed shall neglect so to do for the space of one week, he shall forfeit and pay five dollars. Sweeps to report names of employees.

§ 11. A register shall be kept in the Mayor's office, of the name and place of residence of every person licensed as aforesaid. Register of Licenses.

§ 12. The provisions of this chapter shall apply to those persons who use machinery in sweeping chimneys, for hire, as well as to those who sweep by other methods. Provision.

CHAPTER LIII.

OF CORPORATION ADVERTISEMENTS.

Newspapers to be annually designated

§ 1. Newspapers printed and published in the city of New York, shall be annually designated by the Common Council, in which to publish the official proceedings of each Board of the Common Council, all notices of propositions before the Common Council, involving an assessment upon citizens, and for such period as the ordinances of the Common Council in the discretion of the particular department, shall prescribe, and all resolutions passed by the Common Council involving assessments.

What shall be published.

§ 2. There shall be published in said newspapers all notices of the Board of Supervisors, Board of Health, Commissioners of the Sinking Fund, the messages of the Mayor, and all notices of city and county officers required to be published by law or ordinance, which the said Boards or officers may deem it proper to publish, by virtue of their offices, the expense whereof is to be paid from the funds of the city, except the advertisements for the sale of property for taxes, and the redemption notices in relation to the same; and the proprietors of said newspapers shall agree to furnish, when required, affidavits of the due publication of any notices, ordinances, or advertisements, aforesaid, which are made necessary, or which they may deem are made necessary by law to be published.

CHAPTER LIV.

OF ELECTION DISTRICTS.

§ 1. The twenty-two wards of the city of New York, (comprising seventeen Aldermanic Districts, as constituted under the fiftieth section of the Amended Charter, passed April 14, 1857) shall be, and are hereby severally divided into election districts, the extent and limits of which said election districts shall be as follows, that is to say; Division of Wards into Districts.

§ 2. The First Ward shall be divided into five election districts, the extent and limits of which said election districts shall be as follows: First Ward.

The first election district of the First Ward shall contain all that part of the city bounded by and lying within North, or Hudson river, Morris street, Whitehall street and the East river, including Governor's, Ellis' and Bedloes' Islands, in the bay, and belonging to the city, and within its jurisdiction. First district.

The second election district of the First Ward shall contain all that part of the city bounded by and lying within the Hudson river, Rector, Greenwich and Thames streets, Broadway and Morris streets. Second district.

The third election district of the First Ward shall contain all that part of the city bounded by and lying within Hudson river and Liberty street, Broadway, Thames, Greenwich and Rector streets. Third district

The fourth election district of the First Ward shall contain all that part of the city bounded by and lying within corner of Broadway and Beaver Fourth district.

street, through Broadway to Liberty street, Maiden lane, East river, Old slip and Beaver street to Broadway.

Fifth district. The fifth election district of the First Ward shall contain all that part of the city bounded by and lying within Whitehall, Beaver street, Old slip and East river.

Second Ward. § 3. The Second Ward shall be divided into two election districts, the extent and limits of which said election districts shall be as follows:

First district. The first election district of the Second Ward shall contain all that part of the city bounded by and lying within Broadway, Chatham, Spruce, Gold and Liberty streets.

Second district. The second election district of the Second Ward shall contain all that part of the city bounded by and lying within Gold and Ferry streets, East river and Maiden lane.

Third Ward. § 4. The Third Ward shall be divided into four election districts, the extent and limits of which said election districts shall be as follows:

First district. The first election district of the Third Ward shall contain all that part of the city bounded by and lying within Hudson river, Vesey street, Broadway and Liberty street.

Second district. The second election district of the Third Ward shall contain all that part of the city bounded by and lying within Hudson river, Robinson, Greenwich and Murray streets, Broadway and Vesey street.

Third district The third election district of the Third Ward shall contain all that part of the city bounded by and lying within Hudson river, Chambers street,

Broadway, Murray, Greenwich and Robinson streets.

The fourth election district of the Third Ward shall contain all that part of the city bounded by and lying within Hudson river, Reade street, Broadway and Chambers' street. Fourth district.

§ 5. The Fourth Ward shall be divided into five election districts, the extent and limits of which said election districts shall be as follows: Fourth Ward.

The first election district of the Fourth Ward shall contain all that part of the city bounded by and lying within Chatham, Duane, Rose, Frankfort, and Dover streets, East river, Peck slip, Ferry, Gold and Spruce streets. First district.

The second election district of the Fourth Ward shall contain all that part of the city bounded by and lying within Rose, Duane, Chatham, Roosevelt, Madison and Pearl streets, New Bowery and Frankfort streets. Second district.

The third election district of the Fourth Ward shall contain all that part of the city bounded by and lying within New Bowery, Pearl, Madison and Roosevelt streets, East river and Dover street. Third district

The fourth election district of the Fourth Ward shall contain all that part of the city bounded by and lying within Oak and Catharine streets, East river and Roosevelt street. Fourth district.

The fifth election district of the Fourth Ward shall contain all that part of the city bounded by and lying within Roosevelt, Chatham, Catharine and Oak streets. Fifth district.

Fifth Ward. § 6. The Fifth Ward shall be divided into six election districts, the extent and limit of which said election districts shall be as follows:

First district. The first election district of the Fifth Ward shall contain all that part of the city bounded by and lying within West Broadway, Franklin street, Broadway and Reade street.

Second district. The second election district of the Fifth Ward shall contain all that part of the city bounded by and lying within Franklin, Varick and Beach streets, West Broadway, Canal street and Broadway.

Third district. The third election district of the Fifth Ward shall contain all that part of the city bounded by and lying within Hudson river, Harrison, Hudson and Worth streets, West Broadway and Reade street.

Fourth district. The fourth election district of the Fifth Ward shall contain all that part of the city bounded by and lying within Hudson river, Beach, Hudson, North Moore, Varick and Franklin streets, West Broadway, Worth, Hudson and Harrison streets.

Fifth district. The fifth election district of the Fifth Ward shall contain all that part of the city bounded by and lying within Hudson river, Vestry, Hudson, Laight and Canal streets, West Broadway, Beach, Varick, North Moore, Hudson and Beach streets.

Sixth district. The sixth election district of the Fifth Ward shall contain all that part of the city bounded by and lying within Hudson river, Canal, Laight, Hudson and Vestry streets.

Sixth Ward. § 7. The Sixth Ward shall be divided into eight election districts, the extent and limit of which said election districts shall be as follows:

The first election district of the Sixth Ward shall contain all that part of the city bounded by and lying within Broadway, Chambers and Chatham streets. First district.

The second election district of the Sixth Ward shall contain all that part of the city bounded by and lying within Broadway, Pearl, Chatham and Chambers streets. Second district.

The third election district of the Sixth Ward shall contain all that part of the city bounded by and lying within Broadway, Franklin, Centre and Pearl streets. Third district

The fourth election district of the Sixth Ward shall contain all that part of the city bounded by and lying within Centre, Franklin, Bayard, Mulberry, Park and Worth streets. Fourth district.

The fifth election district of the Sixth Ward shall contain all that part of the city bounded by and lying within Centre, Worth, Park, Mulberry, Chatham and Pearl streets. Fifth district.

The sixth election district of the Sixth Ward shall contain all that part of the city bounded by and lying within Mulberry and Bayard streets, Bowery and Chatham streets. Sixth district.

The seventh election district of the Sixth Ward shall contain all that part of the city bounded by and lying within Broadway, Canal, Baxter and Franklin streets. Seventh district.

The eighth election district of the Sixth Ward shall contain all that part of the city bounded by and lying within Baxter and Canal streets, Bowery and Bayard street. Eighth district.

Seventh Ward.

§ 8. The Seventh Ward shall be divided into nine election districts, the extent and limits of which said election districts shall be as follows :

First district.

The first election district of the Seventh Ward shall contain all that part of the city bounded by and lying within Division, Market, Henry and Catharine streets.

Second district.

The second election district of the Seventh Ward shall contain all that part of the city bounded by and lying within Henry, Market, Monroe and Catharine streets.

Third district

The third election district of the Seventh Ward shall contain all that part of the city bounded by and lying within Monroe and Pike streets, East river and Catharine street.

Fourth district.

The fourth election district of the Seventh Ward shall contain all that part of the city bounded by and lying within Division, Pike, Monroe and Market streets.

Fifth district.

The fifth election district of the Seventh Ward shall contain all that part of the city bounded by and lying within Madison and Clinton streets, East river and Pike street.

Sixth district

The sixth election district of the Seventh Ward shall contain all that part of the city bounded by and lying within Division, Clinton, Madison and Pike streets.

Seventh district.

The seventh election district of the Seventh Ward shall contain all that part of the city bounded by and lying within Division, Gouverneur, Monroe and Scammel streets, East river and Clinton street.

The eighth election district of the Seventh Ward shall contain all that part of the city bounded by and lying within Cherry street, East river and Scammel street. Eighth district.

The ninth election district of the Seventh Ward shall contain all that part of the city bounded by and lying within Division and Grand streets, East river, Cherry, Scammel, Monroe and Gouverneur streets. Ninth district

§ 9. The Eighth Ward shall be divided into eleven election districts, the extent and limits of which said election districts shall be as follows: Eighth Ward.

The first election district of the Eighth Ward shall contain all that part of the city bounded by and lying within Spring street, Broadway, Canal and Wooster streets. First district.

The second election district of the Eighth Ward shall contain all that part of the city bounded by and lying within Spring, Wooster, Canal and Sullivan streets. Second district.

The third election district of the Eighth Ward shall contain all that part of the city bounded by and lying within Spring, Sullivan, Canal and Varick streets. Third district

The fourth election district of the Eighth Ward shall contain all that part of the city bounded by and lying within Spring, Varick, Canal and Hudson streets. Fourth district.

The fifth election district of the Eighth Ward shall contain all that part of the city bounded by and lying within Spring, Hudson and Canal streets and Hudson river. F.f.h district.

30

Sixth district

The sixth election district of the Eighth Ward shall contain all that part of the city bounded by and lying within Houston street, Broadway, Spring and Wooster streets.

Seventh district.

The seventh election district of the Eighth Ward shall contain all that part of the city bounded by and lying within Houston, Wooster, Spring and Sullivan streets.

Eighth district.

The eighth election district of the Eighth Ward shall contain all that part of the city bounded by and lying within Charlton, Prince, Sullivan, Spring and Hudson streets.

Ninth district

The ninth election district of the Eighth Ward shall contain all that part of the city bounded by and lying within Hamersley, Houston, Sullivan, Prince, Charlton and Hudson streets.

Tenth district

The tenth election district of the Eighth Ward shall contain all that part of the city bounded by and lying within Charlton, Hudson and Spring streets and Hudson river.

Eleventh district.

The eleventh election district of the Eighth Ward shall contain all that part of the city bounded by and lying within Hamersley, Hudson and Charlton streets and Hudson river.

Ninth Ward.

§ 10. The Ninth Ward shall be divided into twelve election districts, the extent and limits of which said election districts shall be as follows:

First District.

The first election district of the Ninth Ward shall contain all that part of the city bounded by and lying within Christopher, Hudson and Hamersley streets and the Hudson river.

The second election district of the Ninth Ward shall contain all that part of the city bounded by and lying within Hudson, Christopher, Bedford and Hamersley streets. Second district.

The third election district of the Ninth Ward shall contain all that part of the city bounded by and lying within Bedford, Christopher and Fourth streets, Sixth avenue, Carmine and Bleecker streets and Cottage place. Third district

The fourth election district of the Ninth Ward shall contain all that part of the city bounded by and lying within Fourth and Charles streets, Greenwich avenue, West Tenth street and Sixth avenue. Fourth district.

The fifth election district of the Ninth Ward shall contain all that part of the city bounded by and lying within Greenwich and Eighth avenues, Fourteenth street, Sixth avenue and West Tenth street. Fifth district.

The sixth election district of the Ninth Ward shall contain all that part of the city bounded by and lying within Bleecker, Christopher, Fourth and Charles streets, Greenwich avenue and Hammond street. Sixth district.

The seventh election district of the Ninth Ward shall contain all that part of the city bounded by and lying within Bleecker and Hammond streets, Greenwich and Eighth avenues. Seventh district.

The eighth election district of the Ninth Ward shall contain all that part of the city bounded by and lying within Fourteenth street, Eighth avenue, Horatio street and Hudson river. Eighth district.

Ninth district

The ninth election district of the Ninth Ward shall contain all that part of the city bounded by and lying within Horatio street, Eighth avenue, Troy street and the Hudson river.

Tenth district

The tenth election district of the Ninth Ward shall contain all that part of the city bounded by and lying within Troy street, Eighth avenue, Bleecker and Hammond streets and the Hudson river.

Eleventh district.

The eleventh election district of the Ninth Ward shall contain all that part of the city bounded by and lying within Hammond, Bleecker and Charles streets and the Hudson river.

Twelfth district.

The twelfth election district of the Ninth Ward shall contain all that part of the city bounded by and lying within Charles, Bleecker and Christopher streets and the Hudson river.

Tenth Ward.

§ 11. The Tenth Ward shall be divided into six election districts, the extent and limits of which said election districts shall be as follows:

First district.

The first election district of the Tenth Ward shall contain all that part of the city bounded by and lying within Rivington, Forsyth, Delancey, Eldridge and Grand streets and Bowery.

Second district.

The second election district of the Tenth Ward shall contain all that part of the city bounded by and lying within Rivington, Ludlow, Delancey, Orchard, Grand, Eldridge, Delancey and Forsyth streets.

Third district

The third election district of the Tenth Ward shall contain all that part of the city bounded by and lying within Rivington, Norfolk, Grand, Orchard, Delancey and Ludlow streets.

The fourth election district of the Tenth Ward shall contain all that part of the city bounded by and lying within Grand, Norfolk, Division and Orchard streets. Fourth district.

The fifth election district of the Tenth Ward shall contain all that part of the city bounded by and lying within Grand, Orchard, Canal, Forsyth and Hester streets and Bowery. Fifth district.

The sixth election district of the Tenth Ward shall contain all that part of the city bounded by and lying within Hester, Forsyth, Canal, Orchard and Division streets and Bowery. Sixth district

§12. The Eleventh Ward shall be divided into twelve election districts, the extent and limits of which said election districts shall be as follows: Eleventh Ward.

The first election district of the Eleventh Ward shall contain all that part of the city bounded by and lying within Houston, Pitt, Stanton, Ridge, Rivington and Clinton streets. First district.

The second election district of the Eleventh Ward shall contain all that part of the city bounded by and lying within Houston, Sheriff, Rivington, Ridge, Stanton and Pitt streets. Second district.

The third election district of the Eleventh Ward shall contain all that part of the city bounded by and lying within Houston, Cannon, Rivington and Sheriff streets. Third district.

The fourth election district of the Eleventh Ward shall contain all that part of the city bounded by and lying within Houston street and East river, Rivington and Cannon streets. Fourth district.

Fifth district. The fifth election district of the Eleventh Ward shall contain all that part of the city bounded by and lying within Fifth street, Avenue C, Houston street and Avenue B.

Sixth district. The sixth election district of the Eleventh Ward shall contain all that part of the city bounded by and lying within Ninth street, Avenue C, Fifth street and Avenue B.

Seventh district. The seventh election district of the Eleventh Ward shall contain all that part of the city bounded by and lying within Eleventh street, Avenue D, Ninth street and Avenue B.

Eighth district. The eighth election district of the Eleventh Ward shall contain all that part of the city bounded by and lying within Fourteenth street, East river, Eleventh street and Avenue B.

Ninth district The ninth election district of the Eleventh Ward shall contain all that part of the city bounded by and lying within Fifth street, Avenue D, Houston street and Avenue C.

Tenth district The tenth election district of the Eleventh Ward shall contain all that part of the city bounded by and lying within Ninth street, Avenue D, Fifth street and Avenue C.

Eleventh district. The eleventh election district of the Eleventh Ward shall contain all that part of the city bounded by and lying within Eleventh street, East river, Fifth street and Avenue D.

Twelfth district. The twelfth election district of the Eleventh Ward shall contain all that part of the city bounded by and lying within Fifth street, East river, Houston street and Avenue D.

§ 13. The Twelfth Ward shall be divided into five election districts, the extent and limits of which said election districts shall be as follows: Twelfth Ward

The first election district of the Twelfth Ward shall contain all that part of the city bounded by and lying within One hundred and twentieth street, Fifth avenue, Eighty-sixth street and Hudson river. First district.

The second election district of the Twelfth Ward shall contain all that part of the city bounded by and lying within One hundred and twentieth street, East river, Eighty-sixth street and Fifth avenue, including Ward's Island in the East river, belonging to the city, and within its jurisdiction. Second district.

The third election district of the Twelfth Ward shall contain all that part of the city bounded by and lying within One hundred and forty-fourth street, Harlem river, One hundred and twentieth street and Sixth avenue, including Randall's Island in the East river, belonging to the city, and under its jurisdiction. Third district

The fourth election district of the Twelfth Ward shall contain all that part of the city bounded by and lying within One hundred and forty-fourth street, Sixth avenue, One hundred and twentieth street and Hudson river. Fourth district.

The fifth election district of the Twelfth Ward shall contain all that part of the city bounded by and lying within Spuyten Duyvel Creek, Harlem river, One hundred and forty-fourth street and Hudson river. Fifth district.

§ 14. The Thirteenth Ward shall be divided into seven election districts, the extent and limits of which said election districts shall be as follows: Thirteenth Ward.

First district. The first election district of the Thirteenth Ward shall contain all that part of the city bounded by and lying within Rivington, Clinton, Grand and Norfolk streets.

Second district. The second election district of the Thirteenth Ward shall contain all that part of the city bounded by and lying within Rivington, Ridge, Division and Clinton streets.

Third district. The third election district of the Thirteenth Ward shall contain all that part of the city bounded by and lying within Rivington, Willett, Grand, Division and Ridge streets.

Fourth district. The fourth election district of the Thirteenth Ward shall contain all that part of the city bounded by and lying within Rivington, Columbia, Grand and Willett streets.

Fifth district. The fifth election district of the Thirteenth Ward shall contain all that part of the city bounded by and lying within Rivington, Goerck, Grand and Columbia streets.

Sixth district. The sixth election district of the Thirteenth Ward shall contain all that part of the city bounded by and lying within Rivington street, East river, Grand and Goerck streets.

Seventh district. The seventh election district of the Thirteenth Ward shall contain all that part of the city bounded by and lying within Grand, Clinton, Division and Norfolk streets.

Fourteenth Ward. § 15. The Fourteenth Ward shall be divided into seven election districts, the extent and limits of which said election districts shall be as follows :

The first election district of the Fourteenth Ward shall contain all that part of the city bounded by and lying within Spring, Mulberry, Grand streets and Broadway. First district.

The second election district of the Fourteenth Ward shall contain all that part of the city bounded by and lying within Houston, Mulberry, Spring street and Broadway. Second district.

The third election district of the Fourteenth Ward shall contain all that part of the city bounded by and lying within Spring street, Bowery, Grand and Mulberry streets. Third district

The fourth election district of the Fourteenth Ward shall contain all that part of the city bounded by and lying within Prince street, Bowery, Spring and Mulberry streets. Fourth district.

The fifth election district of the Fourteenth Ward shall contain all that part of the city bounded by and lying within Houston street, Bowery, Prince and Mulberry streets. Fifth district.

The sixth election district of the Fourteenth Ward shall contain all that part of the city bounded by and lying within Grand, Mulberry, Canal street and Broadway. Sixth district

The seventh election district of the Fourteenth Ward shall contain all that part of the city bounded by and lying within Grand street, Bowery, Canal and Mulberry streets. Seventh district.

§ 16. The Fifteenth Ward shall be divided into ten election districts, the extent and limits of which said election districts shall be as follows : Fifteenth Ward.

First district.

The first election district of the Fifteenth Ward shall contain all that part of the city bounded by and lying within Houston, Hancock, Bleecker and Carmine streets and Sixth avenue, Fourth, Thompson, Amity and Sullivan streets.

Second district.

The second election district of the Fifteenth Ward shall contain all that part of the city bounded by and lying within Houston, Sullivan, Amity, Thompson, Fourth and Wooster streets.

Third district

The third election district of the Fifteenth Ward shall contain all that part of the city bounded by and lying within Houston, Wooster and Fourth streets and Broadway.

Fourth district.

The fourth election district of the Fifteenth Ward shall contain all that part of the city bounded by and lying within Fourth street, Sixth avenue, Tenth street and University place.

Fifth district

The fifth election district of the Fifteenth Ward shall contain all that part of the city bounded by and lying within Tenth street, Sixth avenue, Twelfth street and University place.

Sixth district

The sixth election district of the Fifteenth Ward shall contain all that part of the city bounded by and lying within Eighth street, University place, Fourteenth street and Broadway.

Seventh district.

The seventh election district of the Fifteenth Ward shall contain all that part of the city bounded by and lying within Fourth, Wooster and Eighth streets and Broadway.

Eighth district.

The eighth election district of the Fifteenth Ward, shall contain all that part of the city bounded by and lying within Houston street, Broadway Fourth street and the Bowery.

The ninth election district of the Fifteenth Ward shall contain all that part of the city bounded by and lying within Fourth street, Broadway, Fourteenth street, Fourth avenue and the Bowery. Ninth district

The tenth election district of the Fifteenth Ward shall contain all that part of the city bounded by and lying within Twelfth street, Sixth avenue, Fourteenth street and University place. Tenth district

§ 17. The Sixteenth Ward shall be divided into ten election districts, the extent and limits of which said election districts shall be as follows : Sixteenth Ward.

The first election district of the Sixteenth Ward shall contain all that part of the city bounded by and lying within Sixteenth street, Seventh avenue, Seventeenth street, Sixth avenue, Fourteenth street and Eighth avenue. First district.

The second election district of the Sixteenth Ward shall contain all that part of the city bounded by and lying within Nineteenth street, Sixth avenue, Seventeenth street, Seventh avenue, Sixteenth street and Eighth avenue. Second district.

The third election district of the Sixteenth Ward shall contain all that part of the city bounded by and lying within Twenty-second street, Sixth avenue, Nineteenth street and Eighth avenue. Third district

The fourth election district of the Sixteenth Ward shall contain all that part of the city bounded by and lying within Twenty-sixth street, Sixth avenue, Twenty-second street, Eighth avenue, Twenty-fourth street and Seventh avenue. Fourth district.

Fifth district. The fifth election district of the Sixteenth Ward shall contain all that part of the city bounded by and lying within Twenty-sixth street, Seventh avenue, Twenty-fourth street, Eighth avenue, Twenty-third street and Ninth avenue.

Sixth district. The sixth election district of the Sixteenth Ward shall contain all that part of the city bounded by and lying within Twentieth street, Eighth avenue, Fourteenth street and Ninth avenue.

Seventh district. The seventh election district of the Sixteenth Ward shall contain all that part of the city bounded by and lying within Twentieth street, Ninth avenue, Fourteenth street and Tenth avenue.

Eighth district. The eighth election district of the Sixteenth Ward shall contain all that part of the city bounded by and lying within Twentieth street, Tenth avenue, Fourteenth street and Eleventh avenue.

Ninth district The ninth election district of the Sixteenth Ward shall contain all that part of the city bounded by and lying within Twenty-third street, Eighth avenue, Twentieth street and Eleventh avenue.

Tenth district The tenth election district of the Sixteenth Ward shall contain all that part of the city bounded by and lying within Twenty-sixth street, Ninth avenue, Twenty-third street and Eleventh avenue.

Seventeenth Ward. § 18. The Seventeenth Ward shall be divided into fourteen election districts, the extent and limits of which said election districts shall be as follows:

First district. The first election district of the Seventeenth Ward shall contain all that part of the city bounded by and lying within Houston, Eldridge and Rivington streets and the Bowery.

The second election district of the Seventeenth Ward shall contain all that part of the city bounded by and lying within Houston, Essex, Rivington and Eldridge streets. Second district.

The third election district of the Seventeenth Ward shall contain all that part of the city bounded by and lying within Houston, Clinton, Rivington and Essex streets. Third district

The fourth election district of the Seventeenth Ward shall contain all that part of the city bounded by and lying within Third street, First avenue, Houston street and the Bowery. Fourth district.

The fifth election district of the Seventeenth Ward shall contain all that part of the city bounded by and lying within Sixth street, First avenue, Third street, Bowery and Third avenue. Fifth district.

The sixth election district of the Seventeenth Ward shall contain all that part of the city bounded by and lying within Ninth street, First avenue, Sixth street and Fourth avenue. Sixth district

The seventh election district of the Seventeenth Ward shall contain all that part of the city bounded by and lying within Fourteenth street, Second avenue, Ninth street and Fourth avenue. Seventh district.

The eighth election district of the Seventeenth Ward shall contain all that part of the city bounded by and lying within Fourteenth street, First avenue, Ninth street and Second avenue. Eighth district.

The ninth election district of the Seventeenth Ward shall contain all that part of the city bounded by and lying within Fourteenth street, Avenue A, Ninth street and First avenue. Ninth district

Tenth district

The tenth election district of the Seventeenth Ward shall contain all that part of the city bounded by and lying within Ninth street, Avenue A, Fourth street and First avenue.

Eleventh district.

The eleventh election district of the Seventeenth Ward shall contain all that part of the city bounded by and lying within Fourth street, Avenue A, Houston street and First avenue.

Twelfth district.

The twelfth election district of the Seventeenth Ward shall contain all that part of the city bounded by and lying within Fourth street, Avenue B, Houston street and Avenue A.

Thirteenth district.

The thirteenth election district of the Seventeenth Ward shall contain all that part of the city bounded by and lying within Eleventh street, Avenue B, Fourth street and Avenue A.

Fourteenth district.

The fourteenth election district of the Seventeenth Ward shall contain all that part of the city bounded by and lying within Fourteenth street, Avenue B, Eleventh street and Avenue A.

Eighteenth Ward.

§ 19. The Eighteenth Ward shall be divided into ten election districts, the extent and limits of which said election districts shall be as follows :

First district.

The first election district of the Eighteenth Ward shall contain all that part of the city bounded by and lying within Nineteenth street, Broadway, Fourteenth street and Sixth avenue.

Second district.

The second election district of the Eighteenth Ward shall contain all that part of the city bounded by and lying within Nineteenth street, Third avenue, Fourteenth street and Broadway.

The third election district of the Eighteenth Ward shall contain all that part of the city bounded by and lying within Nineteenth street, First avenue, Fourteenth street and Third avenue. Third district

The fourth election district of the Eighteenth Ward shall contain all that part of the city bounded by and lying within Seventeenth street, East river, Fourteenth street and First avenue. Fourth district.

The fifth election district of the Eighteenth Ward shall contain all that part of the city bounded by and lying within Twenty-sixth street, Fifth avenue, Broadway, Nineteenth street and Sixth avenue. Fifth district.

The sixth election district of the Eighteenth Ward shall contain all that part of the city bounded by and lying within Twenty-sixth street, Fourth avenue, Nineteenth street, Broadway and Fifth avenue. Sixth district

The seventh election district of the Eighteenth Ward shall contain all that part of the city bounded by and lying within Twenty-sixth street, Third avenue, Nineteenth street and Fourth avenue. Seventh district.

The eighth election district of the Eighteenth Ward shall contain all that part of the city bounded by and lying within Twenty-sixth street, Second avenue, Twenty-second street, First avenue, Nineteenth street and Third avenue. Eighth district.

The ninth election district of the Eighteenth Ward shall contain all that part of the city bounded by and lying within Twenty-sixth street and the East river, Twenty-second street and Second avenue. Ninth distric

Tenth district

The tenth election district of the Eighteenth Ward shall contain all that part of the city bounded by and lying within Twenty-second street and East river, Seventeenth street and First avenue.

Nineteenth Ward.

§ 20. The Nineteenth Ward shall be divided into five election districts, the extent and limits of which election districts shall be as follows:

First district.

The first election district of the Nineteenth Ward shall contain all that part of the city bounded by and lying within Fifty-second street, Third avenue, Fortieth street and Sixth avenue.

Second district.

The second election district of the Nineteenth Ward shall contain all that part of the city bounded by and lying within Fifty-second street, East river, Fortieth street and Third avenue.

Third district

The third election district of the Nineteenth Ward shall contain all that part of the city bounded by and lying within Sixty-eighth street, East river, Fifty-second street and Sixth avenue, including Blackwell's Island (in the East river) belonging to the city, and within its jurisdiction.

Fourth district.

The fourth election district of the Nineteenth Ward shall contain all that part of the city bounded by and lying within Eighty-sixth street, Third avenue, Sixty-eighth street and Sixth avenue.

Fifth district

The fifth election district of the Nineteenth Ward shall contain all that part of the city bounded by and lying within Eighty sixth street, East river, Sixty-eighth street and Third avenue.

Twentieth Ward.

§ 21. The Twentieth Ward shall be divided into twelve election districts, the extent and limits of which said election districts shall be as follows:

The first election district of the Twentieth Ward shall contain all that part of the city bounded by and lying within Hudson river and Twenty sixth street, Tenth avenue and Thirtieth street. First district.

The second election district of the Twentieth Ward shall contain all that part of the city bounded by and lying within Hudson river and Thirtieth street, Tenth avenue and Fortieth street. Second district.

The third election district of the Twentieth Ward shall contain all that part of the city bounded by and lying within Twenty-sixth street and Tenth avenue, Twenty-eighth street and Eighth avenue. Third district

The fourth election district of the Twentieth Ward shall contain all that part of the city bounded by and lying within Twenty-eighth street and Tenth avenue, Thirty-first street and Eighth avenue. Fourth district.

The fifth election district of the Twentieth Ward shall contain all that part of the city bounded by and lying within Thirty-first street and Tenth avenue, Thirty-fourth street and Eighth avenue. Fifth district.

The sixth election district of the Twentieth Ward shall contain all that part of the city bounded by and lying within Thirty-fourth street and Tenth avenue, Thirty-seventh street and Eighth avenue. Sixth district.

The seventh election district of the Twentieth Ward shall contain all that part of the city bounded by and lying within Thirty-seventh street and Tenth avenue, Fortieth street and Eighth avenue. Seventh district.

The eighth election district of the Twentieth Ward shall contain all that part of the city bounded by and lying within Twenty-sixth street and Eighth avenue, Twenty-ninth street and Sixth avenue. Eighth district.

Ninth district

The ninth election district of the Twentieth Ward shall contain all that part of the city bounded by and lying within Twenty-ninth street and Eighth avenue, Thirty-first street and Sixth avenue.

Tenth district

The tenth election district of the Twentieth Ward shall contain all that part of the city bounded by and lying within Thirty-first street and Eighth avenue, Thirty-third street and Sixth avenue.

Eleventh district.

The eleventh election district of the Twentieth Ward shall contain all that part of the city bounded by and lying within Thirty-third street and Eighth avenue, Thirty-sixth street and Sixth avenue.

Twelfth district.

The twelfth election district of the Twentieth Ward shall contain all that part of the city bounded by and lying within Thirty-sixth street and Eighth avenue, Fortieth street and Sixth avenue.

Twenty-first Ward.

§ 22. The Twenty-first Ward shall be divided into seven election districts, the extent and limits of which said election districts shall be as follows :

First district.

The first election district of the Twenty-first Ward shall contain all that part of the city bounded by and lying within Thirtieth street, Fourth avenue, Twenty-sixth street and Sixth avenue.

Second district.

The second election district of the Twenty-first Ward shall contain all that part of the city bounded by and lying within Twenty-ninth street, East river, Twenty-sixth street and Fourth avenue.

Third district

The third election district of the Twenty-first Ward shall contain all that part of the city bounded by and lying within Thirty-fourth street, Fourth avenue, Thirtieth street and Sixth avenue.

The fourth election district of the Twenty-first Ward shall contain all that part of the city bounded by and lying within Thirty-second street, East river, Twenty-ninth street and Fourth avenue. Fourth district.

The fifth election district of the Twenty-first Ward shall contain all that part of the city bounded by and lying within Fortieth street, Lexington avenue, Thirty-fifth street, Fourth avenue, Thirty-fourth street and Sixth avenue. Fifth district.

The sixth election district of the Twenty-first Ward shall contain all that part of the city bounded by and lying within Thirty-fifth street, East river, Thirty-second street and Fourth avenue. Sixth district.

The seventh election district of the Twenty-first Ward shall contain all that part of the city bounded by and lying within Fortieth street, East river, Thirty-fifth street and Lexington avenue. Seventh district.

§ 23. The Twenty-second Ward shall be divided into eight election districts, the extent and limits of which said election districts shall be as follows: Twenty-second Ward.

The first election district of the Twenty-second Ward shall contain all that part of the city bounded by and lying within Forty-fourth street Sixth avenue, Fortieth street and Ninth avenue. First district.

The second election district of the Twenty-second Ward shall contain all that part of the city bounded by and lying within Forty-ninth street, Sixth avenue, Forty-fourth street and Ninth avenue. Second district.

The third election district of the Twenty-second Ward shall contain all that part of the city bounded by and lying within Fifty-sixth street, Sixth avenue, Forty-ninth street and Ninth avenue. Third district

Fourth district. The fourth election district of the Twenty-second Ward shall contain all that part of the city bounded by and lying within Forty-fourth street, Ninth avenue, Fortieth street and Hudson river.

Fifth district The fifth election district of the Twenty-second Ward shall contain all that part of the city bounded by and lying within Forty-ninth street, Ninth avenue, Forty-fourth street and Hudson river.

Sixth district The sixth election district of the Twenty-second Ward shall contain all that part of the city bounded by and lying within Fifty-sixth street, Ninth avenue Forty-ninth street and Hudson river.

Seventh district. The seventh election district of the Twenty-second Ward shall contain all that part of the city bounded by and lying within Sixty-fifth street, Sixth avenue, Fifty-sixth street and Hudson river.

Eighth district. The eighth election district of the Twenty-second Ward shall contain all that part of the city bounded by and lying within Eighty-sixth street, Sixth avenue, Sixty-fifth street and Hudson river.

The following are the election districts embraced within the seventeen Aldermanic districts, respectively.

First Aldermanic District. § 24. The first Aldermanic district contains the first, second, third, fourth and fifth election districts of the First Ward; the first and second districts of the Second Ward; the first, second and third districts of the Third Ward; the first district of the Fourth Ward, and the first district of the Sixth Ward.

Second Aldermanic District. The second Aldermanic district contains the second, third, fourth and fifth election districts of the Fourth Ward, and the second, third, fourth, fifth and sixth districts of the Sixth Ward.

The third Aldermanic district contains the fourth election district of the Third Ward, the first, second, third, fourth, fifth and sixth districts of the Fifth Ward, and the first, second, third, fourth and fifth districts of the Eighth Ward.

Third Aldermanic District.

The fourth Aldermanic district contains the seventh and eighth election districts of the Sixth Ward; the first, second, third, fourth, fifth and sixth districts of the Seventh Ward; the fourth, fifth and sixth districts of the Tenth Ward; the seventh district of the Thirteenth Ward, and the sixth and seventh districts of the Fourteenth Ward.

Fourth Aldermanic District.

The fifth Aldermanic district contains the sixth, seventh, eighth, ninth, tenth and eleventh election districts of the Eighth Ward; the first, second and third districts of the Ninth Ward, and the first, second and third districts of the Fifteenth Ward.

Fifth Aldermanic District.

The sixth Aldermanic district contains the first, second and third election districts of the Tenth Ward; the first district of the Thirteenth Ward; the first, second, third, fourth and fifth districts of the Fourteenth Ward, and the first, second and third districts of the Seventeenth Ward.

Sixth Aldermanic District

The seventh Aldermanic district contains the fourth, fifth, sixth, seventh, eighth, ninth, tenth, eleventh and twelfth election districts of the Ninth Ward, and the fourth, fifth, sixth and seventh districts of the Fifteenth Ward.

Seventh Aldermanic District.

The eighth Aldermanic district contains the seventh eighth and ninth election districts of the Seventh Ward; the first, second, third and fourth districts of the Eleventh Ward; the second, third, fourth, fifth and sixth districts of the Thirteenth Ward.

Eighth Aldermanic District.

The ninth Aldermanic district contains the first, second, third, fourth, fifth, sixth, seventh, eighth, ninth and tenth election districts of the Sixteenth Ward.

Ninth Aldermanic District.

Tenth Aldermanic District.

The tenth Aldermanic district contains the eighth and ninth election districts of the Fifteenth Ward; the fourth fifth, sixth, seventh, eight, ninth, tenth and eleventh districts of the Seventeenth Ward.

Eleventh Aldermanic District.

The eleventh Aldermanic district contains the first, second, third, fourth, fifth, sixth, seventh, eighth, ninth, tenth, eleventh and twelfth election districts of the Twentieth Ward.

Twelfth Aldermanic District.

The twelfth Aldermanic district contains the fifth, sixth, seventh, eighth, ninth, tenth, eleventh and twelfth election districts of the Eleventh Ward, and the twelfth, thirteenth and fourteenth districts of the Seventeenth Ward.

Thirteenth Aldermanic District.

The thirteenth Aldermanic district contains the first, second, third, fourth, fifth, sixth, seventh and eighth election districts of the Twenty-second Ward.

Fourteenth Aldermanic District.

The fourteenth Aldermanic district contains the first, second, third, fourth, fifth, sixth, seventh, eighth, ninth and tenth election districts of the Eighteenth Ward.

Fifteenth Aldermanic District.

The fifteenth Aldermanic district contains the first, second, third, fourth, fifth, sixth and seventh election districts of the Twenty-first Ward.

Sixteenth Aldermanic District.

The sixteenth Aldermanic district contains the first, second, third, fourth and fifth election districts of the Nineteenth Ward.

Seventeenth Aldermanic District.

The seventeenth Aldermanic district contains the first, second, third, fourth and fifth election districts of the Twelfth Ward.

APPENDIX.

APPENDIX.

OF THE CITY DEBT.*

I.—Of "The New York City Stock."

II.—Of "The Water Stock of the City of New York."

III.—Of "The Fire Loan Stock of the City of New York."

IV.—Of "The Public Building Stock of the City of New York."

V.—Of "The Fire Indemnity Stock of the City of New York."

VI.—Of "The Floating Debt Stock of the City of New York."

VII.—Of "The Croton Water Stock."

VIII.—Of "Building Loan Stock, No. 2."

IX.—Of "Washington Square Iron Railing Stock."

X.—Of "The Water Stock of the City of New York for the year one thousand eight hundred and forty-nine."

XI.—Of "Building Loan Stock No. 3."

XII.—Of "Public Building Stock No. 3."

XIII.—Of "The New York City Five per cent. Stock for Docks and Slips."

XIV.—Of "Building Loan Stock No. 4."

XV.—Of "The Public Education Stock of the City of New York, for the year 1853."

XVI.—Of "The Central Park Fund."

XVII.—Of "The Water Stock of the City of New York, for the year 1854."

XVIII.—Of "The Central Park Improvement Fund."

XIX.—Of "The Public Stock for rebuilding Tompkins Market."

XX.—Of "Assessment Bonds."

XXI.—Of "Miscellaneous Debts of the City."

---

* Note.—It has been thought proper to incorporate the various ordinances relating to the various city stocks, in the volume of city ordinances, in the form of an appendix to the general ordinances. They are different in their character from the latter, as they are, in fact, contracts with the public creditor, and cannot be varied to his detriment. They are given in chronological order, without being classified by chapters, as are the general ordinances.

Of " The New York City Stock."

[By the act of June 8, 1812, 6 Web., 436, the Corporation was authorized to create a public fund or stock not exceeding 900,000 dollars, to be denominated " The New York City Stock." Under this act, the Common Council passed the following resolutions, &c. Min. Com. C. vol. 25, p. 211. For preliminary proceedings, see Ib. p. 197.]

The Mayor, Alderman and Commonalty of the City of New York hereby re-affirm the ordinances heretofore passed in relation to the city debt, and which are hereinafter set forth, as follows, viz :—

(In Common Council, June 29, 1812.)

Resolved, That the Finance Committee and Comptroller be authorized to publish such part of the act of the legislature, regulating the finances of the city of New York, as by them shall be deemed proper; and to advertise the opening of books for subscription for a loan of six hundred thousand dollars of "The New York City Stock," bearing an interest of six per cent. per annum, payable quarter yearly; and that subscriptions be received at the Mechanics' Bank, from the — day of July until the first of August next, unless, previously to the last-mentioned day, the whole sum shall have been subscribed, for any sums from one hundred dollars to the whole amount offered for subscriptions; but that certificates be not issued for a less sum than one hundred dollars, and not for any fractions; therefore the subscriptions must be made for hundreds or thousands.

(In Common Council, August 3, 1812.)

Resolved, That until the further orders of this Board, the Clerk of the Common Council countersign the certificates of the City Stock, issued by this Corporation.

A Law prescribing the form of certificates for " The New York City Stock," and for other purposes. (*Passed September* 28, 1812.)

Be it ordained by the Mayor, Aldermen and Commonalty of the city of New York, in Common Council convened:

That the certificates for " The New York City Stock," which shall be issued under and by virtue of the act of the legislature of the state of New York, entitled " An act to regulate the finances of the city of New York," passed June the eighth, one thousand eight hundred and twelve, shall be signed by the Comptroller and countersigned by the Clerk of the Common Council, and shall be in the form following, that is to say :

"*Be it known that there is due from the Mayor, Aldermen and Commonalty of the city of New York, unto* ———— *or* ———— *assigns, the sum of* ————*dollars, New York City Stock, bearing interest at* — *per cent. per annum, from the* ———— *day of* —— ———— *inclusive, payable quarter yearly, and the principal sum payable on or after the* ————. *This stock is created by virtue of an act of the legislature of the state of New York, entitled 'An act to regulate the finances of the city of New York,' passed the* 8*th day of June,* 1812*; and by a resolution of the Corporation, passed the* —— *day of* ——, 1812: *which debt is recorded in the Comptroller's office, and transferable only by appearance in person, or by attorney, at said office, according to the rules and forms instituted for that purpose.*"

(In Common Council, November 30, 1812.)

Resolved, That the Comptroller be authorized, under the direction of the Finance Committee, to open the books for subscription to the New York City Stock, for the sum of one hundred thousand dollars, at an interest not exceeding six per cent. per annum, payable quarter yearly.*

(In Common Council, June 30, 1817.)

Resolved, That the Comptroller be, and he is hereby authorized, under the direction of the Finance Committee, to dispose of one hundred thousand dollars of City Stock, to be issued for that purpose, at a rate not less than par, from the proceeds of which shall be paid a Corporation bond of ninety thousand dollars, due to the Mechanics' Bank, with the interest thereon, and the residue placed in the treasury.

(In Common Council, June 26, 1820.)

[By act of 24th March, 1820, (Laws p. 85,) the Corporation were authorized to create a public fund or stock, not exceeding $400,000, in addition to that authorized by the act of June 8, 1812, to be denominated "The New York City Stock," bearing interest not exceeding six per cent., payable quarterly. Under this statute, the Common Council passed the following resolution. See Min. C. C. vol. 41, p. 146.]

Resolved, That the Comptroller be authorized to give public notice in the papers employed by the Corporation, that books will be opened and kept during business hours, at the Mechanics' Bank, in this city, from the tenth to the twentieth day of July next, for the purpose of receiving subscriptions for a loan to the Corporation of this city, of any sum not

---

* For proceedings of the Common Council as to loan of $100,000, of Sept. 15, 1819, see Index to Min. C. C. v. 38; also, p. 478; Clerk's rough minutes of Sept. 6, 1819; also, files of Comptroller's office.

less than one hundred dollars, and exceeding two hundred thousand dollars.

That on the closing of such books, should the sum subscribed exceed in amount two hundred thousand dollars, the surplus will be deducted *pro rata*, from the amounts subscribed respectively; that on the twentieth day of July, the subscribers to the loan shall pay to the city treasurer, at the Mechanics' Bank aforesaid, five per cent. on the amount of stock to which they shall be entitled by their subscription, and that on the thirty-first day of July thereafter, the remainder of the sum subscribed shall be paid as aforesaid, when certificates of stock will be issued, bearing an interest of five per cent., payable quarter yearly, from and after the first day of August, one thousand eight hundred and twenty, and not redeemable until the first day of August, one thousand eight hundred and fifty. That in the event of a failure of the subscribers to pay the last installment on the day designated, the previous sums paid will be forfeited to the use of the Corporation of this city.

Resolved, That the Comptroller be authorized, under the instruction of the Finance Committee, to apply the proceeds of the proposed loan to the payment of such of the outstanding bonds of this Corporation, as in their opinion, will be most to the public interest.

(IN COMMON COUNCIL, March 12, 1821.)

1. *Resolved*, That a public market shall be erected upon the ground belonging to the Corporation, between Fulton street and Crane Wharf.

2. *Resolved*, That fifteen thousand dollars be raised annually, for ten years, by tax, which, together with the income from the said market, shall be appropriated to the Sinking Fund for the extinguishment of the debt created by the purchase of said ground, and the erection of suitable buildings, for a market on the same.

* * * * * *

5. *Resolved*, That the two hundred thousand dollars authorized to be funded by the act of one thousand eight hundred and twenty, be funded in such sums and at such times, as the means may be required to defray the aforesaid expense; and that the amount thus funded shall bear an interest of not more than five per cent. per annum, and be redeemable at the pleasure of the Corporation, after ——— years.

6. *Resolved*, That the counsel be instructed to prepare a memorial, to be presented to the legislature, at their next session, praying for an act authorizing the aforesaid; and that the clerk be instructed to give the

necessary notice of the intention of the Corporation to apply for such authority.

7. *Resolved*, That so much of the foregoing resolutions as relates to the City Stock, be referred to the Comptroller and Finance Committee, with authority to adopt the necessary measures for carrying the same into effect.

* * * * * *

(IN COMMON COUNCIL, June 19, 1826.)

[By act of 28th of March, 1826, (Laws 76,) the Corporation was further authorized, as they might find it expedient, to create a public fund or stock, not exceeding, in the whole, $700,000, in addition to the sum authorized by the acts of 1812 and 1820.]

Resolved, That the Finance Committee be authorized to effect a loan, on such terms, and to such an amount, not exceeding five hundred thousand dollars, as they may deem proper, for the purpose of redeeming such part of the City Stock, bearing an interest of six per cent., as is now unredeemed, agreeably to the provisions of "An act of the legislature, authorizing the Corporation of the city of New York to create a public stock," passed 28th March, 1826.

(IN COMMON COUNCIL, December 1, 1828.)

[By act of 19th April, 1828, § 3 and 4, (Laws, 372,) the Corporation were authorized to create a stock not exceeding $200,000, in the like manner, and on the like terms, as are contained in the act of March 28, 1826, except, &c. The only action of the Common Council seems to be the following:]

The Finance Committee presented the following report on the subject of the Six per cent. Stock, &c.:

The Finance Committee respectfully report, that four hundred and sixteen thousand nine hundred dollars of the Six per cent. Stock is redeemable; and that your Committee have directed the Comptroller to advertise for a loan of Five per cent. Stock, redeemable after the first of January, one thousand eight hundred and fifty, in order to substitute the same for the said stock so payable.

The best offer is made by John Jacob Astor, and Prime, Ward, King & Co., viz: four and a half per cent. advance, which your Committee recommend to be accepted, and they therefore respectfully offer the following resolution:

Resolved, That the Comptroller issue the stock certificates in the usual manner, to the said Astor, and King, & Co., and that the Finance Committee instruct the Comptroller and City Treasurer, as to the Six per cent. Stock to be paid off, in such manner as to pay off the Six per cent. Stock at the same time when the moneys of the Five per cent. Stock shall be received.

All of which is respectfully submitted.

W. SEAMAN,
WM. W. MOTT,
W. H. IRELAND.

Which was approved, and the resolutions adopted.

(IN COMMON COUNCIL, August 7, 1835.)

Resolved, That all certificates which may hereafter be issued, for any or either of the stocks of this city, shall be signed by the Comptroller and countersigned by the Mayor, and the Comptroller is hereby directed to cause the form of the certificates to be so prepared, as to designate the officers who are to sign and countersign the same severally.

Of "The Water Stock of the City of New York."

AN ORDINANCE to instruct the Water Commissioners to proceed in the work of supplying the city of New York with water, and to create a public fund or stock, to be called "The Water Stock of the city of New York," for the expense of said work. (*Passed May* 7, 1835.)

The Mayor, Aldermen and Commonalty of the city of New York, in Common Council convened, do ordain as follows:

§ 1. The Water Commissioners of the city of New York are hereby instructed to proceed with the work of supplying the city of New York with a sufficient quantity of pure and wholesome water, for the use of its inhabitants, according to the plan adopted by them, in pursuance of the act of the legislature, entitled "An act to provide for supplying the city of New York with pure and wholesome water," passed May the second, one thousand eight hundred and thirty-four.

§ 2. A public stock or fund, to be called "The Water Stock of the city of New York," shall be created for a loan of two millions five hundred thousand dollars, which shall bear an interest of not exceeding five per cent. per annum, payable quarterly, and shall be redeemable on or after the first day of January, which shall be in the year one thousand eight hundred and sixty.

§ 3. The nominal amount or value of each share of the said stock, shall be one hundred dollars, and the same shall consist of twenty-five thousand shares.

§ 4. The said loan shall be receivable in the following proportions, and at the following periods respectively, that is to say: one million of dollars thereof shall be taken up previous to the tenth day of September, one thousand eight hundred and thirty-five, in sums of two hundred and fifty thousand dollars, payable on the tenth days of June, July, August and September next, respectively; and the remaining one million five hundred thousand dollars thereof, in sums of five hundred thousand dollars, payable half yearly, after the first day of January, one thousand eight hundred and thirty-six.

§ 5. The Comptroller is hereby authorized and directed to advertise for proposals, to be received at any time previous to the twenty-fifth day of May instant, and not to be opened until that day, for the loan of one million of dollars, (a part of the said loan of two millions five hundred thousand dollars) payable in monthly installments of twenty-five per centum, on the tenth days of June, July, August and September next, respectively; and such proposals may be made for any portion of the said one million of dollars, not less than the par value of one share of the said stock.

§ 6. The said Comptroller shall determine, on or after the twenty-fifth day of May instant, which and what proportion of the said proposals shall be accepted; and shall issue certificates for the number of shares necessary to make up the said sum of one million of dollars, to that or those person or persons or companies, whose proposals shall have been accepted; and such certificates shall be, nearly as may be, in the same form as the certificates issued for "The New York City Stock," by virtue of the act entitled "An act to regulate the finances of the city of New York," passed June the eighth, one thousand eight hundred and twelve.

§ 7. The said Comptroller shall receive, from time to time, as the same becomes payable as aforesaid, the said installments of the said loan of one million of dollars, and shall keep a separate and distinct account of the same, and of all sums paid on account thereof.

§ 8. The said moneys so to be received, shall be paid by the said Comptroller to, or on the order of the said Water Commissioners, for the expense of the said work of supplying the city of New York with pure and wholesome water, according to the plan adopted by them for that purpose, as aforesaid.

§ 9. The provisions of the ordinance entitled "A law providing for the redemption of the City Stock," so far as the same can be applied to the "Water Stock of the city of New York," shall be applicable to the same; and all revenue to be received for water, to be procured by the said work, and furnished to the inhabitants of the city of New York, shall be specially appropriated as a Sinking Fund toward the redemption of the said Water Stock.

A Law, in addition to the law "To instruct the Water Commissioners to proceed in the work of supplying the city of New York with water, and to create a public fund or stock, to be called the 'Water Stock of the city of New York,' for the expenses of said work." Approved May 7, 1835. (*Passed March* 27, 1838.)

The Mayor, Aldermen and Commonalty of the city of New York, in Common Council convened, do ordain as follows:

§ 1. That the Comptroller be authorized, under the direction, and with the consent of the Finance Committees of both Boards, to meet the requisitions of the Water Commissioners, to sell or dispose of the "Water Loan Stocks," remaining unsold, upon such terms, and in such manner as they shall deem expedient.

A Law, in addition to the law "To instruct the Water Commissioners to proceed in the work of supplying the city of New York with water, and to create a public fund or stock, to be called 'The Water Stock of the city of New York,' for the expenses of the said work." (*Passed May* 3, 1838.)

The Mayor, Aldermen and Commonalty of the city of New York, in Common Council convened, do ordain as follows:

§ 1. An additional stock or fund, to be called "The Water Stock of the city of New York," shall be created for a loan of three millions of dollars, which shall bear an interest of not exceeding five per cent. per annum, payable quarterly, and shall be redeemable on or after the first day of May, which will be in the year one thousand eight hundred and fifty-eight.

§ 2. The nominal value of each share of said stock shall be one hundred dollars, and the same shall consist of thirty thousand shares.

§ 3. That the Comptroller be authorized, under the direction, and with the consent of the Finance Committees of both Boards, to meet the requisitions on the treasury, for supplying the city with pure and wholesome water, to sell and dispose of five hundred thousand dollars of the above stock, upon such terms, and in such manner as they shall deem expedient.

§ 4. The provisions of the ninth section of the law, to which this is an addition, is applicable, in all respects, to this law.

A Law, in addition to the law, "To instruct the Water Commissioners to proceed in the work of supplying the city of New York with water, and to create a public fund or stock, to be called 'The Water Stock of the city of New York,' for the expenses of said work." Passed May, 3, 1838. (*Passed July* 10, 1838.)

The Mayor, Aldermen and Commonalty of the city of New York, in Common Council convened, do ordain as follows:

That the following section be added to the said law, viz:

§ 5. That the Comptroller be authorized, under the direction, and with the consent of the Finance Committee of both Boards, to meet the requisitions on the treasury, for supplying the city of New York with pure and wholesome water, to sell and dispose of a further amount of five hundred thousand dollars of the above stock, redeemable on or after the year one thousand eight hundred and fifty-eight, upon such terms, and in such manner as they shall deem expedient.

A Law, in addition to the law "To instruct the Water Commissioners to proceed in the work of supplying the city of New York with water, and to create a public fund or stock to be called 'The Water Stock of the city of New York,' for the expenses of said work," passed May 3, 1838. (*Passed November* 2, 1838.)

The Mayor, Aldermen and Commonalty of the city of New York, in Common Council convened, do ordain as follows:

That the following section be added to said law, viz:

§ 6. That the Comptroller be authorized, under the direction, and with the consent of the Finance Committees of both Boards, to meet the requisitions on the treasury, for supplying the city of New York with pure and wholesome water, to sell and dispose of a further amount of two hundred and fifty thousand dollars of the above stock, redeemable on or after the year one thousand eight hundred and fifty-eight, upon such terms, and in such manner as they shall deem expedient.

32

A Law, in addition to the law "To instruct the Water Commissioners to proceed in the work of supplying the city of New York with water, and to create a public fund or stock, to be called 'The Water Stock of the city of New York,' for the expenses of said work." (*Passed February* 26, 1839.)

The Mayor, Aldermen and Commonalty of the city of New York, in Common Council convened, do ordain as follows:

§ 1. That the Comptroller be authorized, under the direction, and with the consent of the Finance Committees of both Boards, to meet the requisitions on the treasury, for supplying the city of New York with pure and wholesome water, to sell and dispose of the balance of one million seven hundred and fifty thousand dollars of the stock, redeemable on or after the year one thousand eight hundred and fifty-eight, upon such terms, and in such manner as they shall deem expedient.

A Law, in addition to the law "To instruct the Water Commissioners to proceed in the work of supplying the city of New York with water, and to create a public fund or stock, to be called 'The Water Stock of the city of New York,' for the expenses of the said work. (*Passed April* 28, 1840.)

The Mayor, Aldermen and Commonalty of the city of New York, do ordain as follows:

§ 1. An additional fund or stock, to be called "The Water Stock of the city of New York, shall be created, for a loan of three millions of dollars, which shall bear an interest of not exceeding six per cent. per annum, payable quarterly, and shall be redeemable on or after the first day of November, in the year of our Lord, one thousand eight hundred and seventy.

§ 2. That no portion of said stock shall be issued for a less sum than one hundred dollars.

§ 3. That to provide for the payment of the interest due, and to grow due upon the Water Stock, to meet the expenses of procuring and laying down water pipes, and to reimburse the City Treasury for all advances it has made, or shall hereafter make, for, or on account of the construction, maintenance and preservation of the "Croton Works," the Comptroller be authorized, under the direction, and with the consent of the Finance Committees of both Boards, to sell and dispose of the above stock upon such terms, and in such manner as they shall deem proper and expedient.

§ 4. The provisions of the ninth section of the law to which this is an addition, are applicable, in all respects, to this law.

§ 5. That at the next regular meeting of either Board of the Common Council, it shall be the duty of the Comptroller, to report to such Board, the amount of stock sold, and the rate at which sold, and the rate of interest such stock bears, and when payable.

An Ordinance, in addition to an ordinance, to instruct the Water Commissioners, &c., passed May 7, 1835. (*Passed September* 24, 1840.)

The Mayor, Aldermen and Commonalty of the the city of New York, do ordain as follows:

§ 1. That the Comptroller shall charge to the Water Loan, the following items of expenditures: All the requisitions of the Water Commissioners, for, or on account of the construction of the Croton Water Works, north of and including the distributing reservoir; all the requisitions of the Croton Aqueduct Commissioner, for or on account of the procuring and laying down water pipes in the city of New York, south of the said distributing reservoir, when the same are ratified by the Croton Aqueduct Committee, and all the interest accruing on the Water Stock of the city of New York, until the further direction of the Common Council.

§ 2. The requisitions of the Water Commissioners, for contingent expenses, shall not exceed five thousand dollars each; but no such requisition shall be paid by the Comptroller, until the former requisition shall be fully and particularly accounted for to that officer; nor until the vouchers and receipts of the respective parties, to whom such moneys have been ultimately paid, shall have been presented to the Croton Aqueduct Committee, and have been approved by the said Committee.

§ 3. No contract that may hereafter be entered into by the Water Commissioners, shall be binding upon the Common Council, until ratified by the Common Council.

§ 4. The powers of the Water Commissioners shall not extend to the making of any contracts for materials or labor, to be used or employed in the city of New York, or in procuring and laying down water pipes in said city, south of the distributing reservoir; and they are hereby instructed, not to enter into any contract for the procuring or laying down mains and water pipes in said city, south of said line—this duty having already been invested in the Croton Aqueduct Commissioner, and Croton Aqueduct Committees of the Corporation.

A Law, in addition to the laws "To instruct the Water Commissioners to proceed in the work of supplying the city of New York with water, and to create a public fund or stock, to be called 'The Water Stock of the city of New York,' for the expenses of the said work," and to complete the same. (*Passed June* 25, 1841.)

The Mayor, Aldermen and Commonalty of the city of New York, do ordain as follows:

§ 1. An additional stock or fund, to be called "The Water Stock of the city of New York," shall be created, for a loan of three million five hundred thousand dollars, which shall bear an interest of not exceeding six per cent. per annum, payable quarterly, and shall be redeemable at such periods, not exceeding forty years, as may be determined by the Finance Committee.

§ 2. The certificates of the said stock shall be issued in such amounts not less than one hundred dollars in each certificate, and in such manner and form as may be decided upon by the Finance Committees, to be the most expedient for the interest of the city.

§ 3. It shall be lawful for the Comptroller, by and with the consent of the Finance Committees of both Boards, to issue the temporary obligations of the city in such sums as they shall deem proper, not under two hundred and fifty dollars each, and therein expressed, to be transferable only on the books of the office of the Comptroller of said city, by the holder thereof in person, or his attorney, duly authorized in writing, for short periods, bearing an interest not exceeding seven per cent. per annum, and in anticipation of the permanent stock authorized by this law, the amount of such temporary obligation not to exceed two millions of dollars.

§ 4. That the Comptroller be authorized, by and with the consent of the Finance Committees of both Boards, to meet the requisitions upon the treasury, for supplying the city of New York with pure and wholesome water, to sell from time to time, and in such sums as they may deem advisable, the stock or temporary obligations of the city, authorized and created by this law, upon such terms, and in such manner as they may deem most expedient; and that he report the amount of such sales, with the price obtained therefor, quarterly, to the Common Council.

§ 5. The moneys to be raised by virtue of this law, shall be applied and expended to and for the purpose of supplying the city with pure and wholesome water, according to the provisions of the law hereby amended, and no part of the funds created by this law, or any other fund raised for the purpose of constructing or completing the Croton Aqueduct, and the works connected therewith, and distributing the water throughout the city, shall be diverted from such object.

§ 6. The provisions of the ninth section of the law to which this is an addition, is applicable, in all respects, to this law.

§ 7. It shall be the duty of the Comptroller, to estimate and report to the Board of Supervisors of the city and county of New York, at their annual meeting, the amount necessary to be raised by tax, on the estates, real and personal, of the freeholders and inhabitants of, and situated within the said city, and to be collected, to defray the deficiency of interest upon the Water Stock of the city of New York, such money to be assessed and collected in the same manner as now provided by law, for the assessment and collection of taxes in the said city.

An Ordinance to raise money by loan. (*Passed January* 25, 1842.)

The Mayor, Aldermen and Commonalty of the city of New York in Common Council convened, do ordain as follows:

That it shall be lawful to raise such further sums of money, as may be necessary to effect the introduction of the Croton Water into this city, in the manner provided by section 3 of the ordinance relating to the Water Stock of the city of New York, passed June 25th, A. D. 1841 The stock certificates to be issued therefor, to be made redeemable at such periods, not exceeding fifteen years, as the Finance Committee may direct.

A Law, to amend a law, in addition to the laws "To instruct the Water Commissioners to proceed in supplying the city of New York with water, and to create a public fund or stock, to be called 'The Water Stock of the city of New York,' for the expenses of said work,' and to complete the same. (*Passed February* 23, 1843.)

The Mayor, Aldermen and Commonalty of the city of New York in Common Council convened, do ordain as follows:

§ 1. That the Comptroller be authorized, by and with the consent of the Finance Committees of both Boards, in order to meet the requisitions upon the treasury, for supplying the city of New York with pure and wholesome water, and to complete the same, to sell from time to time, and in such manner as they may deem advisable, the stock, or obligations of the city, not exceeding the sum of six hundred and forty-seven thousand dollars, authorized and created by the laws heretofore passed by the legislature, 1838, 1840 and 1841, upon such terms, not below the par value thereof, and at an interest not exceeding six per cent. per annum, and in such manner as they may deem most expedient; and that he report the amount of such sales to the Common Council, quarterly.

§ 2. The moneys to be raised, by virtue of this law, shall be applied and expended, to and for the purpose of supplying the city with pure and wholesome water, according to the provisions of the law hereby amended; and no part of the fund created by this law, raised for the purpose of completing the Croton Aqueduct, and the works connected therewith, and distributing the water throughout the city, shall be diverted from such object.

Of the "Fire Loan Stock of the city of New York."

A Law to regulate the the purchase of bonds and mortgages, which belonged, on the 18th day of December, in the year 1835, to any of the Fire Insurance Companies in the city of New York, which have become insolvent, or whose capital may have been impaired, by losses occasioned by the fire of the 16th and 17th of that month, and to provide the funds necessary for that purpose. (*Passed February* 16, 1836.)

The Mayor, Aldermen and Commonalty of the city of New York, in Common Council convened, do ordain as follows:

§ 1. A public stock or fund, to be called "The Fire Loan Stock of the city of New York," shall be created for a loan of four millions of dollars, which shall bear an interest of not exceeding five per cent. per annum, payable half yearly, and shall be redeemable, one-third thereof in two years, one-third thereof in five years, and the remaining third thereof in seven years, or the whole amount in two years, five years, or seven years, under the direction of the Mayor, and the Presidents, and Finance Committees of both Boards of the Common Council, reserving the right to increase the same to the amount prescribed by the act of the legislature, if the same shall be found necessary.

§ 2. The Comptroller is hereby authorized and directed to advertise for proposals, to be received by him at any time previous to the ninth day of March, in the year one thousand eight hundred and thirty-six, and not to be opened until that day, for the said loan of four millions of dollars, receivable at such times as shall be fixed by the said Mayor, Presidents and Finance Committees, and stated in the advertisement for such proposals; and such proposals may be made for any portion of the said loan, and must state whether the amounts and terms thereby offered are intended for a loan of so much, to be secured by the bond or bonds of the Mayor, Aldermen and Commonalty of the city of New York, or stock certificates to be issued by them.

§ 3. The said Comptroller shall, without delay, after the said ninth day of March, in the year one thousand eight hundred and thirty-six, submit such proposals as may have been received by him for the said loan, or portions thereof, to the said Mayor, Presidents and Finance Committees, who shall be a committee to determine whether any, which, and what portion of the said proposals shall be accepted; and such determination shall be in writing, and signed by the members of such committee, or a majority of them.

§ 4. After such determination shall have been made, the Comptroller shall issue certificates, or deliver bonds, according to the proposals which shall have been so accepted, to that or those person or persons, or bodies corporate, who shall have made the same: Provided, that no such bond or certificate shall be so issued or delivered, until the par value, or the amount conditioned to be paid thereby, with any premium to be given therefor, shall have been actually deposited in the Mechanics' Bank of the city of New York, to the credit of the Corporation of the said city, for account of the Fire Loan of the city of New York.

§ 5. All certificates to be issued for any portion of the said loan, shall be made in conformity with the resolution of the Common Council, passed on the seventh day of August, one thousand eight hundred and thirty-five; and shall be signed by the Comptroller, and countersigned by the Mayor; and all bonds which may be delivered for any portion of such loan, shall have affixed thereto the seal of the city, with the signatures of the Clerk of the Common Council and of the Mayor, and shall be made payable to the order of the Comptroller, and indorsed by him.

§ 6. The faith and property of the city of New York, and the proceeds of all bonds and mortgages which may be purchased in pursuance of this law, are hereby pledged for the redemption of the said stock or loan.

§ 7. The Common Council shall appoint seven commissioners, to perform the duties prescribed by the second section of the act of the legislature, entitled "An act to authorize the Mayor, Aldermen and Commonalty of the city of New York, to raise moneys on loan, and for other purposes," passed January sixteenth, one thousand eight hundred and thirty-six; and the said commissioners shall hold their offices until the sixteenth day of July, in the year one thousand eight hundred and thirty-six, unless sooner removed by the Common Council.

§ 8. All applications for the sale, to the Corporation of this city, of any bond and mortgage under the above-mentioned act of the legislature, shall be made to the Comptroller, and shall be accompanied by the said bond and mortgage, together with a written statement or abstract of the title of the mortgaged premises, and the certificates of the Register, and of the clerks of the several courts, showing that such premises were free, and discharged from all prior incumbrances, at the time of the execution of such mortgage; and no such bonds or mortgages shall be purchased, except directly from the Fire Insurance Companies heretofore mentioned.

§ 9. It shall be the duty of the Comptroller, on the receipt of any such application, to furnish to the Commissioners a description of the mortgaged premises, and on receiving from the said commissioners their certificate of the value of such premises, the said Comptroller, shall forthwith submit such application, together with such certificate of the commissioners, to a select committee, to consist of three members from each Board of the Common Council, and to be appointed for that purpose; and such committee shall determine whether such bond and mortgage shall be purchased; and no such purchase shall be made, unless a majority of the persons composing such committee, shall signify their approbation thereof in writing, and under their hands.

§ 10. Every such bond and mortgage, together with the statement or abstract, and certificates respecting the title of the mortgaged premises, and the proposed instrument of assignment or sale thereof, to the Corporation of this city, shall, previous to the purchase thereof, be examined by the Counsel of the Corporation; and no such bond and mortgage shall be purchased until the said counsel shall have certified his opinion, that the form and execution of such bond and mortgage, and of such instrument of assignment are sufficient, and that the title to the mortgaged premises is good and unincumbered.

§ 11. Every assignment of a bond and mortgage, to be made under this law, shall be accompanied, with an admission in writing, from the debtor or debtors thereon, of notice of such assignment, and that he, she or they have no set-off against the same; and all charges and expenses attending the examination of the titles of the mortgaged premises, shall be borne by the companies from whom such bonds and mortgages may be purchased.

§ 12. It shall be the duty of the Comptroller, to pay for every such bond and mortgage, the purchase of which shall be authorized, as hereinbefore mentioned, to such person or officer, as may be duly empowered to receive the same, the amount due upon such bond and mortgage for principal, and for interest accrued since the last time specified therein for the payment of the same; and such payment shall be made out of the moneys to be obtained by loan, on the bonds or stock hereinbefore mentioned.

§ 13. Any of the said companies may, within one year from the date thereof, receive back the bonds and mortgages assigned by them, or such as shall remain unpaid, or a portion thereof, with the consent of the Commissioners of the Sinking Fund, on payment of the amount of the principal and interest thereon, in the Fire Loan Stock of the city of New York, at the same rate at which the same shall be issued by the Corporation.

§ 14. The Mayor and Clerk of the Common Council are hereby authorized to execute a reassignment to any of the said companies, of the bonds and mortgages now held by them, respectively, and which may be sold to the Mayor, Aldermen and Commonalty of the city of New York, and shall remain unpaid, or a portion thereof, on receiving from the Comptroller a certificate, that a portion of the Fire Loan Stock, of the city of New York, had been surrendered to the said Comptroller by the said companies, in payment therefor, to the amount of the principal and interest of the said bonds and mortgages, assigned by them respectively, or such portion as may be so reassigned, deducting the premium received by the Common Council on said stock.

§ 15. It shall be the duty of the Comptroller, to keep a separate and distinct account of all moneys to be received for the said bonds or stock, and of all moneys to be paid for the said bonds and mortgages; also, of all moneys to be received in payment of the principal and interest of such bonds and mortgages, and of all moneys to be paid for the redemption of the bonds or stock to be issued as aforesaid. And the said Comptroller shall furnish a copy of such account, once in every three months, to the Common Council.

§ 16. It shall be the duty of the Comptroller, to collect and receive the interest accruing on the said bonds and mortgages, as the same may become payable; and the principal moneys due thereon, shall be paid into such banks as the Common Council of this city shall, by resolution direct, to the credit of the Commissioners of the Sinking Fund, and on account of the Fire Loan of the city of New York; and a certificate of such payment shall be given by the cashier of such bank; but no payments on account of the principal due on any such bond, shall be received in less sums than five hundred dollars. The Comptroller shall also deposit in such bank, to the credit of the said Commissioners of the Sinking Fund, the interest so to be received by him, and also, any balance of the said loan that may remain, not appropriated under this ordinance, after the sixteenth day of July, in the year one thousand eight hundred and thirty-six.

§ 17. On the payment of all moneys due for principal and interest, upon any such bond and mortgage as aforesaid, it shall be the duty of the Comptroller, on receiving a certificate from the cashier of the said bank, showing such payment of principal, to deliver up the said bond and mortgage to the party making such payment, together with sufficient acknowledgment of the satisfaction of such mortgage; and the Mayor and Clerk of the Common Coumcil are hereby authorized to sign, and cause the seal of the city to be affixed to every such acknowledgment of satisfaction, on the certificate of the Comptroller, that such principal and interest have been paid. But no release of any part of the premises contained in any such mortgage, from the lien created by such mortgage thereon, shall be made or executed, or authorized by the Common Council.

§ 18. The purchase of bonds and mortgages, to be made under this law, shall be confined to bonds secured by mortgage on unincumbered real estate; and whenever any building on the property so mortgaged, shall be estimated by the commissioners, as forming a part of the value of the mortgaged premises, the insurance company from whom such bond and mortgage may be purchased, shall deliver to the Comptroller a policy of insurance, for not less than one year, effected on the said building, by a solvent fire insurance company of this city, with an assignment thereof to the Mayor, Aldermen and Commonalty of the city of New York.

§ 19. All bonds and mortgages which may be purchased under this law, shall be closed, and payment thereof required, within seven years from the sixteenth day of January, in the year one thousand eight hundred and thirty-six; and the right is hereby reserved to the Corporation of this city, to call in or collect, when due, any of the said bonds and mortgages, at any time previous to the expiration of such period; and in case of the non-payment of any interest upon any such bond and mortgage, for more than three months after the same may be due, or the neglect of the owner of any building covered by any such mortgage, to renew any policy of insurance thereon, which may have been assigned to the Corporation of this city as aforesaid, when such policy shall have expired, it shall be the duty of the Comptroller, to deliver the said bond and mortgage to the Counsel of the Corporation, to collect the amount due thereon, for principal and interest.

§ 20. The provisions of the ordinance entitled "A law providing for the redemption of the City Stock," so far as the same can be applied to the Fire Loan Stock of the city of New York, shall be applicable to the same; and the Comptroller shall open and keep a separate account, to be called "The Sinking Fund Account of the Fire Loan Stock of the city of New York;" and the Commissioners of the Sinking Fund of the said city, shall apply the proceeds to be collected and received, on or for all bonds and mortgages which may be purchased by virtue of this law, to the payment of the interest to accrue upon the said loan, and to purchase on redemption, of the said bonds or stock issued therefor; and the whole of the principal and interest of such bonds and mortgages, after the payment of all necessary expenses, is hereby appropriated, as the same shall be paid into the City Treasury, to the said Sinking Fund, for such purpose, and shall not, under any pretense whatever, be diverted therefrom, for any other purpose or use whatsoever.

§ 21. The Comptroller is hereby authorized to employ an additional clerk in his office, who shall be paid at a rate not exceeding one thousand dollars per annum, by the Commissioners of the Sinking Fund, out of the moneys to be received by them under this ordinance.

A Law, to amend a law to "Regulate the purchase of bonds and mortgages, which belonged, on the 18th day of December, in the year 1835, to any of the Fire Insurance Companies in the city of New York, whose capital may have been impaired by losses occasioned by the fire on the 16th and 17th of that month, and to provide the funds necessary for that purpose." (*Passed March* 15, 1836.)

The Mayor, Aldermen and Commonalty of the city of New York, in Common Council convened, do ordain as follows:

§ 1. The Comptroller may, when directed so to do by the Select Committee appointed under the ninth section of the law hereby amended, within sixty days from the passage of this act, accept of any offers for any portion of the stock authorized to be issued by the said law, which has not been subscribed for, nor exceeding, in the whole amount, one and a half millions of dollars, redeemable at a period not longer than five years from the time the said stock shall be issued, and he may issue stock or bonds therefor, in the manner directed by the said law: Provided that no such offer shall be accepted for any portion of the said stock, below the par value thereof.

§ 2. All the provisions of the law hereby amended, shall be applicable to the stock which may be issued in pursuance of the foregoing section, in the same manner as to the stock which may have been subscribed for under the said law, excepting so far as they are inconsistent therewith.

A Law, to provide for loaning the surplus of the Fire Loan Stock of the city of New York, to the Safety Fund Banks of the city. (*Passed March* 3, 1836.)

The Mayor, Aldermen and Commonalty of the city of New York, in Common Council convened, do ordain as follows .

§ 1. The Comptroller may issue, as part of the residue of the stock authorized to be issued by an act of the legislature, entitled " An act to authorize the Mayor, Aldermen and Commonalty of the city of New York, to raise money on loan, and for other purposes," to the amount of one and a half million of dollars in stock.

§ 2. Such stock shall be issued, bearing an interest of five per centum per annum, and shall be redeemable, one-third in two years, and one-third in three years, and one-third in four years from the passage of this law.

§ 3. Such stock may be loaned to such of the banks in this city, as are under the Safety Fund Law, to an amount to be determined by the Joint Committee hereinafter named, not exceeding, to any one bank, the half of the capital of such bank, upon the conditions hereinafter mentioned.

§ 4. Each of the said banks may borrow such portion of the said stock, as may be determined by the said Committee, on delivering to the Comptroller, the obligation of such bank, in the penal sum of double the amount loaned, conditioned for the return of the said stock to the Mayor, Aldermen and Commonalty of the city of New York, at the times when the same shall become redeemable; also, for the payment of the interest on the said stock, at the rate of five and a half per centum per annum, in half yearly payments, at the same time that the interest on the said stock shall become payable; and also, that the said stock shall not, at any time, be sold to any person whatever; that the said stock shall not be used by way of hypothecation, or otherwise, in the state of New York, or to any inhabitant thereof; and that the said bank will save harmless, and indemnify the said Mayor, Aldermen and Commonalty of the city of New York, against any claim whatever, for or on account of the said stock; and also will, when required so to do by the Comptroller, subscribe for a portion of the residue of the said stock, not exceeding one-third of the amount of the stock to be loaned to them by virtue hereof, as is directed by the eighth section of this ordinance.

§ 5. In addition to the obligations of the said banks, there shall also be required, the bond of such of the directors of each bank, as shall be deemed sufficient by the Joint Committee hereafter named, conditioned for the return of the said stock, and payment of the said interest, according to the obligation of each bank, and for the punctual performance of all the covenants and conditions of each bank in regard to the same.

§ 6. Any of the said banks may, at any time, return the said stock loaned to them, and pay up the interest thereon; and on such surrender of all the stock loaned to them, and payment of such interest, the Comptroller may, with the consent of the Mayor and Presidents of both Boards of the Common Council, or a majority of them, deliver up the obligation and bond given by such bank and their directors.

§ 7. The Comptroller may *issue*, for the balance of the stock so authorized as aforesaid, to the amount of five hundred thousand dollars, at an interest of five per centum per annum, redeemable at the pleasure of the Common Council, after one year from the passage of this law, when directed so to do by the said Joint Committee.

§ 8. Each of the said banks, before receiving the said stock so to be loaned as aforesaid, shall, if required so to do by the Joint Committee, appointed under the ninth section of the ordinance of the Common Council, entitled "A law to regulate the purchase of bonds and mortgages, which belonged, on the eighteenth day of December, in the year one thousand eight hundred and thirty-five, to any of the Fire Insurance Companies in the city of New York, which have become insolvent, or whose capital may have been impaired by losses occasioned by the fire of the sixteenth and seventeenth of that month, and to provide the funds necessary for that purpose, 'passed February sixteenth, one thousand eight hundred and thirty-six," subscribe for a portion of said stock, not exceeding one-third of the amount loaned, to be issued as is directed in the *sixth* section of this law, at par, not exceeding one-third of the amount which may be loaned to them respectively.

§ 9. On receiving a certificate of the deposit of the amount, of the par value of the stock so to be subscribed for by any of the said banks, in the Mechanics' Bank, to the credit of the Mayor Aldermen and Commonalty of the city of New York, on account of the Fire Loan Stock of the city of New York, the Comptroller shall deliver to the President of the bank, making such deposit, the amount of stock so subscribed and paid for.

§ 10. On the payment of the said money, in the mode directed in the last section, and the delivery to the Comptroller of the said obligation and bond hereinbefore mentioned, on behalf of any of the said banks, approved of by the Counsel of the Corporation, and the Joint Committee mentioned in the *seventh* section of this law, or in case a subscription for the said stock shall not be required, then, on the delivery of the said obligation and bond as aforesaid, it shall be the duty of the Comptroller to deliver to the President of such bank, the proportion of the stock directed to be issued by the first section of this law, which may have been determined by the said committee to be loaned to such bank, and which shall be secured by the said obligation of the said bank, and bond of the directors thereof.

§ 11. All the provisions of the said ordinance of the Common Council, passed February sixteenth, one thousand eight hundred and thirty-six, and mentioned in the *seventh* section of this law, relating to the charge, custody and deposit of the moneys to be received, and the redemption of the stock, and also to the Sinking Fund, are hereby made applicable to the stock to be issued under this law.

A Law, further to amend a law "To regulate the purchase of bonds and mortgages, which belonged on the 18th day of December, in the year 1835, to any of the Fire Insurance Companies in the city of New York, whose capital may have been impaired by losses occasioned by the fire of the 16th and 17th of that month, and to provide the funds necessary for that purpose. (*Passed July* 12, 1836.)

The Mayor, Aldermen and Commonalty of the city of New York, in Common Council convened, do ordain as follows:

§ 1. The Comptroller is hereby authorized, under the direction of the Select Committee, mentioned in the ninth section of the law hereby amended, to receive and accept proposals, at any time previous to the hour of four o'clock in the afternoon, of the twelfth day of July instant, for a loan of not exceeding seven hundred thousand dollars, at an interest of five per centum per annum, and redeemable within seventeen years from the sixteenth day of January last, upon any portion of the stock authorized to be issued by the law hereby amended, not already subscribed for or issued: Provided, that offers made for the said loan or parts thereof, for the shortest period or periods, and at a rate or rates not less than par, shall be preferred.

§ 2. The Commissioners of the Sinking Fund of the city of New York, are hereby authorized, to invest such moneys as may remain in their hands, belonging to the said fund, in the said loan, or purchase of the said stock, under the direction of the said committee.

§ 3. It shall be lawful for the said Comptroller, when authorized so to do by the said committee, to receive the said stock at par, in payment of the amount due upon any bond and mortgage which shall have been purchased under the law hereby amended, or to sell any such bond and mortgage, and to take the said stock in payment therefor; and the fourteenth section of the law hereby amended shall be applicable to all assignments which may be required to be executed, in pursuance of this section.

§ 4. All the provisions of the law hereby amended, except so far as they may be inconsistent with this law, shall be applicable to the stock which may be issued in pursuance of this law.

Of "The Public Building Stock of the city of New York."

A Law to create a Public Fund or Stock, to be called "The Public Building Stock of the city of New York." (*Passed August* 8, 1836.)

The Mayor, Aldermen and Commonalty of the city of New York, in Common Council convened, do ordain as follows:

§ 1. A public fund or stock, to be called "The Public Building Stock of the city of New York," shall be created for a loan of two hundred and fifty thousand dollars, which shall bear an interest of not exceeding five per centum per annum, payable half yearly, and shall be redeemable on or after the sixth day of May, which shall be in the year one thousand eight hundred and fifty-six.

§ 2. The nominal amount or value of each share of the said stock, shall be one hundred dollars, and the portion of said stock hereby directed to be issued, shall consist of two thousand five hundred shares.

§ 3. The Comptroller is hereby authorized and directed to advertise for proposals, to be received at any time previous to the fifth day of September next, and not to be opened until that day, for the loan of the said sum of two hundred and fifty thousand dollars, payable on the fifteenth day of September next; and such proposals may be made for any portion of the said sum, not less than the par value of one share of the said stock.

§ 4. The Finance Committees of both Boards of the Common Council, and the Comptroller, shall determine, on or after the fifth day of September next, which and what proportion of the said proposals shall be accepted, and the said Comptroller shall issue certificates for the number of shares necessary to make up the said sum of two hundred and fifty thousand dollars, to the person or persons, company or companies, whose proposals shall have been accepted.

§ 5. The said certificates shall be made in conformity with the resolution of the Common Council, passed on the seventh day of August, one thousand eight hundred and thirty-five, and shall be signed by the Comptroller and countersigned by the Mayor.

§ 6. The said Comptroller shall keep a separate and distinct account of all moneys received and paid on account of said stock, and the provisions of the ordinance entitled "A law providing for the redemption of the City Stock," so far as the same can be applied to the stock hereby created, shall be applicable to the same.

A Law to amend a law, entitled "A law to create a Public Fund or Stock, to be called 'The Public Building Stock of the city of New York.'" (*Passed September* 14, 1836.)

The Mayor, Aldermen and Commonalty of the City of New York in Common Council convened, do ordain as follows:

§ 1. The Comptroller is hereby authorized, with the advice and consent of the Finance Committees of the Common Council, to receive and accept such proposals as may be offered to him, for so much of the loan of two hundred and fifty thousand dollars, mentioned in the law hereby amended, as may not have been proposed for and accepted previous to the fifth day of September instant.

A Law, in addition to the law entitled "A law to create a Public Fund or stock, to be called 'The Public Building Stock of the city of New York." (*Passed January* 20, 1838.)

The Mayor, Aldermen and Commonalty of the city of New York, do ordain as follows:

§ 1. An addition to the public fund or stock, called "The Public Building Stock of the city of New York shall be created, for a loan of two hundred and fifty thousand dollars, which shall bear an interest of not exceeding five per centum per annum, payable half yearly, and shall be redeemable on or after the the sixth day of May, which will be in the year one thousand eight hundred and fifty-six.

§ 2. The said stock shall consist of two thousand five hundred shares, and the nominal value of each share of the said stock shall be one hundred dollars.

§ 3. The Comptroller is hereby authorized and directed to receive proposals for said loan of two hundred and fifty thousand dollars, or for any portion of said sum, not less than the par value of one share of said stock, at such times as the Finance Committees of the Common Council shall direct. Said proposals shall be made for cash, or on such terms as shall be directed by the said committees; but no such stock shall be issued under par.

§ 4. The Finance Committees of Both Boards of the Common Council, and the Comptroller, shall determine which and what proportion of the said proposals shall be accepted, and the said Comptroller shall issue the certificates necessary to make up the said sum of two hundred and fifty thousand dollars, to the person or persons, company or companies, whose proposals shall have been accepted.

§ 5. The said certificates shall be made in conformity with the resolution of the Common Council, passed on the seventh day of August, one thousand eight hundred and thirty-five, and shall be signed by the Comptroller, and countersigned by the Mayor.

§ 6. The said Comptroller shall keep a separate and distinct account of all moneys received and paid on account of the Public Building Stock, and the provisions of the ordinance entitled "A law providing for the redemption of the City Stock, so far as the same can be applied to the stock hereby created, shall be applicable to the same.

Of " The Fire Indemnity Stock of the City of New York."

A Law to create a public fund or stock, to be called " The Fire Indemnity Stock of the city of New York.—(*Passed May* 3, 1838.)

The Mayor, Aldermen and Commonalty of the city of New York, in Common Council convened, do ordain as follows:

§ 1. A public fund or stock, to be called " The Fire Indemnity Stock of the city of New York," shall be created, for a loan of not more than six hundred thousand dollars, which shall bear an interest of not exceeding five per centum per annum, payable half yearly ; the one-half of such stock shall be redeemable on or after the tenth day of May, in the year one thousand eight hundred and sixty-eight, and one-half of such stock on or after the tenth day of May, in the year one thousand eight hundred and fifty-eight.

§ 2. The nominal amount or value of each share of the said stock shall be one hundred dollars.

§ 3. The Comptroller is hereby authorized and directed to advertise for proposals, or to dispose of, at private sale, under the direction of the Finance Committees of both Boards, for the whole or either portion of the said stock, at such times, and for such sums, as shall be necessary to be applied to and expended in paying the damages already recovered, and that may hereafter be recovered, against the Mayor, Aldermen and Commonalty of the city of New York, by reason of the blowing up and destruction of sundry buildings in the said city, during the continuance of the great fire in said city, in December, one thousand eight hundred and thirty-five, and the expenses attending such recoveries ; and the stock to be issued under this law shall not exceed the amount necessary for that purpose.

§ 4. The certificates shall be made and signed in conformity with the resolution of the Common Council, passed the seventh day of August, one thousand eight hundred and thirty-five.

§ 5. The Comptroller shall keep a separate and distinct account of all moneys received and paid on account of said stock.

§ 6. The provisions of the ordinance entitled " A law providing for the redemption of the City Stock," as far as the same can be applied to the stock hereby created, shall be applicable to the same.

§ 7. There shall be application made annually to the legislature, for authority to raise, in addition to the amount annually required for taxes, the further sum of twenty-five thousand dollars, which shall be, and hereby is, appropriated to the redemption of the said stock, and shall not be used for any other purpose whatever; and the same shall be paid to the Commissioners of the Sinking Fund therefor.

(*Resolutions, passed November* 30, 1838.)

Resolved, That the suits and claims for damages sustained by the blowing up of buildings during the great fire, be referred to the Finance Committees, together with the Law Committees of both Boards, with power to direct the further prosecution or defense of the same or some of them, or to settle and pay the same, or some of them; and all expenses attending the same, as they in their discretion shall judge proper; and to direct the sale and transfer of so much of the stock of the Fire Indemnity Loan, as shall be necessary to make such payments.

Resolved, That the Comptroller be authorized to sell and dispose of so much of the stock of the Fire Indemnity Loan, and to pay such claims as the Finance Committees, in pursuance of the above resolution, shall direct.

Of "The Floating Debt Stock of the City of New York."

An Ordinance to create a public fund or stock, to be called "The Floating Debt Stock of the city of New York," to be applied exclusively to the payment of the Floating Debt of the said city, contracted before the first day of January, 1840.—(*Passed June* 8, 1840).

The Mayor, Aldermen and Commonalty of the City of New York, in Common Council convened, do ordain as follows:

§ 1. A public fund or stock, to be called "The Floating Debt Stock of the city of New York," shall be created for a loan of four hundred thousand dollars, which shall bear an interest of not exceeding six per cent. per annum, payable semi-annually, on the first day of February and August in each year, hereafter, and shall be redeemable at such periods not exceeding seven years, as may be determined on by the Committees of Finance of both Boards of the Common Council.

§ 2. The Comptroller is hereby authorized, under the direction of the said Committees on Finance, to sell and dispose of the same from time to time, upon such terms, and in such manner, as the said committees shall deem proper, and to apply the proceeds thereof exclusively to the payment of the Floating Debt of the said city, contracted before the first day of January, 1840.

§ 3. The faith of the city of New York, and the taxes authorized to be raised by an act of the Legislature of the State of New York, passed May 14, 1840, authorizing the Mayor, Aldermen and Commonalty of the city of New York, to fund and pay old Floating Debt of the said city, are hereby pledged for the redemption of the said stock or loan, and the interest thereon.

§ 4. The said Comptroller shall keep a separate and distinct account of the said stock, and of all sums received and paid on account, and shall report to each Board of the Common Council, once in every three months, a full and particular statement thereof.

§ 5. The certificates of such stock shall be made in conformity with the resolution of the Common Council, passed August 7, 1835, and shall be signed by the Comptroller and countersigned by the Mayor.

Of " The Croton Water Stock."

An Ordinance to create a public stock or fund, to be called "The Croton Water Stock."—(*Passed December* 24, 1845).

The Mayor, Aldermen and Commonalty of the city of New York, in Common Council convened, do ordain as follows.

§ 1. A public fund or stock, to be called " The Croton Water Stock," shall be created, for a loan of five hundred thousand dollars, which shall bear an interest not exceeding six per centum per annum, payable quarterly, and be redeemable on or before the first day of February, in the year one thousand eight hundred and ninety.

§ 2. The said stock shall consist of five thousand shares, and the nominal value of each share shall be one hundred dollars each.

§ 3. The Comptroller is hereby authorized, with the assent of the Finance Committees of both Boards of the Common Council, to advertise for proposals for the whole or any portion of the said stock ; the proposals so to be received shall be opened in the presence of said committees, who, with the Comptroller, shall determine which and what portions of such proposals shall be accepted.

§ 4. The Comptroller shall issue certificates of stock to the person or persons, company or companies, whose proposals shall have been so accepted; provided, the par value of such stock, together with any premium to be given therefor, shall have been deposited in the City Treasury for the account of "Croton Water Stock."

§ 5. The said certificates shall be made in conformity with the resolution of the Common Council, passed on the seventh day of August, one thousand eight hundred and thirty-five, and shall be signed by the Comptroller, and be countersigned by the Mayor.

§ 6. The money to be loaned by virtue of this ordinance shall be applied to, and expended for, the completion of the Croton Aqueduct, and the payment of claims for damage, by injury to water rights on the Croton river, and the destruction of property by the breaking away of the Croton dam, and the legal expenses attendant thereon; and be drawn only on the requisition of the State Water Commissioners.

§ 7. The provisions of the ordinance, entitled "An ordinance providing for the redemption of the City Debt, and the payment of the interest thereon," approved by the Mayor, February 22, 1844, so far as the same can apply to the stock hereby created, shall be applicable to the same.

An Ordinance to create a public stock or fund, to be called "Croton Water Stock."—(*Passed August* 14, 1851).

The Mayor, Aldermen and Commonalty of the city of New York, in Common Council convened, do ordain as follows:

§ 1. A public fund or stock, to be called "The Croton Water Stock," shall be created for a loan of three hundred and fifty thousand dollars, which shall bear an interest not exceeding five per centum per annum, payable quarterly, and redeemable on or before the first day of February, in the year one thousand eight hundred and ninety.

§ 2. The said stock shall consist of three thousand five hundred shares, and the nominal value of each share shall be one hundred dollars.

§ 3. The Comptroller is hereby authorized to advertise for proposals, for the whole or any portion of said stock; the proposals so to be received, shall be opened in the presence of the Commissioners of the Sinking Fund, who, with the Comptroller, shall determine which and what portions of such proposals shall be accepted.

§ 4. The Comptroller shall issue certificates of stock to the person or persons, company or companies, whose proposals shall have been so accepted; provided the par value of such stock, together with any premium to be given therefor, shall have been deposited in the City Treasury for the account of " Croton Water Stock."

§ 5. The said certificates shall be in conformity with the resolution of the Common Council, passed on the 7th day of August, 1835, and shall be signed by the Comptroller and be countersigned by the Mayor.

§ 6. The moneys to be raised by virtue of this act shall be applied to, and expended for, the purpose of reimbursing the treasury of the city of New York the amount advanced for extending water pipes (mains) in said city, for the distribution of the Croton water, and for the further extension of the same.

§ 7. The provisions of the ordinance, entitled " An ordinance providing for the redemption of the city debt and the payment of the interest thereon," approved by the Mayor, February 22, 1844, so far as the same can apply to the stock hereby created, shall be applicable to the same.

An Ordinance to create a public stock or fund, to be called " Croton Water Stock."—(*Passed May* 20, 1852).

The Mayor, Aldermen and Commonalty of the city of New York, in Common Council convened, do ordain as follows:

§ 1. A public fund or stock, to be called "The Croton Water Stock," shall be created for a loan of one hundred and fifty thousand dollars, which shall bear an interest not exceeding five per cent. per annum, payable quarter-yearly, and redeemable on or before the first day of February, in the year one thousand eight hundred and ninety.

§ 2. The said stock shall consist of one thousand five hundred shares, and the nominal value of each share shall be one hundred dollars.

§ 3. The Comptroller is hereby authorized to advertise for proposals for the whole or any portion of said stock; the proposals, so to be received, shall be opened in the presence of the Commissioners of the Sinking Fund, who, with the Comptroller, shall determine which and what portions of such proposals shall be accepted.

§ 4. The Comptroller shall issue certificates of stock to the person or persons, company or companies, whose proposals shall have been so accepted, provided the par value of such stock, together with any premium to be given therefor, shall have been deposited in the city treasury for the account of "The Croton Water Stock."

§ 5. The said certificates shall be in conformity with the resolution of the Common Council, passed on the 7th day of August, 1835, and shall be signed by the Comptroller, and be countersigned by the Mayor.

§ 6. The moneys to be raised by virtue of this ordinance shall be applied to, and expended for, the purpose of reimbursing the treasury of the city of New York, the amounts advanced for extending water pipes (mains) in said city, for the distribution of the Croton water, and for the further extension of the same.

§ 7. The provisions of an ordinance entitled "An ordinance providing for the redemption of the city debt, and the payment of the interest thereon," approved by the Mayor, February 22, 1844, so far as the same can apply to the stock hereby created, shall be applicable to the same.

Of "Building Loan Stock No. 2."

An Ordinance to create a public stock or fund, to be called "Building Loan Stock No. 2."—(*Passed Nov.* 24, 1845).

The Mayor, Aldermen and Commonalty of the City of New York in Common Council convened, do ordain as follows:

§ 1. A public fund or stock, to be called "Building Loan Stock No. 2," shall be created for a loan of one hundred and fifty thousand dollars, which shall bear an interest not exceeding six per centum per annum payable quarterly, and be redeemable as follows, to wit: fifty thousand dollars on the first day of February, one thousand eight hundred and forty-nine; fifty thousand dollars on the first day of February, one thousand eight hundred and fifty, and fifty thousand dollars on the first day of February, one thousand eight hundred and fifty-one.

§ 2. The said stock shall consist of fifteen hundred shares, and the nominal value of each share shall be one hundred dollars.

§ 3. The Comptroller is hereby authorized, with the assent of the Finance Committees of both Boards of the Common Council, to advertise for proposals for the whole or any portion of the said stock; the proposals so to be received shall be opened in the presence of said committees, who, with the Comptroller, shall determine which, and what proportion of such proposals shall be accepted.

§ 4. The Comptroller shall issue certificates of stock to the person or persons, company or companies, whose proposals shall have been so accepted; provided the par value of such stock, together with any premium to be given therefor, shall have been deposited into the city treasury for the account of "Building Loan Stock No. 2."

§ 5. The said certificates shall be made in conformity with the resolution of the Common Council, passed on the seventh day of August, one thousand eight hundred and thirty-five, and shall be signed by the Comptroller, and be countersigned by the Mayor.

§ 6. The money to be loaned by virtue of this ordinance shall be applied to, and expended for, the erection of the buildings known as the Nurseries and Alms-house; and the Comptroller shall keep a separate and distinct account of such money received and paid on account of said stock and building.

§ 7. The provisions of the ordinance entitled "An ordinance providing for the redemption of the City Debt, and the payment of the interest thereon," approved by the Mayor, February 22, 1844, so far as the same can be applied to the stock hereby created, shall be applicable to the same.

An Ordinance to create a public stock or fund, to be called "Building Loan Stock, No. 2."—(*Passed June* 23, 1847).

The Mayor, Aldermen and Commonalty of the City of New York, in Common Council convened, do ordain as follows:

§ 1. A public fund or stock to be called "Building Loan Stock No. 2," shall be created for a loan of one hundred thousand dollars, which shall bear an interest not exceeding six per cent. per annum, payable quarterly, and be redeemable as follows: Fifty thousand dollars on the first day of February, 1852, and fifty thousand dollars on the first day of February, 1853.

§ 2. The said stock shall consist of one thousand shares, and the nominal value of each share shall be one hundred dollars.

§ 3. The Comptroller is hereby authorized, with the assent of the Finance Committees of both Boards of the Common Council, to advertise for proposals for the whole or any portion of said stock, the proposals so to be received shall be opened in the presence of the said committees, who, with the Comptroller, shall determine which, and what proportions of such proposals shall be accepted.

§ 4. The Comptroller shall issue certificates of stock to the person or persons, company or companies, whose proposals shall have been accepted, provided the par value of such stock, together with any premium to be given therefor, shall have been deposited into the city treasury for the account of "Building Loan Stock No. 2."

§ 5. The said certificate shall be made in conformity with the resolution of the Common Council, passed on the 7th day of August, 1835, and shall be signed by the Comptroller, and countersigned by the Mayor.

§ 6. The money to be loaned by virtue of this Ordinance, shall be applied to and expended for the erection of buildings to be known as the Nurseries and the Mad House, and for the extension of the Lunatic Asylum, and the Comptroller shall keep a separate and distinct account of such money received and paid on account of said stock and buildings.

§ 7. The provisions of the ordinance entitled "An ordinance, providing for the redemption of the City Debt, and the payment of interest thereon," approved by the Mayor, February 22, 1844, so far as the same can be applied to the stock hereby created, shall be applicable to the same.

An Ordinance to create a public stock or fund, to be called "Building Loan Stock No. 2."—(*Passed June* 17, 1848).

The Mayor, Aldermen and Commonalty of the city of New York, in Common Council convened, do ordain as follows:

§ 1. A public fund or stock, to be called "Building Loan Stock No. 2," shall be created, for a loan not exceeding one hundred thousand dollars, which shall bear an interest not exceeding six per cent. per annum, payable quarterly, and be redeemable as follows: Fifty thousand dollars on the first day of February, 1854, and fifty thousand dollars on the first day of February, 1855.

§ 2. The said stock shall consist of one thousand shares, and the nominal value of each share shall be one hundred dollars.

§ 3. The Commissioners of the Sinking Fund are hereby authorized to advertise for proposals for the whole or any portion of said stock, and determine which and what proportions of such proposals shall be accepted.

§ 4. The Comptroller shall issue certificates of stock to the person or persons, company or companies, whose proposals shall have been accepted, provided the par value of such stock, together with any premium to be given therefor, shall have been deposited into the city treasury for the account of "Building Loan Stock No. 2."

§ 5. The said certificates shall be made in conformity with the resolution of the Common Council, passed on the seventh day of August, 1835, and shall be signed by the Comptroller, and countersigned by the Mayor.

§ 6. The money so to be loaned by virtue of this ordinance, shall be applied to, and expended for, the erection of buildings, to be known as the Nurseries and the Mad-house, and for the extension of the Lunatic Asylum; and the Comptroller shall keep a separate and distinct account of such money received and paid on account of said stock and buildings.

§ 7. The provisions of the ordinance entitled "An ordinance providing for the redemption of the City Debt, and payment of interest thereon," approved by the Mayor, February 22, 1844, as far as the same can apply to the stock hereby created, shall be applicable to the same.

An Ordinance to create a public fund or stock, to be called "Building Loan Stock No. 2."—(*Passed January* 26, 1849).

The Mayor, Aldermen and Commonalty of the city of New York, in Common Council convened, do ordain as follows:

§ 1. A public fund or stock, to be called "Building Loan Stock No. 2," shall be created for a loan not exceeding fifty thousand dollars, which shall bear an interest not exceeding six per cent. per annum, payable quarterly, and be redeemable on the first day of February, 1856.

§ 2. The said stock shall consist of five hundred shares, and the nominal value of each share shall be one hundred dollars.

§ 3. The Commissioners of the Sinking Fund are hereby authorized to advertise for proposals for the whole or any portion of said stock, and determine which and what proportion of such proposals shall be accepted.

§ 4. The Comptroller shall issue certificates of stock to the person or persons, company or companies, whose proposals shall have been accepted, provided the par value of such stock, together with any premium to be given therefor, shall have been deposited into the city treasury for the account of "Building Loan Stock No. 2."

§ 5. The said certificates shall be made in conformity with the resolution of the Common Council, passed on the seventh day of August, 1835, and shall be signed by the Comptroller, and countersigned by the Mayor.

§ 6. The money so to be loaned by virtue of this ordinance, shall be applied to, and expended for, the extension of the Lunatic Asylum, and for the erection of buildings to be known as the Nurseries and the Madhouse, and other almshouse buildings, including the Penitentiary Hospital; and the Comptroller shall keep a separate and distinct account of such money received and paid on account of said stock and buildings.

§ 7. The provisions of an ordinance entitled "An ordinance providing for the redemption of the City Debt, and the payment of interest thereon," approved by the Mayor, February 22, 1844, as far as the same can be applied to the stock hereby created, shall be applicable to the same.

Of "Washington Square Iron Railing Stock."

An Ordinance to create a public fund or stock, to be called "Washington square Iron Railing Stock."—(*Passed November* 1, 1848.)

The Mayor, Aldermen and Commonalty of the city of New York, in Common Council convened, do ordain as follows:

§ 1. A public fund or stock, to be called "Washington square Iron Railing Stock," shall be created for a loan not exceeding twenty-five thousand dollars, which shall bear an interest not exceeding six per cent. per annum, payable quarterly, and be redeemable as follows, viz: Five thousand dollars in one year; five thousand dollars in two years; five thousand dollars in three years; five thousand dollars in four years; the remaining five thousand dollars in five years; each period to be reckoned from the day on which said stock bears date.

§ 2. The said stock shall consist of two hundred and fifty shares, and the nominal value of each share shall be one hundred dollars.

§ 3. The Commissioners of the Sinking Fund are hereby authorized to sell and dispose of such shares at public auction, or at private sale, or by subscription to such stock, and on such terms as they shall think proper.

§ 4. The Comptroller shall issue certificates of said stock to the party or parties to whom the same shall have been sold, or awarded by the said commissioners, provided the par value of such stock, together with any premium to be given therefor, shall have been deposited into the city treasury, for the account of "Washington square Iron Railing Stock."

§ 5. The said certificates shall be made in conformity with the resolution of the Common Council, passed on the seventh day of August, 1835, and shall be signed by the Comptroller, and countersigned by the Mayor.

§ 6. The moneys so to be raised by virtue of this ordinance, shall be applied and expended to and for the purpose of building or constructing an iron railing around Washington square, in the city of New York; and the Comptroller shall keep a separate and distinct account of the money received and paid on account of said stock and iron railing.

§ 7. The provisions of this ordinance, entitled "An ordinance providing for the redemption of the city debt, and the payment of interest thereon," approved by the Mayor, February 22, 1844, as far as the same can be applied to the stock hereby created, shall be applicable to the same.

Of "The Water Stock of the City of New York."

An Ordinance relative to "The Water Stock of the City of New York."—(*Passed May* 26, 1849).

The Mayor, Aldermen and Commonalty of the city of New York, in Common Council convened, do ordain as follows:

§ 1. A public fund or stock, to be called "The Water Stock of the City of New York, of the year one thousand eight hundred and forty-nine," shall be created for a loan not exceeding two hundred thousand dollars, which shall bear an interest not to exceed five per cent. per annum, payable quarterly, and be redeemable in the year one thousand eight hundred and seventy-five.

§ 2. The said stock shall consist of two thousand shares, and the nominal value of each share shall be one hundred dollars.

§ 3. That the Commissioners of the Sinking Fund are hereby authorized to sell and dispose of such shares at or above the par value thereof, either at public auction or private sale, or to raise the said sum by subscriptions for such stock in the mode in which such stocks are usually subscribed for.

§ 4. The Comptroller shall issue certificates of stock to the person or persons, company or companies, whose proposals shall have been accepted, provided the par value of such stock, together with any premium to be given therefor, shall have been deposited into the city treasury for the account of "The Water Stock of the city of New York of the year one thousand eight hundred and forty-nine."

§ 5. The said certificates shall be made in conformity with the resolution of the Common Council, passed on the seventh day of August, 1835, and shall be signed by the Comptroller, and countersigned by the Mayor.

§ 6. The moneys to be raised by virtue of this ordinance shall be applied and expended to and for the purpose of increasing the supply of water in the city; in the first place, exclusively for the laying of new mains from the Receiving Reservoir to the city, reserving the surplus (if any there shall be) for the future action of the Common Council.

§ 7. All provisions of the law heretofore passed, pledging the faith of the city of New York, and providing a sinking fund for the redemption of the stock issued by virtue thereof, are hereby made applicable to the stock which shall be issued in pursuance of this ordinance, as far as the same can be done.

An Ordinance to create a public stock or fund, to be called "The Water Stock of the city of New York of the year one thousand eight hundred and forty-nine."—(*Passed December* 19, 1849).

The Mayor, Aldermen and Commonalty of the city of New York, in Common Council convened, do ordain as follows:

§ 1. A public stock or fund, to be called "The Water Stock of the city of New York, for the year one thousand eight hundred and forty-nine," shall be created for a loan not exceeding thirty thousand dollars, which shall bear an interest not to exceed five per cent. per annum, payable quarterly, and be redeemable in the year one thousand eight hundred and fifty-five.

§ 2. The said stock shall consist of three hundred shares, and the nominal value of each share shall be one hundred dollars.

§ 3. The Commissioners of the Sinking Fund are hereby authorized to sell and dispose of such shares at or above the par value thereof either at public auction or private sale, or to raise the said sum by subscriptions for such stock, in the mode in which such stocks are usually subscribed for.

§ 4. The Comptroller shall issue certificates of stock to the person or persons, company or companies, whose proposals shall have been accepted, provided the par value of such stock, together with any premium to be given therefor, shall have been deposited in the city treasury for account of "The Water Stock of the city of New York, of the year one thousand eight hundred and forty-nine."

§ 5. The said certificates shall be made in conformity with the resolution of the Common Council, passed on the seventh day of August, 1835, and shall be signed by the Comptroller and countersigned by the Mayor.

§ 6. The moneys to be raised by virtue of this ordinance shall be applied and expended to and for the purpose of increasing the supply of water in the city; in the first place, exclusively for the laying of new mains from the Receiving Reservoir to the city, reserving the surplus (if any there shall be) for the future action of the Common Council.

§ 7. All the provisions of the law heretofore passed, pledging the faith of the city of New York, and providing a sinking fund for the redemption of the stock issued by virtue thereof, are hereby made applicable to the stock, which shall be issued in pursuance of this ordinance, as far as the same can be done.

An Ordinance to create a public stock or fund, to be called "The Water Stock of the city of New York, of the year one thousand eight hundred and forty-nine."—(*Passed December* 9, 1850).

The Mayor, Aldermen and Commonalty of the city of New York, in Common Council convened, do ordain as follows:

§ 1. A public stock or fund, to be called "The Water Stock of the city of New York, of the year one thousand eight hundred and forty-nine," shall be created for a loan not exceeding twenty-five thousand six hundred dollars, which shall bear an interest not to exceed five per cent. per annum, payable quarterly, and be redeemable in the year one thousand eight hundred and seventy-five.

§ 2. The said stock shall consist of two hundred and fifty-six shares, and the nominal value of each share shall be one hundred dollars.

§ 3. The Commissioners of the Sinking Fund are hereby authorized to sell and dispose of such shares at or above the par value thereof, either at public auction or private sale, or to raise the said sum by subscription for such stock, in the mode in which such stocks are usually subscribed for.

§ 4. The Comptroller shall issue certificates of stock to the person or persons, company or companies, whose proposals shall have been accepted, provided the par value of such stock, together with any premium to be given therefor, shall have been deposited in the city treasury, for account of "The Water stock of the city of New York, of the year one thousand eight hundred and forty-nine."

§ 5. The said certificates shall be made in conformity with the resolution of the Common Council, passed on the seventh day of August, 1835, and shall be signed by the Comptroller, and countersigned by the Mayor.

§ 6. The moneys to be raised by virtue of this ordinance shall be applied and expended to and for the purpose of increasing the supply of water in the city of New York; in the first place, exclusively for the laying of new mains from the Receiving Reservoir to the city, reserving the surplus (if any there shall be) for the future action of the Common Council.

§ 7. All the provisions of the law heretofore passed, pledging the faith of the city of New York, and providing a sinking fund for the redemption of the stock issued by virtue thereof, are hereby made applicable to the stock which shall be issued in pursuance of this ordinance, as far as the same can be done.

Of "Building Loan Stock No. 3."

An Ordinance to create a public fund or stock, to be called "Building Loan Stock No. 3."—(*Passed August* 9, 1850).

The Mayor, Aldermen and Commonalty of the City of New York, in Common Council convened, do ordain as follows:

§ 1. A public fund or stock, to be called "Building Loan Stock No. 3," shall be created for a loan not exceeding fifty thousand dollars, which shall bear an interest not exceeding five per cent. per annum, payable quarterly, and shall be redeemable on the first day of November, in the year 1870.

§ 2. The said stock shall consist of five hundred shares, and the nominal value of each share shall be one hundred dollars.

§ 3. The Commissioners of the Sinking Fund are hereby authorized to advertise for proposals for the whole or any portion of said stock, and determine which and what proportion of such proposals shall be accepted.

§ 4. The Comptroller shall issue certificates of stock to the person or persons, company or companies, whose proposals shall have been accepted, provided the par value of such stock, together with any premium to be given therefor, shall have been deposited into the city treasury, for the account of "Building Loan Stock No. 3."

§ 5. The said certificates shall be made in conformity with the resolution of the Common Council, passed on the seventh day of August, 1835, and shall be signed by the Comptroller, and countersigned by the Mayor.

§ 6. The money so to be raised by virtue of this ordinance, shall be applied to, and expended for, the purpose of "building, or erecting a work-house building or buildings," and the Comptroller shall keep a separate and distinct account of such moneys received and paid on account of said stock and buildings.

§ 7. The provisions of an ordinance entitled "An ordinance providing for the redemption of the City Debt, and the payment of interest thereon," approved by the Mayor, February 22, 1844, as far as the same can be applied to the stock hereby created, shall be applicable to the same.

An Ordinance to create a public fund or stock, to be called "Building Loan Stock No. 3."—(*Passed April* 21, 1852).

The Mayor, Aldermen and Commonalty of the City of New York in Common Council convened, do ordain as follows:

§ 1. A public fund or stock, to be called "Building Loan Stock No. 3," shall be created for a loan not exceeding twenty-five thousand dollars, which shall bear an interest not exceeding five per cent. per annum, payable quarterly, and shall be redeemable on the first day of November, in the year 1870.

§ 2. The said stock shall consist of two hundred and fifty shares, and the nominal value of each share shall be one hundred dollars.

§ 3. The Commissioners of the Sinking Fund are hereby authorized to advertise for proposals for the whole or any portion of said stock, and determine which and what proportion of such proposals shall be accepted.

§ 4. The Comptroller shall issue certificates of stock to the person or persons, company or companies, whose proposals shall have been accepted, provided the par value of such stock, together with any premium to be given therefor, shall have been deposited into the city treasury, for the account of "Building Loan Stock No. 3."

§ 5. The said certificates shall be made in conformity with the resolution of the Common Council, passed on the seventh day of August, 1835, and shall be signed by the Comptroller, and countersigned by the Mayor.

§ 6. The money so to be raised by virtue of this ordinance, shall be applied to, and expended for, the purpose of "building, or erecting a work-house building or buildings," and the Comptroller shall keep a separate and distinct account of such moneys received and paid on account of said stock and buildings.

§ 7. The provisions of an ordinance entitled "An ordinance providing for the redemption of the City Debt, and the payment of interest thereon," approved by the Mayor, February 22, 1844, as far as the same can be applied to the stock hereby created, shall be applicable to the same.

Of "Public Building Stock No. 3."

An Ordinance to create a public fund or stock to be called "Public Building Stock No. 3."—(*Passed August* 14, 1851).

The Mayor, Aldermen and Commonalty of the City of New York in Common Council convened, do ordain as follows:

§ 1. A public fund or stock, to be called "Public Building Stock No. 3," shall be created for a loan of one hundred and fifty thousand dollars, which shall bear an interest not exceeding five per centum per annum,

34

payable quarter yearly, and be redeemable as follows: Fifty thousand dollars on the first day of November, 1857; and fifty thousand dollars on the first day of November, 1858; and fifty thousand dollars on the first day of November, 1859.

§ 2. The said stock shall consist of one thousand five hundred shares, and the nominal value of each share shall be one hundred dollars.

§ 3. The Comptroller is hereby authorized to advertise for proposals for the said stock. The proposals so to be received shall be opened in the presence of the Finance Committees of both Boards, and the Comptroller shall determine which and what proportions of such proposals shall be accepted.

§ 4. The Comptroller shall issue certificates of stock to the person or persons, company or companies, whose proposals shall have been accepted, provided the par value of such stock, together with any premiums to be given therefor, shall have been deposited into the city treasury for the account of "Public Building Stock No. 3."

§ 5. The said certificates shall be made in conformity with the resolution of the Common Council, passed on the seventh day of August, 1835, shall be signed by the Comptroller, and countersigned by the Mayor.

§ 6. The money to be loaned by virtue of this ordinance shall be applied to the reimbursing the city treasury the amount expended therefrom, for the erection of public buildings for the city of New York, and to the erection of such additional public buildings as may be required for the use of said city.

§ 7. The provision of the ordinance entitled "An ordinance providing for the redemption of the City Debt and the payment of interest thereon," approved by the Mayor, February 22, 1844, so far as the same can be applied to the stock hereby created, shall be applied to the same.

An Ordinance to create a public fund or stock to be called "Public Building Stock No. 3."—(*Passed May* 20, 1852).

The Mayor, Aldermen and Commonalty of the city of New York, in Common Council convened, do ordain as follows:

§ 1. A public fund or stock, to be called "Public Building Stock No. 3," shall be created for a loan of one hundred and fifty thousand dollars, which shall bear an interest not exceeding five per cent. per annum, payable quarter yearly, and be redeemable as follows: Fifty thousand dollars on the first day of November, 1860; fifty thousand dollars on the first day of November, 1861, and fifty thousand dollars on the first day of November, 1862.

§ 2. The said stock shall consist of one thousand five hundred shares, and the nominal value of each share shall be one hundred dollars.

§ 3. The Comptroller is hereby authorized to advertise for proposals for the said stock; the proposals so to be received, shall be opened in the presence of the Finance Committees of both Boards and the Comptroller, who shall determine which and what proportions of such proposals shall be accepted.

§ 4. The Comptroller shall issue certificates of stock to the person or persons, company or companies, whose proposals shall have been accepted, provided the par value of such stock, together with any premiums to be given therefor, shall have been deposited in the city treasury for the account of "Public Building Stock No. 3."

§ 5. The said certificates shall be made in conformity with the resolution of the Common Council, passed on the seventh day of August, 1835, and shall be signed by the Comptroller, and countersigned by the Mayor.

§ 6. The money to be loaned by virtue of this ordinance shall be applied to the reimbursing the city treasury the amount expended therefrom, for the erection of public buildings for the city of New York, and to the erection of such additional buildings as may be required for the use of said city.

§ 7. The provision of the ordinance entitled "An ordinance providing for the redemption of the City Debt, and the payment of interest thereon," approved by the Mayor, February 22, 1844, so far as the same can be applied to the stock hereby created, shall be applied to the same.

An Ordinance to create a public fund or stock, to be called "Public Building Stock No. 3."—(*Passed September* 26, 1854).

The Mayor, Aldermen and Commonalty of the city of New York in Common Council convened, do ordain as follows:

§ 1. A public fund or stock, to be called "Public Building Stock No. 3," shall be created for a loan of one hundred thousand dollars ($100,000), which shall bear an interest not exceeding five per centum per annum, payable quarter yearly, and redeemable as follows : Fifty thousand dollars on the first day of November, 1863, and fifty thousand dollars on the first day of November, 1864.

§ 2. The stock shall consist of one thousand shares, and the nominal value of each share shall be one hundred dollars.

§ 3. The Comptroller is hereby authorized to advertise for proposals for the said stock ; the proposals so to be received shall be opened in the presence of the Commissioners of the Sinking Fund, who shall determine which and what proportions of such proposals shall be accepted.

§ 4. The Comptroller shall issue certificates of stock to the person or persons, company or companies, whose proposals shall have been accepted, provided the par value of such stock, together with any premiums to be given therefor, shall have been deposited in the city treasury for the account of " Public Building Stock No. 3."

§ 5. The said certificates shall be made in conformity with the resolution of the Common Council, passed on the seventh day of August, one thousand eight hundred and thirty-five, and shall be signed by the Comptroller and countersigned by the Mayor.

§ 6. The money to be raised by virtue of this ordinance shall be applied to the reimbursing the city treasury the amount expended therefrom for the erection of public buildings for the city of New York, and to the erection of such additional buildings as may be required for the use of said city.

§ 7. The provisions of the ordinance entitled " An ordinance providing for the redemption of the City Debt, and the payment of interest thereon ;" approved by the Mayor, February 22, 1844, so far as the same can apply to the stock hereby created, shall be applicable to the same.

An Ordinance to create a public fund or stock, to be called " Public Building Stock No. 3."—(*Passed April* 13, 1855).

The Mayor, Aldermen and Commonalty of the city of New York in Common Council convened, do ordain as follows:

§ 1. A public fund or stock, to be called " Public Building Stock No. 3," shall be created for a loan of one hundred thousand dollars, which shall bear an interest not exceeding five per cent. per annum, payable quarter yearly, and redeemable as follows : Fifty thousand dollars on the first day of November, 1865, and fifty thousand dollars on the first day of November, 1866.

§ 2. The said stock shall consist of one thousand shares, and the nominal value of each share shall be one hundred dollars.

§ 3. The Comptroller is hereby authorized to advertise for proposals for the said stock; the proposals so to be received shall be opened in the presence of the Commissioners of the Sinking Fund, who shall determine which and what proportions of such proposals shall be accepted.

§ 4. The Comptroller shall issue certificates of stock to the person or persons, company or companies, whose proposals shall have been accepted, provided the par value of such stock, together with any premium to be given therefor, shall have been deposited in the city treasury, for the account of "Public Building Stock No. 3."

§ 5. The certificates shall be made in conformity with the resolution of the Common Council, passed on the seventh day of August, 1835, and shall be signed by the Comptroller, and countersigned by the Mayor.

§ 6. The money to be raised by virtue of this ordinance, shall be applied to the reimbursing the city treasury, the amount expended therefrom, for the erection of public buildings for the Corporation of the city of New York, and to the erection of such additional buildings as may be required for the use of said Corporation.

§ 7. The provisions of the ordinance entitled "An ordinance providing for the redemption of the City Debt, and payment of interest thereon," approved by the Mayor, February 22, 1844, so far as the same can apply to the stock hereby created, shall be applicable to the same.

Of "The New York City Five per cent. Stock for Docks and Slips."

An Ordinance to create a public stock or fund, to be called "The New York City Five per cent. Stock, for Docks and Slips."—(*Passed August* 14, 1851.)

The Mayor, Aldermen and Commonalty of the city of New York, in Common Council convened, do ordain as follows:

§ 1. A public fund or stock, to be called "The New York City Five per cent. Stock, for Docks and Slips," shall be created, for a loan of three hundred thousand dollars, which shall bear an interest not exceeding five per cent. per annum, payable quarterly, and redeemable as follows: fifty thousand dollars on the 1st day of November, 1867, fifty thousand dollars on the 1st day of November, 1868, fifty thousand dollars on the 1st day of November, 1869, fifty thousand dollars on the 1st day of November, 1870, fifty thousand dollars on the 1st day of November, 1871, and fifty thousand dollars on the 1st day of November, 1872.

§ 2. The said stock shall consist of three thousand shares, and the nominal value of each share shall be one hundred dollars.

§ 3. The Comptroller is hereby authorized to advertise for proposals for the said stock. The proposals so to be received, shall be opened in the presence of the Finance Committees of both Boards, and the Comptroller shall determine which, and what proportion of such proposals shall be accepted.

§ 4. The Comptroller shall issue certificates of stock to the person or persons, company or companies, whose proposals shall have been accepted, provided the par value of such stock, together with any premium to be given therefor, shall have been deposited into the city treasury, for the account of "The New York City Five per cent. Stock for Docks and Slips."

§ 5. The said certificates shall be made in conformity with the resolution of the Common Council, passed on the seventh day of August, 1835, and shall be signed by the Comptroller, and countersigned by the Mayor.

§ 6. The money to be loaned by virtue of this ordinance shall be applied to, and expended for, the purpose of building and repairing public docks and slips in the city of New York.

§ 7. The provisions of an ordinance entitled "An ordinance providing for the redemption of the city debt, and the payment of the interest thereon," approved by the Mayor, February 22d, 1844, so far as the same can be applied to the stock hereby created, shall be applied to the same.

An Ordinance to create a public stock, or fund, to be called "The New York City Five per cent. Stock for Docks and Slips."—(*Passed May* 20, 1852.)

The Mayor, Aldermen and Commonalty of the city of New York, in Common Council convened, do ordain as follows:

§ 1. A public fund, or stock, to be called "The New York City Five per cent. Stock for Docks and Slips," shall be created for a loan of two hundred thousand dollars, which shall bear an interest, not exceeding five per cent. per annum, payable quarter-yearly, and redeemable as follows: fifty thousand dollars on the first day of November, 1873; fifty thousand dollars on the first day of November, 1874; fifty thousand dollars on the first day of November, 1875, and fifty thousand dollars on the first day of November, 1876.

§ 2. The Comptroller is hereby authorized to advertise for proposals for said stock. The proposals, so to be received, shall be opened in the presence of the Finance Committees of both Boards and the Comptroller, who shall determine which and what proportion of such proposals shall be accepted.

§ 3. The said stock shall consist of two thousand shares, and the nominal value of each share shall be one hundred dollars.

§ 4. The Comptroller shall issue certificates of stock to the person or persons, company or companies, whose proposals shall have been accepted, provided the par value of such stock, together with any premium to be given therefor, shall have been deposited with the City Treasurer, for the account of "The New York Five per cent. Stock for Docks and Slips."

§ 5. The said certificates shall be made in conformity with the resolution of the Common Council, passed on the 7th day of August, 1835, and shall be signed by the Comptroller, and countersigned by the Mayor.

§ 6. The money to be loaned by virtue of this ordinance shall be applied to, and expended for, the purpose of building and repairing docks and slips in the city of New York.

§ 7. The provision of the ordinance entitled "An ordinance providing for the redemption of the city debt, and the payment of interest thereon," approved by the Mayor, February 22, 1844, so far as the same can be applied to the stock hereby created, shall be applied to the same.

Of "Building Loan Stock No. 4."

An Ordinance to create a public stock, or fund, to be called "Building Loan Stock No. 4."—(*Passed May* 12, 1853.)

The Mayor, Aldermen and Commonalty of the city of New York, in Common Council convened, do ordain as follows:

§ 1. A public stock, or fund, to be called "Building Loan Stock No. 4," shall be created, for a loan not exceeding seventy-five thousand dollars, which shall bear an interest not exceeding six per cent. per annum, payable quarterly, and shall be redeemable on the first day of November, 1873.

§ 2. The said stock shall consist of seven hundred and fifty shares; the nominal value of each share shall be one hundred dollars.

§ 3. The Commissioners of the Sinking Fund are hereby authorized to advertise for proposals for the whole or any portion of said stock, and determine which and what proportions of such proposals shall be accepted.

§ 4. The Comptroller shall issue certificates of stock to the person or persons, company or companies, whose proposals shall have been accepted, provided the par value of such stock, together with any premium to be given therefor, shall have been deposited in the city treasury, for the account of "Building Loan Stock No. 4."

§ 5. The said certificates shall be made in conformity with the resolution of the Common Council, passed on the 7th day of August, 1835, and shall be signed by the Comptroller and countersigned by the Mayor.

§ 6. The money to be raised by virtue of this ordinance shall be applied to, and expended for, the purpose of building or erecting the south wing of the new work-house on Blackwell's Island, and the Comptroller shall keep a separate and distinct account of such moneys received and paid on account of said stock and building.

§ 7. The provisions of the ordinance entitled "An ordinance providing for the redemption of the city debt, and payment of interest thereon," approved by the Mayor, February 22d, 1844, so far as the same can apply to the stock hereby created, shall be applicable to the same.

An Ordinance to create a public stock or fund, to be called "Building Loan Stock No. 4."

The Mayor, Aldermen and Commonalty of the City of New York in Common Council convened, do ordain as follows:

§ 1. A public fund or stock, to be called "Building Loan Stock No. 4," shall be created for a loan not exceeding forty thousand dollars, which shall bear an interest not exceeding five per cent. per annum, payable quarter-yearly, and shall be redeemable on the first day of November, 1873.

§ 2. The said stock shall consist of four hundred shares, the nominal value of each share shall be one hundred dollars.

§ 3. The Comptroller is hereby authorized to advertise for proposals for the said stock; the proposals so to be received, shall be opened in the presence of the Commissioners of the Sinking Fund, who shall determine which and what proportions of such proposals shall be accepted.

§ 4. The Comptroller shall issue certificates of stock to the person or persons, company or companies, whose proposals shall have been accepted; provided, the par value of such stock, together with any premium to be given therefor, shall have been deposited in the City Treasury for the account of "Building Loan Stock No. 4."

§ 5. The said certificates shall be made in conformity with the resolution of the Common Council, passed on the seventh day of August, one thousand eight hundred and thirty-five, and shall be signed by the Comptroller, and be countersigned by the Mayor.

§ 6. The money to be raised by virtue of this ordinance shall be applied to, and expended for, the purpose of completing the south wing of the work-house building on Blackwell's Island.

§ 7. The provisions of the ordinance, entitled "An ordinance providing for the redemption of the City Debt, and the payment of interest thereon," approved by the Mayor, February 22, 1844, so far as the same can apply to the stock hereby created, shall be applicable to the same.

Of "The Public Education Stock for the year one thousand eight hundred and fifty-three."

An Ordinance to create a public stock or fund, to be called "The Public Education Stock of the city of New York for the year one thousand eight hundred and fifty-three."—(*Passed March* 9, 1854).

The Mayor, Aldermen and Commonalty of the city of New York, in Common Council convened, do ordain as follows:

§ 1. A public stock or fund, to be called "The Public Education Stock of the city of New York, for the year one thousand eight hundred and fifty-three," shall be created for a loan not exceeding one hundred and fifty-four thousand dollars, which shall bear an interest of five per cent. per annum, and shall be redeemable on the first day of May, one thousand eight hundred and seventy-three.

§ 2. The said stock shall consist of one thousand five hundred and forty shares; the nominal value of each share shall be one hundred dollars.

§ 3. The Commissioners of the Sinking Fund are hereby authorized to advertise for proposals for the whole or any portion of said stock, and determine which, and what proportions of such proposals shall be accepted.

§ 4. The Comptroller shall issue certificates of stock to the person or persons, company or companies, whose proposals shall have been accepted, provided the par value of such stock, together with any premium to be given therefor, shall have been deposited into the city treasury for the account of "Public Education Stock of the city of New York, of the year one thousand eight hundred and fifty-three."

§ 5. The said certificates shall be made in conformity with the resolution of the Common Council, passed on the seventh day of August, 1835, and shall be signed by the Comptroller, and countersigned by the Mayor.

§ 6. The moneys to be raised by virtue of this ordinance shall be applied and expended for the purpose of paying and discharging all the debts of the Public School Society, as certified by the Board of Supervisors, and filed with the Comptroller of the city.

§ 7. The provisions of the ordinance, entitled "An ordinance providing for the redemption of the city debt, and the payment of interest thereon," approved by the Mayor, February 22, 1844, as far as the same can be applied to the stock hereby created, shall be applicable to the same.

Of "The Central Park Fund."

An Ordinance to create funds for the payment of the public place entitled "The Central Park."—(*Passed February* 29, 1856).

The Mayor, Aldermen and Commonalty of the city of New York, in Common Council convened, do ordain as follows:

§ 1. So much of that piece or parcel of land bounded southerly by Fifty-ninth street; easterly by the Fifth avenue; northerly by One hundred and sixth street, and westerly by the Eighth avenue, as is specially described or referred to in the order for the confirmation of the proceedings of the Commissioners of Estimate and Assessment for taking the same, made by the Supreme Court, and dated the fifth day of February, 1856, shall hereafter be known and entitled as "The Central Park."

§ 2. A public stock or fund, to be called "The Central Park Fund," shall be created for a loan of two millions eight hundred and sixty-seven thousand dollars, which shall bear an interest of five per centum per annum, payable half yearly, and shall be redeemable on the first day of July, in the year one thousand eight hundred and ninety-eight.

§ 3. The nominal amount or value of each share of the said stock shall be one hundred dollars, and the same shall consist of twenty-eight thousand and sixty-seven shares; or portions thereof may be of the nominal amount or value of five hundred, or of one thousand dollars, and the number thereof shall be reduced accordingly.

§ 4. The said loan shall be receivable at any time within sixty days from the passage of this ordinance.

§ 5. The Comptroller is hereby authorized and directed to advertise for proposals to be received at any time within thirty days from the passage of this ordinance, and not to be opened until that day, for the said loan, or for any portion thereof, not less than the par value of one share of the said stock.

§ 6. The said Comptroller shall determine, on and after the expiration of said thirty days, which and what proportion of said proposals shall be accepted, and shall issue certificates for the number of shares necessary to make up the said sum of two millions eight hundred and sixty-seven thousand dollars, to the person or persons, company or companies, whose proposals shall have been accepted; and such certificates shall be as nearly as may be in the form of the certificates issued for "The Water Stock of the City of New York."

§ 7. The said Comptroller shall receive the moneys payable for or upon said loan, and shall pay the same into the city treasury, and keep a separate and distinct account of the same, and of all sums paid on account thereof.

§ 8. The said moneys so to be received shall be applied by the said Comptroller in payment of the awards for the lands aforesaid, as confirmed by the order aforesaid of the Supreme Court.

§ 9. For the payment of the balance of said awards, not exceeding the sum of one million six hundred thousand dollars, being the amount assessed for benefit, and by the order aforesaid, of the Supreme Court, a public stock or fund shall be created, which shall bear an interest not exceeding six per cent. per annum, payable half yearly, and shall be redeemable not exceeding three years from the issuing thereof, and shall be called "The Central Park Assessment Fund."

§ 10. The nominal amount or value of each share of the said stock shall be one hundred dollars; or portions thereof may be of the nominal amount or value of five hundred dollars, or of one thousand dollars.

§ 11. The Comptroller is authorized and directed to issue to any person or persons, company or companies, upon receiving the par value thereof, so much of the said stock as may be necessary to pay the balance of the award aforesaid. For the payment of said stock, the assessments for benefit aforesaid, and all moneys payable on account thereof, are hereby specifically pledged. A separate and distinct account shall be kept by the said Comptroller, of all stock thus issued, of all moneys received therefor, and of all moneys received on account of the assessments aforesaid.

§ 12. The said moneys, so to be received, shall be applied by the said Comptroller in payment of the balance aforesaid of the awards aforesaid.

§ 13. For so much of the awards, as are payable to the Mayor, Aldermen and Commonalty of the city of New York, for mortgages upon lands, within said park, now held by the Commissioners of the Sinking Fund, for lots heretofore sold by the said Commissioners, the Comptroller shall issue and deliver to the said Commissioners of the Sinking Fund, the five per cent. stock, described in the second section of this ordinance, for the amount of the mortgages aforesaid, to be held by said Commissioners in lieu of said mortgages, and as security for the redemption of the city debt.

§ 14. The Collector of Assessments is hereby appointed and directed to proceed forthwith in the collection of the assessments.

An Ordinance to raise funds and provide for the purchase of the State Arsenal, and all the grounds appertaining thereto, in the city of New York.—(*Passed June* 17, 1857).

The Mayor, Aldermen and Commonalty of the city of New York, in Common Council convened, do ordain as follows:

§ 1. A public fund or stock, to be called "The Central Park Fund," and to be an addition to the fund thus entitled and heretofore raised for the purpose of paying the awards for the piece of land known and entitled as "the Central Park Fund," shall be created for a loan of two hundred and seventy-five thousand dollars, which shall bear an interest of six per cent. per annum, and shall be redeemable on the first day of July, in the year 1898.

§ 2. The nominal amount or value of each share of the said stock shall be in sums of one hundred, five hundred, or one thousand dollars, as the Comptroller may deem advisable.

§ 3. The Comptroller is hereby authorized and directed to advertise for proposals to be received at any time within thirty days after the passage of this ordinance, and not to be opened until that day, for the said stock or fund, or for any portion thereof, not less than the par or nominal value thereof.

§ 4. The Comptroller shall determine, on and after the expiration of said thirty days, which and what proportion of said subscriptions shall be accepted, and shall issue certificates for the number of shares necessary to make up the said sum of two hundred and seventy-five thousand dollars, to the person or persons. company or companies, whose proposals shall have been accepted, and such certificates shall be, as nearly as may be, in the form of the certificates issued for "The Water Stock of the city of New York."

§ 5. The subscription to the said stock or fund shall be receivable at any time within sixty days after the passage of this ordinance.

§ 6. The Comptroller shall receive the pledges payable for or upon said stock or fund, and shall pay the same into the city treasury, and keep a separate and distinct account thereof, in addition to, and in continuation of, similar subscriptions and payments, for "the Central Park Fund," heretofore issued.

§ 7. The Comptroller shall pay to the Commissioners of the Land Office the said sum of two hundred and seventy-five thousand dollars, as the price or purchase money for the State Arsenal, and all the lands ap pertaining thereto belonging to the state, situated in the city of New York, upon receiving a good and valid deed or conveyance thereof, vesting the same in the Mayor, Aldermen and Commonalty of the city of New York, free from all incumbrances.

An Ordinance to authorize an additional amount of the Central Park Fund, created for the payment of the public place entitled "The Central Park."—(*Passed December* 30, 1858).

The Mayor, Aldermen and Commonalty of the city of New York, in Common Council convened, do ordain as follows:

§ 1. A public stock or fund, to be called "The Central Park Fund," shall be created, for a loan of three hundred and seventy-three thousand four hundred dollars, which shall bear an interest of six per centum per annum, payable quarter yearly, and shall be redeemable on the first day of July, one thousand eight hundred and eighty-seven.

§ 2. The nominal value of each share of the said stock shall be one hundred dollars, and the same shall consist of three thousand seven hundred and thirty-four shares.

§ 3. The Comptroller is hereby authorized to advertise for sealed proposals for a loan of the sum specified in this ordinance, at such time as in his judgment the interests of the Park Fund may require, giving thirty days' notice of all bids to be made for such loan, or any part thereof.

§ 4. The Comptroller shall determine, on and after the expiration of said thirty days, which, and what proportions of said proposals shall be accepted, and shall issue certificates for the aforesaid number of shares, to the person or persons whose proposals shall have been accepted.

§ 5. The Comptroller shall receive all moneys payable for and upon said stock, and shall pay the same into the city treasury, and keep a separate and distinct account thereof, in addition to, and in continuation of similar payments for the Central Park Fund, heretofore issued.

§ 6. The moneys received on account of the said stock shall be paid and applied by the Comptroller as provided by section 12 of an ordinance of the Common Council, entitled "An ordinance to create funds for the payment of the public place, entitled the Central Park," passed February 29, 1856.

An Ordinance to create funds for the payment of the lands acquired for the construction of a new reservoir for Croton water.—*Passed August* 19, 1856.

The Mayor, Aldermen and Commonalty of the city of New York, in Common Council convened, do ordain as follows:

§ 1. The Croton Aqueduct Board, acting in behalf of the Mayor, Aldermen and Commonalty, as provided by chapter 501 of the laws of 1853, having acquired title to all such lands lying between Eighty-sixth and Ninety-sixth streets, and Fifth and Seventh avenues, as they deem desirable, for the construction of a new reservoir, it is hereby declared that all the lands specially described or referred to, in the order for the confirmation of the proceedings of the Commissioners of Appraisal for taking the same, made on the 14th day of April, 1856, shall hereafter be known as the "New Reservoir for Croton Water."

§ 2. A public fund or stock, to be called "The Water Stock of the city of New York, for the year 1854," shall be created for a loan of five hundred thousand dollars, bearing interest at the rate of five per cent. per annum, payable quarter yearly, and the principal shall be redeemable on the first day of October, in the year one thousand eight hundred and seventy-five, as provided by chapter 342 of the laws of 1854.

§ 3. The nominal amount or value of each share of said stock shall be one hundred dollars, and the same shall consist of five thousand shares.

§ 4. The Comptroller is hereby authorized to advertise for proposals, to be received at any time within thirty days from the passage of this ordinance, and not to be opened until that day, for the said loan, or for any portion thereof, not less than the par value of one share of the said stock.

§ 5. The money subscribed on account of the said loan shall be paid into the city treasury, and applied and paid by the Comptroller, as provided by the 4th section, chapter 342 of the laws of 1854.

§ 6. If money cannot be obtained on the stock authorized to be issued under this ordinance, at the rate of interest prescribed in the act authorizing the loan, the Comptroller is hereby authorized to issue the said stock to persons entitled to the payment of awards on the new reservoir; provided such persons will receive the same at par.

An Ordinance to create funds for the improvement of the Central Park.—(*Passed August* 25, 1857).

The Mayor, Aldermen and Commonalty of the city of New York, in Common Council convened, do ordain as follows:

§ 1. A public stock or fund, to be called "The Central Park Improvement Fund," shall be created for a loan of fifty thousand dollars, which shall bear an interest not exceeding seven per centum per annum, payable quarter yearly, and shall be redeemable in thirty years from the issue thereof.

§ 2. The nominal amount or value of each share of the said stock shall be one hundred dollars, and the same shall consist of five hundred shares, or portions thereof may be of the nominal amount or value of five hundred or of one thousand dollars, and the number thereof shall be reduced accordingly.

§ 3. The said loan shall be receivable at any time within sixty days from the passage of this ordinance.

§ 4. The Comptroller is hereby authorized and directed to advertise for proposals, to be received at any time within thirty days from the passage of this ordinance, and not to be opened until that day for the said loan, or for any portion thereof, not less than the par value of one share of the said stock.

§ 5. The said Comptroller shall determine, on and after the expiration of said thirty days, which and what portions of said proposals shall be accepted, and shall issue certificates for the number of shares necessary to make up the said sum of fifty thousand dollars, to the person or persons, company or companies, whose proposals shall have been accepted, and each certificate shall be, or as nearly as may be, in the form of the certificates issued for the water stock of the city of New York.

§ 6. The Comptroller shall receive all moneys payable for, and upon said fund or stock, and shall deposit the same in accordance with the provisions of an act entitled "An act for the regulation and government of the Central Park in the city of New York," passed April 17, 1857.

An Ordinance to provide money for the improvement of the Central Park.—(*Passed November* 9, 1857).

The Mayor, Aldermen and Commonalty of the City of New York, in Common Council convened, do ordain as follows:

§ 1. A public stock or fund is hereby created for an amount, the annual interest of which, with the interest on the stock of said fund already issued under an ordinance authorizing the same, shall not exceed the sum of one hundred thousand dollars, and shall be issued from time to time, in such amounts as the Common Council shall, from time to time, prescribe by ordinance, which stock or fund shall be designated and known as "The Central Park Improvement Fund;" the interest payable half yearly and shall be redeemable in thirty years from the day on which the same is issued.

§ 2. The Comptroller is hereby authorized and directed to advertise, for thirty days, for proposals for the said fund or stock, or any portion thereof, in such amounts, from time to time, as shall be specially ordered by ordinance of the Common Council; but no proposal shall be received for less than the par value of a single share.

§ 3. The said fund or stock shares shall be divided into shares of the nominal par value of one hundred dollars each.

§ 4. Such proposals shall not be opened until the day designated for the opening thereof, in the advertisement therefor; and on and after the expiration of said thirty days, the Comptroller shall determine which, and what proportion of said proposals shall be accepted; and shall issue certificates in form, as nearly as may be of the certificates issued for the Water Stock of the city of New York, for the amount so accepted, and to the person or persons, or corporation or corporations, whose proposals shall have been accepted.

§ 5. The Comptroller shall receive all moneys payable for and upon said fund or stock, and shall deposit the same in accordance with, and for the purposes specified in the provisions of an act entitled "An act for the regulation and government of the Central Park, in the city of New York," passed April 17, 1857.

§ 6. The Comptroller is hereby authorized to issue stock as aforesaid pursuant to this ordinance, in the sum of two hundred and fifty thousand dollars.

35

An Ordinance to provide a further sum for the improvement of the Central Park.—(*Passed June* 24, 1858).

The Mayor, Aldermen and Commonalty of the City of New York in Common Council convened, do ordain as follows:

§ 1. The Comptroller of the city of New York, is hereby ordered and directed to issue of the stock or fund known as the "Central Park Improvement Fund," created by an ordinance of the Common Council, entitled "An ordinance to provide money for the improvement of the Central Park;" approved by the Mayor, November 9, 1857, the further amount of three hundred thousand dollars in conformity with the provisions of the said ordinance.

An Ordinance to provide a further sum for the improvement of the Central Park.—(*Passed Nov.* 12, 1858).

The Mayor, Aldermen and Commonalty of the City of New York, in Common Council convened, do ordain as follows:

§ 1. The Comptroller of the city of New York is hereby ordered and directed, to issue of the stock or fund, known as the "Central Park Improvement Fund," created by an ordinance of the Common Council, entitled "An ordinance to provide money for the Improvement of the Central Park;" approved by the Mayor, November 9, 1857, the further sum of three hundred thousand dollars, in conformity with the provisions of said ordinance.

An Ordinance to provide a further sum for the improvement of the Central Park.—(*Passed May* 13, 1859).

The Mayor, Aldermen and Commonalty of the city of New York, in Common Council convened, do ordain as follows:

§ 1. The Comptroller of the city of New York is hereby ordered and directed to issue of the stock or fund, known as the "Central Park Improvement Fund," created by an ordinance of the Common Council, entitled "An ordinance to provide money for the Improvement of the Central Park;" approved by the Mayor, November 9, 1857, the further sum of three hundred thousand dollars in conformity with the provisions of said ordinance.

An Ordinance to provide a further sum for the improvement of the Central Park.

The Mayor, Aldermen and Commonalty of the city of New York, in Common Council convened, do ordain as follows:

§ 1. The Comptroller of the city of New York is hereby ordered and directed to issue the balance remaining unissued, being the sum of four hundred and sixty-six thousand six hundred and sixty-six dollars and sixty-six cents of the stock or fund, known as the "Central Park Improvement Fund," created by an ordinance of the Common Council, entitled "An ordinance to provide money for the Improvement of the Central Park;" approved by the Mayor, November 9, 1857, in conformity with the provisions of said ordinance. (Approved July 23, 1859.)

An Ordinance to raise one hundred and seventy thousand dollars by loan, and to fund the same for the rebuilding of Tompkins Market, in pursuance of the act of the Legislature, passed April 11, 1856.—(*Passed Feb.* 11, 1858.)

§ 1. A public fund or stock, to be called "Public Stock for Rebuilding Tompkins Market," shall be created by a loan of one hundred and seventy thousand dollars, which shall bear interest at six per centum per annum, payable half yearly, and shall be redeemable as follows: Seventeen thousand dollars on the first day of July, in the year one thousand eight hundred and sixty, and seventeen thousand dollars on the first day of July in each year thereafter, until the whole sum is redeemed.

§ 2. The nominal amount of each share of the said stock, shall be one hundred dollars, and the total of said stock shall consist of seventeen hundred shares; or portions thereof may be of the nominal amount or value of five hundred dollars, or of one thousand dollars, in which case the number of shares shall be reduced accordingly.

§ 3. The Comptroller is hereby authorized and directed to advertise for proposals to be received at any time, within twenty days from the passage of this ordinance, and not to be opened until that day for the said loan, or for any portion thereof, not less than the par value of one share of said stock.

§ 4. The said Comptroller shall determine on and after the expiration of said twenty days, which and what proportions of said proposals shall be accepted, and shall issue certificates for the number of s hares neces sary to make up the said sum of one hundred and seventy thousand dollars, to the person or persoms, company or companies, whose proposals shall have been accepted, and such certificates shall be as nearly as may be in the form of the certificates issued for the Water Stock of the city of New York; and if the same or any part thereof be not taken by such proposal at or above the par value thereof, then the Comptroller is authorized and directed thereafter at any time, to issue to any person or persons, company or companies, upon receiving not less than the par value thereof, the said stock, or so much thereof as may be necessary to make up the said sum of one hundred and seventy thousand dollars.

§ 5. The said Comptroller shall receive the moneys payable for or upon said loan, and shall pay the same into the city treasury, and keep a separate and distinct account of the same, and of all sums paid on account thereof.

§ 6. The said moneys, when received, shall be applied and expended by the said Comptroller in payment of the amounts due, and which may become due, under the contract entered into with Theodore Hunt, on the 31st of December, 1856, for the rebuilding of said Tompkins market, and for any other work and materials, which may be necessary, for the purpose of rebuilding said market, and for no other purpose whatever.

An Ordinance for the issue of Assessment Bonds, for periods not exceeding five years, on account of deficiencies in collecting arrears of assessment.—(*Passed July* 17, 1856.)

The Mayor, Aldermen and Commonalty of the city of New York, in Common Council convened, do ordain as follows:

§ 1. The Comptroller is hereby authorized to borrow, on the credit of the Corporation, from time to time, such amount as may be required to meet the deficiencies caused by delay in collecting arrears of assessments; not exceeding, at any time, the aggregate amount of said arrears then outstanding, as provided by the 18th section of the act, chapter 579, of the laws of 1853.

§ 2. For the payment of the sums thus borrowed, the Comptroller is authorized to issue Assessment Bonds, for such periods as in his judgment may be required to collect the arrearages of assessment, according to the provisions of the laws and ordinances, not exceeding five years;

the said bonds to bear interest at a rate not exceeding six per cent., payable semi-annually.

§ 3. The amount of bonds authorized to be issued by this ordinance, shall be based on the amount of uncollected assessments returned to the Clerk of Arrears; and the sums borrowed on said bonds shall be applied to the payment of claims against the city, growing out of the performance of any work payable by assessment; provided the assessment for such work has been confirmed by the Common Council.

Of " Miscellaneous Debts of the City."

An Ordinance, passed Oct. 3, 1853.

The Mayor, Aldermen and Commonalty of the city of New York, in Common Council convened, do ordain as follows:

§ 1. The Comptroller is hereby required to borrow, by the issue of bonds, authorized by the act entitled " An act to authorize the Mayor, Aldermen and Commonalty of the city of New York to issue Assessment Bonds," passed April 16, 1852, the sum of two hundred thousand dollars.

§ 2. The proceeds of such bonds are hereby appropriated and applied to the payment of two hundred thousand dollars of the amount due to John Pettigrew, on account of work done by him as assignee of the contract, for regulating section C of Second avenue, under an ordinance adopted the 30th September, 1850, providing for the regulating of Secone avenue, from Twenty-eighth to One hundred and twenty-third street.

§ 3. The Comptroller is directed, upon the receipt of the proceeds of said bonds, to pay the same over to John Pettigrew, on account of work done under said ordinance and contract, and to draw his warrant accordingly to the said John Pettigrew, for the said sum of two hundred thousand dollars.

CITY RAILROADS.

Ordinances and Resolutions Relating to the Different Lines of Railroads Running through the Streets of the City.*

Be it ordained, &c., That the grantees of all railroads within the city, their associates and successors, shall, in the construction, alterations and repairs of such railroads, at all times, furnish such new work, make such additions, and do all such repairs to man-hole heads and covers, receiving basins and stop-cocks and covers, and generally of all fixtures connected with sewers, and the distribution of Croton water, as may, in the process of laying down such rail tracks, be affected thereby; such additions, alterations and repairs to be done under the direction of, and to the satisfaction of the Croton Aqueduct Department, and that in no case shall such rail tracks be laid over the line of Croton water mains, stop-cocks, or sewer man-holes.—(*Ord. May* 16, 1853.)

THE HARLEM RAILROAD.

Resolved, That the maps presented by the New York and Harlem Railroad Company, so far as the same locates the route of the said railroad, from the north side of Twenty-third street, through the centre of the Fourth avenue to Harlem river, and the branch of the same through the centre of One hundred and twenty-fifth street, from the Fourth avenue to the Hudson river, be approved, upon condition that neither this approval, nor anything herein contained, shall be construed into a consent to the said Company to construct the said railroad; but that the said Company shall first obtain the consent of the Mayor, Aldermen and Commonalty of the city of New York, before they commence the construction of said road.—(*Resolution, Oct.* 11, 1831.)

A Law to authorize the New York and Harlem Railroad Company to construct their railway.

§ 1. *Be it ordained, &c.,* That the New York and Harlem Railroad Company be, and they are hereby permitted to construct and lay down, in pursuance of their act of incorporation, a double or single track, or

---

* Resolutions as to laying of bridges and others, which do not affect the general regulations of the roads have been omitted. The provisions here incorporated have been inserted as matters of general interest.

railroad or railway along the Fourth avenue, from Twenty-third street to the Harlem river, in conformity with a map now on file in the Register's office, and a branch thereof along One hundred and twenty-fifth street, from the Fourth avenue to the Hudson river, provided that the width of such double railroad or way shall not exceed twenty-four feet.

§ 2. *And be it further ordained,* That if, at any time after the construction of the aforesaid railways, by the said New York and Harlem Railroad Company, it shall appear to the Mayor, Aldermen and Commonalty of the city of New York, that the said railways, or any part thereof, shall constitute an obstruction or impediment to the future regulation of the city, or the ordinary use of any street or avenue of which the said Mayor, Aldermen and Commonalty shall be the sole judges, the said Railroad Company, or the Directors thereof shall, on the requisition of the said Mayor, Aldermen and Commonalty forthwith provide a remedy for the same, satisfactory to the said Mayor, Aldermen and Commonalty, or if they fail to find such remedy, they shall, within one month after such requisition, proceed to remove such railway, or obstruction, or impediment, and to replace the street or avenue in as good condition as it was before the said railway was laid down; and should the said Directors decline or neglect to obey such requisition, the said Mayor, Aldermen and Commonalty may, upon the expiration of the time limited in such notice, cause the obstruction or impediment to be removed, and the avenues or streets restored as aforesaid, at the expense of the said Railroad Company.

§ 3. That the right of regulating the description of power to be used in propelling carriages on and along said railways, and the speed of the same, as well as all other power reserved to the said Mayor, Aldermen and Commonalty by the act of incorporation of the said Company, or any part thereof, be, and the same are hereby expressly retained and reserved.

§ 4. That it shall especially be incumbent on the said New York and Harlem Railroad Company, at their own cost, to construct stone arches and bridges for all the cross streets now or hereafter to be made, (which will be intersected by the embankments or excavations of the said railroad) and which, in the opinion of the Common Council, the public convenience requires to be arched or bridged; and also to make such embankments or excavations as (in the opinion of the Common Council) may be required to make the passage over the railroad and embankments, at the intersected cross streets, easy and convenient for all the purposes for which streets and roads are usually put to, and also that the said Company shall make, at their own like cost and charges, all such drains and sewers as their embankments and excavations may (in the opinion of the Common Council) make necessary, all which work to be done under the like requisition and under like disabilities, as in the second section of this ordinance mentioned; and, further, that the said Company shall make their railroad path from time to time conform to what may hereafter be the regulation of the avenue and road through which said railroad passes.

§ 5. That it shall be incumbent on the said New York and Harlem Railroad Company to commence and complete their said railroad in the respective times allowed for that purpose in their act of incorporation; and unless they commence and complete the same in the periods of time for the said commencement and completion in said incorporation specified, that then the consent of the Common Council, and all the powers and privileges given in this ordinance shall cease and be null and void.

§ 6. That in case the said railrond should not be completed within the times for that purpose in their charter mentioned, or if any time after the construction of the said railroad, the same should be discontinued, or not kept up, and in repair as a good and sufficient railroad, that then the strip of land to be taken for the said railroad should be thrown open and become a part of the street or public avenue, without any assessment on the owners of the adjoining land or the public therefor.

§ 7. That no building shall be erected on the said strip of land to be taken for said railroad; and that a railing or other erections shall be made on the outer edges of the embankments or railroad path, and also such railing or fences on the edges of the excavations as the Common Council shall, from time to time, deem necessary to prevent accidents and loss of lives to our fellow citizens.

§ 8. That this ordinance shall not be considered as binding on the Common Council, nor shall the said ordinance go into effect until the said Harlem Railroad Company shall first duly execute (under their corporate seal) such an instrument in writing (promising, covenanting and engaging on their part and behalf to stand to, abide by, and perform all the conditions and requirements in this ordinance contained) as the Mayor and the Counsel of the Board shall, by their certificate approve, and not until such instrument shall be filed, so certified in the Comptroller's office of this city.—(*Passed Dec.* 22, 1831).

Resolved, That the New York and Harlem Railroad Company be, and are hereby authorized to take possession of the ground owned by the Common Council, over which the line of said railroad is ordered to be constructed, and that they may be permitted to use the same during the continuance of the present charter, for the purpose of a railroad, and that only, and when they cease so to use it, it shall revert to the Corporation; provided always, that said land shall be so used as not to interfere with the use of the cross streets, and on condition, however, that if the said Corporation shall not commence the said railroad, and complete the same within the time limited by their charter, then the privilege hereby granted shall cease and be void.—(*Resolution, Feb.* 1, 1832).

Resolved, That the New York and Harlem Railroad Company be permitted, and the Common Council hereby consent, so far as their rights extend, that the said Company may extend their rails southerly from the north line of Twenty-third street to Prince street, subject, however, to the same conditions and restrictions which the Common Council heretofore imposed upon said Company in respect to that part of the road above Twenty-third street; that the said Company may forthwith proceed to lay down a single track through the Fourth avenue, south of Twenty-third street, Union place, Bloomingdale road and Broadway, and another single track through the Bowery—both as far south as Prince street; and after two months' use of a single track upon the whole distance south of Twenty-third street, on both Broadway and the Bowery, with convenient turnings at the several terminations as above-mentioned they may, unless otherwise directed by the Common Council, lay down a second track on each of the above-mentioned routes; the same to be maintained by the said Company, subject at all times to the regulations of the Common Council, and also subject to the obligation of removing the whole or any part of the railways hereby permitted to be laid down in case the Common Council shall hereafter see fit to require the same; provided, however, that all the said rails shall be laid down in such manner and in such parts of the said streets as shall be approved by the Street Commissioner, so as to cause no impediment to the common and ordinary use of the streets for all other purposes, and that the water-courses of the streets shall be left free and unobstructed, and that the said Company shall pave the streets in and about the rails in a satisfactory and permanent manner, and keep the width of twenty feet of said paving, including the rails in good repairs at all times during the continuance of their use thereof; and, provided further, that if at any time after the said rails shall have been laid down, the Common Council shall deem it necessary, and shall order the said rails to be taken up, the said Railroad Company shall cause the pavement of the streets to be placed in good and sufficient repair ; and, provided further, that the said Company have their single rail tracks above-mentioned completed on or before the first day of May, 1834, and that they are to charge and receive such tolls, rates or fare for the carrying of passengers or effects upon the said rail tracks south of Twenty-third street, as the said Common Council may prescribe.

Resolved, That the above resolution shall not be considered as binding on the Common Council, nor shall the same go into effect until the said Harlem Railroad Company shall first duly execute, under their corporate seal, such an instrument in writing, promising, covenanting and agreeing on their part and behalf to stand to, abide and perform all the conditions and provisions in the said resolution contained as the Mayor and the Counsel of the Board shall approve of by a certificate under their hands, nor until such instrument shall be filed, so certified in the Comptroller's office of this city.—(*Resolution, May* 10, 1832).

Resolved, That the New York and Harlem Railroad Company be permitted, and the Common Council hereby consent, so far as their rights extend, that the New York and Harlem Railroad Company may continue their rails by single or double track southerly, from the north line of Prince street to the north line of Walker street, subject to the same conditions and restrictions which the Common Council heretofore imposed upon the said Company in respect to that part of the said road between Prince street and Twenty-third street, as provided by the ordinances of the Common Council, May 20, 1832.— (*Resolution, May* 4, 1837).

Resolved, That the New York and Harlem Railroad Company be permitted, and the Common Council hereby consent, that the said Company may continue their rails similar to those laid between Thirteenth and Fourteenth streets by a double track from the Bowery through Broome street to Centre street, and from Broome street through Centre street to Chatham street, subject to the same conditions and restrictions which the Common Council heretofore imposed upon the said Company.

Resolved, That when such rails shall be laid through Centre and Broome streets, the said Company shall cause so much of the rails as are laid in the Bowery south of Broome street, to be removed, and the street repaved under the direction of the Street Commissioner.—(*Resolution, May* 4, 1838.

Resolved, That the New York and Harlem Railroad Company be authorized to lay down rails in Canal street, from their road in Centre street, to a point seventy-five feet east of Broadway, to enable them to afford the increased accommodation for the public, which may be required by the extension of their own road, and by their connection with the New York and New Haven Railroad Company, and for the purpose of establishing a depot for passengers to and from the New York and New Haven Railroad, with permission to cross the sidewalk from the rail tracks into any premises which either of said companies may become the lessees or owners of, all of which to be under the direction of the Street Commissioner, the privileges hereby granted to be enjoyed by said company during the pleasure of the Common Council.—(*Res., Nov.* 15, 1848).

Resolved, That the New York and Harlem Railroad Company be, and they are hereby authorized to take up their double track, from the corner of Grand and Centre streets, to the Bowery, and lay down a single track in the centre of the street, from the corner of Grand street, through Centre and Broome streets to the Bowery; down the Bowery to Grand street, and through Grand street to Centre street, under the direction of the Street Commissioner.—(*Res. Sept.* 13, 1850).

Resolved, That the New York and Harlem Railroad Company be, and they are hereby authorized to lay groove rails in a permanent manner, for a single track, on the westerly side of Chatham street, from the present terminus at Centre street, to the southerly end of the Park, with a turn-out, as shown on a profile on the petitions hereunto attached, for the exclusive use and purpose of running their city line of small passenger cars upon, to that point, subject to the pleasure and order of the Common Council; that when the Common Council may, or shall hereafter, order the said track to be taken up, the Company shall comply therewith at once, and that said Company shall, before said track is laid, execute to the city an agreement to comply therewith at once, when ordered, and that they will not run any but small passenger cars thereon, and that the Comptroller be charged with the preparation and execution of said agreement; said track to be laid under the direction of the Street Commissioner, provided that the said Company shall grade the street through which the said rails shall be laid, at their own expense, and keep the same in repair; that all ordinances heretofore passed relative to the said Company, shall not be deemed to be in any way repealed by such permission hereby granted, except so far as the same conflicts therewith. And that said rails shall not be laid within a distance of twenty feet of the cross walk at the corner of Broadway and the southern end of the Park.—(*Res. Feb.* 6, 1851).

Resolved, That no locomotive or steam engine be allowed to run on the tracks of the Harlem or New Haven Railroad Company, on Fourth avenue, south of Forty-second street, eighteen months after the passage of this ordinance.—(*Res., Dec.* 27, 1854).

Resolved, That the Harlem Railroad Company be directed to station a flagman at the corner of the Bowery and Broome street, for the purpose of warning pedestrians and those persons driving vehicles, of the nigh approach of the rail cars, as they turn the corner of the said Bowery and Broome street.—(*Resolution, Feb.* 3, 1857).

Resolved, That the Harlem Railroad Company be directed to place a flag-man at the corner of Pearl and Centre streets for the protection of persons crossing said streets.—(*Resolution, Feb.* 10, 1857).

Resolved, That the Harlem Railroad Company be, and they are hereby directed to cause their small cars to be run on their track to Forty-second street, as often and as regularly as they are now run between Twenty-seventh street and Park Row, the said Company to commence running small cars as aforesaid, within four months after the approval of this resolution by his Honor the Mayor.—(*Resolution, July* 12, 1858).

Be it Ordained, &c.

§ 1. The New York and Harlem Railroad Company is hereby authorized. empowered and permitted to use steam in the drawing of their passenger and freight cars upon their railroad, on the Fourth avenue, to and from the northern extremity of Manhattan, or New York Island, to the south side of Forty-second street, and to permit the use thereof by the New York and New Haven Railroad Company to the same point, with turn-outs to the engine houses respectively, for a period of thirty years from the passage of this ordinance.

§ 2. Until the completion of their new machine shops, at or above Forty-second street, the New York and Harlem Railroad Company shall be permitted to run their engines with steam, for repairs only, but without any car, truck or other vehicle attached, to and from their present machine shop at Thirty-second street; but such permission shall not extend, in any event, beyond a period of eighteen months from the date of this ordinance.

§ 3. The New York and Harlem Railroad Company are hereby authorized to lay down a double track or railway from their track in the Fourth avenue, at Forty-second street, up said street to Madison avenue, and up Madison avenue to Seventy-ninth street, or as far as it may, from time to time be opened, for the use of their small cars only.

§ 4. The said company is hereby authorized to lay down in the Fourth avenue, between Forty-second and Fiftieth streets, two additional tracks for the use of themselves and the New York and New Haven Railroad Company, to enable them to land and receive their passengers, and may cover that portion thereof which extends from Forty-second to Forty-fourth street, by a neat ornamental roof or shed, to be first approved by the Mayor of the city of New York; and that the sidewalks opposite to said building be reduced to sixteen feet on each side of said avenue in front of the premises of said railroad company.

§ 5. The New York and Harlem Railroad Company shall forthwith complete the title of the Corporation of the city of New York, to the strip of ground twenty feet wide, between Thirty-third and Thirty-fourth streets, on the west side of the Fourth avenue, and also to the strip of ground twenty feet wide, between Thirty-second and Thirty-third streets, agreed by them to be conveyed to the city; and shall, within six months from this date, remove their engine house at Thirty-second street from said last-mentioned strip of land.

§ 6. In the case the New York and Harlem Railroad Company shall fail to carry out in good faith the provisions of the second and fifth sections of this ordinance, within the times in said sections respectively limited, the privileges hereby granted shall cease and determine, and this ordinance shall be null and void.—(*Ordinance, December* 31, 1858.)

THE HUDSON RIVER RAILROAD.

The Mayor, Aldermen and Commonalty of the City of New York, in Common Council convened, do ordain as follows:

§ 1. Permission is hereby granted to the Hudson River Railroad Company to construct a double track of rails, with suitable turn-outs along the line of the Hudson River, from Spuyten Devil Creek to near Sixty-eighth street; occupying so much of the Twelfth avenue as lies along the shore, thence winding from the shore so as to intersect the Eleventh avenue, at or near Sixtieth street; thence through the middle of the Eleventh avenue to about Thirty-second street; thence on a curve across to the Tenth avenue, intersecting the Tenth avenue at or near Thirtieth street; thence through the middle of the Tenth avenue to West street, and thence through the middle of West street to Canal street.

§ 2. The said Hudson River Railroad Company shall grade, regulate, pave and keep in repair a space twenty-five feet in width, in and about the tracks, in all the avenues and streets through which the said track or tracks shall be laid, whenever the Common Council shall deem the interest of the public to require such pavement to be done. The said company shall lay such rail track through the avenues and streets in conformity to such directions as to line and grade as shall be given by the Street Commissioner, and shall conform their said railroad to the grades of the avenues and streets through which it shall extend, or cross, as shall be from time to time established by the Common Council, if the latter so require; and shall lay their rails or tracks in the streets or avenues, in such manner as to cause no unnecessary impediment to the common and ordinary use of the street for all other purposes, and so as to leave all the water courses free and unobstructed. It shall be especially incumbant on the said Hudson River Railroad Company, at their own cost, to construct stone bridges across such of the streets intersected by the railroad as may, by the elevation of their grades above the surface of said road, require to be arched or bridged, whenever, in the opinion of the Common Council, the same shall be necessary for public convenience; and also to make such embankments or excavations as the Common Council may deem necessary to render the passage over the railroad and embankments at the cross streets easy and convenient for all the purposes for which streets and roads are usually put to; and the said company shall also make, at their own cost and charge, all such drains and sewers, as their embankments or excavations may, in the opinion of the Common Council, render necessary; and said company shall be at all times subject to such regulations, with reference to the convenience of public travel through such streets and avenues as are affected by the said railroad, as the Common Council shall, from time to time, by resolution or ordinance, direct; and the Corporation hereby reserves the right to require said company, at any time after the Eleventh avenue shall be made to Fourteenth street, to take up their rails in the Tenth avenue, and lay them in the Eleventh avenue to said Fourteenth street, and through Fourteenth street to connect with West street.

§ 3. The said company shall, within one year from the passage of this ordinance, and before entering upon any contracts for grading, file in the office of the Street Commissioner a map showing the location and intended grade of said railroad.

§ 4. Permission is hereby granted to the Hudson River Railroad Company to run their locomotives as far south as Thirtieth street, and no farther.

§ 5. The said Hudson River Railroad Company shall be and are hereby prohibited from running a stated train between any points below Thirty-second street, for the carrying of passengers between those points, under the penalty of twenty-five dollars for each passenger from whom fare shall be received therefor.

§ 6. This ordinance shall not be construed as binding upon the Corporation, nor shall it go into effect, until the said Hudson River Railroad Company shall first duly execute, under their corporate seal, such an instrument in writing, covenanting and engaging, on their part and behalf, to stand to, abide by, and perform all such conditions and requirements contained in the second and third sections of this ordinance, as the Mayor and the Counsel to the Corporation shall by their certificate approve, and not until such instrument shall be filed, so certified, in the office of the Comptroller of this city.—*Ordinance May* 6, 1847.

Resolved, That the Hudson River Railroad Company be authorized to lay down a double track of rails, with suitable curves and turn-outs, from the northerly line of Canal street, at West street, through Canal and Hudson streets to Chambers street, under the direction of the Street Commissioner, and subject to all the restrictions, obligations, provisions and conditions of the ordinance authorizing said company to lay down rails to Canal street.—(*Res. Sept.* 25, 1849.)

Resolved, That the Hudson River Railroad Company may extend one of their tracks around the country market, (leased to them at foot of Canal street,) with suitable curves and turn-outs, under the direction of the Street Commissioner, so as to connect with the track on West and Canal streets, already constructed by them, subject to all the terms, conditions and restrictions of the annexed resolution passed and approved as stated below. See resolution approved September 25, 1849. (*Res. January* 7, 1850).

Resolved, That the Hudson River Railroad Company be, and they are hereby permitted to propel their cars from Chambers street to Thirty-first street, by their street locomotive, or "Dumb Engine," upon the condition that the same shall not be run at a greater speed than six miles an hour; and also, that they shall employ a proper person to precede the trains on horseback, to give necessary warning, in a suitable manner, of their approach, and be under such further directions as the Common Council may, from time to time, prescribe.—(*Res. December* 4, 1850.)

Resolved, That the Hudson River Railroad Company be directed to take up their rails, and relay them, so that at the southwest corner of Tenth avenue and Thirtieth street they shall be distant from the angle of the curb at least twelve feet.—(*Res. August* 11, 1851).

Resolved, That the Hudson River Railroad Company be, and are hereby required to remove the present high rail in use upon their road, from the corner of Chambers street and West Broadway, up to Fifty-third street, and to lay down in the stead thereof, the rail known as the grooved rail, and that the same be done within six months from the passage of this resolution by the Common Council.

Resolved, That the Hudson River Railroad Company be, and they are hereby authorized and directed to place upon their road, city passenger or small cars, to be run between the depot at Chambers street and Fifty-third street; to take up and set down city passengers between those points; to be governed by the general rules regulating the Eighth Avenue Railroad; and, further, that they run a car thereon each and every day, both ways, as often as every fifteen minutes, from 5 to 6 o'clock, A. M., and every five minutes, from six o'clock, A. M., to 8 o'clock, P. M.; every fifteen minutes, from 8 o'clock, P. M., to 12 o'clock, P. M.; and every thirty minutes, from 12 o'clock, P. M., to five o'clock, A. M. and as much oftener as public convenience may require, under the regulations of the Common Council; and that the said company shall have the right to demand, and receive, from each passenger conveyed in said cars, the sum of five (5) cents, and no more. The aforesaid cars to be placed and run upon said road within six months from the passage of this resolution by the Common Council. It being a special provision and understanding, in making this grant to the Hudson River Railroad Company, that the said company shall not, at any time, either directly or indirectly, in any way alienate from themselves, as a company, or in any manner dispose of the right to run small cars upon their said road hereby granted, unless by consent of the Common Council, under the penalty of the forfeiture of this grant, immediately thereupon.

Resolved, That the Hudson River Railroad Company be, and they are hereby directed to cease the running of locomotives or steam engines below Fifty-third street, immediately upon the small cars being placed upon their road, in accordance with the foregoing resolution.—(*Res. Dec.* 13, 1858).

THE NEW HAVEN RAILROAD.

Resolved, That the block of ground bounded by Centre, Franklin, Elm, and White streets, be leased to the New York and New Haven Railroad Company, for the term of twenty-one years, (the arsenal buildings on Elm and Franklin streets to remain for the use of the military until May 1st, 1851,) at an annual rent of six thousand dollars, payable quarterly, together with the taxes and assessments on the same, with covenants for renewal at the expiration of twenty-one years, at a rent to be fixed by appraisement. The said company to improve the said premises within one year, from the date of their lease. Said premises to continue during said leases for a railroad depot, and the Comptroller is hereby directed to have a lease executed in accordance with this resolution, provided that nothing therein contained shall be construed or taken as a consent or assent on the part of the Corporation of the city of New York, to the use by the said railroad company, of any of the streets and avenues of said city, for the purpose of running cars thereon, by virtue of an agreement with the Harlem Railroad Company, or as a waiver of the right and power of the Common Council of said city, to regulate and control the said New York and New Haven Railroad Company, to the same extent it can now control the New York and Harlem Company.—(*Res. Sept.* 5, 1850.)

Resolved, That the Harlem and New Haven Railroad Companies shall station a man on the north-west corner of Grand street and the Bowery, to warn persons coming down the Bowery on foot, or in vehicles, of the near approach of the cars, toward the corner of Grand street and the Bowery.—(*Res. Feb.* 15, 1853.)

SIXTH AND EIGHTH AVENUE RAILROADS.

Resolved, That the persons to whom permission is granted by the following resolutions, and those who may hereafter become associated with them, have the authority and consent of the Common Council to lay a double track for a railroad in the following streets, viz: From a point at the intersection of Chambers street and West Broadway; thence along West Broadway to Canal street; thence along and down Canal street to Hudson street; along Hudson street and Eighth avenue, to a point at or near Fifty-first street; and that said railroad be continued through the Eighth avenue to Harlem river, whenever required by the

Common Council, and as soon and as fast as said avenue is graded, upon the following stipulations and conditions, viz: Such track or tracks to be laid under the direction of the Street Commissioner, and on such grades as are now established, or may hereafter be established by the Common Council, the said parties to become bound in a sufficient penalty, to keep in good repair the space between the track and the space outside the same, on either side, of at least eight feet in width, of each street in which the rails are laid, and also that no motive power, excepting horses, be used below Fifty-first street; and upon the further condition that said parties shall place new cars on said railroad, with all the modern improvements for the convenience and comfort of passengers, and that they run cars thereon each and every day, both ways, as often as the public convenience may require, under such directions as the Street Commissioner and Common Council may, from time to time, prescribe; and provided also, that the said parties shall, in all respects, comply with the direction of the Street Commissioner, and of the Common Council, in the building of said railroad, and in the running of the cars thereon, and in any other matter connected with the regulation of said railroad; and provided also, that the said parties shall, before this permission takes effect, enter into a good and sufficient agreement with the Mayor, Aldermen and Commonalty of the city of New York, to be drawn and approved of by the Counsel to the Corporation, binding themselves to abide by, and perform the stipulations and provisions herein contained; and also all such other resolutions or ordinances as may be passed by the Common Council relating to the said road; and further, that they run a car thereon each and every day, both ways, as often as every fifteen minutes, from 5 to 6 o'clock, A. M.; every four minutes from 6 o'clock, A. M. to 8 P. M.; every fifteen minutes, from 8 P. M. to 12 P. M.; and every thirty minutes, from 12 P. M. to 5 A. M.; and as much oftener as public convenience may require, under such directions as the Common Council may, from time to time, prescribe; also, that the rate of passage on said railroad shall not exceed a greater sum than five cents for the entire length of said road; and also, that the Common Council shall have the power to cause the same, or any part thereof, to be taken up at any time they may see fit; and also, that the said parties, or either of them, shall not assign their interest in the said road, without first obtaining the consent of the Common Council thereto; also, that such track or tracks shall be laid upon a foundation of concrete, with a grooved rail, or such other rail as may be approved of by the Street Commissioner, even with the surface of the streets through which they may pass, and shall be commenced within three months, and completed to Fifty-first street within one year, and from Fifty-first street to the Harlem river, within three years from the passage of this resolution; also, that the foundation on each side of the rails shall be paved with square grooved blocks of stone, similar to the Russ pavement, as far up as Fifty-first street; that the said parties are to keep an account of the receipts of each road monthly, and report the same to the Comptroller monthly, under oath; that the said parties shall connect their road with such other roads as the Common Council may order to be connected therewith; that they shall file with the Comptroller a statement, under oath, of the cost of each mile of road completed, and agree to surrender, convey and transfer the said road to the Corporation of the city of New York, whenever required so to do, on payment, by the Corporation of the cost of said road, as appears by said statements, with ten per cent. advance thereon; that said parties, on being required at any time by the Corporation, and to such extent as the Common Council shall determine, shall take up, at their own expense said rails, or such part thereof as they shall be required, and in failure so to do, in ten days after such requirement, the same may be done, at their expense, by the Street Commissioner.

Resolved, That the persons to whom permission is granted by the following resolutions, have the authority and consent of the Common Council, to lay a single track in the following streets: Commencing at the corner of Chambers street and West Broadway, through Chambers street to Church street; through Church street to Canal street; and through Canal street to Wooster street; through Wooster street to Fourth street; thence, with a double track, through Fourth street and Sixth avenue to Harlem; also, to lay a single track in Thompson street, from Canal to Fourth street, to connect with the Eighth Avenue Railroad, and extend the same up the Sixth avenue to Harlem river, whenever required by the Common Council, and as soon and as fast as said avenue is graded sufficiently to permit such track to be laid, upon the same terms, stipulations and conditions as are provided in the annexed resolution in relation to the railroad in the Eighth avenue, except that no motive power except horses shall be used below Forty-second street; that said railroad upon the Sixth avenue shall be commenced within three months, and completed to Forty-second street within one year; and from Forty-second street to the Harlem river within three years from the passage of this resolution; also, that the foundation on each side of the rails, shall be paved with square grooved blocks of stone, similar to the

Russ pavement, as far up as Thirty-second street, and that such parts of the Eighth Avenue road, as may be used by the Sixth Avenue Road, from the connection in Canal street and West Broadway to Chambers street, shall be built at the joint expense of said Sixth and Eighth Avenue Roads.

Resolved, That each of said passenger cars, to be used on said road, shall be annually licensed by the Mayor; and there shall be paid annually for such license such sum as the Common Council may hereafter determine.

Resolved, That the permission granted to lay or build a railroad track in the following streets, viz: From a point at the intersection of West Broadway and Chambers street, thence through West Broadway to Canal street, down Canal street to Hudson street, along Hudson street and Eighth avenue to Harlem river, be granted and given to John Pettigrew, Edmund R. Sherman, Solomon Kipp, Abrm. Brown, Washington Smith, Joseph N. Barnes, O'Keefe & Duryea, and Marshalls & Townsend.

Resolved, That the permission granted to lay or build a railroad, in the following streets, viz: Commencing at a point at the intersection of West Broadway and Chambers street, thence through Chambers street to Church street, through Church street to Canal street, and through Canal street to Wooster street, through Wooster street to Fourth street, with a single track; thence through Fourth street to Sixth avenue, and through Sixth avenue to Harlem, with a double track; also to lay a single track in Thompson street, from Fourth street to Canal street, to connect with the Eighth Avenue Railroad, be given to James S. Libby, George R. Howell, William Flagg, William H. Adams, John Post, jr., Edmund Morris, Matthew D. Greene, John Ridley, Wm. Ebbitt, Ward Bolster & Jacacks, and Finch, Sanderson & Beers.—(*Resolution, July* 30, 1851.)

Resolved, That the Eighth Avenue Railroad Company have authority, and the privilege is hereby granted to them, to extend their rail (which is to be constructed in like manner as their present,) through Canal street to Broadway, and also from its present termination at Chambers street through College place to Barclay street, and through Barclay and Church streets, or across Barclay street, and through the buildings which they have rented or procured, or may rent or procure for that purpose, to and into Vesey street; through Vesey street to Broadway, and through Church street, from Vesey street to Chambers street, and through Chambers street to its present termination aforesaid, and to run their cars over the same; and when they shall have made such extension then and thereafter, they shall be at liberty to charge every passenger who may come to and ride any distance upon any part of their road below Fifty-first street, five cents for riding on that part of their road; any thing in the resolutions or agreement under which the said company are now acting inconsistent with any of the privileges granted by this resolution, is hereby modified, so as to conform thereto.

And also resolved, That the Sixth Avenue Railroad Company, upon paying to the said the Eighth Avenue Railroad Company, the one-half part of the cost of that portion of their road lying between Varick street and West Broadway, and of keeping it in repair, from time to time, hereafter; and also, the one-half of the costs and of the repairs, from time to time, of the extensions above authorized, shall be at liberty to use and own one-half of the same, and run their cars thereon, and to charge every passenger who may come to ride any distance upon any part of their road below Forty-third street, the like sum of five cents for riding on that part of the road, and any thing in the resolutions or agreement under which they are now acting inconsistent with the said privileges is hereby modified, so as to conform to this resolution.—(*Resolution, Dec.* 13, 1852).

Resolved, That the route of the Sixth Avenue Railroad be, and the same is hereby changed from the present location, so as to run as follows, viz: Commencing at the intersection of Chambers street and West Broadway, running thence with a double track through West Broadway to Canal street, through Canal street to Varick, through Varick street to Carmine street, through Carmine street and the Sixth avenue to intersect with the original grant of the Sixth Avenue Railroad Company.

Resolved, That the portion of said railroad track to be laid down in West Broadway, from Chambers street to Canal street, shall be built jointly by the Sixth and Eighth Avenue Railroad Companies; and, in the event of either party refusing, or neglecting to unite in the construction of such portion of the road, or pay for their proportionate share of the expense thereof, then it shall be competent for either of said parties to proceed with the work, at their own expense, and for their exclusive benefit, until the other party shall actually pay their proportion of such expense; further, should any difficulty arise between said Sixth and Eigth Avenue Railroad Companies, as to the cost and value of building said road, and rights to run over the same, each party shall have the privilege to select a referee, not interested in any wise in either of said roads, to adjust all difficulties; but, should said referees not be able to make a proper and amicable settlement of any dispute, arising between the parties hereinbefore mentioned, then it shall be competent for the Common Council to select a third person as referee, who shall investigate the subject matter in dispute, and a decision from a majority of said referees shall be final and conclusive; nothing, however, contained in this resolution, shall be construed to interfere with the power and authority of the Common Council to prescribe rules and regulations, from time to time, for the control and management of said railroad.—(*Resolution, June*, 1852).

Whereas, A resolution has passed the Common Council, and which resolution was permitted to become a law, by the non-action of the Mayor, authorizing the Sixth and Eighth Avenue Railroad Companies to extend their road through College place to and across Barclay street, or through Barclay or Vesey street to Broadway, and to return through Church street, to and through Chambers street to its present termination; and

Whereas, It was the understanding, although not specified in the resolution, that said extension should, and was to be only with a single track, yet, the said Eighth Avenue Railroad Company is now engaged in constructing said road with a double track, which will have the effect to shut out from said street all other travel, and be a serious detriment to the interests of the citizens generally, and to the owners of property on the line especially; and, as there seems to be a very serious misunderstanding as to whether there should be constructd a single or a double track; therefore, be it

Resolved, That the Street Commissioner be, and he is hereby directed to cause all further proceedings of said companies, in the construction of said roads through the streets mentioned in the preamble, to be stayed and suspended until the further action of the Common Council, except they build a single track only through said streets; and if that course be not adopted by said companies, that then the said Street Commissioner be, and he is hereby directed to have said streets restored to their former condition, without delay.—(*Resolution, Dec.* 21, 1852).

Whereas, A resolution was passed by the Common Council, on the 21st of December last, by which the Street Commissioner was directed to cause all proceedings on the part of the Sixth and Eighth Avenue

Railroad Companies, in the construction of the extension of their railroads to be, in part, suspended; and

Whereas, The state of the streets, during the last summer, interrupted the travel through Church street, and it now sufficiently appears, that the public convenience, and the wishes of the citizens require some modification of the said resolution, and the laying of tracks, so that a continuous travel can be had, although interruptions and obstructions may happen to occur in Church street, as before mentioned; therefore, it is

Resolved, That the aforesaid resolution be, and the same is hereby rescinded and revoked, and the said companies are hereby authorized and directed to complete the said extensions, and make the connections between the parts thereof, and with the other portion of their road, as the same was begun and unfinished, when the said resolution was passed; the said company shall not lay a double track lengthwise, through Chambers street, Church street, Barclay street or Vesey street.—(*Resolution, Dec.* 31, 1853).

Resolved, That the President, Directors and Company of the Eighth Avenue Railroad be, and they are hereby directed, for the better accommodation of the public, to run their cars, daily, from and to Fifty-ninth street and Eighth avenue, the present terminus of the rails they have already laid, instead of, as they now run, from and to Fifty-first street and Eighth avenue.—(*Resolution Nov.* 30, 1853).

Resolved, That the resolution adopted by this Board, November 21, 1853, directing the Eighth Avenue Railroad to run their cars to Fifty-ninth street, be modified, and so amended as to direct them to run a car once in every twenty minutes during the day, until otherwise directed.—(*Resolution Dec.* 29, 1853).

Resolved, That the Eighth Avenue Railroad Company be, and are hereby directed to run their accommodation cars from Fifty-second to Fifty-ninth street, every ten minutes, so as to start a car every ten minutes, from Fifty-second street up to Fifty-ninth street, and a car every ten minutes, from Fifty-ninth street down to Fifty-second street, daily, from five o'clock, A. M. to ten o'clock, P. M.—(*Resolution, July* 12, 1854).

Resolved, That the Eighth Avenue Railroad Company be, and they are hereby directed to relay the track of said railroad, and to run their cars from Fifty-first street to the junction of Eighth avenue and Broadway, and that said company run their cars from Fifty-first street to Fifty-ninth street, every five minutes, and the Street Commissioner is hereby authorized and directed to carry this resolution into effect.—(*Resolution, Dec.* 20, 1855.

THIRD AVENUE RAILROAD.

1. *Resolved,* That Myndert Van Schaick, Horace M. Dewey, John B. Dingledein, John Murphy, James W. Flynn, James McElvaney, Patrick McElroy, Thomas Murphy, Philip Reynolds, Elijah F. Purdy, Bryant McCahill, George Caplin, Oscar F. Benjamin, and those who may hereafter become associated with them, have the authority and consent of the Common Council, and permission is hereby granted to them to lay a double track for a railroad in the following streets :

From a point at the intersection of Park row and Broadway, near the south-westerly corner of the Park ; thence along Park row to Chatham street ; thence along Chatham street to the Bowery ; thence along the Bowery to the Third avenue, and thence along the Third avenue to the Harlem river, upon the following conditions, viz :

Such track or tracks to be laid under the direction of the Street Commissioner, and on such grades as are now established, or may hereafter be established by the Common Council ; the said parties to become bound in a sufficient penalty to keep in good repair the space inside the tracks, and a space two feet each side of the same, of each street in which the rails are laid ; and also that no steam power be used on any part of the road for propelling cars, and upon the further condition that said parties shall place new cars on said railroad, with all the modern improvements, for the convenience and comfort of passengers, and that they run cars thereon, each and every day, both ways, and as often as the public convenience may require, under such prudential directions as the Common Council and the Street Commissioner may, from time to time prescribe ; and

Provided also, That the said parties shall, in all respects, comply with the directions of the Common Council, in the building of the said railroad, and in any other matter connected with the regulation of said railroad ; and

Provided also, That the said parties shall, before this permission takes effect, enter into a good and sufficient agreement with the Mayor, Aldermen and Commonalty of the city of New York, to be drawn and approved of by the Counsel to the Corporation, binding themselves to abide by and perform the stipulations and provisions herein contained ; and also all such other resolutions or ordinances as may be passed by the Common Council, relating to the running of said cars over the said road ; and

Further, That they run a car thereon, each and every day, both ways, as often as every fifteen minutes, from 5 to 6 o'clock, A. M.; every four minutes, from 6 o'clock, A. M., to 8, P. M.; every fifteen minutes, from 8, P. M., to 12, M., and as much oftener as public convenience may require, under such directions as the Common Council, may, from time to time, prescribe; also,

That the said passage on said railroad shall not exceed a greater sum than five cents for any distance, between the southern point of said railroad, and Sixty-first street; and six cents for the entire length of said railroad; and also,

That said track, or tracks, shall be laid upon a good foundation, with a grooved rail, or such other rail as may be approved of by the Common Council and the Street Commissioner, even with the surface of the streets through which they may pass, and shall be commenced within six months, and completed to Forty-second street, within one year from the passage of this resolution; and from Forty-second street, toward and to the Harlem river, as fast as the Third avenue shall be graded, and in a proper condition to lay rails thereon.

2. *Resolved*, That said parties have the consent of the Common Council, and permission is hereby given to them to connect their said railroad, at the junction of the Bowery and Grand street, with the Second Avenue Railroad, if constructed; and said parties, and those to whom permission may be given by the Common Council, to lay a railroad through the Second avenue, shall have the free use in common of the double track from said junction, through the Bowery to Chatham street; and of one of the tracks to be laid from the southerly termination of the Bowery, through Chatham street to Pearl street; each of said parties to pay one-half the expense of constructing and keeping in repair the double and single track, so to be used by them in common. Either of said parties to have the right to construct said double and single track, so to be used in common, and if constructed by either, the other of said parties shall pay one-half the actual cost thereof; or said parties may, by mutual agreement, construct the same jointly.

3. *Resolved*, That in consideration of the good and faithful performance of the conditions, stipulations and agreements above prescribed, and of such other necessary requirements as may hereafter be made by the Common Council, for the regulations of the said railroad, the said parties shall pay, from the date of opening the said railroad, the annual license fee for each car now allowed by law, and shall have licenses accordingly.

4. *Resolved*, That within a reasonable time after the passage of these resolutions, the said parties, or a majority in interest thereof, may form themselves into an association, which shall be vested, with all the rights and privileges hereby granted; and shall have power, by the votes of at least a majority in interest of the associates, to frame and establish articles of association, providing for the construction, operation and management of said railroad, and to make contracts for the purchase of property, for the use or benefit of said railroad.

5. *Resolved*, That the association shall not be deemed dissolved, by the death or act of any associate, but his successor in interest shall stand in his place, and the rights of each associate shall depend on his own fulfillment of the conditions imposed on him by these restrictions, or the articles of association and by-laws of the association; and in case of his failure to fulfill the same, his rights shall be forfeited to, and devolve upon the remaining associates, after twenty days' notice of such failure, from the secretary of the association, specifying the particulars of his delinquency; and said parties or associates may, at any time, incorporate themselves, under the general railroad act, whenever two-thirds in interest of the associates shall require it.—(*Res. Dec.* 31, 1852).

Resolved, That the time within which, by the provisions of the grant dated January 1, 1853, authorizing the construction of the Third Avenue Railroad, the grantees in said grant named, and their assigns were permitted to lay down a double track in the Bowery, south of Fifth street, and along Park row, be, and the same is hereby extended until the expiration of three months after such time as the Third Avenue Railroad Company shall be deprived by the New York and Harlem Railroad Company, of the privilege now enjoyed by the Third Avenue Railroad Company, of running their cars over the tracks of the New York and Harlem Railroad Company.—(*Res. Dec.* 9, 1853).

THE SECOND AVENUE RAILROAD.

Resolved, That permission is hereby given to Denton Pearsall, Joseph C. Skadon, Abraham B. Rapelyea, Wm. L. Hall, R. T. Mulligan, Charles Miller, Daniel J. Sherwood, Abraham Allen and Henry Goff, to lay a grooved railroad track in the following streets and avenues of the city of New York, viz: Commencing at a point in the Second avenue, at or near to Forty-second street, thence running down the Second avenue to Twenty-third street with a double track; through Twenty-third street, with a single track, to the First avenue; down First avenue to Allen street; through Allen street to Grand street; through Grand street to the Bowery; down the Bowery to Chatham street; across Chatham street to Oliver street; through Oliver street to South street; through South street to Roosevelt street; across Roosevelt street to Front street; through Front street to Peck slip, the terminus. Returning, with a single track, as follows: Through Peck slip to Pearl street; through Pearl street to Chatham street; through Chatham street to the Bowery; through the Bowery to Grand street; through Grand street to Chrystie street; through Chsystie street to the Second avenue, to Twenty-third street, where it intersects the double track, and so on to its termination, opposite the Harlem river, with a double track.

Provided, however, That all the said rails shall be laid down in such manner, and in such parts of the said streets and avenues as shall be approved by the Street Commissioner, so as to cause no impediment to the common and ordinary use of the streets and avenues for all other purposes; and that the water courses of the streets shall be left free and unobstructed, and that the said company shall pave the streets in and about the rails in a permanent manner, and keep the same in repair to the entire satisfaction of said Street Commissioner.

And, provided further, That no motive power, except horses, be used below Forty-second street; and, further, that they run a car on said road, for the convenience of public travel, each and every day, both ways, as often as every fifteen minutes, from 5 to 6 o'clock, A. M.; every four minutes, from 6 o'clock, A. M. to 8 o'clock, P. M.; every fifteen minutes, from 8 o'clock, P. M. to 12 o'clock, P. M., and every thirty minutes, from 12 o'clock, P. M. to 5 o'clock, A. M., and as much oftener as public convenience may require, under such directions as the Common Council may, from time to time, prescribe.

Also, that the rate of passage on said railroad shall not exceed a greater sum than five cents to Forty-second street; and also, that the Common Council shall have power to regulate the fare for the entire length of said road, when it shall be completed to Harlem river.

Also, that said road shall be commenced within six months, and completed to Forty-second street within one year, and from Forty-second street to Harlem river within three years from the passage of this resolution.

Resolved, That the said parties shall, in all respects, comply with the direction of the Street Commissioner, and of the Common Council, in the building of said railroad, and in the running of the cars thereon, and in any other matter connected with the regulation of said railroad.

Resolved, That the said parties shall, before this permission takes effect, enter into a good and sufficient agreement with the Mayor, Aldermen and Commonalty of the city of New York, to be drawn and approved of by the Counsel to the Corporation, binding themselves to abide by and perform the stipulations and provisions herein contained, and also all such other regulations or ordinances as may be passed by the Common Council, relating to the said road.—(*Res. Dec.* 11, 1852).

Resolved, That the route of the Second Avenue Railroad be, and the same is hereby changed from Front street, between Roosevelt street and Peck slip to South street, between the same points.—(*Resolution, July* 20, 1853).

THE NINTH AVENUE RAILROAD.

Resolved, That the Common Council do hereby grant the right and privilege to James Murphy, William Radford and Miner C. Story, and their respective assigns, and to those they may associate with them, to construct a railroad from Fifty-first street to the Battery, and back, in and through the following streets, viz :

With a double track from Fifty-first street through the Ninth avenue to Gansevoort street; thence by a single track through Greenwich street to the Battery; and by a single track through Gansevoort street to Washington street, and through Washington street to the Battery, and through Battery place, between Greenwich and Washington streets, to connect the said single tracks. And also, to run cars for the conveyance of passengers, &c., upon said road each and every day, at such times as they may think proper, subject to provisions hereinafter named.

Provided, said railroad shall be constructed in all respects after the manner of the construction of the Eighth avenue railroad.

Provided, That in no case steam power be used on any part of said railroad ; and also,

Provided, That the said grantees shall begin the construction of said railroad on or before the 1st day of May next, and shall complete the same, and commence running cars thereon, within eighteen months thereafter ; and also,

Provided, That the said grantees shall run cars upon the road so constructed, each way, between Fifty-first street and the Battery, every day, as often as every fifteen minutes from five to six A. M.; and every four minutes from six A. M. to eight P. M.; every fifteen minutes from eight P. M. to twelve M., and as much oftener as public convenience may require, under such direction as the Common Council may, from time to time, prescribe; and

Provided, That no more than five cents be charged for each passenger, riding over the whole, or any portion of the distance of said road; and also

Provided, That said grantees shall keep the space between the tracks, and the space for two feet each side of the same, at all times, in thorough repair; and also,

Provided, That the said cars shall be licensed by the Mayor, and the grantees shall pay the annual fee of twenty dollars per car for such license; and

Also, The said grantees and their associates and assigns, shall have the privilege to organize a joint stock association, either with or without incorporation, to carry out the objects of this grant, and a majority in interest of the grantees, their assigns and associates, shall have the control, management and direction of the road, and the business thereof; and should any or either of the grantees or their associates, or of the shareholders, neglect to pay their respective proportion of the money required for carrying into full effect the grant hereby made, when by such majority thereunto required, the others shall be at liberty to make such payment; and this grant shall enure to the benefit of those who pay in the proportion of their respective contributions.

These resolutions shall be certified by said grantees above-named; and a copy thereof signed by them shall be deemed the agreement between the Mayor, Aldermen and Commonalty of the city of New York, and said associates; and shall be sufficient, in all respects, to give and grant to the said grantees, their associates and assigns aforesaid, the right and privilege above-mentioned, and bind them to conform to the directions herein contained.

And also provided, that said railroad shall be continued from Fifty-first street along the Ninth avenue to the Bloomingdale road, thence along the Bloomingdale road to the Tenth avenue; thence along the Tenth avenue to the Harlem river, whenever required by the Common Council, and as soon and as fast as said avenues are graded.—(*Resolution, Dec.* 28, 1853).

CONTRACTS

WITH

GASLIGHT COMPANIES.

NEW YORK GASLIGHT COMPANY'S CONTRACT.

Articles of Agreement, indented, made and concluded this twelfth day of May, in the year of our Lord, one thousand eight hundred and twenty three, between the Mayor, Aldermen and Commonalty of the city of New York, of the first part, and the New York Gaslight Company, of the second part, Witnesseth : that the said parties of the first part, for and in consideration of the covenants, articles and agreements hereinafter mentioned, on the part of the said parties of the second part, and their successors, to be observed, performed and kept, do hereby grant, demise and to farm let, to the said parties, of the second part, and their successors, all and singular *the sole and exclusive privilege* and right of laying or placing under ground, pipes in all and every of the public streets and parts of streets, of the city of New York, lying and being *south of a line commencing at the East river, at the foot of Grand street, and running through Grand street to Sullivan street, and through Sullivan street to Canal street, and through Canal street to the North or Hudson river*, for conducting gas, for lighting the public lamps in the streets and parts of streets, south of said line, and the houses and buildings, fronting or to front on, or bounded by or adjacent to the streets or part of streets south of said line.

To have and to hold and to enjoy the same unto the said parties of the second part, and their successors, from the day of the date of these presents, for and during and until the 12th day of May, which will be in the year of our Lord one thousand eight hundred and fifty-three,

Provided, nevertheless, and this grant is upon this express condition, that the said parties of the second part, and their successors shall and do in all things well and sufficiently keep, perform and observe all and singular the covenants, articles, agreements and stipulations on their part to be kept, performed and observed as hereinafter is set forth and agreed.

And the said parties of the second part, in consideration of the premises, do for themselves and their successors covenant and agree to and with the said parties of the first part, and their successors, as follows: that is to say, that they, the said parties of the second part, shall and will, before the twelfth day of May, in the year of our Lord, one thousand eight hundred and twenty-five, erect, establish and complete in the said city of New York, good and sufficient buildings, works and apparatus for the preparing and manufacture of gas, and that they will also cause the pipes for conducting the same, and of sufficient capacity, to be laid, and will also manufacture or cause to be manufactured and supplied in the most improved manner, sufficient quantities of the best quality gas, commonly called inflammable gas, for lighting the houses and public lamps in the street called Broadway, in the said city, from the Battery to Grand street, in the manner hereinafter mentioned; AND ALSO MOREOVER, that they, the said parties of the second part, shall and will at all times from and after the twelfth day of May, in the year of our Lord, one thousand eight hundred and twenty-eight, and during the residue of the term of this grant, in like manner cause the pipes of sufficient capacity for conducting the said gas to be laid; and will also manufacture, or cause to be manufactured and supplied in the most approved manner, sufficient quantities of the said gas, of the best quality, for well and sufficiently lighting the streets, parts of streets and public places, and the public lamps and houses adjoining, or to adjoin all and singular the streets and parts of streets lying in the said city, south of the aforesaid line, at such periods as the said parties of the first part shall, from time to time, after the said twelfth day of May, in the year of our Lord one thousand eight hundred and twenty-eight, by resolution or by law reasonably require, of the said parties of the second part.

And that all such pipes to be furnished by the said parties of the second part, and placed under ground for the purpose of conducting the said gas in all or either of the said streets, or parts of streets, shall be made and constructed in the most approved manner, of cast-iron and of the best materials; and also, that the said parties of the second part, shall and will light such and so many of the public lamps with the best quality of gas as are in the streets, or parts of streets of the said city, south of the aforesaid line, whenever they may be required to light the same, or any number of the same, by the said parties of the first part, or their successors; the said lamps to be lighted during such times as the public lamps are now required to be lighted, and in the streets or parts of streets in which the pipes for conducting gas shall be laid according to these presents, at a yearly expense to the said parties of the first part, not exceeding what would be the expense of lighting and supplying an equal number of the said lamps with oil of the quality generally used for that purpose, estimating the price of oil at the average price of the same in the city of New York during the preceding year.

AND FURTHER, That the said parties of the second part, shall likewise furnish at their own expense the necessary conductors of metal of sufficient capacity to the lamp posts, that the lights of the said lamps shall be of a quality, brilliancy, or intensity, equal to the gas in use for the public lamps in the city of London; the said parties of the first part, however, to be at the expense of lamps, lamp irons, and lamp posts, and fittings up, and at no other expense for fixtures, conductors, repairs, or on any other account whatsoever.

And also, that the parties of the second part shall and will, at all times give forty-eight hours' notice to the said parties of the first part, or to their Street Commissioner, of their intention to break up, or open any street, or part of a street, for the purpose of laying or repairing the pipes to conduct the gas; and that they will replace the earth which they may remove in so doing, before sunset of the day on which such opening shall be made, and that they will replace the pavements, and repave and repair the same, in such reasonable time and manner as the said parties of the first part, or their Street Commissioner, may direct, and in as good and firm a manner as the streets were in before being broken up for the aforesaid purpose; and further, that all such repairs as shall, at any time, become necessary by reason of the said pipes or conductors, shall always be made and done by the said parties of the second part, at their own cost and expense.

And also, that the said parties of the second part will so conduct their manufactory or manufactories of gas as not to create a nuisance, and that they will in all things be governed by such reasonable and necessary rules and regulations as the said parties of the first part, or their successors, may, from time to time pass, ordain and establish, relative to the opening of streets, and laying down the pipes and conductors aforesaid.

Provided, always, that nothing in this grant contained shall be construed to prevent any person or persons residing on, adjacent, or near to any of the said streets or parts of streets in the said city, south of the aforesaid line, from erecting in or on his or their own premises, any building or apparatus to light with gas his or their own house or manufactory; and,

Provided further, and the premises hereby granted, are also upon this express condition, any thing herein contained to the contrary, notwithstanding, that if the said parties of the second part, or their successors, shall not well and faithfully observe, perform, fulfill, and keep all and singular the covenants and conditions above contained, on their part and behalf to be observed, performed, fulfilled and kept according to the true intent and meaning of these presents, then and in that case it shall and may be lawful for the said parties of the first part, in Common Council convened, by a resolution or order to annul and vacate this grant, and thereupon the premises hereby demised shall be revested in the said parties of the first part, or their successors, as fully and completely as if this indenture had never been executed.

In witness whereof, to one part of this indenture remaining with the said parties of the first part, the said parties of the second part, have caused the common seal of the said The New York Gaslight Company to be affixed; and to the other part thereof remaining with the said parties of the second part, the said parties of the first part have caused the common seal of the city of New York to be affixed, the day and year first above written.

By the Common Council.

[L. S.] STEPHEN ALLEN.

J. MORTON, *Clerk.*

SAMUEL LEGGETT,

President of the New York Gaslight Company.

MANHATTAN GAS LIGHT COMPANY'S CONTRACT.

THIS INDENTURE, made this eighth day of May, A.D., 1833, between the Mayor, Aldermen and Commonalty of the city of New York, of the first part, and the Manhattan Gas Light Company of the second part, witnesseth: That the said parties of the first part, for and in consideration of the covenants, articles and agreements hereinafter mentioned, on the part of the said parties of the second part, and their successors, to be observed, performed and kept, do hereby grant and demise to the said parties of the second part, and their successors, the privilege and right to lay or place under ground, pipes in any or all of the streets, avenues

37

and public places of the city of New York, lying and being north of a line commencing at the East River, at the foot of Grand street, and running through Grand street to Sullivan street, and through Sullivan street to Canal street, and through Canal street to the North or Hudson river, and in every or any part of such street, avenue or public place, for the purpose of conducting gas, commonly called inflammable gas, for lighting the public lamps in the said streets, avenues and public places, and parts thereof, as hereinafter mentioned, and for lighting the houses or buildings fronting or to front on, or bounded by or adjacent to the said streets, avenues and public places, or parts thereof; to have, hold, use and enjoy the said right and privilege, unto the said parties of the second part, and their successors, from the day of the date of these presents, until the twelfth day of May, which will be A.D., 1853; provided, always, and these presents are upon this express condition, that they, the said parties of the second part, and their successors, shall and do, in all things, well and sufficiently keep, perform and observe, all and singular the covenants, articles, provisions, agreements and stipulations on their part to be kept, performed and observed, as hereinafter specified.

And the said parties of the second part, in consideration of the premises, do, for themselves and their successors, covenant and agree to and with the said parties of the first part, and their successors, as follows, that is to say: that any gas house or works, for the manufactory of such gas, to be erected or established by the said parties of the second part in the city of New York, shall be so erected and established on the margin either of the Hudson or of the East river, not south of Fourteenth street in the said city; and that all pipes for conducting the same which the said parties of the second part may cause to be laid, shall be of sufficient capacity, and made and constructed of the best materials of cast iron, and in the most approved manner; also, that from all such main pipes as they may lay or cause to be laid by virtue of the right and privilege hereby granted, they will supply with gas, and cause to be lighted, such and so many of the public lamps opposite or adjacent to such main pipes, as they may, from time to time, be required to do by the said parties of the first part; and that the said lamps shall be so lighted during such times as the public lamps throughout the city of New York are required to be lighted by the regulation of the said parties of the first part; and that all such public lamps situated north of the line aforesaid, and south of the line of Sixth street, which the parties of the first part may require to be so supplied with gas, and lighted as aforesaid, shall be so supplied and lighted by the said parties of the second part at a yearly expense to the parties of the first part, not exceeding fifteen dollars for supplying each of such lamps with gas, and lighting the same. And it is further agreed, that the said parties of the second part shall furnish at their own expense, the necessary conductors of metal of sufficient capacity to the lamp posts of such public lamps as they may be required to supply with gas and light as aforesaid; and that the light of the said lamps shall be of a quality, brilliancy or intensity equal to the gas in use for the public lamps in the city of London. It is understood, however, that the parties of the first part, are to be at the expense of such lamps, with their lamp-irons, lamp-posts and fittings up, but at no other expense for fixtures, conductors, repairs, or on any other account whatsoever for the same. And it is further agreed, that the said parties of the second part shall, at all times, give forty-eight hours' notice to the said parties of the first part or their Street Commissioner of their intention to break up or open any street, avenue or public place or part thereof, or to remove any part of the pavement therefrom, for the purpose of laying or repairing the pipes to conduct the said gas, and that they will replace the earth which they may remove in so doing, before sunset of the day on which such opening shall be made, and that they will replace the pavement and repave and repair the same in such reasonable time and manner as the said parties of the first part, or their Street Commissioner may direct, and in as good and firm a manner as such streets, avenues or public places or parts thereof were in before being broke up for the purpose aforesaid. Also, that all such repairs as shall at any time become necessary by reason of laying the said pipes or conductors, shall be made and done by the said parties of the second part, at their own cost and expense. Also, that no such street, avenue or public place or part thereof, shall be so broken up or opened, or the pavement thereof removed, or shall be again filled up or repaired, or such pavement replaced, except under the direction and supervision of a competent person to be appointed by the said Street Commissioner, and who shall be considered as in the employ of the said parties of the first part; but who shall be paid for his services by the said parties of th second part, such sum as the said Street Commissioner may direct, not exceeding one dollar and fifty cents per diem, for each day that he may be so employed. Also, that no such street, avenue or public place or part thereof, shall be so broken up or opened, or the pavement thereof removed at any time between the first of December and the first of March, during the continuance of the term mentioned in these presents, without the consent of the said Street Commissioner being first obtained for that purpose.

And it is further agreed, that the said parties of the second part shall and will so conduct their manufactory or manufactories of gas as not to create a nuisance ; and that they will, in all things, be governed by such reasonable and necessary rules and regulations as the said parties of the first part or their successors, may, from time to time, pass, ordain and establish, relative to the opening of such streets, avenues or public places, or parts thereof, and laying down the pipes and conductors aforesaid.

And it is hereby expressly provided that nothing herein contained, shall be construed or deemed as granting to the said parties of the second part, any sole or exclusive right or privilege, or as preventing the said parties of the first part from granting the like privileges as are hereby given to the said parties of the second part, to any other company, persons or parties whatsoever, or as preventing any person or persons residing in, or adjacent, or near to any of the said streets, avenues or public places, or parts thereof, lying north of the line hereinbefore first mentioned, from erecting in or upon his or their own premises any building or apparatus, to light with gas, his or their own house, store, manufactory or premises. And it is further provided, and these presents are upon the express condition, that if the said parties of the second part or their successors, shall not well and truly observe, perform, fulfill and keep all and singular, the covenants and conditions hereinbefore contained, on their part and behalf to be observed, performed, fulfilled and kept, according to the true intent and meaning of these presents, then and in that case, it shall and may be lawful for the said parties of the first part, by a resolution or order to be passed in Common Council, to annul and vacate this grant, and thereupon the premises hereby demised shall be re-vested in the said parties of the first part, or their successors, as fully and completely as if this indenture had never been executed.

In witness whereof, to one part of this indenture, remaining with the said parties of the first part, the said parties of the second part, have caused the common seal of the said the Manhattan Gas Light Company to be affixed, and to the other part thereof, remaining with the said parties of the second part, the said parties of the first part have caused the common seal of the city of New York to be affixed the day and year above written.

[L. S.] LAMBERT SUYDAM,

President M. G. L. Co

MANHATTAN GASLIGHT COMPANY'S CONTRACT.

THIS INDENTURE, made the first day of May, in the year of our Lord one thousand eight hundred and forty-eight, between the Mayor, Aldermen and Commonality of the city of New York, of the first part, and the Manhattan Gaslight Company of the second part, witnesseth: That the said parties of the first part, for and in consideration of the covenants, articles and agreements, hereinafter mentioned on the part of the said parties of the second part, and their successors, to be observed, performed and kept, do hereby grant and demise, to the said parties of the second part, and their successors, the privilege and right to lay or place under ground, pipes in any or all the streets, avenues, and public places of the city of New York, comprised between a line commencing at the East river, at the foot of Grand street, and running through the middle of Grand street, to Sullivan street, and through the middle of Sullivan street, from Grand street to Canal street, and through the middle of Canal street, from Sullivan street to the North or Hudson river, and a line commencing at the East river, at the foot of Forty-second street, on the north side thereof, and running parallel with said street to the North or Hudson river, and embracing both sides of said street, and in any, or every part of any such street, avenue, or public place, for the purpose of conducting gas, commonly called inflammable gas, for lighting the public lamps, in the said streets, avenues and public places and parts thereof, as hereinafter mentioned, and for lighting the houses and buildings, fronting, or to front on, or bounded by or adjacent to the said streets, avenues and public places, or parts thereof. To have, hold, use and enjoy the said right and privilege, with the said parties of the second part, and their successors, from the day of the date of these presents, until the fifth day of May, which will be in the year one thousand eight hundred and sixty-eight; provided always, and these presents are upon this express condition, that they, the said parties of the second part, and their successors, shall and do, in all things well and sufficiently keep, perform and observe all and singular, the covenants, articles, agreements, provisions, stipulations, on their part, to be kept, performed, and observed, as hereinafter specified. And the said parties of the second part, in consideration of the premises, do for themselves and their successors, covenant and agree, to and with said parties of the first part, and their successors, as follows, that is to say: that any gas-house, or works for the manufactory of such gas, which the said parties of the second part, hereafter may use, or erect and establish in the city of New York, shall be located, erected and established, on the margin of either the Hudson or the East river and not south of Fourteenth street, in the said city, and that all pipes for conducting the gas, which the parties of the second part may cause to be laid, shall be of sufficient capacity, and made and constructed of the best materials, of cast iron, and in the most approved manner.

That the said parties of the first part, shall have the right to order the pipes called the mains of the company to be extended in and along all the streets, avenues, and public places in the said city, within the limits aforesaid, commencing at Grand and Canal streets, and continuing through each street in regular succession. Provided, however, that the said parties of the second part, shall not be compelled to expend in the laying of said mains, as last aforesaid, during the continuance of this contract, a yearly sum to exceed six thousand dollars. Also, that the said parties of the second part shall fit up and light all the public lamps required by the Corporation, wherever the pipes of the company are or shall be laid, within the district aforesaid, and that the said lamps shall be so lighted during such times as the public lamps throughout the city of New York are required to be lighted by the regulations of the said parties of the first part; and that all such public lamps, situated within the district aforesaid, which shall be required by the Corporation as aforesaid, shall be so supplied and lighted by the said parties of the second part, at the yearly rate of fifteen dollars for each lamp for the light, and for lighting and extinguishing the same. Also, that the said parties of the first part may direct and require, by notice to that effect, that all or any portion of the said public lamps, shall be lighted, and kept burning at any other time or times during the continuance of this contract; and the said parties of the second part, shall light the same, and continue them burning in accordance with any and every direction of the said parties of the first part, or their proper agent or agents, to that effect; provided that if, in compliance with the direction of the said parties of the first part, the whole number of hours, during which the said lamps, or a portion of them are kept burning in any year, shall exceed the average number of hours during which the public lamps in the city of New York have been kept burning during the last five years, prior to the date of this contract (which the parties hereto estimate to be and fix at two thousand three hundred hours,) then, in that case, the said parties of the second part shall be entitled to claim and receive, for such additional number of hours during which the public lamps, or a portion of them, in the district aforesaid, are kept burning, in accordance with such directions of the said parties of the first part, an additional compensation equivalent to a pro rata increase of the compensation hereinbefore allowed, proportioned to the increased number of hours beyond the said average number.

The burners in the public lamps shall be equal to those heretofore used in the city of New York, equal to an average consumption of three cubic feet per hour. And it is further agreed, that the said parties of the second part shall furnish, at their own expense, the necessary conductors of metal of sufficient capacity to the lamp posts of such public lamps, as they may be required to supply with gas and light as aforesaid. The parties of the second part, shall also fit up the said public lamps, and shall receive, as compensation therefor, the sum of five dollars for each lamp so fitted up. It is agreed, however, that the cost of the posts, lanterns and repairs shall be at the expense of the said parties of the first part; and it is further agreed, that the said parties of the second part, shall have the right to lay pipes at any time within the said district, upon giving forty-eight hours' notice to the said parties of the first part, or to the Street Commissioner, of their intention to break up or open any street, avenue or public place, or part thereof, or to remove any part of the pavement thereof for the purpose of laying or repairing the pipes to conduct the said gas, and that they will replace the earth which they may remove in so doing, before sun-set of the day in which such opening shall be made, and that they will replace the pavement, and repave and repair the same, in such reasonable time and manner as the said parties of the first part, or their Street Commissioner may direct, and in as good and firm a manner as such street, avenue, or public places, or parts thereof, were in before being broken up for the purpose aforesaid. Also, that all such repairs as shall at any time become necessary, by reason of laying the said pipes, or conductors, shall be made and done by said parties of the second part, at their own cost and expense.

Also, that no such street, avenue or public place, or part thereof, shall by so broken up or opened, or the pavement thereof removed, or shall be again filled up or repaved except under the direction and supervision of a competent person, to be appointed by the said Street Commissioner; but the said parties of the second part shall not be called upon to pay any sum to any party or parties, for the inspection of any pavement which they may have occasion to replace. And it is further agreed, that the said parties of the second part, shall and will so conduct the manufactory or manufactories of gas, as not to create a nuisance, and that they will in all things be governed by such reasonable and necessary rules and regulations, as the said parties of the first part, or their successors, may from time to time pass, ordain and establish, relative to the opening of such streets, avenues, or public places, or parts thereof, and laying down the pipes and conductors aforesaid. And it is hereby expressly provided, that nothing herein contained, shall be construed or deemed as granting to the said parties of the second part, any sole or exclusive right or privilege, or as preventing the said parties of the first part from granting the like privileges as are hereby given to the said parties of the second part to any other company, persons or parties whatsoever, or as preventing any person or persons residing in or adjacent, or near to any of the said streets, avenues, or public places, or parts thereof, lying north of the line hereinbefore first mentioned, from erecting in or upon his or their own premises, any building or apparatus, to light with gas his or their own house, store or manufactory, or premises. And it is further covenanted and agreed, by and on the part of the said parties of the first part, that the said parties of the first part and their successors shall and will pass all needful ordinances, which shall be necessary to protect the interests of the said parties of the second part, and which of right ought to be passed for that purpose.

And it is further provided, and these presents are upon the express condition, that if the said parties of the second part, or their successors, shall not well and truly observe, perform and fulfill, and keep all and singular, the covenants and conditions, hereinbefore contained, on their part and behalf to be observed, performed, fulfilled, and kept, according to the true intent and meaning of these presents, then, and in that case, it shall and may be lawful for said parties of the first part, by a resolution or order to be passed in Common Council, to annul and vacate this grant; and thereupon the premises hereby demised shall be re-vested in the said parties of the first part, or their successors, as fully and completely as if this indenture had never been executed.

In witness whereof, to one part of this indenture remaining with the said parties of the first part, the said parties of the second part have caused the common seal of the said the Manhattan Gaslight Company to be affixed; and to the other part thereof remaining with the said parties of the second part, the said parties of the first part have caused the common seal of the city of New York to be affixed, the day and year above written.

Signed,

[L. S.] W. V. BRADY, *Mayor.*

By the Common Council,

Signed, D. T. VALENTINE, *Clerk, C. C.*

To the counterpart, held by the Corporation of the city, is attached the common seal of the Manhattan Gaslight Company, verified by the signatures respectively of the President,

[L. S.] DAVID C. COLDEN,

And Secretary, S. H. Howard.

HARLEM GASLIGHT COMPANY'S CONTRACT.

This Indenture, made this twentieth day of May, in the year of our Lord, one thousand eight hundred and fifty-eight, between the Mayor, Aldermen and Commonalty of the city of New York, parties of the first part, by Edward Cooper, their Street Commissioner, and the Harlem Gaslight Company, of said city, parties of the second part, witnesseth: That the said parties of the first part, for, and in consideration of the covenants, articles and agreements hereinafter mentioned on the part of the said parties of the second part, and their successors, to be observed, performed and kept, do hereby grant and demise to the said parties, of the second part, and their successors, the privilege and right to lay or place under ground pipes in any and all of the streets, avenues and public places of the city of New York, comprised between a line commencing at the centre of Seventy-ninth street, at the East river, running thence through the centre of said Seventy-ninth street to the North or Hudson river, thence along said river to the northern boundary of the city and county of New York, thence along said northern boundary of the city and county of New York to the East river, and thence along said East river to the point of beginning, and in every part of any street, avenue or public place comprised within said limits, for the purpose of conducting gas for lighting the public lamps in the said streets, avenues, and public places and parts thereof as hereinafter mentioned, and for lighting the houses and buildings fronting, or to front on, or bounded by or adjacent to the said streets, avenues and public places or parts thereof, to have and to hold, use and enjoy the said right and privilege unto the said parties of the second part, and their successors, from the 6th of November, one thousand eight hundred and fifty-seven, until the 6th of November, which will be in the year one thousand eight hundred and fifty-eight.

Provided always, and these presents are upon this express condition, that they, the said parties, of the second part, and their successors, shall and will in all things well and sufficiently keep, perform and observe all and singular, the covenants, articles, agreements, provisions and stipulations on their part, to be kept, performed and observed, as hereinafter specified.

And the said parties of the second part, in consideration of the premises, do, for themselves and their successors, covenant and agree to and with the said parties, of the first part, and their successors, as follows: that is to say, that any gas-house or work for the manufacturing of such gas which the said parties of the second part, hereafter may use or erect and establish in the city of New York shall be located, erected, or established on the margin of either the Hudson or North river, or the East or Harlem river, in the said city, and that all pipes for conducting the gas which the said parties of the second part may cause to be laid, shall be of sufficient capacity and made and constructed of the best materials of cast-iron, and in the most approved manner.

That the said parties of the first part shall have the right to order the pipes called the mains of the company to be extended in and along all the streets, avenues, and public places in the said city within the limits aforesaid, commencing at the foot of Seventy-ninth street and the East river, and continuing through such street in regular succession, provided, however, that the said parties of the second part shall not be compelled to expend in the laying of said mains, as last aforesaid, during the continuance of this contract, a yearly sum to exceed six thousand dollars.

Also, that the said parties of the second part shall fit up and light all the public lamps required by the Corporation, wherever the pipes of the company are, or shall be laid within the district aforesaid, and that the said lamps shall be so lighted during such times as the public lamps throughout the city of New York are required to be lighted by the regulations of the said parties of the first part, and that all such public lamps situated within the district aforesaid, which shall be required by the Corporation as aforesaid, shall be so supplied and lighted by the said parties of the second part, at the yearly rate of twenty-eight dollars and eighty cents for each lamp, for the light and for lighting and extinguishing the same, and for keeping the lanterns clean; also that the said parties of the first part may direct and require, by notice to that effect, that all or any portion of said public lamps shall be lighted and kept burning at any other time or times during the continuance of this contract; and the said parties of the second part shall light the same, and continue them burning in accordance with any and every direction of the said parties of the first part, or their proper agent or agents to that effect. Provided that if, in compliance with the direction of the said parties of the first part, the whole number of hours during which the said lamps or a portion of them are kept burning in any year, shall exceed the average number of hours during which the public lamps have been kept burning for three years prior to the date of this contract, (which the parties hereto fix at three thousand eight hundred hours,) then, and in that case, the said parties of the second part shall be entitled to claim and receive for such additional number of hours during which the public lamps, or a portion of them, in the district aforesaid are kept burning, in accordance with such direction of the said parties of the first part, an additional compensation equivalent to a pro-rata increase of the compensation hereinbefore allowed, proportioned to the increased number of hours beyond the said average number.

The burners in the public lamps shall be equal to those heretofore used in the city of New York, equal to an average of consumption of three cubic feet per hour.

And it is further agreed that the said parties of the second part shall furnish, at their own expense, the necessary conductors of metal of sufficient capacity to the lamp-posts of each public lamp, as they may be required, and will make all necessary connections with such conductors and the street mains to supply with gas and light as aforesaid, and will furnish the burner to each lamp-post, such burner to consume three (3) cubic feet of gas per hour. The parties of the second part shall also fit up the said public lamps, and shall receive as compensation therefor the sum of nine dollars and thirty-five cents for each lamp so fitted up. It is agreed, however, that the cost of the posts, lanterns and repairs shall be at the expense of the said parties of the first part, and that said posts, lanterns, &c., are to be delivered to the said parties of the second part, by the said parties of the first part, at the works of said Company, foot of One hundred and eleventh street, Harlem river. And it is further agreed that the said parties of the second part shall have the right to lay pipes at any time within the said district upon giving forty-eight hours' notice to the said parties of the first part, or to the Street Commissioner of said city of their intention to break up or open any street, avenue or public place, or part thereof, or to remove any part of the pavement thereof for the purpose of laying or repairing the pipes to conduct the said gas; and that they will replace the earth which they may remove in so doing before sunset of the day on which such opening shall be made, and that they will replace the pavement, and repave and repair the same in such reasonable time and manner as the said parties of the first part, or the Street Commissioner of said city may direct, and in as good and firm a manner as such streets, avenues, or public places or parts thereof were in before being broken up for the purpose aforesaid.

Also, that all such repairs as shall, at any time, become necessary by reason of laying the said pipes or conductors, shall be made and done by the said parties of the second part at their own cost and expense. Also, that no such street, avenue, or public place or part thereof, shall be so broken up or opened, or the pavement thereof removed, or shall be again filled up or repaired, except under the direction and supervision of a competent person to be appointed by the Street Commissioner of said city; but the said parties of the second part shall not be called upon to pay any sum to any party or parties for such inspection, where, however, any pavement is to be removed or replaced; in such case notice is to be given to the Croton Aqueduct Department.

And it is further agreed that the said parties of the second part shall and will so conduct the manufacture and manufactories of gas as not to create a nuisance; and that they will, in all things, be governed by such reasonable and necessary rules and regulations as the said parties of the first part or their successors may, from time to time, pass, ordain and establish, relative to the opening of such streets, avenues or public places or parts thereof, and laying down the pipes and conductors as aforesaid.

And it is hereby expressly provided that nothing herein contained shall be construed or deemed as granting to the said parties of the second part any sole or exclusive right or privilege, or as preventing the said parties of the first part from granting the like privileges as are hereby given to the said parties of the second part, to any other company, persons or parties whatsoever, or as preventing any person or persons residing on or adjacent or near to any of the said streets, avenues, or public places or parts thereof, lying north of the line hereinbefore mentioned, from erecting on or upon his or their own premises, any building or apparatus to light with gas his or their own house, store, manufactory or premises.

And it is further covenanted and agreed, by and on the part of the said parties of the first part, that the said parties of the first part and their successors, shall and will pass all needful ordinances which shall be necessary to protect the interests of the said parties of the second part, and which of right ought to be passed for that purpose.

And it is further provided, and these presents are upon the express condition that if the said parties of the second part or their successors shall not well and truly observe, perform, fulfill and keep all and singular the covenants and conditions hereinbefore contained on their part, and behalf, to be observed, performed, fulfilled and kept, according to the true intent and meaning of these presents, then, and in that case, it shall and may be lawful for the said parties of the first part, by a resolution or order to be passed in Common Council, to annul and vacate this contract, and thereupon the premises hereby demised shall be vested in the said parties of the first part or their successors, as fully and completely as if this indenture had never been executed.

In witness whereof, the parties hereto have executed triplicate copies of this Indenture, the said Edward Cooper, Street Commissioner, hath hereto set his hand and seal on behalf of the said parties of the first part, and the said parties hereto of the second part have hereunto affixed their corporate seal, and caused the same to be attested by their President and Secretary, one of which copies of this Indenture to remain with the said Street Commissioner, one other to be filed with the Comptroller of the city of New York, and the third to be delivered to the said parties of the second part, the day and date herein first written.

[L. S.] EDWARD COOPER,
Street Commissioner.

Sealed and delivered in the presence of
As to the Harlem Gas Light Co.,
JAS. O. BROWN.

As to Edward Cooper Street Comm'r,
C. H. LAWRENCE.

[L. S.] BARR WAKEMAN, *President.*
HENRY J. MCGOWAN, *Secretary.*

EXTRACTS FROM THE STATE LAWS

RELATING

TO THE POLICE DEPARTMENT,

EMBRACING SUCH PARTS AS CONCERN THE ENFORCEMENT OF THE CITY ORDINANCES.

The Police Board shall guard the public health; preserve order at elections; remove nuisances existing in the public streets, roads, places and highways; provide a proper police at fires; see that all laws relating to the observance of Sunday, and regarding pawnbrokers, mock auctions, emigrants, elections, gambling, and the public health, are promptly enforced. They shall obey and enforce all ordinances which are applicable to police or health.* They shall, when consistent with the rules of the Board, comply with all requests of the Common Council or the Mayor.†

The General Superintendent of Police shall be the superintendent of cabs and cabmen, hackney coaches and hackney cabmen, stages and accommodation coaches or omnibuses and their drivers, carts and cartmen, and all persons employed to drive carts, public porters, hand-cartmen, venders of charcoal, firewood, hard coal, and boats and boatmen. He shall also be inspector of pawnbroker's shops, second-hand dealer's shops, junk shops and intelligence offices.‡ All violations of Corporation ordinances reported to him shall forthwith be reported by him to the Corporation Attorney.§ He shall perform the duties previously performed by the Inspectors of hacks, omnibuses, cabs and public porters; Inspector and Deputy Inspector of stages; Inspector of carts, and keepers of lands and places.‖

The Inspectors or Captains of Police shall be dock masters within their respective districts, and assisted by the Sergeants, shall perform all the duties previously performed by Dock Masters.¶

---

* From § 5 of act of April 15, 1857. † From § 20.—Ibid.
‡ From § 6 of Art. II., Act of April 13, 1853. § From § 7, Art. II., Act of April 13, 1853.
‖ From § 1, Art. II., Act of May 7, 1844. ¶ From § 6, Act April 13, 1853.

Patrolmen shall report through the Inspectors, or Captains, or Sergeants to the General Superintendent all violations of the Corporation ordinances.*

The Police Force shall, in accordance with rules and regulations prescribed in conformity with the laws of the State and the City Ordinances, watch and guard the city day and night.

---

* From § 7, Act April 13, 1853.

INDEX.

G.

M.

N.

T.

V.

www.ingramcontent.com/pod-product-compliance
Lightning Source LLC
LaVergne TN
LVHW021103110826
845150LV00001B/155